GREAT MINDS® WIT & WISDOM

Grade K Module 4:
The Continents

Teacher Edition

Table of Contents

MODULE OVERVIEW

INSTRUCTIONAL LESSONS

Focusing Question: Lessons 1–8

What interesting things can people do in Europe and Asia?

- TEXTS: *Earth from Space*, Stöckli, Reto, et al • "The Seven Continents Song," Silly School Songs • "Where in the World Is Carmen Sandiego? from Smithsonian Folkways," *Smithsonian Folkways* • *Asia*, Rebecca Hirsch • *Europe*, Rebecca Hirsch

    ◦ Vocabulary Deep Dive: Define *Continent* and *Ocean*

- TEXTS: "The Seven Continents Song," Silly School Songs • *Asia*, Rebecca Hirsch • "Traditional Chinese Dance–'Flowers Contend in Beauty'"

    ◦ Vocabulary Deep Dive: Demonstrate Meanings of Adjectives with Opposites

- TEXTS: "The Seven Continents Song," Silly School Song • *Europe*, Rebecca Hirsch • *The Story of Ferdinand*, Munro Leaf; Illustrations, Robert Lawson

    ◦ Vocabulary Deep Dive: Opposite Action Words

- TEXTS: "The Seven Continents Song," Silly School Songs • *Asia*, Rebecca Hirsch

    ◦ Style and Conventions Deep Dive: Examine Writing and Expanding a Sentence

- TEXTS: "The Seven Continents Song," Silly School Songs • *Europe*, Rebecca Hirsch • *The Story of Ferdinand*, Munro Leaf; Illustrations, Robert Lawson

    ◦ Vocabulary Deep Dive: Multiple-Meaning Words: *Stick* and *horns*

Focusing Question: Lessons 9–15

What interesting natural features can people see in Africa and Antarctica?

Focusing Question: Lessons 16–21

How can a story transport you to a different place?

Focusing Question: Lessons 22–27

What amazing animals can people see in South America and Australia?

Focusing Question: Lessons 28–31

Why might people want to visit North America?

Focusing Question: Lessons 32–35

What makes the world fascinating?

Focusing Question: Lesson 36

What is the story of the year?

Appendices

Teacher Edition

GRADE K, MODULE 4

The Continents

Module Summary

You have brains in your head. You have feet in your shoes. You can steer
yourself any direction you choose. You're on your own.
And you know what you know. And YOU are the one who'll decide where to go...

–Dr. Seuss

Have you ever looked at the globe and thought about all the places in the world you could visit? Would you climb high peaks in North America or in Asia? Would you learn to tango in Argentina, or enjoy the beauty of the frescos on the ceiling of the Sistine Chapel? There is, quite literally, a world of possibilities! In this module, students study a group of texts united in theme: what makes the world fascinating?

To build a deep well of world knowledge, students study the seven continents. They begin by considering the texts *Europe* and *Asia*, and the interesting things people can do in these places. In the next set of lessons, students consider another aspect of the world: the various geographical features around which cultures develop. Students learn about these natural features by focusing on two contrasting continents: Africa and Antarctica, and their corresponding texts. A passion for knowledge often develops into a passion for travel, and in the next series of lessons, students experience how elements of a story can help them imagine being in another place. The folktale *Why Mosquitoes Buzz in People's Ears* prompts students to explore how specifics of language and illustration can transport them to the sights and sounds of African animals. Students continue to learn about amazing animals in *Australia* and *South America*, and about aspects of South American customs and culture through another fictional folktale: *Moon Rope*, featuring Peruvian textiles as well as storytelling. In the last group of lessons, students lay groundwork for synthesizing information into an opinion through the study of *Introducing North America*. Throughout the module, the text *World Atlas* provides supplemental information on the continents and reinforces how readers collect various sorts of information from maps. Art studies (*Earth from Space, Carta Marina*) layered within the lessons provide alleyways into visual perspectives on the continents.

In addition to content knowledge, the continent study fosters skill development. Images that convey information about the continents from *World Atlas* teach students to compare and contrast two sources of information about the same topic. While students analyze the different characteristics of the continents, they consider the transferable knowledge of how an author supports a point. After collecting text evidence about aspects of each continent, students refer to it to first make and then support informed decisions in a new form of writing: the opinion paragraph. Students use the skills of reading maps, collecting and organizing evidence, and making connections between texts to build their knowledge of the continents and develop an appreciation and passion for exploring the world beyond their classroom.

This work culminates with the End-of-Module (EOM) Task, in which students take evidence they have gathered and opinions they have formed while studying the Essential Question—*What makes the world fascinating*?– and create a travel brochure about which continent they would most like to visit. Students fuse informative and opinion writing to share information about the natural features, animals, and things to do which make their favorite continent a "must-see!"

Essential Question

What makes the world fascinating?

Suggested Student Understandings

- The world is a large place with diverse people and places.

- Each continent is characterized by its own animals, natural features, and things to do.

- Maps and photographs can visually transport viewers to different locations around the world.

- Stories can transport readers to another place through language and illustrations.

- Collecting and reflecting upon information allows a person to make and support an informed opinion with reasons.

Texts

CORE TEXTS

Picture Books (Informational)
- *Africa*, Rebecca Hirsch
- *Antarctica*, Rebecca Hirsch
- *Asia*, Rebecca Hirsch
- *Australia*, Rebecca Hirsch
- *Europe*, Rebecca Hirsch
- *Introducing North America*, Chris Oxlade
- *South America*, Rebecca Hirsch
- *World Atlas*, Nick Crane; Illustrations, David Dean

Picture Books (Literary)

- *Moon Rope*, Lois Ehlert

- *The Story of Ferdinand*, Munro Leaf; Illustrations, Robert Lawson

- *Why Mosquitoes Buzz in People's Ears: A West African Tale*, Verna Aardema; Illustrations, Leo and Diane Dillon

SUPPLEMENTARY TEXTS

Article

- "5 Reasons Why Animal Moms Are Awesome," April Capochino Myers

Painting

- *Carta Marina*, Olaus Magnus

Photographs

- *Earth from Space*, Stöckli, Reto, et al.

- "Grand Canyon Scenic Splendor," *National Park Service*

- "Patterns of Chinchero," *Descendants of the Incas*

Picture Books (Informational)

- *When I Was Young in the Mountains*, Cynthia Rylant; Illustrations, Diane Goode

Poem

- "Lions Roar," *CanTeach*

Quotation

- "What is life?" Crowfoot

Songs

- "Penguin Song," *Preschool Education*

- "Where in the World Is Carmen Sandiego? from Smithsonian Folkways," *Smithsonian Folkways*

Videos

- "Antarctic Sights and Sounds," James Napoli

- "Burkina Faso: Music," *Our Africa*

- "Explore Views of the Burj Khalifa with Google Maps," Google Maps

- "The Seven Continents Song," Silly School Songs

- "Storm-Proofing the World's Biggest Mud Building," BBC Earth

- "Traditional Chinese Dance—'Flowers Contend in Beauty' by Li Qian, Lin Chen..."

Web Pages

- "Americas—Fact Files," *Go Wild*

- "Moles," *DK Find Out!*

Module Learning Goals

Knowledge Goals

- Identify the seven continents.

- Describe the different natural features, things to do, and animals on each continent.

- Demonstrate understanding of maps and their purpose.

- Understand how illustrations, photographs, and words in a text communicate important information.

Reading Goals

- Ask and answer questions about unknown words in a text. (RL.K.4)

- Recognize and sort common types of text. (RL.K.5)

- Describe the relationship between the words and illustrations in a text. (RI.K.7, RL.K.7)

- Identify the reasons an author gives to support a point in the text. (RI.K.8)

- Identify similarities and differences between two texts on the same topic. (RI.K.9)

Writing Goals

- Use a combination of drawing, dictating, and writing to name a topic and state an opinion about the topic. (W.K.1)

- Respond to questions and suggestions from a peer and add detail based on feedback. (W.K.5)

- Collect evidence from the texts and use it support responses to a prompt. (W.K.8)

Speaking and Listening Goals

- Confirm understanding of a text read aloud or information presented orally by giving an example of something heard or understood. (SL.K.2)

- Describe familiar people, places, things, and events to provide additional detail. (SL.K.4)

Language Goals

- Produce and expand complete sentences beginning each sentence with a capital letter. (L.K.1.f, L.K.2.a)

- Recognize and name end punctuation. (L.K.2.b)

- Identify new meanings of familiar words and use them accurately. (L.K.4.a)

- Use the most frequently occurring inflections and affixes to determine the meaning of an unknown word. (L.K.4.b)

- Demonstrate understanding of frequently occurring verbs and adjectives by relating them to their opposites. (L.K.5.b)

- Distinguish between shades of meaning of verbs describing the same general action by acting out their meanings. (L.K.5.d)

Module in Context

Knowledge: In this fourth module of Kindergarten, students build knowledge of the world by embarking on an exploration of the seven continents. Informational texts provide the backbone of this module, allowing students to gather information about the different characteristics of each continent. They use the words and photographs to conduct research on the topics of natural features, animals, and things to do on each of the seven continents. They reflect upon these findings and use the information to develop opinions about each continent, ultimately using the information to write an opinion piece about one of the seven continents.

Reading: In Module 3, students formed an understanding of an informational text's structure and how key details, contained in the words and illustrations, support a text's main topic. In this module, students demonstrate independence using words and illustrations in both informational and literary texts to understand key information in the text. Familiarity with different types of texts allows them to use the words and photographs to think more deeply about a text. They compare and contrast two texts on the same topic, as well as develop an understanding of how an author supports a point with reasons. Students engage with informational and literary texts through Text-Dependent Questions (TDQs), annotating, and charting details. They use the structure of an informational text to guide evidence collection and collect details about the different characteristics of each continent.

Writing: The primary writing focus of this module is text-based opinion writing. Students use the familiar structure of an informative writing piece to engage in another form of informative writing: opinion writing. They collect evidence from the text and learn the process of crafting an opinion about a specific topic. They learn through the Opinion Sandwich writing model how to begin with an opinion statement and support that statement with information from the text. Students continue producing and expanding sentences using details from the text. In addition, students learn to share their writing with their peers as well as give feedback to another. Students reflect upon feedback and learn strategies to implement changes to improve writing. Because writing development varies widely, students work toward independence from where they are, engaging in productive struggle without frustration. Throughout this module, students have frequent opportunities to write, draw, and dictate. These efforts include brief responses in their Response Journals, recording evidence to post on class charts, and answering prompts about the text. In the EOM Task, students create their own travel brochure about which continent they would most like to visit, forming an opinion and supporting it with evidence from the texts.

Speaking and Listening: Students have frequent opportunities to develop listening and speaking skills in multiple settings, including whole group, small group, and pairs. During discussions about the texts, students practice sharing ideas in a group setting. Students learn the importance of confirming their understanding of a text read aloud or information presented orally to demonstrate their ability to listen to their peers and reflect upon their discussion. They also demonstrate an ability to use information from the text to describe familiar people, places, things, and events to provide additional detail while discussing a topic. Students engage in conversations about the texts both in class discussions and in Socratic Seminars. These opportunities give students a chance to build their knowledge of the content and support their ideas with text evidence while responding to classmates thoughtfully and respectfully.

Standards

FOCUS STANDARDS

Reading Literature	
RL.K.4	Ask and answer questions about unknown words in a text.
RL.K.5	Recognize common types of texts (e.g., storybooks, poems).
RL.K.7	With prompting and support, describe the relationship between illustrations and the story in which they appear (e.g., what moment in a story an illustration depicts).
Reading Informational	
RI.K.7	With prompting and support, describe the relationship between illustrations and the text in which they appear (e.g., what person, place, thing, or idea in the text an illustration depicts).
RI.K.8	With prompting and support, identify the reasons an author gives to support points in a text.
RI.K.9	With prompting and support, identify basic similarities in and differences between two texts on the same topic (e.g., in illustrations, descriptions, or procedures).
Writing	
W.K.1	Use a combination of drawing, dictating, and writing to compose opinion pieces in which they tell a reader the topic or the name of the book they are writing about and state an opinion or preference about the topic or book.
W.K.5	With guidance and support from adults, respond to questions and suggestions from peers and add details to strengthen writing as needed.
W.K.8	With guidance and support from adults, recall information from experiences or gather information from provided sources to answer a question.

Language	
L.K.1.f	Produce and expand complete sentences in shared language activities.
L.K.2.a	Capitalize the first word in a sentence and the pronoun *I*.
L.K.2.b	Recognize and name end punctuation.
L.K.4.a	Identify new meanings for familiar words and apply them accurately (e.g., knowing *duck* is a bird and learning the verb *to duck*).
L.K.4.b	Use the most frequently occurring inflections and affixes (e.g., *-ed, -s, re-, un-, pre-, -ful, -less*) as a clue to the meaning of an unknown word.
L.K.5.b	Demonstrate understanding of frequently occurring verbs and adjectives by relating them to their opposites (antonyms).
L.K.5.d	Distinguish shades of meaning among verbs describing the same general action (e.g., *walk, march, strut, prance*) by acting out the meanings.
Speaking and Listening	
SL.K.2	Confirm understanding of a text read aloud or information presented orally or through other media by asking and answering questions about key details and requesting clarification if something is not understood.
SL.K.4	Describe familiar people, places, things, and events and, with prompting and support, provide additional detail.

CONTINUING STANDARDS

Reading Literature	
RL.K.10	Actively engage in group reading activities with purpose and understanding.
Reading Informational Text	
RI.K.10	Actively engage in group reading activities with purpose and understanding.
Language	
L.K.6	Use words and phrases acquired through conversations, reading and being read to, and responding to texts.

Major Assessments

Focusing Question Task	Elements That Support Success on the EOM Task	Standards
1. Write an opinion statement about which continent, Asia or Europe, has the most interesting things to do.	▪ Use informational texts to gather information in order to form an opinion. ▪ Demonstrate understanding of how to form an opinion statement.	RI.K.1; W.K.1, W.K.8
2. Write an opinion paragraph about which continent, Africa or Antarctica, has the most interesting natural features.	▪ Demonstrate an understanding of the opinion paragraph structure. ▪ Use information from the text to form and support an opinion. ▪ Demonstrate understanding of how adjectives add detail to a sentence.	RI.K.1; W.K.1, W.K.8
3. Part 1: Write a sentence about what moment in the story the illustration on pages 17–18 depicts. Part 2: Write an opinion paragraph about a favorite character in *Why Mosquitoes Buzz in People's Ears*. Part 3: In small groups, distinguish shades of meaning among the verbs *tiptoe*, *walk*, *lumber*, and *scurry* by acting them out.	▪ Use evidence from the text to support an opinion. ▪ Use the illustrations to guide understanding and collect information. ▪ Demonstrate understanding of the opinion paragraph structure. ▪ Demonstrate understanding of how adjectives provide detail in a sentence.	RL.K.1, RL.K.7; W.K.1, W.K.2 W.K.8; L.K.5.d
4. Part 1: Use understanding of the words and pictures in *South America* to respond to questions about the text. Part 2: Write an opinion paragraph about which continent, South America or Australia, has the most interesting animals.	▪ Use informational texts to gather information and form an opinion about a topic. ▪ Support an opinion statement with evidence from the text. ▪ Add details to writing based on peer feedback.	RI.K.1, RI.K.7; W.K.1, W.K.5, W.K.8

Focusing Question Task	Elements That Support Success on the EOM Task	Standards
5. Part 1: Write an opinion paragraph in the form of a letter to convince someone to visit North America. Part 2: Identify the different forms of end punctuation by circling examples from the text.	▪ Use informational texts to gather information and form an opinion about a topic. ▪ Support an opinion statement with evidence from the text. ▪ Demonstrate understanding of the part of a complete sentence, including using a capital letter to signal the start of a sentence. ▪ Demonstrate understanding of the opinion paragraph structure by restating an opinion to conclude the paragraph.	RI.K.1; W.K.1, W.K.8; L.K.1.f, L.K.2.a, L.K.2.b

New-Read Assessment	Elements That Support Success on the EOM Task	Standards
1. After listening to a read-aloud of "5 Reasons Why Animal Moms Are Awesome," identify two reasons the author gives to support the point, "African Elephant moms are awesome!"	▪ Demonstrate an understanding of how reasons or information support a point made by the author.	RI.K.8
2. After listening to a read-aloud of *Moon Rope*, use knowledge of word relationships and the illustrations to define key vocabulary.	▪ Understand how illustrations can help determine the meaning of unknown words. ▪ Develop an understanding of familiar words by relating them to their opposites. ▪ Understand that certain words can have multiple meanings.	RL.K.4; L.K.4.a, L.K.4.b, L.K.5.b
3. Use the map on pages 38–39 of *World Atlas* to compare and contrast information that appears on the map of North America with information collected from *Introducing North America*.	▪ Identify how two sources on the same topic can provide similar and different information. ▪ Understand that using multiple sources can enhance understanding of a topic.	RI.K.9

Socratic Seminar	Elements That Support Success on the EOM Task	Standards
1. Describe which natural feature in Antarctica you would most like to explore and give an example from the text to support your opinion.	▪ Use information from the text to form an opinion about a topic. ▪ Demonstrate understanding of how providing an example helps support an opinion statement. ▪ Demonstrate the importance of confirming understanding.	SL.K.2
2. After sharing the EOM Task, describe how the continent you chose is similar to and different from North America.	▪ Demonstrate an ability to make connections between information gathered on two different continents. ▪ Use examples from the text to describe similarities and differences. ▪ Demonstrate understanding of how describing details on a topic provides more information.	SL.K.4

End-of-Module Task	Criteria for Success	Standards
Part 1: Use knowledge of various text types to sort each module text into one of the following categories: informational text or storybook. Part 2: Choosing from one of the following continents–Asia, Africa, Antarctica, Europe, Australia, and South America–create a travel brochure to explain why someone should visit that continent.	▪ Sort the module texts by genre. ▪ Use the Opinion Sandwich writing model to structure the opinion paragraph. ▪ Support an opinion statement with details from the text as part of a shared research piece. ▪ Use drawings to support and add detail to each sentence. ▪ Produce and expand complete sentences with information from the text, including capitalizing the first letter of each sentence.	RI.K.1; RL.K.5 W.K.1, W.K.8; L.K.1.f, L.K.2.a

Module Map

Focusing Question 1: What interesting things can people do in Europe and Asia?				
	TEXT(S)	**CONTENT FRAMING QUESTION**	**CRAFT QUESTION(S)**	**LEARNING GOALS**
1	*Earth from Space*, Stöckli, Reto, et al. "The Seven Continents Song ," Silly School Songs "*Where in the World Is Carmen Sandiego?* from Smithsonian Folkways ," Smithsonian Folkways *Asia*, Rebecca Hirsch *Europe*, Rebecca Hirsch	<u>Wonder</u> What do I notice and wonder about *Europe* and *Asia*?		▪ Use a variety of question words to ask questions about *Asia*. (RI.K.1, L.K.1.d) ▪ Represent learning through writing and drawing. (W.10*) ▪ Identify land and water items by the categories *continent* and *ocean* to gain a sense of these vocabulary words. (L.K.5.a)
2	"The Seven Continents Song ," Silly School Songs *Asia*, Rebecca Hirsch "Traditional Chinese Dance– 'Flowers Contend in Beauty'"	<u>Organize</u> What is happening in *Asia*?	<u>Examine</u> Why is opinion writing important?	▪ Use text features to identify the main topic and key details in sections of *Asia*. (RI.K.2) ▪ Write a sentence to state an opinion. (W.K.1, L.K.1.f) ▪ Demonstrate understanding of frequently occurring adjectives by relating them to their opposites. (L.K.5.b)
3	"The Seven Continents Song ," Silly School Songs *Europe*, Rebecca Hirsch *The Story of Ferdinand*, Munro Leaf; Illustrations, Robert Lawson	<u>Organize</u> What is happening in *Europe*?		▪ Use text features to identify the main topic and key details in a section of *Europe*. (RI.K.2) ▪ Identify unknown words in The Story of Ferdinand. (RL.K.4) ▪ Demonstrate understanding of *sit, pick,* and *shout* by stating and acting out each word's opposite. (L.K.5.b)

Focusing Question 1: What interesting things can people do in Europe and Asia?				
4	"The Seven Continents Song ," Silly School Songs *Asia*, Rebecca Hirsch	<u>Reveal</u> What does a deeper exploration of the words and photographs in *Asia* reveal?	<u>Experiment</u> How do I write an opinion statement? <u>Examine</u> Why is it important to create and expand complete sentences?	▪ Use photographs and details from the text to describe things people can do in Asia. (RI.K.7) ▪ Use the pictures and words in the text to form an opinion statement. (RI.K.1, W.K.1, W.K.8, L.K.1.f) ▪ Identify the parts of a complete sentence and describe how a given sentence was expanded. (L.K.1.f)
5	"The Seven Continents Song ," Silly School Songs *Europe*, Rebecca Hirsch *The Story of Ferdinand*, Munro Leaf; Illustrations, Robert Lawson	<u>Reveal</u> What does a deeper exploration of the words and photographs in *Europe* reveal?	<u>Experiment</u> How do I write an opinion statement?	▪ Use photographs and details from the text to describe things people can do in Europe. (RI.K.7) ▪ Use the illustrations and details from the text to describe events in *The Story of Ferdinand*. (RL.K.1, RL.K.7, W.K.8) ▪ Identify new meanings for the words *stick* and *horns* and apply them accurately. (L.K.4.a)
6	"The Seven Continents Song," Silly School Songs *When I Was Young in the Mountains*, Cynthia Rylant *Asia*, Rebecca Hirsch "Explore Views of the Burj Khalifa with Google Maps," Google Maps *The Story of Ferdinand*, Munro Leaf; Illustrations, Robert Lawson	<u>Reveal</u> What does a deeper exploration of *Asia* reveal about a point the author makes?	<u>Experiment</u> How do I write an opinion statement?	▪ Identify reasons the author gives to support a point in Asia. (RI.K.8) ▪ Use the photographs and details from the text to state an opinion about the text. (W.K.1, W.K.8) ▪ Distinguish shades of meaning between *stick*, *touch*, and *poke* by acting out their meanings. (L.K.5.d)

Focusing Question 1: What interesting things can people do in Europe and Asia?				
7 ✔FQT	"The Seven Continents Song," Silly School Songs *Europe*, Rebecca Hirsch *Asia*, Rebecca Hirsch	**Reveal** What does a deeper exploration of *Europe* reveal about a point the author makes?	**Execute** How do I write an opinion statement for my Focusing Question Task?	▪ Identify reasons the author gives to support a point in *Europe*. (RI.K.8) ▪ Reflect upon evidence collected from *Asia* and *Europe* to form and write an opinion statement. (RI.K.1, W.K.1, W.K.8) ▪ Distinguish shades of meaning between *speak*, *whisper*, and *yell* by acting out their meanings. (L.K.5.d)
8	"The Seven Continents Song," Silly School Songs *Earth from Space*, Stöckli, Reto, et al. *Asia*, Rebecca Hirsch *Europe*, Rebecca Hirsch *World Atlas*, Nick Crane; Illustrations, David Dean "Explore Views of the Burj Khalifa with Google Maps," Google Maps	**Know** How do *Europe* and *Asia* build my knowledge of the continents?	**Experiment** How does creating and expanding sentences with prepositions work?	▪ Use the evidence organizer and photographs from the text to reflect upon and share important learning from *Asia*. (RI.K.2) ▪ Identify basic similarities between *Europe* and *World Atlas*. (RI.K.9) ▪ Create a complete sentence and expand it by adding a preposition. (L.K.1.e, L.K.1.f)

Focusing Question 2: What interesting natural features can people see in Africa and Antarctica?				
	TEXT(S)	CONTENT FRAMING QUESTION	CRAFT QUESTION(S)	LEARNING GOALS
9	"Antarctic Sights and Sounds," James Napoli "*Where in the World Is Carmen Sandiego?* from Smithsonian Folkways," Smithsonian Folkways *Africa*, Rebecca Hirsch *Antarctica*, Rebecca Hirsch "Penguin Song," Preschool Education	Wonder What do I notice and wonder about *Antarctica* and *Africa*?		▪ Represent learning through writing and drawing. (W.10*) ▪ Use a variety of question words to ask questions about *Africa*. (RI.K.1, L.K.1.d) ▪ Demonstrate understanding of frequently occurring adjectives, or describing words, by matching them to their opposites. (L.K.5.b)
10	"Penguin Song," Preschool Education *Africa*, Rebecca Hirsch *Antarctica*, Rebecca Hirsch	Organize What is happening in *Africa* and *Antarctica*?	Examine Why is supporting an opinion important? Examine Why is it important to make sure you understand something?	▪ Use text features to identify the main topic and key details in a section of *Africa*. (RI.K.2) ▪ Demonstrate understanding of frequently occurring adjectives, or describing words, by matching them to their opposites. (L.K.5.b)
11	"Penguin Song," Preschool Education *Africa*, Rebecca Hirsch "Storm-Proofing the World's Biggest Mud Building," BBC Earth	Reveal What does a deeper exploration of the words and illustrations reveal in *Africa*?	Experiment How do I support an opinion with reasons from the text? Experiment How can I show I understand something?	▪ Use photographs and details from the text to describe natural features in Africa. (RI.K.7, L.K.5.c) ▪ Use details from the words and illustrations to support an opinion statement. (RI.K.1, W.K.1, W.K.8) ▪ Demonstrate understanding of *work*, *grow*, and *climb* by acting out their opposites. (L.K.5.b)

Focusing Question 2: What interesting natural features can people see in Africa and Antarctica?			
12	"Penguin Song," Preschool Education *Antarctica*, Rebecca Hirsch	Reveal What does a deeper exploration of the words and illustrations reveal in *Antarctica*?	Experiment How do I support an opinion with reasons from the text?	▪ Use photographs and details from the text to describe natural features in *Antarctica*. (RI.K.7, L.K.5.c) ▪ Use details from the words and illustrations to support an opinion statement. (RI.K.1, W.K.1, W.K.8) ▪ Distinguish shades of meaning between *blow*, *swirl*, and *flow* by acting out their meanings. (L.K.5.d)
13 ✔NR ✔FQT	"Penguin Song," Preschool Education *Africa*, Rebecca Hirsch "5 Reasons Why Animal Moms Are Awesome," April Capochino Myers	Reveal What does a deeper exploration of *Africa* reveal about a point the author makes?	Execute How do I write an opinion statement for my Focusing Question Task? Experiment How does writing and expanding sentences by adding describing words work?	▪ Identify reasons the author gives to support a point in *Africa*. (RI.K.8) ▪ Identify reasons the author gives to support the point "African elephant moms are awesome!" (RI.K.8) ▪ Create a complete sentence and expand it by adding a describing word. (L.K.1.f)
14 ✔FQT	"Penguin Song," Preschool Education *Africa*, Rebecca Hirsch *World Atlas*, Nick Crane; Illustrations, David Dean "5 Reasons Why Animal Moms Are Awesome," April Capochino Myers	Know How does *Africa* build my knowledge of the continents?	Execute How do I support my opinion statement in my Focusing Question Task?	▪ Use information gathered from *Africa* and *Antarctica* to provide supporting reasons for an opinion statement. (RI.K.1, W.K.1, W.K.8) ▪ Identify basic similarities in and differences between *Africa* and *World Atlas*. (RI.K.9) ▪ Use the meaning of the word ending *-ful* as a clue to find the meaning of a new describing word. (L.K.4.b)

Focusing Question 2: What interesting natural features can people see in Africa and Antarctica?

| 15 ✔FQT ✔SS | "Penguin Song," Preschool Education

Africa, Rebecca Hirsch

Antarctica, Rebecca Hirsch | <u>Know</u>

How does *Antarctica* build my knowledge of the continents? | <u>Execute</u>

How do I support my opinion statement in my Focusing Question Task?

<u>Execute</u>

How can I show my understanding in a Socratic Seminar? | ▪ Use information gathered from *Africa* and *Antarctica* to provide supporting reasons for an opinion statement. (RI.K.1, W.K.1, W.K.8)

▪ Confirm understanding of a text read aloud by answering questions during a group discussion. (RI.K.1, SL.K.1, SL.K.2, SL.K.6)

▪ Use the meaning of the word ending *-less* as a clue to figure out the meaning of an unknown describing word. (L.K.4.b) |

Focusing Question 3: How can a story transport you to a different place?

	TEXT(S)	CONTENT FRAMING QUESTION	CRAFT QUESTION(S)	LEARNING GOALS
16	*Why Mosquitoes Buzz in People's Ears: A West African Tale*, Verna Aardem; Illustrations Leo and Diane Dillon *Carta Marina*, Olaus Magnus	<u>Wonder</u> What do I notice and wonder about *Why Mosquitoes Buzz in People's Ears*?	<u>Examine</u> Why is it important to share your writing?	▪ Use familiar words in *Why Mosquitoes Buzz in People's Ears* to determine the meaning of unknown words. (RL.K.4, L.K.5.d) ▪ Use a variety of question words to ask questions about *Carta Marina*. (RL.K.1, L.K.1.d) ▪ Apply both meanings of the words *bear* and *lumber*. (L.K.4.a)

Focusing Question 3: How can a story transport you to a different place?				
17	"Lions Roar," *CanTeach* *Why Mosquitoes Buzz in People's Ears: A West African Tale*, Verna Aardema; Illustrations Leo and Diane Dillon *Carta Marina*, Olaus Magnus "Burkina Faso: Music," *Our Africa*	<u>Organize</u> What is happening in *Why Mosquitoes Buzz in People's Ears*?	<u>Experiment</u> How can I share my writing with others?	▪ Use illustrations from *Why Mosquitoes Buzz in People's Ears* to better understand the events in the story. (RL.K.2, RL.K.7) ▪ Follow agreed-upon rules for discussion when sharing writing with a peer. (W.K.5, SL.K.1.a) ▪ Use the meaning of the prefix *re-* as a clue to find the meaning of an unknown word. (L.K.4.b)
18	"Lions Roar," *CanTeach* *Why Mosquitoes Buzz in People's Ears: A West African Tale*, Verna Aardema; Illustrations Leo and Diane Dillon *Carta Marina*, Olaus Magnus	<u>Reveal</u> What does a deeper exploration of the words and illustrations reveal about unknown words in *Why Mosquitoes Buzz in People's Ears*?	<u>Experiment</u> How do I respond to someone's writing?	▪ Use context clues from the words and illustrations to define unknown words in *Why Mosquitoes Buzz in People's Ears*. (RL.K.4, RL.K.7) ▪ Provide feedback to a peer about their writing. (W.K.5) ▪ Demonstrate understanding of *lumbered*, *scurried*, *returned*, and *left* by acting out their opposites. (L.K.5.b)
19 ✔FQT	"Lions Roar," *CanTeach* *Why Mosquitoes Buzz in People's Ears: A West African Tale*, Verna Aardema; Illustrations Leo and Diane Dillon	<u>Reveal</u> What does a deeper exploration of the words and illustrations reveal in *Why Mosquitoes Buzz in People's Ears*?	<u>Experiment</u> How do I respond to someone's writing?	▪ Use the words and illustrations in the text to describe the characters' actions. (RL.K.4, RL.K.7) ▪ Use the illustrations to determine what is happening in one scene of the text. (RL.K.7, W.K.2) ▪ Use the meaning of the prefix *un-* as a clue to find the meaning of an unknown word. (L.K.4.b)

Focusing Question 3: How can a story transport you to a different place?			
20 ✔ FQT	"Lions Roar," *CanTeach* *Why Mosquitoes Buzz in People's Ears: A West African Tale*, Verna Aardema; Illustrations Leo and Diane Dillon *Carta Marina*, Olaus Magnus *Earth from Space*, Stöckli, Reto, et al. "Burkina Faso: Music," *Our Africa*	<u>Distill</u> What is the essential meaning of *Why Mosquitoes Buzz in People's Ears*?	<u>Execute</u> How do I execute my Focusing Question Task?	▪ Determine essential meanings of *Why Mosquitoes Buzz in People's Ears*. (RL.K.1) ▪ Express understanding of the characters in *Why Mosquitoes Buzz in People's Ears* by writing an opinion piece about a favorite character. (RL.K.1, W.K.1, W.K.8) ▪ Describe multiple meanings of the words snap and mind. (L.K.4.a)
21 ✔ FQT	"Lions Roar," *CanTeach* *Why Mosquitoes Buzz in People's Ears: A West African Tale*, Verna Aardema *Carta Marina*, Olaus Magnus *Earth from Space*, Stöckli, Reto, et al. *World Atlas*, Nick Crane; Illustrated by David Dean	<u>Know</u> How does *Why Mosquitoes Buzz in People's Ears* build my knowledge?	<u>Execute</u> How do I execute my Focusing Question Task? <u>Execute</u> How do I respond to my peer's Focusing Question Task? <u>Experiment</u> How do I create and expand complete sentences?	▪ Express understanding of the characters in *Why Mosquitoes Buzz in People's Ears* by writing an opinion piece about a favorite character. (RL.K.1, W.K.1, W.K.8) ▪ Distinguish the different shades of meaning between verbs of movement. (L.K.5.d) ▪ Write a complete sentence and expand it by adding an adjective and preposition. (L.K.1.f)

Focusing Question 4: What amazing animals can people see in South America and Australia?				
	TEXT(S)	**CONTENT FRAMING QUESTION**	**CRAFT QUESTION(S)**	**LEARNING GOALS**
22	*"Where in the World Is Carmen Sandiego?* from Smithsonian Folkways," Smithsonian Folkways *South America*, Rebecca Hirsch *Australia*, Rebecca Hirsch	<u>Wonder</u> What do I notice and wonder about *South America* and *Australia*?	<u>Examine</u> Why do writers add to their writing?	▪ Represent learning through writing and drawing. (W.10*) ▪ Use a variety of question words to ask questions about *Australia*. (RI.K.1, L.K.1.d) ▪ Use the meaning of the prefix *un-* as a clue to figure out the meaning of an unknown word. (L.K.4.b)
23 ✔NR	"Americas–Fact Files," *Go Wild* *South America*, Rebecca Hirsch *Moon Rope*, Lois Ehlert "Moles," *DK Find Out!*	<u>Organize</u> What is happening in *South America*?		▪ Use text features to identify the main topic and key details in sections of *South America*. (RI.K.2) ▪ Use knowledge of word relationships and the illustrations in *Moon Rope* to define key vocabulary. (RL.K.4, L.K.4.a, L.K.4.b, L.K.5.b) ▪ Distinguish shades of meaning between *hitch* and *hang* by acting out their meanings and analyzing how the meaning of the words change the meaning of the story. (L.K.5.d)

Focusing Question 4: What amazing animals can people see in South America and Australia?				
24	*Moon Rope*, Lois Ehlert *Australia*, Rebecca Hirsch	<u>Organize</u> What is happening in *Australia*?	<u>Experiment</u> How do writers add to their writing? <u>Examine</u> Why is it important write a complete sentence that begins with a capital letter?	▪ Use text features to identify the main topic and key details in a section of *Australia*. (RI.K.2) ▪ Add details to strengthen a piece of writing. (W.K.5) ▪ Distinguish between a phrase and a complete sentence and identify the letter that should be capitalized in a complete sentence. (L.K.1.f, L.K.2.a)
25	*Moon Rope*, Lois Ehlert *Earth from Space*, Stöckli, Reto, et al. *South America*, Rebecca Hirsch "Patterns of Chinchero" *Descendants of the Incas*	<u>Reveal</u> What does a deeper exploration of the words and illustrations reveal in *South America*?	<u>Experiment</u> How do I add to my writing? <u>Experiment</u> How does writing a complete sentence that begins with a capital letter work?	▪ Use photographs and details from the text to describe animals in *South America*. (RI.K.7) ▪ Respond to suggestions from a peer to improve writing. (W.K.5) ▪ Write a complete sentence caption that begins with a capital letter. (L.K.1.f, L.K.2.a)
26 ✔FQT ✔VOC	*Moon Rope*, Lois Ehlert *Australia*, Rebecca Hirsch *South America*, Rebecca Hirsch	<u>Reveal</u> What does a deeper exploration of the words and illustrations reveal in *Australia*?	<u>Execute</u> How do I execute my Focusing Question Task?	▪ Use photographs and details from the text to respond to questions about *South America*. (RI.K.7) ▪ Use information gathered from *South America* and *Australia* to form an opinion about the animals on those continents. (RI.K.1, W.K.1, W.K.8) ▪ Demonstrate understanding of grade-level vocabulary. (L.K.6)

Focusing Question 4: What amazing animals can people see in South America and Australia?				
27 ✔FQT	*Moon Rope*, Lois Ehlert *Australia*, Rebecca Hirsch *South America*, Rebecca Hirsch *World Atlas*, Nick Crane; Illustrations, David Dean	<u>Know</u> How do *Australia* and *South America* build my knowledge of the continents?	<u>Execute</u> How do I add to my writing in my Focusing Question Task? <u>Experiment</u> How do I write a complete sentence that begins with a capital letter?	▪ Use information gathered from *South America* and *Australia* to support an opinion about the continent. (RI.K.1, W.K.1, W.K.8) ▪ Respond to suggestions from a peer to improve writing for the Focusing Question Task. (W.K.5) ▪ Identify basic similarities in and differences between *South America* and *World Atlas*. (RI.K.9) ▪ Write a complete sentence that begins with a capital letter. (L.K.1.f, L.K.2.a)

Focusing Question 5: Why might people want to visit North America?				
	TEXT(S)	**CONTENT FRAMING QUESTION**	**CRAFT QUESTION(S)**	**LEARNING GOALS**
28	"*Where in the World Is Carmen Sandiego?* from Smithsonian Folkways," *Smithsonian Folkways* *Introducing North America*, Chris Oxlade "What is life?" Crowfoot "Grand Canyon Scenic Splendor," *National Park Service*	<u>Wonder</u> What do I notice and wonder about *Introducing North America?*	<u>Examine</u> Why is restating an opinion important? <u>Examine</u> Why is it important to use a punctuation mark at the end of a complete sentence?	▪ Use a variety of question words to ask questions about *Introducing North America*. (RI.K.1, L.K.1.d) ▪ Examine the importance of writing a conclusion sentence in an opinion paragraph. (W.K.1) ▪ Identify a complete sentence and describe the end punctuation. (L.K.1.f, L.K.2.b)

Focusing Question 5: Why might people want to visit North America?				
29	"What is life?" Crowfoot *Introducing North America*, Chris Oxlade	<u>Organize</u> What is happening in *Introducing North America*?	<u>Experiment</u> How can I restate my opinion? <u>Experiment</u> How does using a punctuation mark at the end of a complete sentence work?	▪ Use text features to identify the main topic and key details in sections of *Introducing North America*. (RI.K.2) ▪ Restate an opinion to provide a conclusion for an opinion paragraph. (W.K.1) ▪ Create a complete sentence and describe the end punctuation. (L.K.1.f, L.K.2.b)
30 ✔ FQT	"What is life?" Crowfoot *Introducing North America*, Chris Oxlade	<u>Reveal:</u> What does a deeper exploration of the words and illustrations reveal in *Introducing North America*?	<u>Execute</u> How do I execute my Focusing Question Task? <u>Experiment</u> How do I end a complete sentence with the correct punctuation mark?	▪ Use photographs and details from the text to describe natural features and animals in *Introducing North America*. (RI.K.7) ▪ Use information gathered from *Introducing North America* to form an opinion about the continent. (W.K.1, W.K.8, L.K.2.a) ▪ Write a complete sentence that ends with the correct punctuation mark. (L.K.1.f, L.K.2.b)
31 ✔ FQT ✔ NR	"What is life?" Crowfoot *Introducing North America*, Chris Oxlade *World Atlas*, Nick Crane; Illustrations, David Dean	<u>Know</u> How does *Introducing North America* build my knowledge of the continents?	<u>Execute</u> How do I execute using capital letters in my Focusing Question Task?	▪ Recognize and annotate end punctuation. (L.K.2.b) ▪ Use information gathered from *Introducing North America* to support an opinion about the continent. (RI.K.1, W.K.1, W.K.8, L.K.1.f, L.K.2.a) ▪ Identify basic similarities in and differences between *Introducing North America* and *World Atlas*. (RI.K.9) ▪ Sort photographs from the text into categories based on the type of natural feature it depicts. (L.K.5.a)

Essential Question: What makes the world fascinating?				
	TEXT(S)	CONTENT FRAMING QUESTION	CRAFT QUESTION(S)	LEARNING GOALS
32 ✔EOM	All Module Texts	Know How do Module 4 texts build my knowledge the continents?	Examine Why is it important to describe things in detail when I speak? Excel How do I improve at writing a complete sentence?	▪ Recognize common text types and sort module texts into genres. (RL.K.5) ▪ Examine the importance of verbal descriptions in providing details. (RI.K.7, SL.K.4) ▪ Write and expand a complete sentence that begins with a capital letter and ends with the correct punctuation mark. (L.K.1.f, L.K.2.a, L.K.2.b)
33 ✔VOC ✔EOM	All Module Texts	Know How do Module 4 texts build my knowledge of the continents?	Experiment How do I describe things when I speak? Execute How do I use complete sentences in my End-of-Module Task?	▪ Express understanding of the unique natural features, animals, and things to do on the different continents. (RI.K.1, W.K.1, W.K.8, L.K.1.f, L.K.2.a) ▪ Use descriptive words to verbally describe familiar places. (SL.K.4) ▪ Demonstrate understanding of grade-level vocabulary. (L.K.6)
34 ✔EOM	All Module Texts	Know How do Module 4 texts build my knowledge of the continents?	Execute How do I use complete sentences for my End-of-Module Task? Excel How do I improve my opinion writing?	▪ Express understanding of the unique natural features, animals, and things to do on the different continents. (RI.K.1, W.K.1, W.K.8, L.K.1.f, L.K.2.a) ▪ With support, evaluate writing and use complete sentences to share reflections. (L.K.1.f)

Essential Question: What makes the world fascinating?				
35 ✔ EOM ✔ SS	All Module Texts	<u>Know</u> How do Module 4 texts build my knowledge of the continents?	<u>Execute</u> How do I describe things in a Socratic Seminar? <u>Excel</u> How do I improve my opinion writing?	• Express understanding of the unique natural features, animals, and things to do on different continents. (RI.K.1, W.K.1, W.K.8, L.K.1.f, L.K.2.a) • Verbally describe how a detail in one supporting reason from the EOM Task compares to a characteristic of North America. (SL.K.4, SL.K.6) • With support, evaluate writing and use complete sentences to share reflections. (L.K.1.f)

Focusing Question: What is the story of the year?				
	TEXT(S)	**CONTENT FRAMING QUESTION**	**CRAFT QUESTION(S)**	**LEARNING GOALS**
36	All Module 1–4 Core Texts *The Cornell Farm*, Edward Hicks *Washington Crossing the Delaware*, Emanuel Leutze *Carta Marina*, Olaus Magnus	<u>Know</u> How do this year's texts build my knowledge?		• Reflect on learning over the course of the year and verbally describe something from a text that sparked a sense of wonder. (RI.K.1, RL.K.1, SL.K.2, SL.K.4) • Draw and label one detail from a module text that sparks a sense of wonder. (RI.K.1, RL.K.1, W.K.8, L.K.2.c, L.K.2.d)

*In alignment with the CCSS, W.10 formally begins in Grade 3. However, K–2 students write routinely for a variety of time frames, tasks, purposes, and audiences. As a result, this lesson contains instruction related to W.10 in an effort to familiarize students with a range of writing.

■ FOCUSING QUESTION: LESSONS 1–8

What interesting things can people do in Europe and Asia?

1 2 3 4 5 6 7 8 9 10 11 12 13 14 15 16 17 18 19 20 21 22 23 24 25 26 27 28 29 30 31 32 33 34 35 36

Lesson 1

TEXTS

- *Earth from Space*, Stöckli, Reto, et al. (**http://witeng.link/0373**)

- "The Seven Continents Song," Silly School Songs (video) (**http://witeng.link/0374**)

- "*Where in the World Is Carmen Sandiego?* from Smithsonian Folkways," Smithsonian Folkways (playlist) (**http://witeng.link/0375**)

- *Asia*, Rebecca Hirsch

- *Europe*, Rebecca Hirsch

Lesson 1: At a Glance

AGENDA

Welcome (8 min.)

Read the Essential Question

Launch (9 min.)

Learn (55 min.)

Listen Actively and Share Observations about Europe (15 min.)

Share Questions about Europe (10 min.)

Listen Actively and Share Observations about Asia (12 min.)

Share Questions about Asia (10 min.)

Examine Earth from Space (8 min.)

Land (2 min.)

Answer the Content Framing Question

Wrap (1 min.)

Assign Homework

Vocabulary Deep Dive: Define *Continent* and *Ocean* (15 min.)

STANDARDS ADDRESSED

The full text of ELA Standards can be found in the Module Overview.

Reading

- RI.K.1

Writing

- W.10*

Speaking and Listening

- SL.K.1.a, SL.K.2

Language

- L.K.1.d
- ⬇ L.K.5.a

MATERIALS

- Volume of Reading Reflection Questions
- Large map of the world (retained for the remainder of the module)
- Image of a small airplane (retained for the remainder of the module)
- Question Corner signs (created in Module 1)
- Wonder Chart for *Europe* and *Asia*
- Question Grab Bags (created in Module 3)
- Globe
- Sticky notes

Learning Goals

Use a variety of question words to ask questions about *Asia*. (RI.K.1, L.K.1.d)

✔ Generate questions using Question Grab Bags.

Represent learning through writing and drawing. (W.10*)

✔ Record questions about the *Earth from Space* in Response Journals.

⬇ Identify land and water items by the categories *continent* and *ocean* to gain a sense of these vocabulary words. (L.K.5.a)

✔ Use Nonverbal Signals to identify if an item is found on a continent or in an ocean.

*In alignment with the CCSS, W.10 formally begins in Grade 3. However, Kindergarten–Grade 2 students write routinely to a variety of time frames, tasks, purposes, and audiences. This lesson contains instruction related to W.10 to familiarize students with a range of writing.

✔ Checks for Understanding

ESSENTIAL QUESTION

What makes the world fascinating?

FOCUSING QUESTION: Lessons 1–8

What interesting things can people do in Europe and Asia?

CONTENT FRAMING QUESTION: Lesson 1

Wonder: *What do I notice and wonder about* Europe and Asia?

Students begin Module 4 by considering the beauty and mystery of our world, exploring a NASA image of Earth taken from space. They embark on an exploration of Earth's continents by reading the texts *Europe* and *Asia.* Students continue to build strong habits of mind by observing and generating questions about the texts. Throughout the module, students explore and analyze texts about the seven continents to collect information about the natural features, animals, and activities on each.

Welcome 8 MIN.

READ THE ESSENTIAL QUESTION

Display the image *Earth from Space* (**http://witeng.link/0373**). Students consider the image silently for thirty seconds, holding questions and comments.

Ask: "What do you see in this picture?" Volunteers respond. Confirm that the image shows Earth, the moon, and stars.

Direct students to look at the blue areas of the image, and ask: "What are the blue areas of our Earth?" Volunteers respond. Confirm that the blue areas indicate areas of water on Earth.

Direct students to look at the green and brown parts of the image, and ask: "What are these green and brown areas?" Volunteers respond. Confirm that the green and brown areas indicate land.

Instruct students to Think-Pair-Share, and ask: "How does this picture make you feel? Why?" Use Equity Sticks to call on students to respond.

Tell students that as long as people have lived on Earth, they have been curious about the variety of people, places, and animals of the planet. Many explorers have traveled the world to discover answers to some of their questions, meeting people, trying to understand their culture and the features of their land, making maps as they go.

Explain that students will join the exploration during this module as they travel on an adventure around the world. They will travel using books, videos, songs, and pictures to learn about Earth's people, places, and animals.

Display and read aloud the Essential Question, pointing to each word as you say it. As you read the word *world*, model a Nonverbal Signal by using your hands to outline an imaginary globe.

Students Echo Read the Essential Question using the Nonverbal Signal for *world*. Remind students that the Essential Question is the big question they will be trying to answer over the course of this module.

TEACHER NOTE	Leave the Essential Question posted for reference throughout the module.

Launch 9 MIN.

Reference the areas of land on the *Earth from Space* image and explain that when you look at the world from far away, you see huge pieces of land separated by water. Explain that these pieces of land are called <u>continents</u>.

Students repeat the word *continent* several times. Place *continent* on the Word Wall as a module word.

Explain that Earth has seven continents and students will explore each one of them over the course of the module. Play "The Seven Continents Song" video (**http://witeng.link/0374**) to introduce the continents.

Foundational Skills Connection

Invite students to clap out the syllables as they repeat the word *continent*. Ask: "How many syllables does the word *continent* have?" If needed, repeat this activity for the names of the seven continents for additional practice counting syllables. If some students need help blending syllables, practice with continent names. Say the syllables in a word, pausing for a second between each syllable. After saying all the syllables, signal students to say the full word. For example, after hearing Ant...arc...ti...ca, students say *Antarctica*.

TEACHER NOTE	Students will use the first part of "The Seven Continents Song" for fluency practice beginning in Lesson 2.

Instruct students to Mix and Mingle, and ask: "What did you notice about 'The Seven Continents Song'?" Call on several students to share their observations with the whole class.

Display and read aloud the Focusing Question. Students Echo Read the question. Underline or highlight the words *Europe* and *Asia*.

Explain that students will start their adventure by exploring Europe and Asia, and that students will read two informational texts as an introduction to these continents. Display the front covers of *Europe* and *Asia*. Ask: "What will our jobs be as we read these books for the first time today?" Volunteers respond.

- *We should notice things about the books.*
- *We will talk about what we notice.*
- *Our job is to ask questions about the books.*

Use student responses to confirm that during this lesson they will notice and wonder about *Europe* and *Asia*. Display and read aloud the Content Framing Question.

Learn 55 MIN.

LISTEN ACTIVELY AND SHARE OBSERVATIONS ABOUT EUROPE 15 MIN.

Whole Group

Tell students they will start their world adventure by exploring the continent of Europe. Display a large map of the world and explain that explorers use maps to help them travel from place to place. Ask: "What is a map? How do maps help people travel?" Volunteers respond.

- *A map shows you where places are.*
- *Maps help you know where to go.*
- *Maps show you how to get where you want to go.*

Foundational Skills Connection

Encourage students to decode the word by demonstrating 1-1 letter-sound correspondence for each letter in the word *map*. Ask students to isolate each sound and then blend the sounds back together to read the word. Consider using a nonverbal cue for segmenting and blending (e.g., tapping each sound on a different finger) and make that motion while saying each phoneme and blending the word.

Use responses to define *map* as "an image of the land or sky that is designed to give information about a place." Place *map* on the Word Wall as a module word.

Identify the location of your city on the world map and place a mark on the map that students can use as reference throughout the module. Point out the location of Europe. Ask: "Could we walk to Europe? Why or why not?" Use Equity Sticks to call on students to respond.

- No, it's too far away.
- No, we can't walk on the ocean!

Hold one finger on the location of your city and another finger on Europe. Remove your hands and hold them up in front of the class showing the distance between the two points on the map. Ask: "Looking at my hand, does Europe seem far away? Is it really just this far from us?" Volunteers respond. Use responses to reinforce that distances on a map are different than they are in real life. This map is an image of the world made smaller so people can look at it and see how big things are in relation to other things–the whole world cannot fit inside a classroom! Reinforce that short distances on a map can actually be very far apart in real life.

Explain that students will need to fly in an airplane in order to travel to Europe. Mark the class's first destination by placing an image of an airplane on Europe on the world map. Invite students to walk around the room, pretending to fly in an airplane. As they "fly," play music from Europe using the link for "Where in the World Is Carmen Sandiego? from Smithsonian Folkways" (**http://witeng. link/0375**). Scroll down for clips of music from a variety of countries in Europe. Consider using track 157, "Spain - La Liviana; La Serrana." Stop the music to indicate that students should "land" at the whole-group gathering area.

| TEACHER NOTE | The above link is a suggestion. Substitute different European music if desired. |

Display the front cover of *Europe* as you read aloud the title and author's name. Ask: "What do you think you already know about Europe? Do you know anyone who has ever been to Europe?" Volunteers respond.

💬 * Read the book aloud with minimal interruptions. Students sit in "listening position," focusing eyes and ears on you as you read.

This icon indicates an opportunity to practice Speaking and Listening skills.

- Remind students of the protocol for sharing texts and engaging in group discussions. If needed, refer back to the skills they have learned and cataloged on the Speaking and Listening Anchor Chart.

- Consider projecting the pages of the book in front of the class on a document camera. The pages are small and may not be easily seen from where students sit. If your classroom does not have a way to project the book, organize chairs to allow students to have a better view of the pages.

Instruct students to Think-Pair-Share, and ask: "What did you learn about Europe that surprised you?" Use Equity Sticks to call on students to respond.

Distribute copies of the text to pairs of students. Instruct students to take turns sharing what they notice about the text with their partner. Students use the sentence frame **I notice** _____ and point to the relevant illustration in the text to share observations. Invite several students to share one of their observations with the whole class.

SHARE QUESTIONS ABOUT *EUROPE* 10 MIN.

Pairs

Explain that students will use Question Corners to ask questions about the text. Assign pairs a starting Question Corner, and review the routine as needed.

Pairs move to their assigned Question Corner and generate questions about *Europe* using the designated question word. Place a few copies of the text at each corner.

Circulate to support pairs in reading the question words as needed, calling attention to key letters and sounds. Encourage students to return to the text to develop questions. Listen in and choose four to six student-generated questions to record on sticky notes, labeling with students' initials.

Post a blank Wonder Chart for *Europe* and *Asia*. Add students' questions.

Working with one question at a time, students Echo Read the question and Think-Pair-Share about details they remember from the text. Students use the following Nonverbal Signals to indicate whether they are able to answer the question:

- Thumbs-up: we remember the answer from the text.

- Thumbs-sideways: we remember part of the answer from the text.

- Thumbs-down: we don't remember the answer.

Call on students to share their thinking. Return to the text to confirm and clarify their thinking. Move sticky notes along the progression to indicate the extent to which each question has been answered.

LISTEN ACTIVELY AND SHARE OBSERVATIONS ABOUT ASIA 12 MIN.

Whole Group

Tell students that they will continue their world exploration by traveling to another continent: Asia. Identify Asia on the world map. Direct students to look at the placement of the airplane over Europe and at the location of Asia, and ask: "Could we walk to Asia from Europe? Why or why not?" Use Equity Sticks to call on students to respond.

- *Yes, they are right next to each other.*
- *Yes, it looks like they are attached.*
- *No, I think it is too far to walk.*

Explain that people can travel to Asia from Europe by walking, because the two continents are connected by land. However, both continents are very large, and that would not be the most convenient way to travel! Today students will get to Asia in their imaginary airplanes.

Mark the destination by moving the airplane image to Asia. Invite students to walk around the room, pretending to fly in an airplane. As they "fly," play music from Asia using the link for "Where in the World Is Carmen Sandiego? from Smithsonian Folkways" (**http://witeng.link/0375**). Scroll down for clips of music from a variety of Asian countries. Consider using track 27, "China - Yeung Choi-hei." Stop the music to indicate that students should "land" at the whole-group gathering area.

TEACHER NOTE	• The above link is a suggestion. Explain that a continent as large as Asia has all different styles of music. This music is from a large country called China (indicate on map). Substitute different Asian music if desired. • Continue to use the airplane image daily to note the continent students are exploring. Move the airplane image between the continents as appropriate.

Display the front cover of *Asia* as you read aloud the title and author's name. Ask: "What do you think you already know about Asia? Do you know anyone who has ever been to Asia?" Volunteers respond.

Read the book aloud with minimal interruptions. Students sit in "listening position," focusing eyes and ears on you as you read.

Instruct students to Think-Pair-Share, and ask: "What did you learn about Asia that surprised you?" Use Equity Sticks to call on students to respond.

Instruct students to Mix and Mingle, and ask: "What else did you notice about the text?" Spread copies of the text around the room for students to reference as needed.

SHARE QUESTIONS ABOUT *ASIA* 10 MIN.

Small Groups

Explain that now students will use Question Grab Bags to generate questions about the text. Divide the class into five small groups and distribute a Question Grab Bag and a copy of the text to each group. Revisit the procedure for the Question Grab Bag routine if needed.

✔ Small groups of students take turns pulling a question word from the Question Grab Bag and using the word to ask a question about *Asia*.

Circulate to support groups in reading the question words as needed, calling attention to key letters and sounds. Encourage them to return to the text to develop their questions, and listen in on questions. Choose four to six student-generated questions to record on sticky notes, labeling them with students' initials.

Post the Wonder Chart for *Europe* and *Asia*. Add students' questions underneath the questions recorded earlier in the lesson.

Working with one question at a time, students Echo Read the question and Think-Pair-Share about details they remember from the text. Students use the following Nonverbal Signals to indicate whether they are able to answer the question:

- Thumbs-up: we remember the answer from the text.

- Thumbs-sideways: we remember part of the answer from the text.

- Thumbs-down: we don't remember the answer.

Call on students to share their thinking. Return to the text to confirm and clarify their thinking. Move sticky notes along the progression to indicate the extent to which each question has been answered.

SAMPLE WONDER CHART FOR *EUROPE* AND *ASIA*

Wonders for *Europe* and *Asia*		
Questions ?	Answers in Progress ⟷	Complete Answers ✓
• Who lives in the big castle? • Why doesn't the place in Italy have cars? • Where do bears live in Europe? • How tall is Mount Everest? • What do tigers eat? • When was the tallest building made?		

EXAMINE *EARTH FROM SPACE* 8 MIN.

Whole Group

Display the image called *Earth from Space* (**http://witeng.link/0373**). Explain that after looking at a few continents more closely, students will take a step back and look again at the world as a whole.

Ask: "Is this a map? Why or why not?" Call on several students to respond.

  ▪ *Yes, because it shows Earth.*
  ▪ *Yes, because we can see part of Earth and the sky.*
  ▪ *No, because you can't see details about the land.*
  ▪ *No, it looks like a photo.*

Scaffold

Remind students that a map is an image of the earth or sky, which is designed to give information about a place.

Ask: "How do you think this picture was made?" Volunteers respond. Use responses to explain that the picture is a photograph taken from space.

Ask: "Looking at this photograph, what shape does the world seem to be?" Students chorally respond.

Explain that Earth has a spherical shape, which means something that is round like a ball, but the maps we usually use are flat, so it seems to be round. Use a globe to demonstrate Earth's spherical shape. Identify the continents of Asia and Europe on the globe.

Distribute Response Journals to students. Provide time for students to think about one question they wonder about the image *Earth from Space.*

✔ Students record one question about *Earth from Space.* As time permits, use Equity Sticks to call on several students to share their question with the class.

Land 2 MIN.

ANSWER THE CONTENT FRAMING QUESTION

Instruct students to Mix and Mingle, and ask: "Do you think *Europe* and *Asia* are storybooks or informational texts? What makes you say that?" Call on several students to share their responses with the whole class.

Wrap 1 MIN.

ASSIGN HOMEWORK

Continue the home-reading routine. Use this time in each lesson to remind students of expectations. Once this routine is in place, distribute and review the Volume of Reading Reflection Questions. Explain that students should consider these questions as they read and explain classroom systems for sharing their responses.

Analyze

Context and Alignment

Students utilize Question Grab Bags to generate questions about *Asia*. This questioning tool supports students in developing the habit of "wondering" as they read a text (RI.K.1, L.K.1.d). Each student:

- Generates text-based questions.

- Correctly uses the question word presented on the Question Card.

Next Steps

If students struggle to generate questions, focus on one question word, such as *how* or *why*. Work with small groups and go through the text together, one page spread at a time. Support students in generating one question per page spread.

⬇ LESSON 1 DEEP DIVE: VOCABULARY

Define *Continent* and *Ocean*

- **Time:** 15 min.

- **Texts:** *Earth from Space*, Stöckli, Reto, et al. (**http://witeng.link/0373**), *World Atlas*, Nick Crane; Illustrations, David Dean

- **Vocabulary Learning Goal:** Identify land and water items by the categories *continent* and *ocean* to gain a sense of these vocabulary words. (L.K.5.a)

Launch

Reinforce that students are learning about the world in this module. Remind students that they learned the meaning of the words *world* and *map* during today's lesson. Display the image *Earth from Space* (**http://witeng.link/0373**).

Reinforce that students explored this image during today's lesson. Ask: "What are the blue parts, and what are the green and brown parts you see?"

- *The blue parts are water.*
- *The green and brown parts are land.*

Explain that the green and brown parts are pieces of land called <u>continents</u> and the blue parts are bodies of water called <u>oceans</u>. Students are going to use a special book called a *World Atlas* to find out more about continents and oceans.

Learn

Display the cover of *World Atlas*. Explain that this is a special book that has maps and information about the whole world. Reinforce that students will be exploring many of these places throughout this module. They will sometimes use this book to learn new things about the places they "visit."

Display "The Oceans and Continents of the World" map on pages 8–9 of *World Atlas*. If possible use a document camera to project these pages in front of the class.

Alternate Activity

Divide the class into small groups and distribute a copy of *World Atlas* to each group in order to share the text and get a closer look at the illustrations.

Point to the green and brown areas and reinforce that these large areas of land are called continents. Write *continent* in large letters on the board. Instruct students to Think-Pair-Share, and ask: "What pictures do you see on the continents?" Volunteers respond.

- *I see different buildings.*
- *There are some trees and bushes.*
- *I see people dancing and walking.*
- *There are lots of different animals.*

Record appropriate responses as a list underneath the word *continent*. Teach students a Nonverbal Signal for *continent*, such as "air writing" a large letter *c*.

Use student responses to reinforce that these things live on or can be found on <u>land</u>. Ask: "What do you notice about the land? What do you think land is?" Volunteers respond.

- *I think it is the ground.*
- *Maybe it is the place where people can walk and build.*
- *It is hard and maybe has dirt and grass.*

Add *land* to the Word Wall as a yearlong word.

Redirect student attention to "The Oceans and Continents of the World" map. Point to the blue areas and reinforce that these large bodies of water are called <u>oceans</u>. Write *ocean* in large letters on the board. Instruct students to Think-Pair-Share, and ask: "What pictures do you see on the oceans?" Volunteers respond.

- *I see different types of boats.*
- *There is a hot air balloon and an airplane.*
- *I see fish, whales, and dolphins.*

Use student responses to reinforce that these things live in water or are used to travel on or over water. Record appropriate responses as a list underneath the word *ocean*. Teach students a Nonverbal Signal for *ocean*, such as "air writing" a large letter *o*.

Prompt students to look at the map on pages 8–9 displayed in front of the class. Explain that students will determine if an item would be found on a continent or in an ocean.

✔ As you call out the following land or water items from "The Oceans and Continents of the World" map, students identify whether you would find the item on a continent or in an ocean by making the correct Nonverbal Signal.

- Tall buildings
- Dolphins
- Panda bears
- Sailboats
- People dancing

Land

Reinforce that students will learn all about the continents and oceans of the world throughout Module 4.

Point to the word *continent* on the board. Ask students to respond chorally to complete the sentence: **Continents are large areas of _____.**

  ▪ *Land!*

Point to the word *ocean* on the board. Ask students to respond chorally to complete the sentence: **Oceans are large areas of _____.**

  ▪ *Water!*

■ FOCUSING QUESTION: LESSONS 1-8

What interesting things can people do in Europe and Asia?

1 2 3 4 5 6 7 8 9 10 11 12 13 14 15 16 17 18 19 20 21 22 23 24 25 26 27 28 29 30 31 32 33 34 35 36

Lesson 2

TEXTS

- "The Seven Continents Song," Silly School Songs (video) (**http://witeng.link/0374**)

- *Asia*, Rebecca Hirsch

- "Traditional Chinese Dance–'Flowers Contend in Beauty' by Li Qian, Lin Chen…" (video) (**http://witeng.link/0376**)

Lesson 2: At a Glance

AGENDA

Welcome (10 min.)

Practice Fluency

Launch (3 min.)

Learn (55 min.)

Identify Text Features (20 min.)

Identify the Main Topic and Key Details (20 min.)

Examine Opinion Writing (15 min.)

Land (6 min.)

Answer the Content Framing Question

Wrap (1 min.)

Assign Homework

Vocabulary Deep Dive: Demonstrate Meanings of Adjectives with Opposites (15 min.)

STANDARDS ADDRESSED

The full text of ELA Standards can be found in the Module Overview.

Reading

- RI.K.1, RI.K.2, RI.K.4

Writing

- W.K.1, W.K.7

Speaking and Listening

- SL.K.1, SL.K.2

Language

- L.K.1.f
- ⬇ L.K.5.b

MATERIALS

- Repeated Language Chart (see lesson for details; retain for future lessons)
- World map
- Compass rose
- Index cards
- Document camera or projector

Learning Goals

Use text features to identify the main topic and key details in sections of *Asia*. (RI.K.2)

✔ Use Nonverbal Signals to identify and retell the main topic and key details of a section in the text.

Write a sentence to state an opinion. (W.K.1, L.K.1.f)

✔ Complete a sentence frame to write an opinion about the best thing to do at recess.

⬇ Demonstrate understanding of frequently occurring adjectives by relating them to their opposites. (L.K.5.b)

✔ State the opposite of a given adjective from the text.

✔ Checks for Understanding

Prepare

FOCUSING QUESTION: Lessons 1–8

What interesting things can people do in Europe and Asia?

CONTENT FRAMING QUESTION: Lesson 2

Organize: *What is happening in Asia?*

CRAFT QUESTION: Lesson 2

Examine: *Why is opinion writing important?*

In this lesson students build their understanding of informational text features by exploring headings in *Asia*. After identifying headings, students begin to analyze the relationship between the heading and the main topic of those sections of the text. This transferrable knowledge develops an understanding of the structure and organization of informational texts. In addition, students share opinions as an introduction to the genre of opinion writing.

Welcome 10 MIN.

PRACTICE FLUENCY

Post and read the Essential Question aloud, pointing to each word as you say it. As you read the word *what*, model a Nonverbal Signal by holding your hands out in a questioning manner. As you read the word *fascinating*, model a Nonverbal Signal by holding your hands up near the sides of your head and wiggling your fingers in a twinkling manner.

Students Echo Read the Essential Question using the Nonverbal Signals for *what*, *world*, (hands create an outline of a globe), and *fascinating*.

Ask: "What does it mean for something to be <u>fascinating</u>?" Volunteers respond.

Use responses to explain that when something is <u>fascinating</u> it grabs your attention and makes you feel curious.

Direct students to demonstrate what their facial expressions might look like if they saw something fascinating. Ask: "How do you feel when you see something fascinating?" Volunteers respond.

- *I feel excited.*
- *It makes me want to know more.*

Explain that students will explore many fascinating things about the world over the course of the module. Emphasize that this learning is a starting place and they will continue to explore fascinating things about the world all throughout their lives as they have experiences with reading, exploring different foods music and art, travel, and meeting people from other countries.

Remind students that they will explore the world by learning about different continents. Instruct students to Think-Pair-Share, and ask: "What is a continent?" Call on several students to respond.

- *It's a big piece of land.*
- *You can see continents on maps of Earth.*

Invite volunteers to point out continents on the world map.

Explain that students will use the words from the beginning of "The Seven Continents Song" as their fluency passage. Play "The Seven Continents Song" video (**http://witeng.link/0374**).

Display the Repeated Language Chart and read aloud the title and the first line of "The Seven Continents Song," tracking the words with your finger.

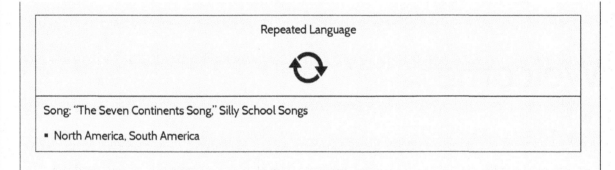

Repeated Language
Song: "The Seven Continents Song," Silly School Songs ■ North America, South America

Students Echo Read the line. Highlight the locations of North America and South America on the world map.

Ask: "We live on one of these continents. Which one?" Volunteers respond. Invite a volunteer to point to the location of your city or town on the map. Confirm that students live in North America.

Ask: "What do *north* and *south* mean?" Volunteers respond. Display a compass rose and explain that *north* and *south* are words that describe where something is in relation to something else, similar to the idea of left and right. Emphasize that North and South America are connected to each other. When people look at both continents, together, North America is the area of land that is located to the north while South America is to the south.

Work with students to create a simple dance move that goes along with the rhythm of the first line of text. For example, sway forward and back, or take a step forward and then back.

Students Choral Read the first line of text several times while practicing the corresponding dance moves.

Launch <small>3 MIN.</small>

Post and read aloud the Focusing Question. Remind students that they are beginning their world adventure by exploring two continents–Europe and Asia.

Ask: "Where is the continent of Asia?" Students respond by pointing to Asia on the map. Confirm that Asia is the continent marked with the image of an airplane (placed during the previous lesson).

Display the front cover of *Asia* and tell students that today they will build their knowledge about the continent by digging deeper into the text. Post and read aloud the Content Framing Question. Students Echo Read the question.

Learn <small>55 MIN.</small>

IDENTIFY TEXT FEATURES <small>20 MIN.</small>

Whole Group

Explain that students will use text features to help them think about what is happening in the text. Remind students that text features are special parts of a book that help focus a reader's attention on important information. Ask: "What text features do you already know?" Volunteers respond.

- *I know about photos.*
- *I remember bold words.*
- *There are glossaries.*

Tell students that they will use a new text feature to look at what is happening in *Asia*: headings. Students repeat the word *headings*. Explain that headings introduce readers to different topics in the text.

Use a document camera or projector to display page 9 of the text. Ask: "Which part of the page might be the heading?" Invite a volunteer to approach the text and point to the heading. Ask: "How does the heading stand out from the rest of the text?" Volunteers respond.

- *The words are blue.*
- *The letters are bigger than the other letters.*

Explain that headings are important text features that stand out from the rest of the text. The words in a heading can be bigger than the other words on the page, or they could be written in bold or colored print.

Read the heading aloud and explain that the heading helps readers know what a section of the text is about by naming the topic. Highlight the connection between the heading and the information in the text. For example:

The heading tells me what kind of information will be in the next part of the text. Since the heading says, "People of Asia," I know that this section of the book will tell me details about the people of Asia.

Tell students that they will go on a scavenger hunt through the text to find more headings. Divide students into small groups and distribute a copy of the text to each group. Students take turns looking through the book for headings. When they find a heading they show it to the group and share how they know it is a heading. They then pass it to the next person in the group and the pattern repeats.

Extension

If students are ready, encourage them to read aloud the words they know in the headings.

Read *Asia* aloud to the class. After reading each heading, pause and ask: "What information will this section tell us? How do you know?" Use Equity Sticks to call on students to respond.

TEACHER NOTE

The heading for the first section in *Asia* ("Welcome to Asia!") is not linked to the main topic as directly as the other headings in the text. Consider waiting until the second section of the text to begin the questioning procedure outlined above.

IDENTIFY THE MAIN TOPIC AND KEY DETAILS 20 MIN.

Whole Group

Explain that readers can use headings to help them understand the main topic of sections in a text. Display page 15 of *Asia* and read the heading aloud. Instruct students to Think-Pair-Share, and ask: "What do you think the main topic of this section might be? What is this section mostly about?" Volunteers respond.

- *The main topic is wild weather.*
- *It is about the wild weather in Asia.*

Confirm that the main topic of the section is wild weather. Define *wild* as out of control. Explain that the heading of a section will often be the same as the section's main topic because they are both explaining what the section is mostly about.

Tell students that readers can find key details about the main topic in the section that follows the heading. Ask: "What are key details? How do they relate to the main topic?" Volunteers respond.

- *They are the details about the topic.*

> *They tell us more about the topic.*

> *We can find them in the text to give us more information.*

💬 Ask students to listen for key details about Asia's wild weather while you reread the "Wild Weather" section.

Read pages 14–15 aloud. Ask: "What is a <u>monsoon</u>? How do you know?" Volunteers respond.

> *It's a big storm.*

> *A monsoon has strong wind and rain.*

> *I heard the words strong winds.*

> *I see children running through the rain in the picture.*

Instruct students to Think-Pair-Share, and ask: "What key detail did you hear on this page about Asia's wild weather?" Use Equity Sticks to call on students to respond.

> *Asia has monsoons.*

> *There are strong winds.*

> *In the summer there are heavy rains.*

Use responses to confirm the key detail that Asia has monsoons.

Read pages 16–17 aloud. Instruct students to Think-Pair-Share, and ask: "What key detail did you hear on this page about Asia's wild weather?" Use Equity Sticks to call on students to respond.

> *Asia has snow.*

> *In the winter it is cold and snowy.*

Use responses to confirm the key detail that Asia has cold, snowy winters.

Tell students that they will use Nonverbal Signals when retelling the main topic and key details of the "Wild Weather" section. Model the Nonverbal Signal for main topic by placing your hand on the top of your head. Ask: "Why might it make sense to put your hand on your head while saying the main topic?" Volunteers respond.

> *The main topic is first, like your head is on top.*

> *Because it's the heading. That sounds like head.*

Students practice naming the main topic for the "Wild Weather" section while making the Nonverbal Signal.

Explain that, just like your body has one head and several limbs, sections in the text have one main topic and several key details about the topic.

Model Nonverbal Signals for showing key details by waving your arms or hands, one at a time.

Alternate Activity

Incorporate feet as well as hands into the Nonverbal Signals for key details. After waving each arm or hand, wave or wiggle your feet, one foot at a time.

Demonstrate how to retell the main topic and key details of the section while using the Nonverbal Signals. Place your hand on your head while naming the main topic, then wave one hand at a time while you retell the key details.

Pairs take turns using the Nonverbal Signals to retell the main topic and key details of the section to each other. Display pages from the "Wild Weather" section for students to use as reference.

TEACHER NOTE	If students have difficulty speaking and moving at the same time, instruct students to say the key detail aloud, then wave their hand or arm. This will allow students to focus on retelling the key details first, which is the main purpose of this lesson.

Explain that students can use the same process to identify the main topic and key details of other sections of the text. Display pages 18–19 of the text. Use the process outlined above to identify the main topic and key details of the "Amazing Animals" section.

✔ Pairs take turns using Nonverbal Signals to retell the main topic and key details of the "Amazing Animals" section. Display pages from the section for students to use as reference.

EXAMINE OPINION WRITING 15 MIN.

Whole Group

Tell students that in this module they will learn about a new kind of writing: opinion writing. Display and read aloud the Craft Question: *Why is opinion writing important?*

Underline or highlight the word *opinion*. Explain that an opinion is what you think or how you feel about a person or a thing. Students repeat the word *opinion* several times. Provide an example, such as:

I like to eat waffles for breakfast. I think they are the best breakfast food! It is my opinion that waffles are the best breakfast food.

Instruct students to Think-Pair-Share about the following questions. Students use the following sentence frame to respond: **It is my opinion that _____.** For each question, call on several students to respond.

What is the best breakfast food?

Who is the best superhero?

Do cats or dogs make better pets?

Place the word *opinion* on the Word Wall as a yearlong word. Ask: "Did everyone in class have the same opinion?" Volunteers respond. Emphasize that it is normal for people to have different opinions. Every person has their own thoughts and their own opinions.

Ask: "Why might it be important to share your opinion? What can you learn by listening to other people's opinions?" Volunteers respond.

- *You can tell someone what you think.*
- *You can learn what someone else thinks.*
- *You might learn more about the world.*
- *You can listen to different ideas.*

Explain that people don't always say the word *opinion* when they are giving an opinion. Another way to share an opinion is with the sentence frame: **I think _____.** When a speaker or writer starts a sentence with "I think," it's a clue that they might be about to share an opinion.

Provide an example, such as:

I think dogs make better pets than cats.

Explain that students will use this sentence frame to write an opinion in their Response Journals.

Direct students to think about all the activities they can do when they are at recess. Instruct students to Mix and Mingle, and ask: What is the best thing to do at recess?

Students respond using the sentence frame: **I think _____.**

Distribute Response Journals and explain that students will write a sentence to share their opinion about recess.

✔ Students write their opinion about recess in their Response Journals using the sentence frame: **I think _____.** If time permits, students draw an illustration to support their sentence.

Land 6 MIN.

ANSWER THE CONTENT FRAMING QUESTION

Students Echo Read the Content Framing Question. Ask: "What did you do to answer this question? Which text feature helped you today?" Volunteers respond.

- *We looked at the headings.*
- *The headings helped us find the main topic.*
- *The words told us key details.*
- *We moved our bodies to talk about the main topic and key details.*

Ask: "Which continent did you learn about today?" Students chorally respond.

Explain that people on each continent have different ways of doing things. For example, people from around the world might have different ways of dancing, cooking, working, or building homes. One way we can explore the world is by learning about the many ways people live in different parts of the world. During this module, students will watch several videos to build their knowledge about the question: "How do people around the world dance?" Tell students they will learn about a different style of dancing by watching a traditional dance from one country in Asia: China.

Display the questions: "What do I see in this dance performance? What do I hear in this dance performance?" Tell students they can focus their video observations either on what they see or hear, which will help the class learn about different aspects of the dance. Individual students raise their hands to indicate whether they choose to focus on what they see, or what they hear.

Play a clip from the "Traditional Chinese Dance" video (**http://witeng.link/0376**).

Instruct students to Mix and Mingle, and ask: "What did you see or hear in the Chinese dance?"

TEACHER NOTE	Consider broadening student understanding of the variety of cultures in Asia by playing video clips of dances from other Asian countries.

Wrap 1 MIN.

ASSIGN HOMEWORK

Continue the class home-reading routine.

Analyze

Context and Alignment

Students use the heading of a section in *Asia* to identify the main topic. After reading the section they retell key details (RI.K.2). Each student:

- Uses the heading to identify the main topic.
- Uses Nonverbal Signals to retell the main topic and key details.

Next Steps

If students have difficulty retelling key details in the text, work with small groups and reread the section. Stop after each page spread and ask: "What details did you learn about the main topic from this page?" After students gain confidence with the key details of the section, support them in using the Nonverbal Signals to retell the main topic and key details of the section as a whole.

⬇ LESSON 2 DEEP DIVE: VOCABULARY

Demonstrate Meanings of Adjectives with Opposites

- **Time:** 15 min.

- **Text:** *Asia*, Rebecca Hirsch

- **Vocabulary Learning Goal:** Demonstrate understanding of frequently occurring adjectives by relating them to their opposites. (L.K.5.b)

Launch

Remind students that they learned the meaning of words by exploring opposites in previous modules. Instruct students to Think-Pair-Share, and ask: "What are opposites?" Volunteers respond.

- *Things that are very different.*

- *Two things that are as unlike each other as possible.*

- *Big and small are opposites.*

Emphasize that Rebecca Hirsch used many describing words in *Asia* to tell about the continent.

Explain that students are going to show that they understand the meaning of some of the describing words by finding opposites in the text.

Learn

Draw a large T-chart on the board. On the top left side write *Word*. On the top right side write *Opposite*. Under *Word* write *shortest*. Call on a volunteer to define the word *short*. Reinforce that if something is the *shortest* it is "the most short." Instruct students to listen for the opposite of the word *shortest* as you read aloud. Students stand when they hear the opposite.

Read the first bullet on page 28 of the text. Call on a standing student to identify the opposite of *shortest*. Write *tallest* on the right side of the T-chart.

Word	Opposite
shortest	tallest

Display the photograph on page 26. Ask: "How does this picture show us how the building is the opposite of *shortest*? How does this picture show us that it is the *tallest*?" Volunteers respond. Confirm that the building is the tallest because there is not another building that goes higher. Explain that now they will practice identifying the opposites of words and using the photographs to reinforce the meaning of the word.

Organize students in five small groups. Distribute a text to each group and an index card with one of the following describing words written on it: *calm, weak, light, hot,* and *wet.* Echo Read the word on the index card with each group to ensure understanding.

TEACHER NOTE	Consider pairing each word with an image to help students read the card independently.

Prompt groups to look at the word on their index card. Instruct groups to discuss: "What does your word mean? What is the opposite of your word?" Circulate to ensure students understand the correct meaning of the word for this lesson, as some words may have multiple meanings.

After groups identify the opposite of the word on their card, instruct groups to find an illustration demonstrating that particular opposite in the text. Provide two minutes for groups to find the correct opposite photograph. Circulate to provide support as needed.

In order to support students, prompt students to look at the following page numbers:

Calm/Busy page 8 (photograph of a busy market).

Weak/Strong page 14 (photograph of strong storm); page 20 (photograph of a *strong* tiger).

Light/Heavy page 14 (photograph of heavy rain); page 18 (photograph of a *heavy* panda).

Hot/Cold page 16 (photograph of a snowy day).

Wet/Dry page 24 (photograph of a dry desert).

Use Equity Sticks to call on each group to share their findings. Record each group's original describing word and use student responses to identify the correct opposite word from the text on the T-chart.

Word	Opposite
shortest	tallest
calm	busy
weak	strong
light	heavy
hot	cold
wet	dry

Extension

Invite each group to create a Nonverbal Signal for the opposite word they found in the text. Encourage students to use the photograph from the text to create their signal. Group members teach the nonverbal signal to the rest of the class. The class mimics the signal while saying the opposite word.

Land

Collect the index cards from each group and put them into a container or bag. Reorganize the class into one large group. Explain that students are going to show they understand the meaning of these describing words by saying the opposite and making the matching Nonverbal Signal.

Pull out an index card and call out the describing word written on the card. Students state the opposite of the word. Repeat for each index card.

Extension

In order to challenge students, erase the T-chart prior to completing the "check for understanding" activity.

■ FOCUSING QUESTION: LESSONS 1–8

What interesting things can people do in Europe and Asia?

Lesson 3

TEXTS

- "The Seven Continents Song," Silly School Songs (video) (**http://witeng.link/0374**)

- *Europe*, Rebecca Hirsch

- *The Story of Ferdinand*, Munro Leaf; Illustrations, Robert Lawson

Lesson 3: At a Glance

AGENDA

Welcome (8 min.)

Practice Fluency

Launch (2 min.)

Learn (60 min.)

Use Text Features in Europe (15 min.)

Identify the Main Topic and Key Details in Europe (20 min.)

Listen Actively to The Story of Ferdinand (17 min.)

Identify Unknown Words in The Story of Ferdinand (8 min.)

Land (4 min.)

Answer the Content Framing Question

Wrap (1 min.)

Assign Homework

Vocabulary Deep Dive: Opposite Action Words (15 min.)

STANDARDS ADDRESSED

The full text of ELA Standards can be found in the Module Overview.

Reading

- RL.K.3, RL.K.4, RL.K.7, RI.K.1, RI.K.2

Writing

- W.K.1

Speaking and Listening

- SL.K.1, SL.K.2

Language

- ⬇ L.K.5.b

MATERIALS

- Repeated Language Chart
- World map
- Compass rose

Learning Goals

Use text features to identify the main topic and key details in a section of *Europe*. (RI.K.2)

✔ Use Nonverbal Signals to identify and retell the main topic and key details of a section in the text.

Identify unknown words in *The Story of Ferdinand*. (RL.K.4)

✔ Signal unknown words while listening to part of *The Story of Ferdinand* read aloud.

⬇ Demonstrate understanding of *sit*, *pick*, and *shout* by stating and acting out each word's opposite. (L.K.5.b)

✔ Complete given sentences by stating and acting out the correct opposite.

✔ Checks for Understanding

FOCUSING QUESTION: Lessons 1–8

What interesting things can people do in Europe and Asia?

CONTENT FRAMING QUESTION: Lesson 3

Organize: *What is happening in Europe?*

Students build on their learning from the previous lesson by using the headings in *Europe* to identify the main topic of sections in the text. They also explore another text feature: the table of contents. They practice using the table of contents in *Europe* to locate specific sections in the text. In addition, students begin to explore the setting and customs of Spain through the read-aloud text, *The Story of Ferdinand.*

Welcome 8 MIN.

PRACTICE FLUENCY

Display the Repeated Language Chart with the next line of the song added. Read the first two lines of the song. Students Echo Read the lines.

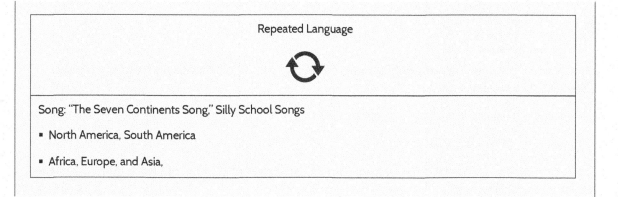

Repeated Language
Song: "The Seven Continents Song," Silly School Songs • North America, South America • Africa, Europe, and Asia,

Highlight the locations of Africa, Europe, and Asia on the world map.

Ask: "What do you notice about Europe and Asia that makes those continents different from the others?" Volunteers respond.

• *They are connected.*

• *It's like they are one piece.*

Use responses to confirm that Europe and Asia are connected as one large landmass. Point out that most of the other continents are surrounded on all sides by water, rather than being up against another one.

Display a compass rose and remind students of their learning from the previous lesson about north and south. Point to the east and west markings on the compass rose and explain that people also use the terms *east* and *west* to describe where something is in relation to something else.

When people look at Europe and Asia together, Asia is the area of land that is to the <u>east</u> while Europe is to the <u>west</u>.

Extension

Identify where the directions of north, south, east, and west are in relation to the classroom.

Work with students to create simple dance moves to go along with the rhythm of the second line of text. For example, sway back and forth or march in place.

Students Echo Read the first two lines several times while practicing the corresponding dance moves.

Play the first part of "The Seven Continents Song" video (**http://witeng.link/0374**) and ask students to join along with the words and movements they know.

Launch 2 MIN.

Display and read aloud the Content Framing Question. Ask: "What do you notice about today's question?" Volunteers respond.

- *It's the same question we had yesterday about Asia.*
- *Today's question is about Europe.*

Use responses to confirm that today students will dig deeper into *Europe* to learn more about the text and the continent.

Ask: "Where is the continent called Europe?" Students respond by pointing to Europe on the map. Invite a student to approach the map and move the airplane to Europe.

Learn 60 MIN.

USE TEXT FEATURES IN *EUROPE* 15 MIN.

Whole Group

Remind students that they used headings to help them think about *Asia* in the previous lesson. Ask: "How do headings stand out from the rest of the text? Where can you find headings in a text?" Volunteers respond.

- *The headings look different from the other words.*
- *The headings are a different color.*
- *Headings come at the beginning.*
- *You can see a heading when the book starts a new topic.*

Display a copy of *Europe* and invite a volunteer to identify a heading in the text. Emphasize that students will see headings in many informational texts. They will always stand out from the rest of the text, but they won't always be in a different color. The words in a heading could be bigger than the other words on the page, or they could be written in bold print.

Instruct students to Think-Pair-Share, and ask: "How can headings help you understand the text? What do headings tell readers?" Call on several students to respond.

- *A heading helps you know what part of the book is about.*
- *Headings tell you the topic.*

Distribute copies of the text to pairs of students. Direct pairs to look through the text to find a heading.

Call on pairs to hold up their page spread and indicate the heading they found. Read aloud the heading that each pair displays, and ask: "What information will this section of the text tell us about?" Use Equity Sticks to call on students to respond.

Direct pairs to turn to the table of contents page at the beginning of *Europe*. Read aloud the first four sections from the list. Ask: "Do these topics sound familiar? Where have you heard these topics?" Volunteers respond.

- *Yes, we just heard those topics!*
- *They sound like the headings.*

Explain that a table of contents is a text feature that many informational texts use. It is a list of all the headings, or section names, in text. The table of contents makes finding information in the text easier by telling readers which page number they can turn to for each section.

Model how to use the table of contents in *Europe* to find the page number of a section. For example, say:

The first section in the book is "Welcome to Europe!" If I trace my finger along the dots after the section name, I see the number 5. That tells me that the "Welcome to Europe!" section starts on page 5.

Turn to page 5 and confirm that it is the start of the "Welcome to Europe!" section.

Ask students to place a finger on the second section listed in the table of contents. Read the name of the section aloud. Instruct students to trace their fingers across the page to find the starting page number for the "People of Europe" section. Ask: "Which page can you turn to for the 'People of Europe' section?" Volunteers respond.

- *Page 9.*

As time permits, repeat the process outlined above to find the starting page for other sections in the text.

IDENTIFY THE MAIN TOPIC AND KEY DETAILS IN *EUROPE* 20 MIN.

Pairs

Remind students that they can use headings to help them understand the main topic of sections in the text. Ask: "How can a heading help you understand the main topic of a section?" Volunteers respond.

- *Headings tell you what it will be about.*
- *The heading tells you what the main topic is.*
- *The heading and main topic are the same.*

Explain that students will use headings to help them find the main topic and key details of a section in *Europe*.

Display page 15 of *Europe* and read the heading aloud. Ask: "What do you think the main topic of this section is? What will this section mostly be about?" Use Equity Sticks to call on students to respond.

- *The main topic is places to see.*
- *It will be about places to see in Europe.*

Remind students that readers can find key details about the main topic in the section that follows the heading. Ask students to listen for key details about places to see in Europe while you read the "Places to See" section.

💬 Direct students to get into position for Partner Reading. Review the procedure for Partner Reading as needed.

Read pages 15–17 aloud while pairs follow along in their copies of the text. Ask: "Why do people visit Europe's museums?" Volunteers respond.

- *They go to see art.*
- *There are famous paintings.*

Extension

Tell students to think about the different pieces of art they have explored throughout the year. Ask: "Which piece of art would you most like to see in person in a museum? Why?"

Read the remainder of the section aloud. Instruct students to Think-Pair-Share, and ask: "What key details did you hear on these pages about places to see in Europe?" Use Equity Sticks to call on students to respond.

- *People can visit beautiful parks.*
- *You can go to museums to see art.*
- *There are castles!*

Remind students how to use Nonverbal Signals to retell the main topic and key details. Demonstrate how to place your hand on your head to signal the main topic, then wave one arm or hand at a time to indicate each key detail.

Alternate Activity

Incorporate feet as well as hands into the Nonverbal Signals for key details. After waving each arm or hand, wave or wiggle your feet, one foot at a time.

✔ Pairs take turns using Nonverbal Signals to retell the main topic and key details of the "Places to See" section, using the text for reference.

Instruct students to Mix and Mingle, and ask: "Imagine that you are going to visit Europe. Which place from the 'Places to See' section would you most like to visit? Why?"

Distribute Response Journals. Students write a sentence to share which place they would like to visit. As time permits, they draw an illustration to support their sentence.

LISTEN ACTIVELY TO *THE STORY OF FERDINAND* 17 MIN.

Whole Group

Display the map on page 6 of *Europe* and read aloud the text on page 7. Ask: "What do you notice about this map? What does the map show readers?" Volunteers respond.

- *There are a lot of colors.*
- *There are a lot of words, too.*
- *It shows readers what Europe looks like.*
- *Maybe the colors show different countries.*

Use student responses to confirm that the map shows the continent of Europe divided into its different countries. Remind students that the continent of Europe is made up of many countries, each with its own language, food, and way of life. Explain that each country on the map is labeled with its name. Provide an example by pointing to a country and reading its name aloud.

| **TEACHER NOTE** | Maps present abstract concepts, which students need not fully grasp to succeed with this lesson. This line of questioning is designed to highlight the visual representation showing that continents can be made up of smaller countries. |

Extension

Display the front cover of *Europe* and point out the three photographs of European monuments. Explain that the photographs show places people can see in different countries in Europe—the Eiffel Tower in France, Big Ben in England, and the Coliseum in Italy. Support students in identifying the locations of France, the United Kingdom, and Italy on the map in the text.

Point to Spain on the map. Explain that students will read a story set in Spain. Emphasize that reading a story with a setting in a different country can help readers imagine what it might be like to visit or live in that country.

Display the front cover of *The Story of Ferdinand* and read aloud the title, author's name, and illustrator's name. Instruct students to Mix and Mingle, and ask: "What do you think this story might be about? What makes you think that?"

After completing the Mix and Mingle routine, students sit in the whole-group gathering area. Read the text aloud with minimal interruptions.

Ask: "Who is the main character in the story?" Volunteers respond.

- *Ferdinand.*
- *The bull Ferdinand.*

Instruct students to Think-Pair-Share, and ask: "What did you notice about Ferdinand? How is he different from the other bulls?" Use Equity Sticks to call on students to respond.

- *Ferdinand likes to sit under a tree.*
- *He likes to smell.*
- *Ferdinand is happy.*
- *He is different because the other bulls like to butt their heads together. But Ferdinand doesn't like to do that.*
- *The other bulls run around and fight each other. Ferdinand likes to sit by himself.*

Ask: "What else did you notice about the text?" Volunteers respond.

TEACHER NOTE	If needed, display page spreads from the text to support students with making observations. Consider using pages 4–5, 14–15, 18–19, and 26–27.

Instruct students to Think-Pair-Share, and ask: "What questions do you have about the text?" Call on several students to respond.

Play music and invite students to walk or dance around the room like they imagine Ferdinand would move. Then have students switch and walk or dance around the room as they imagine the other bulls would move (without touching each other).

IDENTIFY UNKNOWN WORDS IN *THE STORY OF FERDINAND*   8 MIN.

Whole Group

Tell students that when good readers read a text, they pay attention to unfamiliar or new words. They notice when they read a word that they do not know, and try to figure out what the unknown word means to better understand the text.

Explain that students will practice thinking about the words in *The Story of Ferdinand*. Tell students that they will listen to part of the text read aloud and identify words that they do not know the meaning of by making a Nonverbal Signal. Demonstrate a Nonverbal Signal, such as raising one finger, that students will use to indicate unknown words.

Model how to use the Nonverbal Signal by reading aloud page 4. Use the signal after reading the word *pasture*. Students practice using the Nonverbal Signal.

Use a Think Aloud to describe how one might question an unknown word. For example,

> *Pasture.* Hmm, I'm not sure what that word means. Let me read the sentence again to look for clues. "He had a favorite spot out in the <u>pasture</u> under a cork tree." So, a <u>pasture</u> is something outside, and it could be under a tree. Let me check the illustration to see if it has any clues to help me. I see Ferdinand sitting on the ground under a tree, with grass and flowers around him. Maybe *pasture* means land that is covered with grass and flowers.

✔ Read pages 14–15 aloud. Students use the Nonverbal Signal to indicate unknown words they hear in the text. Call on students who signal to share the word that is unfamiliar to them.

Support students in looking for context clues in the surrounding sentences and illustrations to help determine the meaning of each unknown word. Possible unfamiliar words include *snorting*, *butting*, and *fierce*.

After defining the unknown words, reread pages 14–15. Ask: "How did thinking about the words help you better understand these pages?" Volunteers respond.

Tell students that they will return to *The Story of Ferdinand* in a few days to go deeper into the story and to learn more about Spain and Europe.

Land 4 MIN.

ANSWER THE CONTENT FRAMING QUESTION

Display and read aloud the Content Framing Question.

Instruct students to Mix and Mingle, and ask: "What did you learn about Europe today?"

If time permits, play "The Seven Continents Song" **(http://witeng.link/0374)** and invite students to join in with the words and dance moves they know.

Wrap 1 MIN.

ASSIGN HOMEWORK

Continue the classroom home-reading routine.

Analyze

Context and Alignment

Students use the heading of a section in *Europe* to identify the main topic. After reading the section they retell key details (RI.K.2). Each student:

- Uses the heading to identify the main topic.

- Uses Nonverbal Signals to retell the main topic and key details.

Next Steps

If students have difficulty retelling key details in the text, work with small groups to identify the main topic and key details of the "Places to See" section. Use the heading to support students in identifying the main topic. As you read the text, stop after each page spread and ask: "What details did you learn about the main topic from this page? Is that a detail about a place people can see in Europe?" After students gain confidence with the key details of the section, support them in using the Nonverbal Signals to retell the main topic and key details of the whole section.

⬇ LESSON 3 DEEP DIVE: VOCABULARY

Opposite Action Words

- **Time:** 15 min.

- **Text:** *The Story of Ferdinand*, Munro Leaf; Illustrations, Robert Lawson

- **Vocabulary Learning Goal:** Demonstrate understanding of *sit*, *pick*, and *shout* by stating and acting out each word's opposite. (L.K.5.b)

Launch

Remind students that in the previous Deep Dive they studied opposite describing words. Reinforce that opposites are words that are as unlike each other as possible.

Display the cover of the text and remind students that they read a new story today about a bull named Ferdinand. Instruct students to Think-Pair-Share, and ask: "Was Ferdinand opposite of the other bulls in the story? Why or why not?"

- *Yes, because he was very different from them.*
- *Yes, because they liked to fight and he liked to smell flowers.*
- *Yes, because they liked to run and jump and he liked to sit quietly.*

Explain that students are going to explore the opposites of other action words in the story.

Learn

Display and read page 12 of the text. As you read aloud, students act out the part of Ferdinand, pretending to <u>sit</u> under a tree. Emphasize that Ferdinand liked to <u>sit</u>. Reinforce that Ferdinand was the opposite of the other bulls. Ask: "What did the other bulls do that is opposite of *sit*?" Call on a different volunteer to say and act out the opposite of the word *sit*. If needed, reread page 3 or 14 to remind students of how the other bulls act. Use student responses to identify the opposite of *sit* as *stand*. Invite the class to move from <u>sit</u> to <u>stand</u>, saying the word while doing each action.

Ask: "What did you learn about Ferdinand by exploring how his actions are the opposite of the other bulls?" Volunteers respond.

- *He is a lot different than the other bulls.*

Display and read page 13 of the text. As you read aloud, students act out the part of the men, pretending to <u>pick</u> Ferdinand as the best bull. Ask: "How does Ferdinand feel about getting picked?" Volunteers respond.

- *He doesn't like it because he doesn't want to go fight.*
- *He is nervous about going to the fight.*

Point out that the opposite happened to the other bulls on the farm. Call on a student volunteer to say and act out the opposite of *pick*. Reinforce that the opposite of *pick* is *leave out*. Ask: "How do you think the other bulls feel being *left out*?"

- *They are sad because they wanted to go fight.*

Invite the class to say and act out the opposites *pick* and *leave out*.

Display and read page 27 of the text. As you read aloud, students act out the part of the crowd silently pretending to *shout*. Ask: "Why does the crowd *shout*?" Volunteers respond.

- *Because they are excited to see Ferdinand fight.*

Point out that at other events crowds do the opposite of *shout*. Call on a student volunteer to say and act out the opposite of *shout*. Reinforce that the opposite of *shout* is *whisper*. Ask: "At what events would a crowd *whisper*?"

- *At a movie.*
- *At a play.*

Invite the class to say and act out the opposites *shout* and *whisper*.

Land

✔ Students stand and find space in the classroom. As you read the following, students respond by stating and acting out the correct opposite to complete the sentence.

Ferdinand is different than the other bulls. He likes to sit and they want to _____.

The men come to pick the best bull. They will _____ the other bulls, and they will be sad.

At the bullfight, the crowd likes to shout. At movies, crowds prefer to _____.

█ FOCUSING QUESTION: LESSONS 1–8

What interesting things can people do in Europe and Asia?

1 2 3 **4** 5 6 7 8 9 10 11 12 13 14 15 16 17 18 19 20 21 22 23 24 25 26 27 28 29 30 31 32 33 34 35 36

Lesson 4

TEXTS

- "The Seven Continents Song," Silly School Songs (video) (**http://witeng.link/0374**)

- *Asia*, Rebecca Hirsch

Lesson 4: At a Glance

AGENDA

Welcome (5 min.)

Practice Fluency

Launch (4 min.)

Learn (60 min.)

Analyze Words and Photographs in Asia (18 min.)

Collect Evidence for Focusing Question Task 1 (20 min.)

Experiment with Writing an Opinion Statement (22 min.)

Land (5 min.)

Answer the Content Framing Question

Wrap (1 min.)

Assign Homework

Style and Conventions Deep Dive: Examine Writing and Expanding a Sentence (15 min.)

STANDARDS ADDRESSED

The full text of ELA Standards can be found in the Module Overview.

Reading

- RI.K.1, RI.K.4, RI.K.7

Writing

- W.K.1, W.K.8

Speaking and Listening

- SL.K.1, SL.K.2

Language

- L.K.1.f
- ⬇ L.K.1.f

MATERIALS

- Repeated Language Chart
- Document camera (if available)
- Evidence Organizer for *Asia*
- Sticky notes

Learning Goals

Use photographs and details from the text to describe things people can do in Asia. (RI.K.7)

✔ Use a Nonverbal Signal to identify text evidence.

Use the pictures and words in the text to form an opinion statement. (RI.K.1, W.K.1, W.K.8, L.K.1.f)

✔ Write an opinion statement about animals in Asia.

⬇ Identify the parts of a complete sentence and describe how a given sentence was expanded. (L.K.1.f)

✔ Work in partners to answer questions about a complete sentence.

✔ Checks for Understanding

Prepare

FOCUSING QUESTION: Lessons 1–8

What interesting things can people do in Europe and Asia?

CONTENT FRAMING QUESTION: Lesson 4

Reveal: *What does a deeper exploration of the words and photographs in* Asia *reveal?*

CRAFT QUESTION: Lesson 4

Experiment: *How do I write an opinion statement?*

In this lesson, students continue their exploration of *Asia* by looking closely at the relationship between the words and photographs in the text. Students deepen their understanding of how a text's words and pictures work together to provide different sorts of details—descriptive and visual—to build understanding. Students use this knowledge to collect evidence for the Focusing Question Task. Finally, students explore opinion statements by identifying examples and writing their own opinion statements in their Response Journals.

Welcome 5 MIN.

PRACTICE FLUENCY

Display the Repeated Language Chart with the last two continents in the song added. Read the lines aloud.

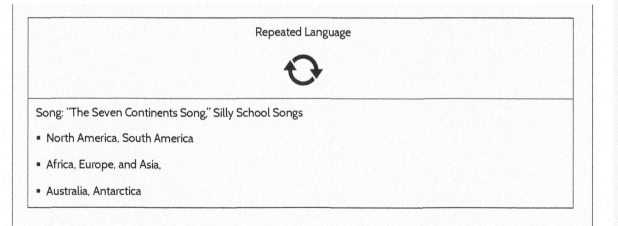

Repeated Language
Song: "The Seven Continents Song," Silly School Songs
▪ North America, South America
▪ Africa, Europe, and Asia,
▪ Australia, Antarctica

Read the added line of the song aloud, emphasizing the different syllables in *Antarctica* the way the song does. Ask: "What do you notice about the syllables in these words? Are these long words or short words? How do you know?" Volunteers respond.

- *I can hear lots of sounds.*
- *I can count the sounds.*
- *The words have more than one sound.*

Model breaking down a student's name into syllables. Clap your hands to the different syllables to emphasize the different parts. Ask students to turn to a partner to break down the syllables of each other's names by saying the name aloud and breaking it into different parts.

Ask students to stand up from their seats. Explain that they will now use their feet to stomp the different syllables in *Australia* and *Antarctica*.

As a class, students stomp the different syllables. If needed, model this first for the class or count the syllables first on your fingers.

Reread the third line of the song aloud again. Create simple dance moves for the third line. Students Echo Read the line using the agreed-upon dance moves.

Launch 4 MIN.

Display the front cover of *Asia*. Ask: "Is this a photograph or a drawing on the front cover? How do you know?" Volunteers respond.

Ask: "Why do you think this text included real photographs instead of drawings? How do real photographs help us as readers?" Call on several students to respond. If needed, flip through the pages of the text to prompt student thinking.

- *The photos help us see what it is really like.*
- *They show us real life, not pretend.*

Turn to page 20 in the text. Ask: "If someone had never seen a real tiger or a picture of a tiger before, how might this image help them?" Volunteers respond.

- *They can see the tiger's stripes.*
- *They learn it has orange and black stripes.*
- *They can see what the tiger looks like so they know next time.*

Use student responses to reinforce that the pictures often add additional detail to the information in the text. The fact that the author chose to use photographs in these informational texts helps readers see what these things look like in real life, especially since they probably have not visited this continent before.

Display and read aloud the Content Framing Question. Tell students that today they will explore the words and pictures in *Asia* to help them better understand the information in the text and collect evidence for the Focusing Question Task.

Learn 60 MIN.

ANALYZE WORDS AND PHOTOGRAPHS IN *ASIA* 18 MIN.

Whole Group

Explain that as students take a closer look at the words and photographs in *Asia*, they will think about how the words and pictures work together to add to their understanding of the continent.

If possible, use a document camera to display page 28 for the class, hiding the photo on page 29. Read the heading at the top of the page. Ask: "What does *modern* mean? Where have we heard this word before?" Volunteers respond.

- *It means new.*
- *It means something that is made now.*
- *It isn't from a long time ago.*
- *We heard it in* Now & Ben.

Reinforce the definition of *modern* as something that relates to the present.

Reread the word *marvel* aloud. Explain that a marvel is a something or someone amazing. It is something which, when people look at it, they might say "Wow!"

Ask: "Putting those two words together, what might this page be about?" Volunteers respond.

- *Something new that makes us say "Wow!"*
- *It is something that we will like to see.*
- *It is something new that people will like to see.*

💬 Prompt students to sit in "listening position" and look at the copy of the text in front of the class. Read page 28 aloud, prompting students to pay close attention to the words they hear to describe this "Modern Marvel." Instruct students to Think-Pair-Share, and ask the following TDQs. Call on volunteers to respond.

1 What do you think the Burj Khalifa looks like? What words make you think that?

- *It is super tall. They said it is the tallest building in the world!*
- *I think it has windows because it said glass.*
- *I think it is very big. They said it took 6 years to make it.*

Use a document camera to display the picture of the Burj Khalifa on page 29. Call on a volunteer to approach the text and point to the Burj Khalifa. Ask the student to explain their rationale for choosing that building.

> **TEACHER NOTE** | If a document camera is not available in your classroom, divide students into small groups. Distribute a copy of the text to each group for better visibility.

2 **The text tells us that this modern marvel is the tallest building in the world. How does this photograph help us better understand how tall it is?**

- *I see it is taller than the buildings.*
- *It looks like it reaches the clouds.*
- *It makes the other buildings look really small.*

Ask: "What details did you learn from the picture that you did not hear in the words?" Volunteers respond. Use the document camera to zoom in close to certain areas of the picture to allow students to gain a better sense of what they are looking at.

- *There is a pool in front of it.*
- *It gets very pointy at the top.*
- *It goes up like a triangle.*
- *The buildings around it are small.*

Ask: "How did the words and the picture in this section work together to build your knowledge of the Burj Khalifa?" Volunteers respond.

- *We could learn details about it in the words.*
- *The picture showed us.*
- *The picture showed us things in the words and things not in the words.*

Use responses to reinforce that the picture played an important part in enhancing their understanding of this building.

Turn to pages 24–25 in the text. Use the document camera to display the photograph on page 24. Explain that this is a picture of the Gobi Desert.

3 **What does this photograph teach us about the Gobi Desert in Asia? Use specific examples.**

- *There aren't any trees.*
- *I see a lot of sand.*
- *There are mountains and little hills.*
- *There are camels there.*
- *I don't see any houses or people.*

Point to the sand dunes in the picture on page 24 but do not refer to them by name. Ask: "What are these called?" Volunteers respond.

Read page 25 aloud. Instruct students to Think-Pair-Share, and ask: "What are dunes? What do we learn about dunes from the words and pictures?" Use Equity Sticks to call on students to respond.

- *They are hills made of sand.*
- *The wind blows the sand into a hill.*
- *They are not as big as the mountains.*
- *They look soft.*

Call on a volunteer to approach the text and point to the dunes in the picture to confirm their understanding.

Extension

Turn to the "Words You Know" section on page 31 in the text. Explain that this section is similar to a glossary but it does not tell readers the definitions of words. Instead it pairs words from the text with a picture to remind readers of the words they learned while reading this text. Call on a volunteer to use the pictures to locate the word *dunes*.

Refer quickly to pages 26–27. Point to the picture and label this as a mountain.

4 What is a mountain? How does this picture give us information about what a mountain is?

- *It is really tall and goes up to the clouds.*
- *It isn't like the ground. It goes up high.*
- *There is snow on it so it is cold.*
- *There are rocks too.*

Turn back to page 31 and point to the picture and word for *mountain*. Ask: "How does putting these pictures next to each other help us see the differences between a mountain and a dune?" Volunteers respond.

- *The dunes are made of sand.*
- *The mountain has rocks and snow.*
- *There is no snow on the dunes.*
- *The dunes are hot and dry.*
- *The mountains are cold.*

Ask: "How did the words and the picture in this text work together to build your knowledge of the Gobi Dessert?" Volunteers respond.

- *We learned that there are dunes.*
- *We learned the wind blows sand into hills.*
- *The words told us about the sand.*
- *The picture showed us there are camels and no trees.*

The picture showed us things in the words and things not in the words.

The words told us things about the picture.

Use responses to reinforce that the words and pictures work together in this informational text to convey information to readers. They can work together to help readers understand new words, or they can add details when just the words or just the pictures are not enough.

Explain that this understanding of the words and illustrations will help them collect evidence in preparation for the Focusing Question Task.

COLLECT EVIDENCE FOR FOCUSING QUESTION TASK 1 20 MIN.

Whole Group

Post and read the Focusing Question aloud.

Ask: "What does *interesting* mean? What does it mean when something is *interesting*?" Volunteers respond.

It means it's cool.

It means we want to learn about it.

It means we like it and want to know more.

It means we are excited to learn more.

Use responses to explain that in this Focusing Question Task they will be thinking about the different and interesting things people can do in Europe and Asia.

Post a blank Evidence Organizer for *Asia* in front of the class.

Ask: "Why is it important to collect evidence from the text to answer our Focusing Questions?" Volunteers respond.

It supports our topic.

It gives an example.

It helps us show why our answer is right.

| **TEACHER NOTE** | Over the course of this module, students will collect evidence on three categories: Things to Do, Natural Features, and Animals. In Lessons 1–8 they begin by collecting evidence for the category Things to Do in the continents of Europe and Asia. To focus student attention, cover up, or leave the labels blank, for the categories that are not the studied in this section of lessons. These will be revealed and revisited as students progress through the module.

Prepare this evidence organizer prior to the lesson to save time. |

Read the title of the first column, "Things to Do," aloud. Explain that now they will look back through the text as a class to collect evidence on things to do in Asia.

Remind students that "things to do" can mean a lot of different things; it can mean things people do every day for work, it can mean places they can visit, and it can be things they can do for fun. Reinforce that this category includes things both visitors as well as people who live there can do.

Instruct students to Think-Pair-Share, and ask: "Why do you think we are collecting evidence on the different things to do in Asia? How does this help us learn more about the continent?" Volunteers respond.

- *Maybe things are different than what we can do here.*
- *Maybe they have things that we can't do here.*
- *They could have things to do that are the same.*
- *It helps us learn more about what the people like to do there.*
- *Maybe we will want to go there one day and do it too.*

Scaffold

Remind students of how they compared their own life to that of Cynthia Rylant's in *When I Was Young in the Mountains*. Ask: "Why was it helpful to learn about how her life and how it was different or the same? What did that teach us?"

Reinforce that it is important to learn about things people do on different continents because it helps them learn more about these different places. Perhaps students will find that some things are the same, and perhaps they will find that some things are different. It will help them form a bigger picture of the places they are learning about, and ultimately write about them.

Explain that now they will use both the words and the photographs to collect evidence for the Focusing Question Task.

Turn to pages 28–29 in the text. Model looking at the photograph and thinking about whether this qualifies as things to do in Asia. For example,

This is the tallest building in the whole world. That would be an amazing thing to see! I bet it goes straight up into the clouds. It says in the text that people work here and they can live here. I think a very interesting thing to do in Asia would be to visit the tallest building in the world, the Burj Khalifa.

Quickly draw a picture of the Burj Khalifa and add the phrase "visit Burj Khalifa" to a sticky note. Add this evidence to the evidence organizer.

Divide the class into five small groups and distribute a text for reference to each group. Explain that they will share these copies of the text with their group in order to get a closer look at the pictures.

Explain that students will go back through the text as a class to collect evidence. While following along in their group copies of the text, students will make a Nonverbal Signal, such as stretching their arms up in a point above their heads, mimicking the Burj Khalifa, when they hear a piece of evidence in the text.

✔ Read the text aloud, with students following along with their groups. Students make a Nonverbal Signal when they hear or see evidence about things to do in Asia. Call on students who signal to share their evidence. After each response, students consider whether or not that piece of evidence is an example of things to do in Asia. They indicate a level of agreement by holding up anywhere from one to five fingers, with one finger showing the lowest level of agreement and five fingers showing the strongest level of agreement.

TEACHER NOTE	Use this time to help students evaluate whether this evidence belongs in this category before placing it on the chart. This will help them be thoughtful about their choices and consider the information in front of them. Consider using actual photographs as pieces of evidence instead of drawing and labeling. This will save time as well as help students easily access the evidence organizer independently. Consider using the example below to prerecord or print out images to include on the evidence organizer.

Record this evidence quickly on a sticky note and add it to the evidence organizer.

SAMPLE EVIDENCE ORGANIZER FOR *ASIA*

Evidence Organizer for *Asia*		
Things to Do	Natural Features	Animals
▪ visit Burj Khalifa ▪ build computer parts ▪ grow rice ▪ walk the Great Wall of China ▪ shop at street market ▪ walk in a park		

EXPERIMENT WITH WRITING AN OPINION STATEMENT 22 MIN.

Whole Group

Post and read the Craft Question: *How do I write an opinion statement?*

Explain that students will look to the evidence they collected from *Asia* to practice creating opinion statements as a class.

Instruct students to Think-Pair-Share, and ask: "What is an <u>opinion</u>? Why is it important to share your opinion?" Volunteers respond.

- *It tells people what we think.*
- *It tells people how we feel.*
- *Maybe people can learn from what we think.*

Use responses to reinforce that an opinion conveys information about how a person thinks or feels about something.

Ask: "Does the sentence, 'I am wearing [insert article of clothing]' give my opinion? Why or why not?" Volunteers respond.

- *No, because it doesn't tell us what you think.*
- *No, because it doesn't tell us how you feel about it.*
- *You are just telling us about something true.*

Reinforce that the sentence is not an opinion sentence because it just gives information about clothes. It doesn't give information about how you think or feel.

Ask: "Does the sentence 'I think blue is the best color in the world' give my opinion? Why or why not?" Volunteers respond.

- *Yes, because it tells us what you think.*
- *It tells us what you think about the color blue.*
- *It tells us how you feel about blue.*

Confirm that this sentence is an opinion statement because it tells people how you feel about the color blue.

Instruct students to turn to a partner and answer the following question: "What color do you think is the best color in the world? What is your favorite color?" Use Equity Sticks to call on three students to share their answers. After each student shares, ask students to stand up if they think that color is the best color in the world, too.

Ask: "Did we all think that one color was the best in the world?" Volunteer responds. Reinforce that one person's opinion can be different from another's.

Practice recognizing opinion statements using the following examples:

- My favorite ice cream is chocolate. (yes)

- I have a brother. (no)

- I think the best sport to play is baseball. (yes)

- Asia is the best continent in the world. (yes)

- I think the most interesting place to see in Asia is the Gobi Desert. (yes)

- I think I'll drink some water now. (no)

Instruct students to stand up if they think the sentence is an opinion statement; students stay seated if they do not think the sentence is an opinion. Call on a volunteer to explain their thinking for each sentence.

Explain that they will use the text to practice creating an opinion statement. Post and read the following prompt.

Which animal from Asia is your favorite, the giant panda or the Bengal tiger?

Read pages 18–21 aloud. Prompt students to listen closely to the descriptions of the two animals in the text. After the read, model a Think Aloud about the text you read to form your own opinion. For example,

Which animal is my favorite? I don't know. I will have to look at both animals to try to make that choice. The text explains that the giant panda loves bamboo. I think the picture of the panda is funny, too. He looks comfortable. The text also says that the Bengal tiger is a good hunter and likes to swim. I also like to swim! I think it is amazing that tigers are so good at both things. They also have pretty stripes. After thinking about what I heard, I think the Bengal tiger is my favorite animal!

TEACHER NOTE | Modeling this Think Aloud is important because it shows students that one forms an opinion based on the evidence they already know, rather than forming an opinion and then searching for reasons to support it. The purpose of this lesson is to model the process for students so that later in the module they will be familiar with the thought process.

Explain that now students will think about the prompt and form their own opinion about which animal in Asia is their favorite. Remind students that they do not need to have the same opinion as you or their peers!

Instruct students to Mix and Mingle about the prompt. If needed, distribute copies of the text to small groups for them to share.

> **Scaffold**
>
> Post the following sentence frame for students to use during their verbal rehearsal and writing: **My favorite animal in Asia is _____.** In the next lessons, students will experiment with writing an opinion statement and using the question as a guide to form complete sentences.

✔ Students write an opinion statement in response to the above prompt in their Response Journals. If time allows, students include a drawing to support their sentence.

Land 5 MIN.

ANSWER THE CONTENT FRAMING QUESTION

Display and read aloud the Content Framing Question. Ask: "How did the words and pictures work together in this text to help us learn more about Asia?" Volunteers respond.

Instruct students to Mix and Mingle, and ask: "If you were traveling to Asia, what would you need to pack? Why?" Encourage students to look at the evidence organizer and consider the different things they would do while in Asia. If needed, allow students to look back through the pictures in the text. Use Equity Sticks to call on students to share their answers.

Wrap 1 MIN.

ASSIGN HOMEWORK

Continue the class home-reading routine.

Analyze

Context and Alignment

Students use the words and photographs in *Asia* to learn more about the continent and collect evidence on the different things to do in Asia (RI.K.1, RI.K.7). Each student:

- Makes a Nonverbal Signal when hearing a piece of evidence from the text.

Next Steps

If students have difficulty understanding which evidence qualifies as things to do, consider the root of the problem. Does the student understand what the category means? If not, redefine the category and provide concrete examples from the text. Does the student have trouble locating evidence in the text? If so, go back through the text slowly, focusing largely on the photographs. Encourage students to think about the people in the pictures and what they are doing in the pictures.

⬇ LESSON 4 DEEP DIVE: STYLE AND CONVENTIONS

Examine Writing and Expanding a Sentence

- **Time:** 15 min.

- **Text:** *Asia*, Rebecca Hirsch

- **Style and Conventions Learning Goal:** Identify the parts of a complete sentence and describe how a given sentence was expanded. (L.K.1.f)

   STYLE AND CONVENTIONS CRAFT QUESTION: Lesson 4
   Examine: *Why is it important to create and expand complete sentences?*

Launch

Post and read the Style and Conventions Craft Question.

Remind students that they have worked hard at becoming writers throughout all the previous modules. Ask: "What questions need to be answered to make a sentence?" Volunteers respond.

Use student responses to reinforce that a sentence answers the questions "who?" and "does what?"

Explain that students are going to look at sentences from *Asia* to see how authors write complete sentences and add details to tell more information.

Learn

	Consider writing the following sentences or phrases from *Asia* on sentence strips ahead of time to maximize instructional time.
TEACHER NOTE	A giant panda eats bamboo. (page 18)
	A Bengal tiger. (page 20)
	Other forests grow bamboo plants. (page 23)

Instruct students to listen closely to determine if the information from the book is a complete sentence or not.

Display page 18, point out the illustration and read the caption. Display the caption on the board. Instruct students to Think-Pair-Share, and ask: "Is this a complete sentence? Why or why not?"

Volunteers respond.

  ▪ *Yes, because it tells who does what.*

  ▪ *Yes, because it tells that a giant panda eats.*

Display page 20, point out the illustration, and read the caption. Display the caption on the board. Instruct students to Think-Pair-Share, and ask: "Is this a complete sentence? Why or why not?" Volunteers respond.

  ▪ *No, because it only says who.*

  ▪ *No, because it doesn't tell what the tiger does.*

Point out that authors do not always write in complete sentences when describing illustrations.

However, they always write in complete sentences when telling a story or sharing information so that readers understand clearly.

Explain that authors usually add details to their sentences and tell more than just the "who" and "does what" so their writing is more interesting and shares more information.

Display page 11, and say, "People work." Write the sentence on the board. Ask students to give a thumbs-up signal if this is a complete sentence. Ask: "Does it tell a lot of information?" Students respond chorally.

  ▪ *No!*

Read the first sentence on page 11: "Many people work in modern factories." Record the sentence on the board, writing the describing word *many* and the prepositional phrase *in modern factories* in a color different than *people work.*

Ask: "What other information did the author include in this sentence?" Volunteers respond.

  ▪ *She tells that it is many people.*

  ▪ *She tells that the people work in factories.*

  ▪ *She tells that the factories are modern.*

Use student responses to emphasize that these details made the sentence more interesting and gave important information. Reinforce that *many* describes how many and *in modern factories* tells where.

Organize students into pairs. Display page 23 and read the last sentence, "Other forests grow bamboo plants." Post the sentence on the board.

✔ Students give a thumbs-up signal if they hear a complete sentence or a thumbs-down signal if not. Post the following questions:

Who is the sentence about?

What is the who doing in the sentence?

How did the author add more information?

Students work in partners to determine the answers to the questions. Circulate to provide support and ensure understanding. Call on pairs who demonstrate a strong understanding to share their findings with the class.

Land

Direct student attention back to Style and Conventions Craft Question, and ask: "Why do authors add details to their sentences?" Volunteers respond.

- *Because then we can understand the book better.*
- *Because they make it more interesting.*
- *Because then we could learn even more information.*

■ FOCUSING QUESTION: LESSONS 1–8

What interesting things can people do in Europe and Asia?

| 1 | 2 | 3 | 4 | 5 | 6 | 7 | 8 | 9 | 10 | 11 | 12 | 13 | 14 | 15 | 16 | 17 | 18 | 19 | 20 | 21 | 22 | 23 | 24 | 25 | 26 | 27 | 28 | 29 | 30 | 31 | 32 | 33 | 34 | 35 | 36 |

Lesson 5

TEXTS

- "The Seven Continents Song," Silly School Songs (video) (**http://witeng.link/0374**)
- *Europe*, Rebecca Hirsch
- *The Story of Ferdinand*, Munro Leaf; Illustrations, Robert Lawson

Lesson 5: At a Glance

AGENDA

Welcome (5 min.)

Practice Fluency

Launch (4 min.)

Learn (60 min.)

Analyze Words and Photographs in Europe (15 min.)

Collect Evidence for Focusing Question Task 1 (15 min.)

Experiment with Expressing an Opinion (10 min.)

Analyze Words and Illustrations in The Story of Ferdinand (20 min.)

Land (5 min.)

Answer the Content Framing Question

Wrap (1 min.)

Assign Homework

Vocabulary Deep Dive: Multiple-Meaning Words: *Stick* and *horns* (15 min.)

STANDARDS ADDRESSED

The full text of ELA Standards can be found in the Module Overview.

Reading

- RL.K.1, RL.K.7, RI.K.1, RI.K.4, RI.K.7

Writing

- W.K.1, W.K.8

Speaking and Listening

- SL.K.1, SL.K.2

Language

- L.K.1.f
- ⬇ L.K.4.a

MATERIALS

- Repeated Language Chart
- Evidence Organizer for *Europe*
- Evidence Organizer for *Asia*
- Sticky notes
- Sentence strips
- Document camera (if available)

Learning Goals

Use photographs and details from the text to describe things people can do in Europe. (RI.K.7)

✔ Annotate evidence for the Focusing Question Task.

Use the illustrations and details from the text to describe events in *The Story of Ferdinand*. (RL.K.1, RL.K.7, W.K.8)

✔ Write a sentence about a detail found in an illustration.

⬇ Identify new meanings for the words *stick* and *horns* and apply them accurately. (L.K.4.a)

✔ Mix and Mingle, sharing complete sentences using each word correctly.

✔ Checks for Understanding

Prepare

FOCUSING QUESTION: Lessons 1–8

What interesting things can people do in Europe and Asia?

CONTENT FRAMING QUESTION: Lesson 5

Reveal: *What does a deeper exploration of the words and photographs in* Europe *reveal?*

CRAFT QUESTION

Experiment: *How do I write an opinion statement?*

In this lesson, students continue their exploration of *Europe*, deepening understanding of how a text's words and illustrations work together to build understanding. Students use this knowledge to collect evidence for the Focusing Question Task. In addition, students experiment with how to create an opinion statement by including key words from the prompt. Finally, students use their experience analyzing illustrations to help them analyze *The Story of Ferdinand* and learn more about the events in the story.

Welcome 5 MIN.

PRACTICE FLUENCY

Play the first 10 seconds of the video "The Seven Continents Song" (**http://witeng.link/0374**). Display the Repeated Language Chart with the last line in the song added. Read the line aloud. Students Echo Read the last line.

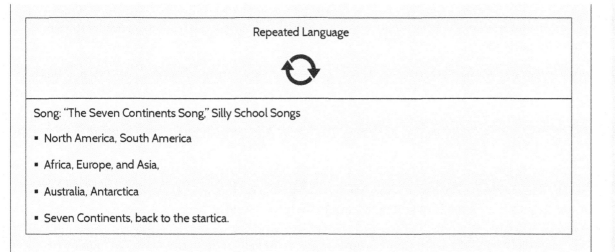

Repeated Language
Song: "The Seven Continents Song," Silly School Songs • North America, South America • Africa, Europe, and Asia, • Australia, Antarctica • Seven Continents, back to the startica.

Read the added line of the song aloud. Ask: "Is *startica* a real word? What continent name does it rhyme with?" Volunteers respond.

- *I think it is pretend.*
- *It is like* Antarctica.
- *It rhymes with* Antarctica.

Ask: "Why do you think they created this word for the song? What word do you think they really mean?" Volunteers respond.

- *I think they wanted it to rhyme.*
- *They mean go back to the start.*
- *They are being funny.*
- *The song repeats so it goes back to the start.*

Confirm that *startica* isn't a real word, but one invented to create a rhyme in the song. It is a silly way of telling listeners that they will go back to the start of the song.

Instruct students to Think-Pair-Share, and ask: "How do rhymes in songs help listeners? Why do you think hearing rhymes in songs?" Volunteers respond.

- *It is like a beat.*
- *It makes me feel like I am dancing.*
- *The rhymes are fun to listen to.*

Foundational Skills Connection

Listen to the next verse of the song and ask students to make a Nonverbal Signal when they hear a rhyming pair. Ask: "What are the rhyming words you heard?" Volunteers respond. If students need support, provide one of the words in the rhyming pair and ask them to listen for the word that rhymes with it.

Create simple dance moves for the last line of the song, such as holding up seven fingers for "seven continents" and gesturing with a thumb over your shoulder for "back to the startica."

Reread all four lines of the song aloud. Students Echo Read the song while incorporating the dance moves for each line.

Launch 4 MIN.

Explain that authors choose words in a song or story for a reason. Paying close attention to the words an author uses can help students learn more from a song or text.

Ask: "How did we use the words and pictures together to help understand *Asia*?" Volunteers respond.

- *We looked at the pictures for more detail.*
- *We listened to the words to learn more, too.*
- *Sometimes the picture helped us understand the words we read.*

Ask: "Why do you think the author included photos instead of drawings?" Volunteers respond.

- *The photos show us real life.*
- *A drawing is just what people remember.*
- *Photos show us more.*

Display and read aloud the Content Framing Question. Tell students that today they will explore the words and pictures in *Europe* to help them better understand the information in the text and collect evidence for the Focusing Question Task.

Learn 60 MIN.

ANALYZE WORDS AND PHOTOGRAPHS IN *EUROPE* 15 MIN.

Pairs

Explain that as students take a closer look at the words and photographs in *Europe*, they will think about how the words and pictures work together add to their knowledge of the continent.

💬 Divide the class into pairs and distribute copies of the text to each pair. Explain that students will now engage in Partner Reading and share responsibility for the text as they respond to TDQs about the words and pictures in the text.

Prompt students to turn pages 8–9 in the text. Read the heading on the top of page 9. Students Echo Read the heading. Explain that now students will read through this section of the text as a class and respond to questions about how the words and pictures in this section work together to communicate key details in the text.

Instruct students to Think-Pair-Share about the following TDQs. Use Equity Sticks to call on students to answer.

Read the first sentence on page 9 aloud. Ask: "What is a *language*? What language do you speak? Have you heard of any other languages?" Volunteers respond.

Define *language* as "the words that people put together to communicate their ideas"; languages are not the same for everyone. There are many different languages spoken all over the world. Explain that in Europe each country has its own language. While they may be all the same continent, they aren't always able to talk to each other without help!

93

Define a *custom* as "a way of doing something that is accepted by a group." For example, explain that having fireworks or a big celebration on the Fourth of July is an American custom; it is something that lots of people do in the United States. Your family might have a custom of eating dinner together every Sunday afternoon.

Read the rest of page 9 aloud. Ask: "Is celebrating Oktoberfest a custom? Is this something we do in America?" Volunteers respond. Reinforce that celebrating Oktoberfest is a German custom because it is something that is done in Germany, but not in many other places.

1   **How does the picture on page 8 help us understand what this festival might be like?**

- *They wear pretty clothes and the girls have braids.*
- *The girls are wearing the same clothes.*
- *It looks like they are dancing.*
- *It looks a like a big party.*

Extension

Ask: "What month do you think Oktoberfest takes place in?" Volunteers respond.

Organize students into two lines across from each other. Instruct students to match with the person across from them, and dance down the line together, stopping at the ends of the line and going back to their side. This will allow students to act out the actions in the picture and get a better sense of the celebration.

Read pages 10–11. Ask: "What language do they speak in the United Kingdom? Do you recognize that language?" Volunteers respond.

- *They speak English!*
- *That is just like us. We speak English here.*

Use responses to confirm that some countries, even on different continents, can speak the same language. Explain that this is because a long time ago, people would travel to discover new places around the world. When they found a new place and decided to stay there, they would often bring their languages and customs with them.

Read pages 12–13.

2   **How does the picture on page 12 help us understand what a waterway is?**

- *There are no roads.*
- *They are streets made of water.*
- *A waterway is water that is like a road, but without pavement.*

Extension

Ask: "What two words do you hear in the word *waterway*?" If needed, define *way* as "a street or path that goes from one place to another." Ask: "How does putting those two words together help us understand what a waterway is?" Volunteers respond.

Instruct students to Think-Pair-Share, and ask: "How is this city different from the cities you know? Use the picture to help you answer." Use Equity Sticks to call on students to answer.

- *There are no sidewalks. The houses go into the water.*
- *The boats are the cars. They have to wait in line.*
- *A man has to drive the boat.*

Instruct students to Think-Pair-Share, and ask: "How did the pictures help you understand the words we read in 'People of Europe'? How do people in Europe live differently than you?" Volunteers respond.

- *The pictures show us what places look like.*
- *Pictures show us the real life.*
- *We don't have boats, we have cars.*
- *We don't have Oktoberfest and wear those clothes.*

Explain that now they will use this understanding help them collect evidence for the Focusing Question Task.

COLLECT EVIDENCE FOR FOCUSING QUESTION TASK 1 15 MIN.

Pairs

Post and read the Focusing Question. Students Echo Read the question.

Display the Evidence Organizer for *Asia*.

Ask: "What do we mean by 'things to do'? What evidence did we find in the previous lesson that is an example of things to do?" Volunteers respond. Encourage those answering to approach the Evidence Organizer for *Asia* and point to the example they are naming.

Display the blank Evidence Organizer for *Europe*.

Divide the class into pairs and distribute copies of the text. Prompt students to turn to pages 8–9 and look at the photograph on page 8. Model a Think Aloud about whether or not this photograph demonstrates an example of things to do in Europe. For example,

> **I see that there are children dancing in special clothing. This must be a festival! I think if I went to Europe I could see a lot of festivals. I think this is an example of things to do in Europe.**

Record this evidence on a sticky note and add it to the "Things to Do" column.

Prompt students to turn to pages 12–13 and look at the photograph on page 12. Ask: "What is happening in this photograph? Is this an example of something people can do in Europe?" Volunteers respond.

- *People are driving boats.*
- *They are riding in boats instead of cars.*
- *This is something people can do in Europe.*

As students respond, briefly record this answer on a sticky note and add it to the "Things to Do" column on the Evidence Organizer for *Europe*.

Extension

Prompt students to look at the photograph on page 10. Ask: "What is happening in this picture? Is this an example of a thing people can do in Europe?" Volunteers respond. Read the caption at the bottom of the photograph. Reinforce that this is not an example of things that people can do in Europe. While people do get married, the photograph is showing readers a picture of the royal family instead.

Divide the class into pairs and give each pair two sticky notes. Explain that they will go back through the photographs in the text to look for examples of other things to do in Europe.

Prompt pairs to turn to page 14–15 in the text. Instruct pairs to turn through the section "Places to See" and annotate one photograph that is an example of something people can do in Europe. Give students two minutes to Think-Pair-Share about the photographs and place a sticky note on one photograph. Use Equity Sticks to call on pairs to share their annotations. As pairs answer, record their evidence on a sticky note and add it to the evidence organizer.

Scaffold

If students have difficulty identifying evidence, use this time to provide support by going through each photograph in this section as a class, instead of individually annotating.

✔ Prompt pairs to turn to page 20–21. Instruct pairs to turn through the section "Land and Water" and annotate one photograph that is an example of something people can do in Europe. Give students two minutes to Think-Pair-Share about the photographs and place a sticky note on one photograph. Use Equity Sticks to call on pairs to share their annotations.

After each pair shares their annotation, students consider whether or not that piece of evidence is an example of things to do by indicating a level of agreement by holding up anywhere from one to five fingers, with one finger showing the lowest level of agreement and five fingers showing the strongest level of agreement.

As pairs answer, record their evidence on a sticky note and add it to the evidence organizer.

<table>
<tr><td>TEACHER NOTE</td><td>Consider using actual photographs as pieces of evidence instead of drawing and labeling. This will save time as well as help students easily access the evidence organizer independently. Consider using the example below to prerecord or print out images to include on the evidence organizer.

The chart below is an example. It includes most of the answers students may find. It is not critical that students collect every piece of evidence in the text, only that there are enough examples for students to choose from and form their own opinions based on that information.</td></tr>
</table>

SAMPLE EVIDENCE ORGANIZER FOR *EUROPE*

Evidence Organizer for *Europe*		
Things to Do	**Natural Features**	**Animals**
• ride in boats • go to festivals • visit museums • see pretty buildings • visit old castles • ski • pick grapes		

EXPERIMENT WITH EXPRESSING AN OPINION 10 MIN.

Whole Group

Ask: "Why do you think we are collecting evidence from the text on the different things to do in Asia and Europe?" Volunteers respond.

- We are going to write about it.

Ask: "What is an opinion?" Volunteer respond.

- It is when you say what you like.
- It is when you choose something you like the best.
- It is what you think
- It could be how you feel about something.

Use responses to reinforce the definition of an opinion.

Post and read the Craft Question: *How do I write an opinion statement?*

Explain that students will practice creating an opinion statement by looking at how to respond to the prompt.

Ask: "How do you respond to a prompt?" Volunteers respond.

- *We use the text.*
- *We have to answer the question.*
- *We can't answer a different question.*
- *It is important to answer the question being asked.*

Reinforce the importance of responding to the question asked and not a different question. Reactivate knowledge from Module 1.

Post and read the following question aloud: "What is your favorite place to see in Europe?" Students Echo Read the question.

Post the following sentences, in this order, on sentence strips underneath the question:

- My favorite snack is yogurt.
- I don't think museums are fun to see.
- My favorite place to see in Europe is a castle.

TEACHER NOTE	Considering lining up the strips so students can see where similar words line up. For example, the word *favorite* from the question and two of the responses should be in the same vertical eye line. This will help students see how one forms an opinion statement by using the words from the prompt.

Read the first sample response aloud. Students Echo Read the sentence. Ask: "Does this opinion statement answer the question?" Students stand up if they think "yes," and stay seated if they think "no." Call on a volunteer to explain their thinking.

- *That doesn't answer the question. The question is about Europe, not about snacks.*

Confirm that this opinion statement does not answer the question. Remove the sentence strip from the front of the class.

Read the second sample response aloud. Students Echo Read the sentence. Ask: "Does this opinion statement answer the question?" Students stand up if they think "yes," and stay seated if they think "no." Call on a volunteer to explain their thinking.

- *That doesn't answer the question. That says what you don't like to see.*

Confirm that this opinion statement does not answer the question. Remove the sentence strip from the front of the class.

Read the final sample response aloud. Students Echo Read the sentence. Ask: "Does this opinion statement answer the question?" Students stand up if they think "yes," and stay seated if they think "no." Call on a volunteer to explain their thinking.

 ▪ *Yes it does!*

Ask: "What do you notice about the words in my answer? How did you know that this answered the question?" Volunteers respond.

 ▪ *The words are the same.*

 ▪ *I heard a lot of the same words.*

 ▪ *The words are the same, but it is not a question.*

Reinforce that the words in the answer are the same as in the question by demonstrating how the words in the question line up with the words in the answer.

Alternate Activity

Call on volunteers to approach the sentence strips and identify the words that are the same in the question and in the answer.

Instruct students to Think-Pair-Share, and ask: "How do I write an opinion statement?" Use Equity Sticks to call on students to share their thinking.

 ▪ *You can use the question to help you.*

 ▪ *You say what you like the best or how you feel.*

 ▪ *You use the words from the question to make a sentence.*

Use responses to reinforce that when responding to an opinion question it is important to use the words in the question so readers understand what you are responding to.

Read the following question: "What is your favorite thing to do after school?"

Instruct students to Think-Pair-Share about the question and practice verbally stating their opinion using the words from the question. If needed, post the sentence frame, **My favorite thing to do after school is _____.**, as a guide.

Extension

If time allows, pose more opinion questions so students can practice forming their opinions using key words from the question. This will give students practice with different types of opinion questions.

ANALYZE WORDS AND ILLUSTRATIONS IN *THE STORY OF FERDINAND*
20 MIN.

Whole Group

Explain that now students will use their knowledge of the relationship between the words and illustrations to enhance their understanding of events in *The Story of Ferdinand*.

Bring students together in front of the book, or use a document camera to display the pages of the text.

Locate an image of a matador on the Internet and provide a brief background on bullfighting. For example, explain that bullfighting is an ancient custom in areas of Europe, such as Spain. It was a big show put on for the people of a city where a man, also known as the Matador, would fight a bull.

TEACHER NOTE	Use this to provide insight into the different outfits and movements of the matador, but exclude images of the bull getting hurt, which might be difficult for students to understand.

Explain that now they will read back through the text and use the illustrations to help them understand different events in the text.

Read the text aloud. Stop on the selected pages, and instruct students to Think-Pair-Share about the following TDQs. Use Equity Sticks to call on students to answer.

Read through page 15.

3 How does this illustration help us know which bull is Ferdinand? What in the picture makes you think so?

- *The bull near the flowers. He smells the flower.*
- *The other bulls are jumping and snorting.*
- *I see the bulls butting their heads. Ferdinand doesn't do that.*
- *The butterflies are near him because he is gentle.*

Confirm their answers by pointing to Ferdinand on page 15.

Continue reading through page 17.

4   What is happening in this picture on page 17? How does the illustration help us understand what happened to Ferdinand?

  ▪ *He looks surprised.*

  ▪ *His eyes are really big because he got stung!*

  ▪ *We can't see the bee sting him, but his face says it does.*

  ▪ *He looks like it hurt him.*

Use responses to reinforce that while the illustrator does not actually show Ferdinand getting stung by the bee, they see a change in his facial expression that tell them something has happened. Ask students to mimic Ferdinand and make a face like a bee has just stung them.

Continue reading through page 27. Explain that illustrators often create pictures to help readers understand how big something is in real life. For example, the illustrator could not draw the whole ring on page 27 because it wouldn't fit!

5   How does this illustration show us how big the ring is?

  ▪ *Ferdinand looks really small, but we know he is big.*

  ▪ *I can't see any people. They are dots.*

  ▪ *The matador is tiny, too.*

Use response to reinforce that the illustrator wanted to show how many people were there, but he couldn't fit everyone in the picture. He needed to draw the people very small. Also, the story tells readers that Ferdinand is very big, but he looks small in this picture. This is to show readers how big the ring is in comparison to Ferdinand.

Ask: "How would you feel if you were Ferdinand and you walked into a ring that big?" Volunteers respond.

Read page 28. Display the illustration on page 28 in front of the class. Ask: "How does Ferdinand feel about being in the ring?" Explain that students will record their answer to this question in their Response Journals.

> **Scaffold**
>
> Using a document camera, zoom in on Ferdinand's facial expression to help students get a better sense of his emotions.

✔ Students respond to following questions in their Response Journals: "How does Ferdinand feel about being in the ring? How do you know?" Encourage students to support their answer with one example from the illustration.

Land 5 MIN.

ANSWER THE CONTENT FRAMING QUESTION

Display and read aloud the Content Framing Question. Ask: "How did the words and pictures in *Europe* work together to help us learn more about Europe?" Volunteers respond.

Ask: "How did the words and pictures in *The Story of Ferdinand* work together in this text to help us understand the story?" Volunteers respond.

Instruct students to Mix and Mingle, and ask: "If you were traveling to Europe, what would you need to pack? Why?" Encourage students to look at the evidence organizer and consider the different things they would do while in Europe. If needed, allow students to look back through the pictures in the text. Use Equity Sticks to call on students to share their answers.

Wrap 1 MIN.

ASSIGN HOMEWORK

Continue the classroom home-reading routine.

Analyze

Context and Alignment

Students use the words and pictures in *Europe* to learn more about the continent and collect evidence on the different things to do in Europe (RI.K.1, RI.K.7). Each student:

- Annotates one piece of evidence from the text.

Next Steps

If students have difficulty understanding what evidence qualifies as things to do, consider the root of the problem. Does the student understand what the category means? If not, redefine the category and provide concrete examples from the text. Does the student have trouble locating evidence in the text? If so, go back through the text slowly, focusing largely on the photographs. Encourage students to think about the people in the pictures and what they are doing in the picture. Reread pages of the text as needed to remind students of what the photographs show.

⬇ LESSON 5 DEEP DIVE: VOCABULARY

Multiple-Meaning Words: *Stick* and *horns*

- **Time:** 15 min.

- **Text:** *The Story of Ferdinand*, Munro Leaf; Illustrations, Robert Lawson

- **Vocabulary Learning Goal:** Identify new meanings for the words *stick* and *horns* and apply them accurately. (L.K.4.a)

Launch

Remind students that during the earlier lesson they learned the word *language*. Ask: "What is a language?" Volunteers respond.

- *How people talk to each other.*
- *The words people use to say things.*
- *The way that people can share information.*

Use student responses to reinforce that language is the words people use to share thoughts and ideas. Remind students that we speak English at school and in our language, words can have more than one meaning.

Display the cover of *The Story of Ferdinand* and explain that students are going to use the words and illustrations to discover the new meanings of some words in the story.

Learn

Post the words:

horns

stick

Point to and read the word *horns*. Ask: "What are musical *horns*?" Volunteers respond.

- *Instruments you hear in a band.*
- *Things that make a loud noise.*
- *A trumpet is a horn!*

Use student responses to draw a picture of musical *horns* next to the word.

Reinforce that this story is not about music or noise so *horns* has a different meaning in the book. Display and read page 11 of the text, emphasizing the word *horns*. Instruct students to Think-Pair-Share, and ask: "What does *horns* mean in this sentence?" Volunteers respond.

> *The pointy things on top of the bull's head.*

Use student responses to reinforce that *horns* is also the name of the hard, pointy objects that grown on some animals' heads. Draw a picture of animal horns next to the word.

Point to and read the word *stick*. Ask: "What is a stick?" Volunteers respond.

> *A long piece of wood.*
> *A branch or a twig.*

Use student responses to draw a picture of a stick next to the word.

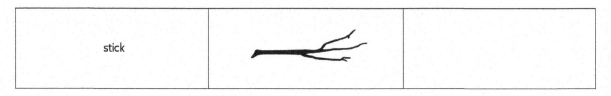

Reinforce that this story is not about trees or wood so *stick* has a different meaning in the book. Display and read pages 22–23 of the text, emphasizing the word *stick*. Instruct students to Think-Pair-Share and ask: "What does *stick* mean in this sentence?" Volunteers respond.

> *To poke with something sharp.*

Use student responses to reinforce that *stick* also means "to poke with something sharp or pointy." Draw a picture of *stick* next to the word.

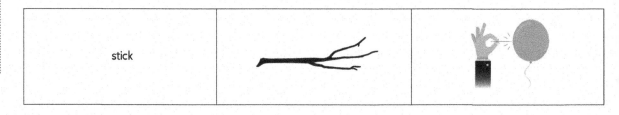

Explain that students are going to use the words in sentences to show they understand both meanings of the words.

✔ Call out a word and point to a picture representing one meaning. Instruct students to Mix and Mingle and share a sentence using that word correctly. Circulate to provide support as needed and to ensure that students are using the words correctly in their sentences. Repeat this for each meaning of the words *stick* and *horn*.

Land

Reorganize students back into a whole group. Review each word and its meanings.

Use Equity Sticks to call on several students to share their sentences for each word and meaning.

What interesting things can people do in Europe and Asia?

1 2 3 4 5 **6** 7 8 9 10 11 12 13 14 15 16 17 18 19 20 21 22 23 24 25 26 27 28 29 30 31 32 33 34 35 36

Lesson 6

TEXTS

- "The Seven Continents Song," Silly School Songs (video) (**http://witeng.link/0374**)
- *When I Was Young in the Mountains*, Cynthia Rylant; Illustrations, Diane Goode
- *Asia*, Rebecca Hirsch
- "Explore Views of the Burj Khalifa with Google Maps," Google Maps (video) (**http://witeng.link/0390**)
- *The Story of Ferdinand*, Munro Leaf; Illustrations, Robert Lawson

Lesson 6: At a Glance

AGENDA

Welcome (5 min.)

Practice Fluency

Launch (10 min.)

Learn (54 min.)

Identify a Point in the Text (15 min.)

Identify Reasons That Support a Point (20 min.)

Experiment with Writing an Opinion Statement (19 min.)

Land (5 min.)

Answer the Content Framing Question

Wrap (1 min.)

Assign Homework

Vocabulary Deep Dive: Shades of Meaning: *Stick*, *touch*, and *poke* (15 min.)

STANDARDS ADDRESSED

The full text of ELA Standards can be found in the Module Overview.

Reading

- RI.K.1, RI.K.4, RI.K.8

Writing

- W.K.1, W.K.8

Speaking and Listening

- SL.K.1, SL.K.2

Language

- L.K.1.f
- ⬇ L.K.5.d

MATERIALS

- Repeated Language Chart
- Document camera (if available)

Learning Goals

Identify reasons the author gives to support a point in *Asia*. (RI.K.8)

✔ Use a Nonverbal Signal to indicate a reason that supports the author's point.

Use the photographs and details from the text to state an opinion about the text. (W.K.1, W.K.8)

✔ Write an opinion statement responding to a detail in the text.

⬇ Distinguish shades of meaning between *stick*, *touch*, and *poke* by acting out their meanings. (L.K.5.d)

✔ Take turns choosing a word, saying it, and acting out its meaning.

✔ Checks for Understanding

Prepare

FOCUSING QUESTION: Lessons 1–8

What interesting things can people do in Europe and Asia?

CONTENT FRAMING QUESTION: Lesson 6

Reveal: *What does a deeper exploration of Asia reveal about a point the author makes?*

CRAFT QUESTION: Lesson 6

Experiment: *How do I write an opinion statement?*

In this lesson, students explore a new aspect of text analysis: looking for reasons that support an author's point. Students' work with opinions, main topic, and key details has prepared them for this. After being given the author's point, students identify reasons that support it. This structural understanding of nonfiction texts supports them in their own opinion writing as the module develops. Students complete the lesson by experimenting with writing an opinion statement.

Welcome 5 MIN.

PRACTICE FLUENCY

Play the video of "The Seven Continents Song" (**http://witeng.link/0374**).

Display the Repeated Language Chart. Read first four lines of the song aloud. Students Echo Read the song.

Repeated Language

⟳

Song: "The Seven Continents Song," Silly School Songs

- North America, South America
- Africa, Europe, and Asia,
- Australia, Antarctica
- Seven Continents, back to the startica.

Divide the class into seven groups, assigning each group one of the seven continents. Explain that they will now practice the song while clapping the syllables of each continent. Students clap the syllables and say their assigned continent when it is their turn. Each group focuses on the one continent they have been assigned.

Remind students that learning the different syllables can also help them keep the beat of the song.

Reread the first four lines of the song aloud without clapping the syllables. Students Echo Read while doing the dance moves for each line.

Launch 10 MIN.

Display and read aloud the Content Framing Question. Explain that a point is something the author believes and will try to convince the reader of in the text.

Display the front cover of *When I Was Young in the Mountains*. Call on a volunteer to remind the class briefly what the text is about. Turn to the last page and read it aloud. Ask: "What does *enough* mean? What was Cynthia Rylant telling us in this text?" Volunteers respond.

- *She was telling us that she liked the mountains.*
- *She didn't want to go anywhere else.*
- *She really liked it there and didn't need any more.*
- *She is telling us that she doesn't need anything else.*

Scaffold

If needed, quickly reread portions of the text or turn through the pages to remind students of the different things the author did while young in the mountains.

Reinforce that one point Cynthia Rylant makes in this text is that life in the mountains was enough for her, and she didn't need anything else. Explain that through the pictures and words in the text, Cynthia Rylant gave reasons to support this point, or help the reader understand why she thought that her life in the mountains was enough. Provide students with a few examples such as she enjoyed swimming in the swimming hole, she could get plenty of food from Mr. Crawford's store, and she happily sat on the porch with her grandmother and grandfather.

Ask: "If we only read the last page, would we have been able to understand why Cynthia Rylant enjoyed life in the mountains? What did we need to understand her point?" Volunteers respond.

Reinforce that authors, like Cynthia Rylant, give reasons or examples to support their points so readers understand why. They will put these reasons in the text so the reader can better understand the point they are making.

Explain that in this lesson they will work together as a class to identify a point the author makes in *Asia*. Then, they will search the text—both words and pictures—for specific reasons the author gives to support the point and help readers better understand it.

Learn 54 MIN.

IDENTIFY A POINT IN THE TEXT 15 MIN.

Whole Group

💬 Divide the class into small groups to share the text. Explain that students will go back through the book as a class to identify the point the author is trying to make. Read through the whole text.

Reread the last sentence on page 27, emphasizing the word *unique*. Define *unique* as "something that is one of a kind, or the only one of something." If something is unique, there is nothing else exactly like it—like a snowflake or a personality. Explain that when the author says it is a "unique continent," she is saying that this continent has certain features that no other continent in the world has.

Read the first two sentences on page 27. Ask: "What does *tallest* mean?" Volunteers respond.

Ask: "What word do you recognize in the word *tallest*?" Volunteers respond.

▪ *I know the word* tall.

Confirm that the root word of *tallest* is *tall*. Write *tall* on the board in front of the class. Confirm that Mount Everest is a tall mountain. Explain that when writers add the ending –*est* to a word it changes the meaning; instead of saying the mountain is tall, the –*est* ending tells readers that it is the most tall mountain. When readers hear the ending –*est* it means "the most." For example, when something is the highest it is "the most high." If needed, reinforce this concept with other adjectives.

Confirm that *tallest* means that there is nothing higher. Everything else is shorter. Ask: "How does this make Asia unique? Can there be another tallest mountain in the world on another continent?" Volunteers respond.

- *It is the only one with the tallest mountain in the world.*
- *The other continents don't have a mountain this tall.*
- *Asia is unique because it has the tallest mountain.*

Reinforce that the point the author is making in this text is that Asia is a unique continent. On the board, write the sentence: *Asia is a unique continent.*

Explain that now they will use the text to look for reasons the author gives to support this point.

IDENTIFY REASONS THAT SUPPORT A POINT 20 MIN.

Whole Group

Point to the picture of Mount Everest on page 26. If needed, read the first two sentences on page 27. Ask: "What did we learn about this mountain? How did this show us one way that Asia is unique?" Volunteers respond.

- *It is the tallest in the whole world!*
- *Nowhere else has a mountain this big.*
- *Asia is unique because it is the only one that has this.*

Reinforce that the words on the page, with the help of the photograph, help readers understand why Asia is a unique continent. Explain that the details in the text that answer why are called <u>reasons</u>. Just like authors use key details from the text to support a topic, they also use details or evidence from the text to support their point.

Reinforce that the author states that Asia is unique and then supports this point by giving a reason that shows how Asia is not like the other continents. Write this reason underneath the author's point.

Read the word *tallest* aloud. Ask: "What does this word mean? What does the ending *–est* signal to us?" Volunteers respond.

- *It means there is nothing taller.*
- *The –est means the most.*
- *It means that there is nothing that is above it.*

Reinforce that when writers use the ending *–est* they are telling the reader that this is "the most."

Explain that now students are going to go back through the text as a class to identify the different reasons the author gives to support the point: Asia is a unique continent. When students hear a reason to support the author's point in the text, they make a triangle with their hands high above their heads, like they are the tallest mountain in the world, Mount Everest.

Prompt students to listen for words ending in –*est*. These words signal to readers that the author is describing something in Asia that is "the most."

✔ Read the text aloud through the end of page 30. Students make a Nonverbal Signal when they hear a reason in the text. Use Equity Sticks to call on students who signal to share their answers. Record student responses on the chart paper underneath the author's point.

SAMPLE RESPONSES

Asia is a unique continent.			
It has the tallest mountain in the world.	It is the biggest continent.	It has the tallest building in the world.	It has the biggest lizard in the world.

Extension

Locate images of Mount Everest, the Burj Khalifa, and a Komodo dragon. Divide the class into small groups and distribute copies of each image to the group in a container. Students take turns picking the image out of the pile and playing charades. Group members guess which unique feature the student is acting out.

EXPERIMENT WITH WRITING AN OPINION STATEMENT 19 MIN.

Individuals

Explain that students have done a lot of work reading people's opinions and learning how to create an opinion statement. Now they will practice writing their own opinion statement by responding to the following prompt.

If you were going to visit Asia, what would you like to see the most: the tallest mountain, the tallest building, or the biggest lizard?

Ask: "How do we write an opinion statement?" Volunteers respond.

- *We use words from the question.*
- *We say what we think or feel.*

Model looking at the pictures of Mount Everest and the Komodo dragon. Think Aloud about why it would be fun to see both these things, but that in the end it would be more interesting to see the tallest mountain. For example,

I think it would be fun to see the tallest mountain and the biggest lizard. I have never seen a lizard that big, and it smells with its tongue! But I also like the tallest mountain in the world. I wonder if I got up high enough if I could see everything. I also love to climb. I think I would most like to see the tallest mountain in the world.

In small groups, students discuss the prompt, using the pictures in the test to help them decide their answer.

Students turn to a partner and share their opinion statement and explain why they choose that unique feature.

✔ Students record their opinion statement in their Response Journals. If time allows, students add a drawing to support their sentence.

Land 5 MIN.

ANSWER THE CONTENT FRAMING QUESTION

Display and read aloud the Content Framing Question. Ask: "How did the words in the text help us identify the reasons the author gave to support her point?" Volunteers respond.

- *She uses* tallest *and* biggest.
- *The words told us it was the most.*
- *The pictures helped us see this, too.*

Access and play the video: "Explore Views of the Burj Khalifa with Google Maps" (**http://witeng. link/0390**).

Ask: "What do you notice about the views from the tallest building in the world? How does going up higher help you see things?" Volunteers respond.

Wrap 1 MIN.

ASSIGN HOMEWORK

Continue the class home-reading routine.

Analyze

Context and Alignment

Students use the words in *Asia* to identify the reasons an author gives to support a point in the text (RI.K.8). Each student:

- Makes a Nonverbal Signal to indicate a reason given in the text.

Next Steps

If students have difficulty identifying the reason the author gives to support the point, focus on smaller portions of the text. Because students can listen for words ending in –*est*, focus on specific pages in which the author uses a superlative. Reinforce the definition of *unique* in conjunction with the –*est* ending to help students understand why these reasons explain why Asia is one of a kind. This is the first time students are encountering this standard and may need heavy support. If students continue to struggle, identify the reasons verbally as a class, instead of using Nonverbal Signals, which require students to process the information themselves.

⬇ LESSON 6 DEEP DIVE: VOCABULARY

Shades of Meaning: *Stick*, *touch*, and *poke*

- **Time:** 15 min.

- **Text:** *The Story of Ferdinand*, Munro Leaf; Illustrations, Robert Lawson

- **Vocabulary Learning Goal:** Distinguish shades of meaning between *stick*, *touch*, and *poke* by acting out their meanings. (L.K.5.d)

Launch

Remind students that in the previous Deep Dive they learned a new meaning for the word *stick* that is different than "a piece of wood." Call on a volunteer to act out the new meaning of *stick*. Invite the class to stand and say *stick* as they mimic the action.

Reinforce that *stick* also means "to poke with something sharp and pointy."

Explain that today students are going to learn the meaning of other words that are similar to the new meaning of the word *stick*.

Learn

Instruct students to Think-Pair-Share, and ask: "What other action words may have a similar meaning to *stick*?" Provide prompts as needed to elicit correct responses. Volunteers respond.

Use student responses to identify the words as *touch* and *poke*. Post the words on the board.

Display page 6 of *The Story of Ferdinand*, using a document camera if available. Point out the action of Ferdinand in the illustration and ask: "What is Ferdinand doing in this illustration?" Volunteers respond.

- *He is trying to touch her.*
- *He is putting his hoof on her nose.*
- *He is being gentle.*

Use student responses to identify and develop the definition for *touch*. Post the definition on the board:

- touch: to put one's hands or fingers on something

Use Equity Sticks to choose a student to create a safe action for *touch*. Invite the class to mimic the action while saying the word aloud.

Display page 16 of *The Story of Ferdinand*, using a document camera if available. Point out the action of the bumblebee in the illustration and ask: "What is the bee going to do to Ferdinand with his stinger?" Volunteers respond.

- *He is going to push the stinger in him.*
- *He is going to poke him with the stinger.*

Use student responses to identify and develop the definition for *poke*. Post the definition on the board:

- poke: to push with a thin, sharp object

Use Equity Sticks to choose a student to create a safe action for *poke*. Encourage the student to develop an action that is distinct from the action for *touch*. Invite the class to mimic the action while saying the word aloud.

Explain that students are going to play a game to show the meaning of each word by saying and acting out each word.

✔ Organize students into one large circle. Use Equity Sticks to choose a student to begin the game. Students take turns saying one of the words and acting out its meaning. After their turn, they pass the turn to a fellow classmate who has not yet had a turn by pointing their hand at them and saying their name. Repeat until all students have had the opportunity to say and act out one of the vocabulary words.

Land

Students Think-Pair-Share to respond to the following prompts:

- Use the word *stick* in a sentence.
- Use the word *touch* in a sentence.
- Use the word *poke* in a sentence.

Call on volunteers to share their ideas for each prompt.

■ FOCUSING QUESTION: LESSONS 1–8

What interesting things can people do in Europe and Asia?

1 2 3 4 5 6 **7** 8 9 10 11 12 13 14 15 16 17 18 19 20 21 22 23 24 25 26 27 28 29 30 31 32 33 34 35 36

Lesson 7

TEXTS

- "The Seven Continents Song," Silly School Songs (video) (**http://witeng.link/0374**)
- *Europe*, Rebecca Hirsch
- *Asia*, Rebecca Hirsch

Lesson 7: At a Glance

AGENDA

Welcome (5 min.)

Practice Fluency

Launch (4 min.)

Learn (62 min.)

Identify a Point in the Text (15 min.)

Identify Reasons That Support a Point (22 min.)

Execute Focusing Question Task 1 (25 min.)

Land (3 min.)

Answer the Content Framing Question

Wrap (1 min.)

Assign Homework

Vocabulary Deep Dive: Shades of Meaning: *Speak, whisper,* and *yell* (15 min.)

STANDARDS ADDRESSED

The full text of ELA Standards can be found in the Module Overview.

Reading

- RI.K.1, RI.K.4, RI.K.8

Writing

- W.K.1, W.K.8

Speaking and Listening

- SL.K.1, SL.K.2, SL.K.3

Language

- ↓ L.K.5.d

MATERIALS

- Assessment 7A: Focusing Question Task 1

- Repeated Language Chart

- Sticky notes

- Evidence Organizer for *Asia*

- Evidence Organizer for *Europe*

Learning Goals

Identify reasons the author gives to support a point in *Europe*. (RI.K.8)

✔ Annotate one page in the text.

Reflect upon evidence collected from *Asia* and *Europe* to form and write an opinion statement. (RI.K.1, W.K.1, W.K.8)

✔ Complete Focusing Question Task 1.

↓ Distinguish shades of meaning between *speak, whisper,* and *yell* by acting out their meanings. (L.K.5.d)

✔ Find a word on a sticky note and act it out.

✔ Checks for Understanding

Prepare

FOCUSING QUESTION: Lessons 1–8

What interesting things can people do in Europe and Asia?

CONTENT FRAMING QUESTION: Lesson 7

Reveal: *What does a deeper exploration of Europe reveal about a point the author makes?*

CRAFT QUESTION: Lesson 7

Execute: *How do I write an opinion statement for my Focusing Question Task?*

In this lesson, students develop further understanding of how authors give reasons to support a point. Students are given the author's point, then use words and pictures in the text to identify reasons supporting that point. Students annotate the examples in the text. Students prepare for the Focusing Question Task by reflecting upon their collected evidence, responding to questions with a partner to form an opinion about either Europe or Asia. Finally, students complete the Focusing Question Task by writing an opinion statement.

Welcome 5 MIN.

PRACTICE FLUENCY

Play the video of "The Seven Continents Song" (**http://witeng.link/0374**).

Display the Repeated Language Chart. Read first four lines of the song aloud. Students Echo Read the song.

Repeated Language
Song: "The Seven Continents Song," Silly School Songs ▪ North America, South America ▪ Africa, Europe, and Asia, ▪ Australia, Antarctica ▪ Seven Continents, back to the startica.

Divide the class into small groups. Groups practice the lines on the chart at least three times together. Encourage students to articulate the different syllables, stomping their feet if needed. Groups incorporate the class dance moves for each line.

> **Alternate Activity**
>
> If students feel comfortable with the song, encourage them to create their own dance moves to accompany each line.

Launch 4 MIN.

Display the front cover of *Asia*, and ask: "What did we learn from reading *Asia*? What point did the author make, and what information did she tell us that supports her point?" Volunteers respond.

- ▪ *We learned about the tallest mountain.*
- ▪ *We learned that it has the biggest lizards.*
- ▪ *The author told us that Asia is unique.*

Display and read aloud the Content Framing Question. Explain that in this lesson, students will be told a point the author is making in *Europe*. Then, they will work with a partner to look at the words and pictures in the text to help them identify specific reasons the author gives to support the point and help readers understand it.

Learn 62 MIN.

IDENTIFY A POINT IN THE TEXT 15 MIN.

Whole Group

Divide the class into pairs to share copies of the text. Explain that students will go back through the text as a class to identify the point the author is trying to make in this text.

Instruct students to Think-Pair-Share, and ask: "What is the author teaching us in this text? What do we learn about Europe?" Use Equity Sticks to call on students to answer.

- ▪ *She is teaching us about the continent of Europe.*
- ▪ *We are learning information about Europe.*
- ▪ *We are learning about the different things you can do there.*

Explain that now students will reread the text to explore a specific point the author makes in the text.

💬 Read through the entire text with students following along in their group copies. Prompt students to listen to the words they hear and think about how the author feels about the continent Europe. Read the text through page 27.

Reread the last sentence on page 27, emphasizing the phrase *interesting places*. Ask: "What does *interesting* mean? Where have we heard this word before?" Volunteers respond.

- *It is in our Focusing Question.*
- *It means things that we want to learn about.*
- *It is something that makes us want to know more.*
- Interesting *means we like it and want to learn about it.*

Instruct students to Think-Pair-Share, and ask: "Do you think Europe has interesting places? Why do you think this?" Use Equity Sticks to call on students to answer.

Explain that the point the author is making in this text is that people visit Europe to see all the interesting places. On the board, write the sentence: *Europe has interesting places.*

Explain that now they will use the text to look for reasons the author gives to support this point.

IDENTIFY REASONS THAT SUPPORT A POINT 22 MIN.

Whole Group

Ask: "Why do authors support a point? How does supporting their point help readers?" Volunteers respond.

- *They tell readers why.*
- *A point needs reasons so we know why they think that.*
- *They give us evidence.*

Confirm that authors often give reasons to support a point or opinion so readers can understand their thoughts.

Read the caption underneath the picture on page 26. Model thinking aloud about the picture to help students understand why this could be interesting, or why you would want to learn more about this place. For example,

Wow, look at that building! It looks very big. I see a car in the picture, and that shows me how huge the building is. The outside has lots of sharp parts on it, too. I wonder what is on the inside of such a beautiful building. People can ride boats on the river and look at this building. I think this building in Budapest certainly is an interesting place.

Reinforce that this is an example that supports the author's point. The author states that Europe has interesting places and then supports this point by showing an interesting place in Europe. Briefly write "beautiful buildings" on a sticky note, and add it under the author's point.

Explain that now students are going to go back through the text with a partner to identify different reasons the author gives to support this point: *Europe has interesting places.*

Distribute two sticky notes to each pair, or one per student. Explain that they will look through the photographs in the section "Places to See" with a partner and each student will annotate one page in the text that supports the author's point. Instruct students to Think-Pair-Share as they turn through the pages, and ask: "How could this be an interesting place? Does this support the author's point that 'Europe has interesting places'?"

✔ Students use a sticky note to annotate one reason in the "Places to See" section of the text.

Call on each pair to share the reason they annotated. After each response, students jump up high if they believe the response is a reason to support the author's opinion and crouch down low if they disagree or are unsure. Record student responses on the chart.

SAMPLE RESPONSE

Europe has interesting places.
▪ beautiful buildings
▪ museums in France
▪ beautiful parks
▪ old castles

EXECUTE FOCUSING QUESTION TASK 1   25 MIN.

Individuals

Point to the chart created by the class and remind students that visiting interesting places is just one of the many things people can do in Europe!

Display the Evidence Organizers for *Asia* and *Europe* in front of the class. Ask: "What type of information did we collect from these texts?" Volunteers respond.

Confirm that the class collected information on the different things to do in Asia and Europe.

Explain that now students will think about all that they have learned about Asia and Europe and prepare to form an opinion about these continents for their Focusing Question Task.

Post and read aloud the Focusing Question. Students Echo Read the question. Ask: "What do we mean by *interesting things to do?*" Volunteers respond. Confirm that *interesting things to do* means "activities that make people curious or want to learn more." Interesting things keep your interest, or attention.

Introduce the Focusing Question Task. Explain that students will be writing an opinion statement to answer the following prompt.

> Which continent do you think has the most interesting things to do?

Reference the prompt as you instruct students to Think-Pair-Share, and ask: "Does this question have one right answer, or could there be different answers? What makes you say that?" Call on several students to respond.

- *There could be different answers.*
- *People could have different ideas.*
- *Someone might think Europe has the most interesting things to do. Someone else might think Asia does.*
- *Maybe people have different opinions.*

Use responses to reinforce that the prompt is asking what students think, or their opinion, about Europe and Asia. The choice of continent is not "right" or "wrong," it's up to each student to decide what they think.

Display and read aloud the Craft Question: *How do I write an opinion statement for my Focusing Question Task?*

Introduce the criteria for success.

- Students use the evidence organizers to form an opinion and choose between Europe and Asia.
- Students write one sentence stating which continent they believe has the most interesting things for people to do.

Divide the class into pairs. Explain that they will now use the evidence they collected about different things to do in Asia and in Europe. Instruct students to Think-Pair-Share about the following questions as their verbal rehearsal for the Focusing Question Task.

- If you visited Asia, what things would you like to do?
- If you visit Europe, what things would you like to do?
- Which continent do you think has the most interesting things to do? Why?

Pairs verbally rehearse for the Focusing Question Task by responding to the previous questions. Encourage students to use the evidence organizers and copies of the texts for reference. Students verbally share their opinion statement.

Scaffold

If students are not using complete sentences to answer the prompts, provide the following sentence frames for them to use during their verbal rehearsal:

- I would like _____ in Europe.

- I would like _____ in Asia.

- I think _____ has the most interesting things to do because_____.

While they will not have a frame for the Focusing Question Task, using a frame during the verbal rehearsal allows students to practice communicating in complete sentences and form good habits of mind.

Place the Evidence Organizer for *Europe* on one side of the room and the Evidence Organizer for *Asia* on the other. Instruct students to think about the choice they made earlier in the lesson. Direct students to "fly" to the organizer showing the continent they think has the most interesting things to do.

✔ Distribute Assessment 7A. Students respond to the prompt by writing their opinion statement.

> Name: _____
>
> **Assessment 7A: Focusing Question Task 1**
>
> Directions: Write your opinion statement on the lines provided.
>
> Opinion Statement:

TEACHER NOTE	As students write their opinion statement, encourage them to reference their classroom resources, such as the evidence organizers or the texts, to help them spell the name of the continent they are writing about.

Land 3 MIN.

ANSWER THE CONTENT FRAMING QUESTION

Display and read aloud the Content Framing Question. Ask: "How did the words in the text help us identify the reasons the author gave to support her point?" Volunteers respond.

- *She told us all the different things you can do.*
- *The words told us what places people could see.*
- *It talked about a lot of different things.*
- *People can learn about a lot of different places.*

Explain that while they have been learning a lot about Europe and Asia, there are still five more continents to learn about and there will be a lot more to capture their interest and attention.

Extension

Divide the class into small groups and provide each group with a soft ball such as a beach ball. Explain that they will now practice naming the different continents. Groups toss the ball around. When a student catches the ball they name one of the seven continents. Groups repeat this for two minutes.

Wrap 1 MIN.

ASSIGN HOMEWORK

Continue the class home-reading routine.

Analyze

Context and Alignment

Students use evidence from *Europe* and *Asia* to express an opinion about the continent they believe has the most interesting things to do (RI.K.1, W.K.1, W.K.8). Each student:

- Uses the evidence organizers to form an opinion and choose between Europe and Asia.

- Writes one sentence stating which continent they believe has the most interesting things for people to do.

Next Steps

If students have difficulty using text evidence to form an opinion, offer support by providing additional opportunities to practice with different sections of the continent texts. For example, reread the "Land and Water" section of *Europe*, and ask: "What is the most beautiful place in Europe?" Think Aloud as you model the process of selecting one of the places from the text and stating an opinion. Support students with verbally stating their opinion, then with transferring their thinking into writing.

Group students with similar needs and plan small-group support for these skills to set students up for success with their Focusing Question Task.

⬇ LESSON 7 DEEP DIVE: VOCABULARY

Shades of Meaning: *Speak, whisper,* and *yell*

- **Time:** 15 min.

- **Text:** *Europe*, Rebecca Hirsch

- **Vocabulary Learning Goal:** Distinguish shades of meaning between *speak, whisper,* and *yell* by acting out their meanings. (L.K.5.d)

Launch

Reinforce that in this module students are pretending to travel the world's continents to learn more about them. Ask: "What have you learned about the way people talk around the world?"

- *That people talk differently.*

- *That people use different words.*

- *That people speak different languages in different places.*

Post *speak* on the board. Use Equity Sticks to call on a student to develop an action for *speak*, such as pretending to have a calm conversation. Students mimic the action and say the word *speak*.

Reinforce that in the book *Europe*, the author describes the languages people speak in different countries. Explain that there are other words that describe how languages can be shared by people.

Tell the students that they are going to find and act out words that describe other ways to speak.

Learn

Instruct students to listen as you read for a word that describes a way that words are shared. Students should stand when they hear the word.

Display the image on page 16 in *Europe* and say the following sentence: "The children whisper quietly in the museum." Ask: "What word describes how the children speak?" Call on a standing student to answer.

- *Whisper.*

Post the word *whisper* and explain that *whisper* means "to speak softly and quietly." Call on another standing student to create an action for *whisper*. Students mimic the action and whisper, "*whisper.*"

Instruct students to sit down and listen for another word that describes a way to speak. Students should stand when they hear the word.

Display the image and read the caption on page 24 in *Europe*. Say the following sentence: "The children <u>yell</u> with joy as they ski down the hill." Ask: "What word describes how the children speak?" Call on a standing student to answer.

▪ *Yell.*

Post the word *yell* and explain that *yell* means "to speak in a very loud voice." Call on another standing student to create an action for *yell*. Students mimic the action and say, "*yell*" in an appropriate raised voice.

TEACHER NOTE	To maximize instructional time, write *speak*, *whisper*, and *yell* on sticky notes. There should be at least one sticky note for every student in your class and an equal number of sticky notes featuring each word.

Instruct all students to stand. Echo Read *speak*, *whisper*, and *yell*. Explain that students are going to go on a hunt around the classroom to find and act out these words.

✔ Post sticky notes with the words *speak*, *whisper*, and *yell* throughout the classroom. Students move about the room to locate a sticky note as you count down from five. As you get to 1, students read the word on the sticky note they found and act out the word. Circulate to provide support and to ensure that students are acting out the correct word. Repeat as time allows.

Land

Reorganize the class back to a whole group.

Instruct students to Think-Pair-Share, and ask: "When is it appropriate to <u>whisper</u>?" Call on a few pairs to share their responses.

▪ *In the library.*
▪ *During a movie.*
▪ *In a museum.*

Instruct students to Think-Pair-Share, and ask: "When is it appropriate to <u>yell</u>?" Call on a few pairs to share their responses.

▪ *When you feel really excited or happy.*
▪ *At a game or sporting event.*
▪ *When it is loud.*

■ FOCUSING QUESTION: LESSONS 1–8

What interesting things can people do in Europe and Asia?

Lesson 8

TEXTS

- "The Seven Continents Song," Silly School Songs (video) (**http://witeng.link/0374**)

- *Earth from Space*, Stöckli, Reto, et al. (**http://witeng.link/0373**)

- *Asia*, Rebecca Hirsch

- *Europe*, Rebecca Hirsch

- *World Atlas*, Nick Crane; Illustrations, David Dean

- "Explore Views of the Burj Khalifa with Google Maps," Google Maps (video) (**http://witeng.link/0390**)

Lesson 8: At a Glance

AGENDA

Welcome (7 min.)

Perform Fluency

Launch (6 min.)

Learn (55 min.)

Record Knowledge (25 min.)

Explain an Opinion (10 min.)

Compare Europe with World Atlas (20 min.)

Land (6 min.)

Answer the Content Framing Question

Wrap (1 min.)

Assign Homework

Style and Conventions Deep Dive: Experiment with Expanding a Sentence (15 min.)

STANDARDS ADDRESSED

The full text of ELA Standards can be found in the Module Overview.

Reading

- RI.K.1, RI.K.2, RI.K.7, RI.K.9

Writing

- W.K.1, W.K.8, W.10*

Speaking and Listening

- SL.K.1

Language

- ⬇ L.K.1.e, L.K.1.f

MATERIALS

- Assessment 7A: Focusing Question Task 1

- Handout 8A: Passport Journal (retain for future lessons)

- Repeated Language Chart

- Passport (real or online image; see lesson for details)

- Knowledge Journal

- Evidence Organizer for *Asia*

- Evidence Organizer for *Europe*

- Stamps or stickers (see lesson for details)

- Sticky notes

Learning Goals

Use the evidence organizer and photographs from the text to reflect upon and share important learning from *Asia*. (RI.K.2)

✔ Draw and label one detail about Asia in a Passport Journal.

Identify basic similarities between *Europe* and *World Atlas*. (RI.K.9)

✔ Identify a detail that appears both in *Europe* and on the map of Europe in *World Atlas*.

⬇ Create a complete sentence and expand it by adding a preposition. (L.K.1.e, L.K.1.f)

✔ Write a complete sentence caption and expand it with a preposition.

In alignment with the CCSS, W.10 formally begins in Grade 3. However, K–2 students write routinely for a variety of time frames, tasks, purposes, and audiences. As a result, this lesson contains instruction related to W.10 in an effort to familiarize students with a range of writing.

✔ Checks for Understanding

FOCUSING QUESTION: Lessons 1–8

What interesting things can people do in Europe and Asia?

CONTENT FRAMING QUESTION: Lesson 8

Know: *How do Europe and Asia build my knowledge of the continents?*

In this lesson the Knowledge Journal routine is expanded, as students reflect on important learning they have gained and record it in individual Passport Journals. They deepen their work with Focusing Question Task 1 by verbally supporting their opinion with text evidence. In addition, students explore the *World Atlas* text and compare it with *Europe*.

TEACHER NOTE	Lessons 1–15 and 22–31 contain no instruction for the Distill Stage due to the difficulty of discerning the essential meanings of these texts and the focus of instruction in Module 4.
	In these informational texts, knowledge growth comes primarily from analyzing the words and photographs in the text. Understanding how the words and pictures in an informational text enhance understanding and communicate important information is a key skill of this module as students develop skills with focus standards RI.K.7, RI.K.8, and RI.K.9.

Welcome 7 MIN.

PERFORM FLUENCY

Display the Repeated Language Chart. Explain that students will conclude their hard work with this song by performing for each other.

The class conducts a rehearsal by Choral Reading the Repeated Language Chart. Divide the class into two groups. Each group takes a turn performing "The Seven Continents Song" from the Repeated Language Chart for their peers.

Play the entire song (**http://witeng.link/0374**) for the class and invite students to sing along as a whole group, using the words and dance moves they know.

Extension

Record the performances and share with families or other classes via an approved outlet.

Launch 6 MIN.

Display the *Earth from Space* image (**http://witeng.link/0373**) and remind students that the image shows a picture of what Earth looks like from space. Ask: "How long do you think it would take to walk around the whole planet?" Volunteers respond.

Tell students that it would take about three years to walk around the world if you walked along the equator, or the middle of the earth, for eight hours a day. They would be in Grade 3 by the time they finished their walk.

Explain that the books, videos, and pictures students are exploring during this module are helping them travel around the world much more quickly, through their minds and imaginations.

Tell students that when people travel to different continents and countries in real life, they need to bring a *passport* to be allowed in and out. Define *passport* as "a document that shows a person is a citizen of a certain country" and explain that a person must show their passport to enter and exit a different country.

Provide an example by displaying a copy of a real passport, or showing online images. Point out that passports contain identifying information and a photograph. Explain that passports are stamped to show when a person travels to a new country. This is a fun way that people can keep track of all the places they have been!

Tell students that they will make their own passport books to record their travels around the continents. Students will use their passport books to create individual Knowledge Journals and will write down important learning about the continents they explore. Their passports will be stamped to show that they visited each continent, just like real passports.

Remind students that they have already explored two of the seven continents. Post and read aloud the Content Framing Question. Students Echo Read the question. Tell students that today they will think about their learning and create the first few pages for their passport books.

Learn 55 MIN.

RECORD KNOWLEDGE 25 MIN.

Individuals

Distribute page 1 of Handout 8A. Students complete the first page of their Passport Journal by filling in their name and continent.

Name:

Handout 8A: Passport Journal

Directions: Write your name and home continent on the lines provided on page 1. On pages 2–8, draw and label one detail about the continent pictured in the top right corner.

Student Picture

Name: _____

Continent: _____

TEACHER NOTE	As one's passport also contains an individual's photograph, find time to insert a photo of each student into his or her Passport Journal. Or, each student may draw a self-portrait in the space provided on the passport.

Remind students that thinking about the knowledge and skills they gain with each text is an important part of learning. Talking about new knowledge helps them remember what they learned, and makes it easier to use and build on that knowledge in the future.

TEACHER NOTE	Research on brain science has indicated that active reflection about learning promotes the creation and strengthening of neural connections, serving as a boost for future learning on that subject. As students reflect on the important learning they have gained about the continents, they develop connections in the brain that will foster ownership of that learning and better prepare them for future knowledge and growth.

Display a copy of *Europe*. Provide time for students to think about the important knowledge they learned while exploring the text. Instruct students to Mix and Mingle, and ask: "What important knowledge did you learn about Europe?" Encourage students to use the Evidence Organizer for *Europe* as a reference.

Repeat the questioning process outlined above for *Asia*.

Distribute pages 2 and 3 of Handout 8A to each student. Explain that students will record the knowledge they gained from reading *Europe* and *Asia*.

Instruct students to point to the page on which they think they should write about Europe. Ask: "How did you know which page goes with Europe?" Volunteers respond.

- *I see that it says "Europe" at the top part of the page.*
- *There is a map of Europe there, too.*

Use responses to confirm that students will draw and label an illustration to share what they learned about Europe on page 2 of the handout.

Students draw and label an illustration to share one thing they learned about Europe. Make copies of the text available for students to reference as needed. As students complete their journals, place a stamp or sticker on this section to mark their visit to the continent.

Alternate Activity

Depending on the needs of the class, students may write and illustrate sentences in their Passport Journals instead of drawing and labeling illustrations.

Display page 3 of Handout 8A. Explain that this is where they will write about Asia.

✔ Students draw and label an illustration to share one thing they learned about Asia. Make copies of the text available for students to reference as needed. As students complete their journals, place a stamp or sticker on this section to mark their visit to the continent.

Use Equity Sticks to call on several students to share their Passport Journals with the class.

Display the class Knowledge Journal. Point to the left part of the journal and explain that students have already completed this part by writing important learning in their Passport Journals.

Tell students that they will add new items to the "What I Can Do" column by thinking about the new skills they learned as readers and writers.

Ask: "What did you learn to do as a reader? What did you learn to do as a writer?"

Scaffold

Ask: "What did you learn about points in a text? What did you learn about opinion writing?"

Use Equity Sticks to call on pairs to share responses. After each response, students consider whether or not that piece of learning is something important that they want to remember and include in the Knowledge Journal. They indicate a level of agreement by holding up anywhere from one to five fingers, with one finger showing the lowest level of agreement and five fingers showing the strongest level of agreement.

Use votes to choose one or two refined responses to record in the Knowledge Journal.

SAMPLE KNOWLEDGE JOURNAL

What I Know	What I Can Do
	• I can state an opinion. • I can find reasons to support a point.

TEACHER NOTE

Students record important learning individually in their Passport Journals instead of on the "What I Know" section of the class Knowledge Journal. If time permits, consider selecting several strong responses from the individual journals to add to the class journal.

EXPLAIN AN OPINION 10 MIN.

Pairs

Reference the Evidence Organizers for *Europe* and *Asia*. Ask: "How did we use the evidence from the text in our Focusing Question Task?" Volunteers respond.

- *We looked at the different things to do.*
- *We wrote about which has the most interesting ones.*
- *We said our opinion about the continent with the most interesting things to do.*

Ask: "How does an author support their point in the text?" Volunteers respond. Using responses to support a point is important so readers can understand why one might think that.

Move the evidence organizers to opposite sides of the room. Distribute completed copies of Assessment 7A. Place copies of the text near each evidence organizer. Instruct students to "fly" to the evidence organizer of the continent they chose for their Focusing Question Task.

Once each student is on either side of the room, instruct students to find a partner from the opposite side of the room.

Name: _____

Assessment 7A: Focusing Question Task 1

Directions: Write your opinion statement on the lines provided.

Opinion Statement:

_____

_____

_____

_____

137

TEACHER NOTE	In a class with an odd number of students, a group of three will suffice. The purpose of this exercise is to share an opinion statement and verbally support the opinion.

Students share their opinion sentence with their partner.

Instruct students to Think-Pair-Share, and ask: "Why do you think that continent has the most interesting things to do? Find a piece of evidence from the evidence organizer or a photograph in the text to support your answer." Pairs locate a piece of evidence and verbally explain why they think that their continent of choice has the most interesting things to do.

Ask: "How did hearing your partner's example help you understand their opinion?" Volunteers respond. Use responses to reinforce that supporting an opinion is an important part of opinion writing. Explain that in the next few lessons students will explore more about supporting their opinion with reasons from the text.

Extension

If time allows, encourage students to add a drawing to Assessment 7A of the most interesting thing to do from their continent of choice. This will help students practice supporting their opinion statements, a skill they will address in Lessons 9–15 and practice throughout the module.

COMPARE *EUROPE* WITH *WORLD ATLAS*   20 MIN.

Small Groups

Display the front cover of *World Atlas*, and read the title, author, and illustrator aloud. Ask: "What is a *map*?" Volunteers respond.

Turn slowly through the pages of *World Atlas*. Ask: "Do you see any maps on these pages?" Students chorally respond.

Define *atlas* as "a book of maps." Add *atlas* to the Word Wall as a module word.

Explain that there are many kinds of atlases with collections of maps designed for different purposes. For example, road atlases have maps showing roads and ocean atlases have detailed maps of the oceans. A world atlas contains maps of Earth's continents and oceans.

Alternate Activity

Display or show images of different kinds of atlases. Ask students to predict what kind of maps they might find in each atlas.

Extension

Divide students into small groups and distribute a copy of *World Atlas* to each group. Instruct students to open to the first page spread of *World Atlas*. Read the heading "Contents" aloud, and ask: "What is this page? What information does a table of contents tell us?"

- *This page is the table of contents.*
- *It tells us where to find things in the book.*
- *It tells us which page to go to.*

Confirm that a table of contents is a list of the different sections in a book. Ask students to look at the second page of the table of contents to find the section for Europe, providing support as needed. Instruct students to use their finger to trace along the page next to the word *Europe* to find the page number for the section.

Groups open the atlas to the map of Europe on page 32. Allow students to observe the map for thirty seconds. Ask: "What do you notice about the map of Europe?" Students take turns sharing their observations in their small groups. Call on several students to share their response with the whole class.

TEACHER NOTE	Due to the complexity of the written text, instruction with *World Atlas* will focus primarily on the maps and illustrations. Depending on the needs of your class, incorporate portions of the written text as desired.

Explain that the illustrations on the map show readers where interesting things in Europe are located. Instruct students to place a finger on an illustration of mountains. Tell students that the mapmaker put the pictures of mountains in those spots to show where mountains are located in Europe.

Ask: "What do you think the dotted red lines are showing us about Europe?" Volunteers respond. Use responses to explain that the dotted red lines show the borders of Europe's many countries. A border shows where one country ends and another begins.

Tell students that they will compare the map of Europe from *World Atlas* with the map from *Europe*. Distribute several copies of *Europe* to each group and ask students to open to the map of Europe on page 6.

Ask: "How are these two maps the same? How are they different?" Students take turns sharing their responses in their small groups. Call on several students with strong responses to share with the whole class.

- *They both show Europe.*
- *They both show different countries.*
- *The map in the atlas is different because it has pictures of things like mountains and people.*
- *The map in Europe is different because it uses different colors to show different countries.*

Direct students to think about the whole *Europe* book, not only the map page, and ask: "Both texts show illustrations of people, places, and animals in Europe. How are the illustrations in *World Atlas* different from the illustrations in *Europe*?" Volunteers respond.

- *The illustrations in* World Atlas *are all on one page. The pictures in* Europe *are on different pages.*
- *The illustrations in* World Atlas *are drawings. The pictures in* Europe *are photographs.*

Explain that the texts are sharing some of the same information, just in different ways. Provide an example such as pointing out the picture of the Eiffel Tower on the front cover of *Europe* and the illustration of the Eiffel Tower on the map in *World Atlas*.

Ask: "Can you find an illustration on the atlas map that shows one of the same details you read about in *Europe*?"

✔ Students identify a matching detail present in both texts. Instruct students to open their copy of *Europe* to the page showing the detail and point to the corresponding detail on the map in *World Atlas*.

TEACHER NOTE	For ease of management, consider pairing students within each small group. Direct each pair to work together and share a copy of *Europe.*

Use Equity Sticks to call on students to share the matching detail they found with the whole class. As time permits, instruct students to identify additional details that appear in both texts.

Extension

Direct students to find details that are unique to each text. Ask: "What details can you find in *Europe* that are not shown on the map in *World Atlas*? What details can you find on the map in *World Atlas* that cannot be found in *Europe*?"

Foundational Skills Connection

If students need additional work identifying the initial or final sounds of words, use the illustrations throughout the text to practice. Call out a letter or sound and have students find an item in a specific map that begins or ends with the given sound. Repeat for any letter or sounds that would benefit students.

Land 6 MIN.

ANSWER THE CONTENT FRAMING QUESTION

Display the illustration on the bottom of page 6 in *World Atlas*, and explain that people have been creating maps and atlases for hundreds of years. Ask: "This illustration shows a mapmaker from long ago. What tools do you see him using to create his map?" Volunteers respond.

- *I see a globe.*
- *It looks like he's writing with a feather!*
- *There are books open near him.*
- *I think I see a compass.*

Ask: "What tools do you think mapmakers might use today?" Volunteers respond.

Explain that today mapmakers often use technology to help them create maps. For example, they might use cameras, computers, and satellites. Play part of the "Explore Views of the Burj Khalifa with Google Maps" video (**http://witeng.link/0390**) and tell students to look for modern mapmaking tools.

Ask: "What mapmaking tools did you see in the video?" Volunteers respond.

Emphasize that mapmakers and explorers are still working to help people understand more about Earth today.

Congratulate students on the learning and exploration they have done with *Europe* and *Asia*. Instruct students to Mix and Mingle, and ask: "Which continent do you hope to explore next? Why?"

Wrap <small>1 MIN.</small>

ASSIGN HOMEWORK

Continue the class home-reading routine.

Analyze

Context and Alignment

Students compare and contrast information about Europe presented in *Europe* and *World Atlas* (RI.K.9). Each student:

- Matches a photograph in *Europe* to an illustration on the map of Europe in *World Atlas*.

Next Steps

This is the first encounter *Wit & Wisdom* presents for students to compare and contrast texts using photos. If they have difficulty identifying similarities in the text, scaffold this exercise by revisiting specific pages in *Europe* as a class and locating images in *World Atlas* together. Model this skill for the class prior to asking them to do it independently. *World Atlas* contains a lot of information in its pictures. If students continue to have difficulty locating similarities, consider focusing students' attention to the different structures or buildings on the *World Atlas* map and relating them to the photographs in "Places to See" in *Europe*.

⬇ LESSON 8 DEEP DIVE: STYLE AND CONVENTIONS

Experiment with Expanding a Sentence

- **Time:** 15 min.

- **Text:** *Europe*, Rebecca Hirsch

- **Style and Conventions Learning Goal:** Create a complete sentence and expand it by adding a preposition. (L.K.1.e, L.K.1.f)

   STYLE AND CONVENTIONS CRAFT QUESTION: Lesson 8
   Experiment: *How does creating and expanding sentences with prepositions work?*

Launch

TEACHER NOTE	In Modules 1 and 2, students explored how to add details using prepositions. Deep Dive Lesson 8 builds on this knowledge to help students expand sentences in their own writing. Use your understanding of student knowledge to determine if a more thorough review of prepositions would be beneficial prior to teaching this Deep Dive.

Post and read the Style and Conventions Craft Question.

Remind students that authors write in complete sentences by telling "who, does what." Reinforce that authors also expand sentences by adding more information. Reinforce the meaning of *expand* by repeating the movement presented in Deep Dive Lesson 4. Emphasize that *expand* means "to add more information to make a sentence longer."

Explain that one way authors expand sentences and add information is by using <u>prepositions</u>.

Remind students that they learned about prepositions in Modules 1 and 2. Emphasize that prepositions tell when or where something happens.

Scaffold

As a refresher on the different prepositions and their meanings, see Handout 26B from Module 1.

Instruct students to Mix and Mingle, and ask: "What are words that tell when or where something happens?" Provide examples or prompts to facilitate correct answers. Call on students to share their ideas.

- *In*
- *At*
- *On*

Use student responses to record *in*, *at*, and *on* on the board. Explain that students are going to practice making and expanding complete sentences by telling "who, does what" and "where" or "when."

Learn

Display the cover of *Europe*. Instruct students to Think-Pair-Share, and ask: "Who is doing what in the photograph?" Volunteers respond.

- *The girl smiles.*
- *The girl dances.*
- *The girl plays.*

Record two student responses on the board for examples. Confirm that students created complete sentences about the illustration by pointing out the "who, does what" in their sentences.

Remind students they can expand their sentences by adding prepositions to tell where or when information about the illustration.

Ask: "Where is the little girl? How can we expand our sentence to add information about where she is?" Volunteers respond.

- *She is outside.*
- *She is in a park.*

Use a student response to model how to expand the first example sentence by telling where. For example, "The girl smiles in a park." Record the sentence on the board and underline the prepositional phrase *in the park*.

Ask: "When is this picture taken? How can we expand our sentence to add information about when this girl is in a park?" Volunteers respond. Encourage students to think about her clothing and what that tells them about the time of year.

- *It is warm out.*
- *I think it is in the summer.*
- *I think it is in the spring.*

Use a student response to model how to expand the second example sentence by telling when. For example, "The girl plays in the summer." Record the sentence on the board and underline the prepositional phrase in the summer.

Explain that students are going to work with a partner to practice making a complete sentence and expanding it by telling "where" or "when" information.

Organize class into pairs. Distribute a copy of *Europe* and a sticky note to each pair.

✔ Students turn to page 12 in the text. One partner writes on the sticky note "who, does what" in the photograph. The other partner expands the sentence by writing where or when the sentence happens. Circulate to provide support as needed.

Scaffold

There are some photographs in the text that do not show people or animals. Explain that pairs should look for photographs that have people or animals in them to complete the "who" in the sentence.

Use Equity Sticks to call on pairs to share their sentences with the class.

Land

Reorganize the class into whole group setting. Direct students' attention to the Style and Conventions Craft Question. Ask: "How did you make complete sentences?" Volunteers respond.

- *By telling who, did what.*

Ask: "How did you expand your sentences with prepositions?" Volunteers respond.

- *By telling where or when information.*

■ FOCUSING QUESTION: LESSONS 9–15

What interesting natural features can people see in Africa and Antarctica?

1 2 3 4 5 6 7 8 **9 10 11 12 13 14 15** 16 17 18 19 20 21 22 23 24 25 26 27 28 29 30 31 32 33 34 35 36

Lesson 9

TEXTS

- "Antarctic Sights and Sounds," James Napoli (video) (**http://witeng.link/0392**)

- "*Where in the World Is Carmen Sandiego?* from Smithsonian Folkways," Smithsonian Folkways (playlist) (**http://witeng.link/0375**)

- *Africa*, Rebecca Hirsch

- *Antarctica*, Rebecca Hirsch

- "Penguin Song," *Preschool Education* (**http://witeng.link/0393**)

Lesson 9: At a Glance

AGENDA

Welcome (6 min.)

Explore the Focusing Question

Launch (4 min.)

Learn (59 min.)

Listen Actively and Share Observations about Antarctica (12 min.)

Share Questions about Antarctica (12 min.)

Listen Actively and Share Observations about Africa (20 min.)

Share Questions about Africa (10 min.)

Read the Fluency Passage (5 min.)

Land (5 min.)

Answer the Content Framing Question

Wrap (1 min.)

Assign Homework

Vocabulary Deep Dive: Opposite Adjectives: *Africa* (15 min.)

STANDARDS ADDRESSED

The full text of ELA Standards can be found in the Module Overview.

Reading

- RI.K.1

Writing

- W.10*

Speaking and Listening

- SL.K.1.a, SL.K.2

Language

- L.K.1.d
- ⬇ L.K.5.b

MATERIALS

- Handout 9A: Opposite Describing Words
- Suitcase containing cold-weather items (see lesson for details)
- World map
- Question Grab Bags
- Sticky notes
- Compass rose
- Question Corner signs
- Wonder Chart for *Antarctica* and *Africa*
- Repeated Language Chart (see lesson for details; retain for future lessons)
- Document camera (if available)

Learning Goals

Represent learning through writing and drawing. (W.10*)

✔ Record an observation about *Africa* in Response Journals.

Use a variety of question words to ask questions about *Africa*. (RI.K.1, L.K.1.d)

✔ Generate questions using Question Corners.

⬇ Demonstrate understanding of frequently occurring adjectives, or describing words, by matching them to their opposites. (L.K.5.b)

✔ Complete Handout 9A.

*In alignment with the CCSS, W.10 formally begins in Grade 3. However, K–2 students write routinely for a variety of time frames, tasks, purposes, and audiences. As a result, this lesson contains instruction related to W.10 in an effort to familiarize students with a range of writing.

✔ Checks for Understanding

FOCUSING QUESTION: Lessons 9–15

What interesting natural features can people see in Africa and Antarctica?

CONTENT FRAMING QUESTION: Lesson 9

Wonder: *What do I notice and wonder about Antarctica and Africa?*

Students continue their exploration of the continents by reading the informational texts *Antarctica* and *Africa*. The familiar structure of the texts contributes to accessibility and aids in comprehension. Students make observations about and generate questions for each text. They also contrast the two continents by sharing their initial observations about the differences they notice.

Welcome 6 MIN.

EXPLORE THE FOCUSING QUESTION

TEACHER NOTE	Use a "mystery suitcase" to build anticipation and excitement for learning about new texts and continents. Prior to the lesson, gather materials that provide hints about Antarctica and place them in a suitcase. For example, pack a warm jacket, gloves, winter hat, and a stuffed penguin (or image of a penguin).

Display the closed suitcase for students. Explain that it's time to travel to a different continent for new exploration and adventure, and that the suitcase contains clues about where the class will go next.

Direct students to observe each item as it is pulled out of the suitcase. Ask: "Which continent do you think we are heading to? What makes you say that?" Volunteers respond.

Confirm that students will explore the continent of Antarctica, the coldest place on Earth.

Display and read aloud the Focusing Question. Students Echo Read the question. Ask: "What other continent will we explore? What did you hear in the Focusing Question?" Volunteers respond.

Confirm that students will also explore Africa. Explain that Africa contains the hottest place on Earth—they will go from one extreme to another!

Highlight or underline the words *natural features* in the Focusing Question. Students repeat the words *natural features* several times. Explain that just like text <u>features</u> are special parts of a book, natural <u>features</u> are special parts of nature on Earth.

Provide examples of natural features such as mountains, rivers, and forests. Explain that these <u>features</u> are the special parts that make up a continent. Add context by displaying familiar pictures of natural features from *Asia* or *Europe* (e.g., display the photographs of Mount Everest, the Alps, the Gobi Desert).

Launch 4 MIN.

Tell students they will explore Antarctica and Africa through books, videos, music, and pictures. Post and read aloud the Content Framing Question.

Display the front covers of *Antarctica* and *Africa* and read the titles and author's name aloud. Ask: "What seems familiar about these texts? When have you seen books like these?" Volunteers respond.

- *They look like the books we read about Europe and Asia.*
- *I think they have the same author as the other continent books.*

Confirm that the books are from the same series as the books students have already read about Europe and Asia.

Instruct students to Mix and Mingle, and ask: "Antarctica and Africa are very different from each other. What differences do you see in the pictures on the front covers of the texts?"

Learn 59 MIN.

LISTEN ACTIVELY AND SHARE OBSERVATIONS ABOUT *ANTARCTICA*
12 MIN.

Whole Group

Tell students they will start their adventure today by exploring the continent of Antarctica. Display the world map and remind students that explorers use maps to help them travel from place to place.

Call on a volunteer to approach the world map and to point to where they believe Antarctica is located. Confirm the location by placing the image of an airplane on Antarctica.

Invite students to travel to Antarctica by pretending to fly there in an airplane. Students walk around the room, pretending to fly in an airplane while listening to a small portion of "Antarctic Sights and

Sounds" (**http://witeng.link/0392**). Stop playing the sounds to indicate that students should "land" at the whole-group gathering area.

Extension

After listening to "Antarctic Sights and Sounds," ask: "What did you notice about the sounds you heard? What did you hear? What did you not hear?" Explain that over the next few lessons they will learn more about Antarctica and understand why it is such a quiet continent!

Display the front cover of *Antarctica* as you read aloud the title and author's name. Ask: "What do you think you already know about Antarctica? Do you know anyone who has ever been to Antarctica?" Volunteers respond.

💬 Read the book aloud with minimal interruptions. Students sit in "listening position," focusing eyes and ears on you as you read.

TEACHER NOTE	Consider using a document camera to project the pages of the book in the front of the class. The pages are small and may not easily be seen from where students sit. If your classroom does not have a way to project the book, organize chairs in a way that will allow students to get a better view the pages.

Instruct students to Think-Pair-Share, and ask: "What did you learn about Antarctica that surprised you?" Use Equity Sticks to call on students to respond.

Ask: "Do many people live in Antarctica? Why or why not?" Volunteers respond.

- *No, because it is so cold.*
- *No, because it is made of ice.*

Instruct students to Mix and Mingle, and ask: "What else did you notice about the text?" Spread copies of the text around the room for students to reference as needed.

SHARE QUESTIONS ABOUT *ANTARCTICA* 12 MIN.

Small Groups

Remind students that it is important for both readers and explorers to ask good questions. Tell students they will use Question Grab Bags to ask questions about the text.

Divide the class into five small groups. Distribute a Question Grab Bag and a copy of the text to each group. Students take turns pulling a question word from the Question Grab Bag and using the word to ask a question about *Antarctica*.

Foundational Skills Connection

Many foundational skills curriculums will include many, or all, question words as part of their high-frequency word lists. Additionally, students have been working on asking and answering questions in previous modules and have had a lot of exposure to question words. Therefore, students could use the Question Grab Bag activity as an additional opportunity to practice reading question words.

Circulate to support groups in reading the question words as needed, calling attention to key letters and sounds. Encourage them to return to the text to develop questions. Listen in and choose four to six student-generated questions to record on sticky notes, labeling them with students' initials.

Post a blank Wonder Chart for *Antarctica* and *Africa*. Add students' questions.

Working with one question at a time, students Echo Read the question and Think-Pair-Share about details they remember from the text. Students use the following Nonverbal Signals to indicate whether they are able to answer the question:

- Thumbs-up: we remember the answer from the text.

- Thumbs-sideways: we remember part of the answer from the text.

- Thumbs-down: we don't remember the answer.

Call on students to share their thinking. Return to the text to confirm and clarify students' thinking. Move sticky notes along the progression to indicate the extent to which each question has been answered.

LISTEN ACTIVELY AND SHARE OBSERVATIONS ABOUT *AFRICA*　20 MIN.

Whole Group

Tell students that they will continue their world exploration by traveling to the next continent: Africa. Identify Africa on the world map and circle around the continent with your finger.

Direct students to look at the placement of the airplane over Antarctica and at the location of Africa, and ask: "What do you notice about the location of these continents on the map?" Volunteers respond.

- *They are kind of like neighbors.*
- *There is water between them.*

Display a compass rose and remind students that people often use the directions of north, south, west, and east to describe where something is in relation to something else. Highlight the directions of north and south on the compass rose. Highlight north and south on the map. Reinforce that when looking at a map, north is usually up, or at the top of the map, and south is down, or at the bottom of the map.

Reference the locations of Africa and Antarctica on the world map, and ask: "To travel to Africa from Antarctica, do we need to fly north or south?" Volunteers respond.

▪ *North.*

Mark the destination by moving the airplane image to Africa. Invite students to walk around the room, pretending to fly in an airplane. As they "fly," play music from Africa using the "Where in the World Is Carmen Sandiego? from Smithsonian Folkways" link (**http://witeng.link/0375**). Scroll down for clips of music from a variety of countries in Africa. Consider using track 115, "Nigeria - Music of the Anaguta and Jarawa." Stop the music to indicate that students should "land" at the whole-group gathering area.

TEACHER NOTE	The above link is a suggestion. Substitute different African music if desired.
	Continue to use the airplane image daily to note the continent students are exploring. Move the airplane image between the continents as appropriate.

Display the front cover of *Africa* as you read aloud the title and author's name. Ask: "What do you think you already know about Africa? Do you know anyone who has ever been to Africa?" Volunteers respond.

Read the book aloud with minimal interruptions. Students sit in "listening position," focusing eyes and ears on you as you read.

Instruct students to Think-Pair-Share, and ask: "What did you learn about Africa that surprised you?" Use Equity Sticks to call on students to respond.

Distribute copies of the text to pairs of students. Instruct students to take turns sharing what they notice about the text with their partner. Students use the sentence frame **I notice** _____., and point to the relevant illustration in the text to share observations.

✔ Distribute Response Journals to students and ask students to record one of their observations about *Africa* in their journals. They write a sentence about something they noticed in the text and illustrate the sentence as time permits.

SHARE QUESTIONS ABOUT *AFRICA* 10 MIN.

Pairs

As students complete their Response Journal entries, join them into pairs and explain that they will use Question Corners to ask questions about the text. Assign pairs a starting Question Corner, and review the routine as needed.

✔ Pairs move to their assigned Question Corner and generate questions about *Africa* using the designated question word. Place a few copies of the text at each corner.

Circulate to support students in reading the question words as needed, calling attention to key letters and sounds. Encourage them to return to the text to develop questions. Listen in and choose four to six student-generated questions to record on sticky notes, labeling with students' initials.

Display the Wonder Chart for *Antarctica* and *Africa*. Add students' questions underneath the questions recorded earlier in the lesson.

Working with one question at a time, students Echo Read the question and Think-Pair-Share about details they remember from the text. Students use the following Nonverbal Signals to indicate whether they are able to answer the question:

- Thumbs-up: we remember the answer from the text.

- Thumbs-sideways: we remember part of the answer from the text.

- Thumbs-down: we don't remember the answer.

Call on students to share their thinking. Return to the text to confirm and clarify their thinking. Move sticky notes along the progression to indicate the extent to which each question has been answered.

SAMPLE WONDER CHART FOR *ANTARCTICA* AND *AFRICA*

Wonders for *Antarctica* and *Africa*		
Questions ?	Answers in Progress ⟵⟶	Complete Answers ✓
- *How do people in Antarctica get food?* - *Why is Antarctica so cold?* - *When did people start exploring Antarctica* - *Where do zebras live in Africa?* - *How big is the biggest desert?* - *What is a savanna?*		

READ THE FLUENCY PASSAGE   5 MIN.

Whole Group

Explain that the fluency passage for *Antarctica* and *Africa* is a poem about an animal from Antarctica. Play "Who Am I?" and ask students to guess which animal the poem might be about. Provide clues such as:

I am black and white. I eat fish. I'm a bird but I can't fly.

Confirm that the poem is about penguins. Display the Repeated Language Chart and read the poem aloud. Explain that students will learn to read the poem line by line over the next week.

Repeated Language

Song: "Penguin Song," Original author unknown

- I'm a little penguin

- In the sea.

- I can swim as fast as can be!

- When I catch a fish, just look at me.

- I'm as proud as I can be!

TEACHER NOTE | The poem is titled "Penguin Song" and can be found at the following link: (**http://witeng.link/0393**) . There are many songs and poems listed on this page. "Penguin Song" is the sixth poem listed on the page.

Play the first thirty seconds of the "Antarctic Sights and Sounds" video (**http://witeng.link/0392**), and direct students to pay attention to the different ways the penguins move.

Ask: "Describe how you saw the penguins moving." Use Equity Sticks to call on students to respond.

- *I saw them walking on the ground.*

- *It looked like they were leaping through the water!*

- *They were flapping their wings.*

- *They did a belly flop on the shore.*

Invite students to imitate some of their favorite penguin movements.

Land  5 MIN.

ANSWER THE CONTENT FRAMING QUESTION

Display and read aloud the Content Framing Question. Instruct students to Think-Pair-Share, and ask: "Why is it important for readers to notice and wonder about texts?" Call on several students to respond.

- *It helps us think about the text.*
- *It helps us understand.*
- *It makes us interested to learn more.*

Remind students that they looked at the covers of *Antarctica* and *Africa* at the beginning of the lesson to think about how the continents might be different.

Instruct students to Mix and Mingle, and ask: "Now that you have read *Antarctica* and *Africa*, what other differences do you know? How are Antarctica and Africa different from each other?"

Wrap 1 MIN.

ASSIGN HOMEWORK

Continue the class home-reading routine.

Analyze

Context and Alignment

Students utilize Question Corners to generate questions about *Africa*. This questioning tool supports students in developing the habit of "wondering" as they read a text (RI.K.1, L.K.1.d). Each student:

- Generates text-based questions.
- Correctly uses the question word presented on the Question Corner sign.

Next Steps

If students have difficulty generating questions, focus on one question word, such as *how* or *why*. Work with small groups and go through the text together, one page spread at a time. Support students in generating one question per page spread.

⬇ LESSON 9 DEEP DIVE: VOCABULARY

Opposite Adjectives: *Africa*

- **Time:** 15 min.

- **Text:** *Africa*, Rebecca Hirsch

- **Vocabulary Learning Goal:** Demonstrate understanding of frequently occurring adjectives, or describing words, by matching them to their opposites. (L.K.5.b)

Launch

Display the cover of the text. Explain that the author uses a lot of describing words in her books to tell about the continents. Emphasize that she uses many describing words in *Africa* to help readers better understand what it feels and looks like to visit the continent.

Instruct students to Mix and Mingle and share an example of a describing word. Provide prompts as needed. Call on volunteers to share their examples. Use student responses to reinforce that describing words give more information about a person, place, or thing.

Explain that students are again going to show their understanding of describing words from the text by finding opposites. Students may recognize some of the words from Deep Dive Lesson 2.

Learn

Instruct students to sit and listen closely as you read sentences from *Africa*. As you read, students should stand when they hear a describing word.

Display pages 14–15 and read: "Africa has <u>hot</u> deserts." Call on a standing student to identify the describing word *hot*. Record the word on the board. Call on a different standing student to identify the opposite of *hot*. Use student responses to identify *cold* as the opposite and record next to *hot*, leaving space between. Draw a horizontal line between the words.

hot ----------------------------------- cold

All students return to sitting position. Display pages 16–17 and read: "Savannas have <u>wet</u> seasons." Repeat the previous activity, using student responses to identify the opposite pair *wet* and *dry*. Record on the board in the same manner as described, below *hot* and *cold*.

All students return to sitting position. Display pages 20–21 and read: "Africa has <u>wild</u> animals." Repeat the activity, using student responses to identify the opposite pair *wild* and *calm*. Record on the board in the same manner as described, below *wet* and *dry*.

All students return to sitting position. Display pages 20–21 and read: "They visit Africa to see its <u>amazing</u> animals, people, and places." Repeat the activity, using student responses to identify the opposite pair *amazing* and *ordinary*. Record on the board in the same manner as described, below *wild* and *calm*.

Echo Read the opposite pairs on the board. Explain that students are going to complete a matching activity to show they understand the meaning of these describing words.

Land

Erase the board to encourage independence as students complete Handout 9A.

✔ Distribute Handout 9A. Students Echo Read the directions at the top. Instruct students to point to each picture as you read each describing word. Allow students time to complete the handout independently. Circulate to provide support as needed.

Once all students are finished, ask: "How did these describing words help you better understand *Africa*?" Volunteers respond.

- *It helped us imagine what Africa looked like*
- *It helped us imagine what it feels like to be in Africa.*

What interesting natural features can people see in Africa and Antarctica?

1 | 2 | 3 | 4 | 5 | 6 | 7 | 8 | **9** | **10** | **11** | **12** | **13** | **14** | **15** | 16 | 17 | 18 | 19 | 20 | 21 | 22 | 23 | 24 | 25 | 26 | 27 | 28 | 29 | 30 | 31 | 32 | 33 | 34 | 35 | 36

Lesson 10

TEXTS

- "Penguin Song," *Preschool Education* (**http://witeng.link/0393**)

- *Africa*, Rebecca Hirsch

- *Antarctica*, Rebecca Hirsch

Lesson 10: At a Glance

AGENDA

Welcome (5 min.)

Practice Fluency

Launch (3 min.)

Learn (61 min.)

Identify the Main Topic and Key Details in Antarctica (18 min.)

Identify the Main Topic and Key Details in Africa (25 min.)

Examine the Importance of Supporting an Opinion (10 min.)

Examine the Importance of Showing Understanding (8 min.)

Land (5 min.)

Answer the Content Framing Question

Wrap (1 min.)

Assign Homework

Vocabulary Deep Dive: Opposite Adjectives: *Antarctica* (15 min.)

STANDARDS ADDRESSED

The full text of ELA Standards can be found in the Module Overview.

Reading

- RI.K.1, RI.K.2

Writing

- W.K.1

Speaking and Listening

- SL.K.1, SL.K.2

Language

- ⬇ L.K.5.b

MATERIALS

- Repeated Language Chart
- World map
- Opinion Sandwich Anchor Chart (see lesson for details)
- Puppets (see lesson for details)
- Building blocks
- Index cards

Learning Goals

Use text features to identify the main topic and key details in a section of *Africa*. (RI.K.2)

✔ Use Nonverbal Signals to identify and retell the main topic and key details of a section in the text.

⬇ Demonstrate understanding of frequently occurring adjectives, or describing words, by matching them to their opposites. (L.K.5.b)

✔ Mix and Mingle to find opposite pairs.

✔ Checks for Understanding

Prepare

FOCUSING QUESTION: Lessons 9–15

What interesting natural features can people see in Africa and Antarctica?

CONTENT FRAMING QUESTION: Lesson 10

Organize: *What is happening in Africa and Antarctica?*

CRAFT QUESTIONS: Lesson 10

Examine: *Why is supporting an opinion important?*
Examine: *Why is it important to make sure you understand something?*

Students continue to develop confidence in and facility with identifying the main topic and key details of informational texts. They use headings in *Antarctica* and *Africa* to identify the main topic of sections in the texts. Students read sections of the texts to identify corresponding key details. In addition, students expand their understanding of opinion writing by examining the importance of supporting an opinion with strong reasons. Finally, students reflect upon demonstrating understanding of a text read aloud and how important it is for building knowledge.

Welcome 5 MIN.

PRACTICE FLUENCY

Display the Repeated Language Chart and read aloud the title and the first line of "Penguin Song," tracking the words with your finger. Students Echo Read the line.

TEACHER NOTE	Cover the remainder of the poem to focus student attention on the first line.

Repeated Language
Song: "Penguin Song," Original author unknown   ▪ I'm a little penguin

Remind students of the video from the previous lesson, and ask: "Did it look like it's easier for penguins to swim or walk? How do penguins look when they walk?" Volunteers respond.

- *It looks like swimming is easier.*
- *They look funny when they walk!*
- *They wobble.*
- *They waddle side to side.*
- *They hold their wings out.*

Scaffold

Replay the first thirty seconds of the "Antarctic Sights and Sounds" video (**http://witeng.link/0392**) to refresh students' memories about penguin movements.

Confirm that it is easier for penguins to swim through water than it is for them to walk on land. Explain that when penguins walk, they waddle from side to side. Penguins have short legs and big feet. Waddling from side to side helps them move more easily on land.

Work with students to create a movement for the first line of the poem, such as waddling in place like a penguin.

Students Echo Read the first line of the poem several times while incorporating the movement.

Launch 3 MIN.

Display and read aloud the Content Framing Question. Explain that after reading, noticing, and wondering about *Antarctica* and *Africa* in the previous lesson, students are now ready to read more closely and learn more about the texts and the continents.

Tell students they will use headings to help them think about what is happening in the texts, similar to what they did with *Europe* and *Asia*.

Display the front cover of *Antarctica* and explain that today's exploration will begin with the continent of Antarctica.

Ask: "Where is the continent called Antarctica?" Students respond by pointing to the location of the continent on the world map. Invite a student to approach the map and move the airplane to Antarctica.

Learn 61 MIN.

IDENTIFY THE MAIN TOPIC AND KEY DETAILS IN *ANTARCTICA* 18 MIN.

Whole Group

Display page 9 of *Antarctica*, and ask: "Where is the heading on this page? How do you know?" Invite a volunteer to approach the text, point out the heading, and explain their thinking.

Instruct students to Think-Pair-Share, and ask: "How can headings help you understand the text? What do headings tell readers?" Call on several students to respond.

- *A heading helps you know what part of the book is about.*
- *Headings tell you the topic.*

Use responses to reinforce that headings introduce readers to new topics in the text. Headings tell readers what they will read about. They know to get ready to read details about that topic.

Explain that students will use headings to help them find the main topic and key details of sections in *Antarctica*.

Read aloud the heading from page 9, and ask: "What do you think this part of the text will tell us about? What is the main topic of this section?" Use Equity Sticks to call on students to respond.

- *This part is about people.*
- *It will tell us about people who live in Antarctica.*
- *The main topic is the people of Antarctica.*

Confirm that the main topic of the section is the people of Antarctica. Explain that the heading of a section will often be the same as the section's main topic because they are both explaining what the section is mostly about.

Remind students that readers can find key details about the main topic in the section that follows the heading. Ask students to listen for key details about the people of Antarctica while you read the "People of Antarctica" section.

Read pages 8–9 aloud. Instruct students to Think-Pair-Share, and ask: "What key detail did you hear on this page about people in Antarctica?" Use Equity Sticks to call on students to respond.

- *Most people in Antarctica are scientists.*
- *People come to Antarctica to study it.*

Use responses to confirm the key detail that scientists study Antarctica.

Read pages 10–11 aloud. Instruct students to Think-Pair-Share, and ask: "What key detail did you hear on this page about people in Antarctica?" Use Equity Sticks to call on students to respond.

- *Visitors come to Antarctica.*
- *People come to Antarctica to see animals.*

Use responses to confirm the key detail that visitors watch animals in Antarctica.

Read pages 12–13 aloud. Instruct students to Think-Pair-Share, and ask: "What key detail did you hear on this page about people in Antarctica?" Use Equity Sticks to call on students to respond.

- *Adventurers come to Antarctica.*
- *People come to Antarctica to ski.*

Use responses to confirm the key detail that people ski in Antarctica.

Tell students that they will use Nonverbal Signals to retell the main topic and key details of the "People of Antarctica" section. Model the Nonverbal Signal for main topic by placing your hand on the top of your head. Ask: "Why do we put our hands on our heads while saying the main topic?" Volunteers respond.

- *The main topic is first, like your head is on top.*
- *Because it's the heading. That sounds like head.*

Students practice naming the main topic for the "People of Antarctica" section while making the Nonverbal Signal.

Explain that, just like your body has one head and several limbs, sections in the text have one main topic and several key details about the topic.

Model Nonverbal Signals for showing key details by waving your arms or hands, one at a time.

TEACHER NOTE	If students have difficulty speaking and moving at the same time, instruct students to say the key detail aloud, then wave their hand or arm. This will allow students to focus on retelling the key details first, which is the main purpose of this part of the lesson.

Alternate Activity

Incorporate feet as well as hands into the Nonverbal Signals for key details. After waving each arm or hand, wave or wiggle your feet, one foot at a time.

Pairs take turns using the Nonverbal Signals to retell the main topic and key details of the section to each other. Display pages from the "People of Antarctica" section for students to use as reference.

IDENTIFY THE MAIN TOPIC AND KEY DETAILS IN *AFRICA* 25 MIN.

Whole Group

Display the front cover of *Africa* and tell students that they will continue their exploration by reading about the African continent.

Reference the world map, and ask: "Where is the continent called Africa?" Students respond by pointing to the location of the continent on the map. Invite a student to approach the map and move the airplane back to Africa.

Explain that students will continue using headings to help them find the main topic and key details of a section in *Africa*. Distribute copies of the text to pairs of students and instruct them to open the book to the table of contents.

Ask: "What is a table of contents? What can readers learn from the information on this page?" Volunteers respond.

Use responses to confirm that a table of contents lists all the headings, or section names, in the text. The table of contents makes finding information in the text easier by telling readers which page number they can turn to for each section.

Scaffold

If needed, model how to use the table of contents to find the page number of a section.

For example, say:

The first section in the book is "Welcome to Africa!" If I trace my finger along the dots after the section name, I see the number 5. That tells me that the "Welcome to Africa!" section starts on page 5.

Turn to page 5 and confirm that it is start of the "Welcome to Africa!" section.

Direct pairs to look for the "Amazing Animals" section in the table of contents. Encourage students to use their knowledge of letter-sound relationships to identify the section name, providing support as needed.

Once students find the listing for "Amazing Animals," instruct them to trace their fingers across the page to find the starting page number for the section. Ask: "Which page can you turn to for the 'Amazing Animals' section?" Volunteers respond.

▪ *Page 21.*

Pairs open their books to the "Amazing Animals" section on page 21. Read the heading aloud, and ask: "What do you think the main topic of this section is? What will this section mostly be about?" Use Equity Sticks to call on students to respond.

▪ *The main topic is amazing animals.*

▪ *It will be about animals in Africa.*

Remind students that readers can find key details about the main topic in the section that follows the heading. Ask students to listen for key details about animals in Africa while you read the "Amazing Animals" section.

Direct students to get into position for Partner Reading. Review the procedure for Partner Reading as needed.

Read pages 21–23 aloud while pairs follow along in their copies of the text.

Instruct students to Think-Pair-Share, and ask: "What key details did you hear on these pages about amazing animals in Africa?" Use Equity Sticks to call on students to respond.

- *There are gorillas in Africa.*
- *People can see zebras.*
- *There are giraffes and lions, too!*

As needed, remind students how to use Nonverbal Signals to retell the main topic and key details.

✔ Pairs take turns using Nonverbal Signals to retell the main topic and key details of the "Amazing Animals" section, using the text for reference.

Instruct students to Mix and Mingle, and ask: "Imagine that you are going to visit Africa. Which animal from the 'Amazing Animals' section would you most like to see? Why?"

Distribute Response Journals. Students write a sentence to share which animal they would like to see. As time permits, they draw an illustration to support their sentence.

EXAMINE THE IMPORTANCE OF SUPPORTING AN OPINION 10 MIN.

Whole Group

Reference the Response Journal entries completed in the previous section. Emphasize that students in the class had different responses because they had different opinions about which animal they would like to see in Africa.

Explain that this week students will continue their work with opinion writing and will learn how to add information to support their opinion statements.

Display and read aloud the first Craft Question: *Why is supporting an opinion important?* Students Echo Read the question.

Explain that to think about this question, students will listen in as some friends discuss their opinion about the best animal in Antarctica. Introduce the friends (two puppets) to the class.

TEACHER NOTE	If you do not have access to puppets, use figurines or print out images and attach them to popsicle sticks.

Develop a script for supporting an opinion and use the puppets to act it out.

For example:

- Puppet 1: "Which animal do you think is the best animal in Antarctica?"

- Puppet 2: "I'm glad you asked, I've been thinking about this a lot. I think the penguin is the best animal in Antarctica!"

- Puppet 1: "Really? Why?"

- Puppet 2: "One reason is that penguins are great swimmers. Penguins can also walk on the ice. That's why penguins are the best!"

- Puppet 1: "Oh, I get it! Those are really great reasons. I understand why you like penguins the best."

Instruct students to Think-Pair-Share, and ask: "How did [Puppet 2] support, or explain, his/her opinion?" Call on several students to respond.

- *He told why penguins are the best.*
- *He explained why he likes penguins.*
- *He gave information about penguins.*
- *He said penguins walk on ice.*

Ask: "When you heard [Puppet 2's] supporting reasons, did that help you understand why he/she picked penguins as the best animal in Antarctica? How did it help you?" Volunteers respond.

- *Yes, it gave me more details.*
- *Yes, he explained the reasons why he picked penguins.*

Instruct students to Think-Pair-Share, and ask: "Why is supporting an opinion important?" Use Equity Sticks to call on students to respond.

- *It helps people understand your thinking.*
- *To give more information.*
- *It explains reasons why.*

Display the Opinion Sandwich Anchor Chart. Explain that the image on the chart represents the shape of opinion writing. Just like they used a sandwich to learn the shape of an informative paragraph, they can use the way this cookie is built to remember the parts of an opinion paragraph.

SAMPLE OPINION SANDWICH ANCHOR CHART

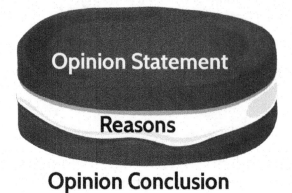

Explain that students have already learned about the top and bottom parts of writing an opinion piece: the opinion. This is like the topic statement; it tells what the paragraph will be about. Point to the middle of the sandwich. Explain that in the next few lessons, students will add the "good stuff" in the center: supporting reasons. These sentences help answer the question "What makes you think that?"

Point to each part of the cookie sandwich as you identify the sequence of "opinion statement, reasons, opinion conclusion." Students Echo Read this sequence. Point to the parts again and explain it's what you think, why you think it, and what you think, once again.

EXAMINE THE IMPORTANCE OF SHOWING UNDERSTANDING 8 MIN.

Whole Group

Remind students that when great writers talk to each other about their writing, they practice their best speaking and listening. Share that today, students will examine another way to speak and listen well.

Display and read aloud the second Craft Question: *Why is it important to make sure you understand something?*

Use blocks to create a simple tower or building. As you build, talk about the way learning is like building with blocks. For example:

> **As you learn new things, you are building on things you already know. When you were very little, you didn't know how to read. Most people start learning to read by learning the letters in the alphabet. Then they have to learn the sounds each letter makes. After that, they can put those sounds together and read words. Each new block of learning builds on the one before it.**

Ask: "What would happen if I pulled the bottom blocks out from the tower?" Volunteers respond.

- *The tower would fall!*

Invite a student to pull the bottom blocks out from the tower to confirm students' predictions.

Explain that as students learn new things, it's important to really understand what they're learning. If they don't "get it," they won't be able to build on that learning. They'll be missing important building blocks.

Instruct students to Think-Pair-Share, and ask: "Why do we read each text several times? Why not read it just once?" Call on several students to respond.

- *Reading a book over helps us understand it better.*
- *We notice things that we didn't notice at first.*
- *We can enjoy it more when we really understand it.*

Ask: "What else do we do to help us understand and build on our learning?" Volunteers respond.

- *We talk about what we are reading.*
- *We share our writing.*
- *We learn from each other.*
- *We ask questions when we don't understand.*

Ask: "Why do teachers ask you questions about the text? What are they learning by asking you questions?" Volunteers respond.

- *They know if we know it.*
- *Then they know if we listened.*
- *We can answer and tell them what they know.*

Confirm that teachers ask questions of their students to understand what students know or are learning. By asking questions, teachers learn more. By answering the questions, students show what they know. This is one way students and teachers work together to build knowledge.

Land 5 MIN.

ANSWER THE CONTENT FRAMING QUESTION

Display and read aloud the Content Framing Question.

Instruct students to Mix and Mingle, and ask: "What did you learn about Antarctica today? Africa?"

> **Extension**
>
> Explore additional facts, pictures, and videos about African animals with the interactive "Africa-Fact Files" website (**http://witeng.link/0395**).

Wrap 1 MIN.

ASSIGN HOMEWORK

Continue the class home-reading routine.

Analyze

Context and Alignment

Students use the heading of a section in *Africa* to identify the main topic. After reading the section they retell key details (RI.K.2). Each student:

- Uses the heading to identify the main topic.

- Uses Nonverbal Signals to retell the main topic and key details.

Next Steps

If students have difficulty making the connection between headings and main topics, work with small groups to provide focused practice with this skill. Read sections of *Africa* or *Antarctica* aloud to the group, pausing after each heading to ask: "What information will this section tell us? How do you know?" After reading the section, reflect on the relationship between the heading and the details in the section. Create a graphic organizer with the main topic listed at the top of the page and direct each student to illustrate a related detail from the section.

⬇ LESSON 10 DEEP DIVE: VOCABULARY

Opposite Adjectives: *Antarctica*

- **Time:** 15 min.

- **Text:** *Antarctica*, Rebecca Hirsch

- **Vocabulary Learning Goal:** Demonstrate understanding of frequently occurring adjectives, or describing words, by matching them to their opposites. (L.K.5.b)

Launch

Display the cover of the text. Remind students that Rebecca Hirsch uses a lot of describing words in her books to tell about the continents. Reinforce that she also uses many describing words in *Antarctica* to help readers better understand what it feels and looks like to visit the continent.

Instruct students to Think-Pair-Share and ask: "Do you think the describing words in *Antarctica* will be the same or different that the words in *Africa*? Why or why not?"

- *Yes, because they are written by the same person.*

- *No, because the continents are very different.*

Use student responses to acknowledge that some describing words may be the same and some may be different. Point out that *Africa* and *Antarctica* are opposite continents because one is very hot and one is very cold.

Explain that students are again going to show their understanding of describing words from the text by finding opposites. Students may recognize some of the words from Deep Dive Lessons 2 and 9.

Learn

Instruct students to sit and listen closely as you read sentences from *Antarctica*. As you read, students should stand when they hear a describing word.

Display pages 14–15 and read: "Penguins live by the *rocky* shore." Call on a standing student to identify the describing word *rocky*. Record the word on the board. Call on a different standing student to describe the opposite of *rocky*. Use the student's response to identify *smooth* as the opposite. Record both words on the board and draw a simple image underneath each.

ROCKY	SMOOTH

All students return to sitting position. Display pages 20–21 and read: "Antarctica has <u>tall</u> mountains." Repeat the activity, using student responses to identify the opposite pair *tall* and *short*. Record on the board in same manner as described, below *rocky* and *smooth*.

All students return to sitting position. Display pages 22–23 and read: "Antarctica has <u>thick</u> sheets of ice." Repeat the activity, using student responses to identify the opposite pair *thick* and *thin*. Record on the board in the same manner as described, below *tall* and *short*.

All students return to sitting position. Display pages 22–23 and read: "<u>Giant</u> ice chunks break off into the ocean." Repeat the activity, using student responses to identify the opposite pair *giant* and *tiny*. Record on the board in the same manner as described, below *thick* and *thin*.

Echo Read the opposite pairs on the board. Explain that students are going to complete a matching activity to show they understand the meaning of these describing words.

Land

TEACHER NOTE	Consider preparing index cards ahead of time to maximize instructional time.

Write each word from the opposite pairs on index cards. Prepare enough cards so each student will receive one card, with one word written on it. Words from opposite pairs need to be represented equally for matching purposes.

Distribute an index card to each student. Read the word to each student as you hand out the card. If time allows, students can draw the matching image on their card from the board.

✔ Students Mix and Mingle to find a student with the opposite describing word. Call on pairs to share their opposite pairs.

Ask: "How did these describing words help you better understand *Antarctica*?" Volunteers respond.

- *It helped us imagine what Antarctica looked like.*
- *It helped us imagine what it feels like to be in Antarctica.*

■ FOCUSING QUESTION: LESSONS 9–15

What interesting natural features can people see in Africa and Antarctica?

| 1 | 2 | 3 | 4 | 5 | 6 | 7 | 8 | 9 | 10 | 11 | 12 | 13 | 14 | 15 | 16 | 17 | 18 | 19 | 20 | 21 | 22 | 23 | 24 | 25 | 26 | 27 | 28 | 29 | 30 | 31 | 32 | 33 | 34 | 35 | 36 |

Lesson 11

TEXTS

- "Penguin Song," *Preschool Education* (**http://witeng.link/0393**)

- *Africa*, Rebecca Hirsch

- "Storm-Proofing the World's Biggest Mud Building," BBC Earth (video) (**http://witeng.link/0396**)

Lesson 11: At a Glance

AGENDA

Welcome (5 min.)

Practice Fluency

Launch (4 min.)

Learn (60 min.)

Analyze Words and Photographs (17 min.)

Collect Evidence for Focusing Question Task 2 (20 min.)

Experiment with Supporting an Opinion (15 min.)

Experiment with Giving an Example to Show Understanding (8 min.)

Land (5 min.)

Answer the Content Framing Question

Wrap (1 min.)

Assign Homework

Vocabulary Deep Dive: Opposite Verbs: *Africa* **(15 min.)**

STANDARDS ADDRESSED

The full text of ELA Standards can be found in the Module Overview.

Reading

- RI.K.1, RI.K.4, RI.K.7

Writing

- W.K.1, W.K.8

Speaking and Listening

- SL.K.1, SL.K.2

Language

- L.K.1.f, L.K.5.c
- ⬇ L.K.5.b

MATERIALS

- Repeated Language Chart
- Evidence Organizer for *Africa*
- Sticky notes
- Opinion Sandwich Anchor Chart
- Speaking and Listening Anchor Chart

Learning Goals

Use photographs and details from the text to describe natural features in Africa. (RI.K.7, L.K.5.c)

✔ Record evidence for the Focusing Question Task.

Use details from the words and illustrations to support an opinion statement. (RI.K.1, W.K.1, W.K.8)

✔ Verbally support an opinion statement with details from the text.

⬇ Demonstrate understanding of *work*, *grow*, and *climb* by acting out their opposites. (L.K.5.b)

✔ Mix and Mingle to act out opposite action words.

✔ Checks for Understanding

Prepare

FOCUSING QUESTION: Lessons 9–15

What interesting natural features can people see in Africa and Antarctica?

CONTENT FRAMING QUESTION: Lesson 11

Reveal: *What does a deeper exploration of the words and illustrations reveal in Africa?*

CRAFT QUESTIONS: Lesson 11

Experiment: *How do I support an opinion with reasons from the text?*
Experiment: *How can I show I understand something?*

In this lesson, students continue exploring *Africa* by looking closely at the pictures to understand key descriptive words in the text, which help them to understand the natural features of this continent. Students use the words and pictures in the text to collect evidence for the Focusing Question Task. Students continue to prepare for the Focusing Question Task by practicing providing reasons to support an opinion in the text. Finally, students share their sentences in small groups to develop their ability to confirm understanding of information presented aloud.

Welcome 5 MIN.

PRACTICE FLUENCY

Display the Repeated Language Chart with the second line of the poem added. Read the line aloud. Students Echo Read the line.

Repeated Language
Song: "Penguin Song," Original author unknown
• I'm a little penguin
• In the sea.

Foundational Skills Connection

Use Equity Sticks to call on students to approach the chart and point to the words they recognize from the High-Frequency Word list. As the student points to each high-frequency word, students read the word chorally. As you add more lines of the poem, repeat this exercise to reinforce these skills.

Ask: "What is a sea?" Volunteers respond.

- *I think it is like the ocean.*
- *I think it is water because penguins like to swim.*

Confirm that *sea* is another word for the ocean. It is a large area of salt water.

Ask: "What does the line 'in the sea' mean? What does that tell us about the penguin?" Volunteers respond.

- *It means it is swimming inside the sea.*
- *I think it means they are swimming.*
- *In means you are inside it.*

Reread the second line again, emphasizing the word *sea*, and create a movement for the second line. For example, moving your hands in an undulating wave motion.

Reread the first two lines of the poem aloud. Students Echo Read while incorporating the movements for each line.

Launch 4 MIN.

Ask: "How did you use text features in the previous lesson? What is a text feature?" Volunteers respond.

- *They are special parts of the book.*
- *They help us find the key details.*
- *They help us find information.*

Confirm that text features are the different parts of a book that help readers organize and understand what they are reading. Explain that a feature is an important part of something; text features are important parts of a text that help a reader understand it better. They often stand out from the rest of the text because they are meant to catch a reader's attention.

Read the Focusing Question aloud. Remind students that natural features are an important part of a place, and that they are created over time by changes in Earth. Mountains and rivers are both examples of natural features. Understanding a continent's natural features helps one understand more about that continent and the shape of its land.

Display and read aloud the Content Framing Question. Tell students that today they will explore the words and pictures in *Africa* to help them better understand the natural features in Africa and collect evidence for the Focusing Question Task.

Learn 60 MIN.

ANALYZE WORDS AND PHOTOGRAPHS 17 MIN.

Pairs

Divide the class into pairs and distribute a copy of the text to each. Explain that students will now engage in Partner Reading, sharing responsibility for the text as they respond to TDQs about the words and pictures.

Prompt students to turn to pages 14–15. Read the heading on the top of page 15. Students Echo Read. Explain that now students will read through this section as a class and respond to questions about how the words and pictures work together to communicate key details.

Alternate Activity

Rather than giving students the page numbers, ask pairs to use the table of contents to locate the section "Wild Places." Encourage students to use their knowledge of letter sounds to find the heading on the list, and then turn to the corresponding page.

Instruct students to Think-Pair-Share about the following TDQs. Use Equity Sticks to call on students to answer.

Read page 15.

1   How does the picture on page 14 help us understand what *dry* means?

   ▪ *There is no water.*

   ▪ *There are not a lot of plants because they need water.*

   ▪ *It is really sandy because there is no water.*

Ask: "What else do we learn about the desert from this picture that the words do not tell us?" Volunteers respond.

   ▪ *There are camels there.*

   ▪ *There aren't any trees.*

   ▪ *It is really sandy.*

   ▪ *There are dunes.*

Extension

Consider doing an experiment with sand and water. Allow students to make observations about dry sand by holding it in their hands, blowing on it, and filling containers or sifters. Then add water to the sand and ask students to make observations about the differences between dry and wet sand. Allow them to hold it in their hands, try blowing on it, and sifting it. Ask: "What do you notice about the sand when water is added to it? The Sahara Desert does not have any water nearby. What does that tell us about the sand there?"

Read page 17, then the caption underneath the photo on page 16.

2 How does this picture help us understand what *few* means?

- *There aren't a lot.*
- *I only see one tree.*
- *Few means "a little."*
- *The picture only shows one tree, not a lot.*
- *Few means not a lot.*

Confirm the definition of *few*. Explain that the savannas are large, grassy areas where there are not many trees. Instead, there are large areas of land with thick grass.

Read page 19. Ask: "What two words do you hear in the word *rainforest*?" Volunteers respond.

Ask: "Thinking about those two words, what do you think a rainforest is? What characteristics might a rainforest have?" Volunteers respond.

- *I think it has tall trees like a forest.*
- *I think it rains a lot.*
- *Maybe it is a really rainy forest.*
- *Maybe it has a lot of plants because plants like rain.*

3 What do the words and picture teach us about rainforests?

- *It rains a lot there.*
- *It is a forest and it is rainy.*
- *There are a lot of plants.*
- *Everything is really green.*
- *There are big trees and leaves.*

Prompt students to look at the pictures of the desert and the rainforest. Instruct students to Think-Pair-Share, and ask: "What differences to do you notice between the desert and the rainforest? Why do you think they are so different?" Use Equity Sticks to call on students to share their answers.

- *The desert is dry. It doesn't have trees.*
- *The rainforest has lots of plants.*
- *The rainforest is really green, but the desert is orange.*

- *It rains a lot in the rainforest, so there are more plants.*
- *It doesn't rain in the desert, so it gets very sandy.*

Confirm the differences between the rainforest and the desert. Reinforce that while these natural features are very different, they both exist on the same continent. Most continents have very different natural features in different places.

Instruct students to Think-Pair-Share, and ask: "How did the pictures help you understand the words we read in 'Wild Places'?" Volunteers respond.

- *They show us what places look like.*
- *We could see how they are different.*
- *It showed us real life.*

Use responses to reinforce that photographs play a big role in this text. They can do as much work as descriptive words do in helping the reader picture Africa.

Explain that now they will use this understanding to help them collect evidence for the Focusing Question Task.

COLLECT EVIDENCE FOR FOCUSING QUESTION TASK 2   20 MIN.

Pairs

Post and read the Focusing Question. Students Echo Read the question.

Display the blank Evidence Organizer for *Africa* (see the following example).

TEACHER NOTE	Prepare this evidence organizer beforehand. In Lessons 11 and 12, students will focus their evidence collection on natural features. Consider covering the other two columns on the chart to focus students' attention. Students will revisit the text in Lessons 14 and 15 in order to collect evidence for the "Things to Do" column. This is preparation for the EOM Task, but not crucial to the completion of Focusing Question Task 2.

Point to the second column. Ask: "What do we mean by *natural features*?" Volunteers respond.

Divide the class into pairs, giving each five sticky notes. Explain that now they will go back through the whole text to look for examples of other natural features in Africa. As they listen, pairs use sticky notes to annotate the text when they see and hear examples of natural features in Africa.

Read pages 15–19 aloud with pairs following along in their copies of the text. Pairs use sticky notes to annotate picture evidence in the text.

Prompt students to turn to pages 24–25 and the section "Water and Land." Explain that while the previous section, "Wild Places," clearly discussed the natural features, not all sections are as clear—but they still contain important information about the natural features. Briefly remind students of the definition of *natural feature.*

Prompt students to listen closely to the words they hear in the text. The words will give them hints as to what natural feature they hear about in the text.

Read pages 24–27 aloud. After each page spread in this section, use Equity Sticks to call on students to share the natural feature they hear about in the text. Confirm the natural feature in the text and instruct pairs to place a sticky note on the photograph to annotate the example.

✔ After the read, pairs go back to the photographs they marked and choose two natural features to record, using drawing and labeling, as the evidence on the sticky note provided. Instruct pairs to divide responsibility by having one student record one piece of evidence and their partner recording the second. Use Equity Sticks to call on pairs share the natural features they recorded.

Group similar responses together to add to the evidence organizer.

TEACHER NOTE

Pair pieces of evidence with photograph to help students access the evidence organizer independently. Consider using the example below to prerecord or print out images to include on the evidence organizer.

The example below is comprehensive. It is not critical that students collect every piece of evidence in the text, only that there are enough examples for students to base opinions upon.

Point to the evidence recorded on the evidence organizer. Ask: "Did the text just tell us 'there are deserts' or did the text give us more information about the desert in Africa?" Volunteers respond.

Confirm that the text did not just list the natural features, but used descriptive words to give more detail. Explain that now they will go back through the text as a class and add more detail to the evidence collected.

Scaffold

Reactivate knowledge of adjectives or descriptive words from the Lesson 9 and 10 Deep Dives.

Prompt pairs to follow along in their copies of the text. Instruct students to listen closely for descriptive words used to describe these natural features in the text.

Read pages 15–19 and 24–27 aloud. Instruct students to make a Nonverbal Signal, such as reaching their arms up high like the lone tree in the savanna, when they hear a descriptive word. Call on students who signal to answer the following questions:

- "What descriptive word did you hear in the text?"

- "What natural feature does this word tell us more about?"

Record the descriptive words students hear on the Evidence Organizer for *Africa* next to the corresponding natural feature.

Foundational Skills Connection

If students are ready, encourage group participation in helping you label the evidence with descriptive words. As you segment the word verbally into phonemes, invite students to chorally share the letter that makes each sound. Record the letters shared to model how to use knowledge of one-to-one letter-sound correspondence to write words.

TEACHER NOTE	Descriptive words are seen in bold below. This is to note which information should be collected in the first half of the evidence collection and which words should be added in the second half of the evidence collection.

SAMPLE EVIDENCE ORGANIZER FOR *AFRICA*

Evidence Organizer for *Africa*		
Things to Do	**Natural Features**	**Animals**
	• **hot and dry** *deserts* • **grassy** *savannas* • **green** *rainforests* • **long** *Nile River* • **tall** *mountains*	

EXPERIMENT WITH SUPPORTING AN OPINION   15 MIN.

Individuals

Explain that now students will reflect upon the evidence they collected and use it to form an opinion.

Post and read the first Craft Question: *How do I support an opinion with reasons from the text?*

Display the Opinion Sandwich Anchor Chart. Ask: "Why do we need to include reason sentences?" Volunteers respond.

- *They tell why.*
- *We need reasons to explain our opinion.*
- *They say why we think that.*
- *It is so people know why we think that.*

Reinforce that supporting an opinion with reason sentences helps readers understand why you formed that opinion.

Scaffold

Display the Opinion Sandwich Anchor Chart and reinforce the "opinion statement, reasons, opinion conclusion" sequence of writing an opinion paragraph. Point to the matching cookies at the top and bottom confirming that these are the opinion sentences that tell readers what you think. Point to the cream filling in the middle of the cookie sandwich and confirm this represents the reason sentences. The reason sentences support the opinion by answering the question: "Why do you think that?"

Ask: "How can we find reasons to support our opinion?" Volunteers respond.

- *We can use the words.*
- *We can look at the pictures.*
- *We need to use the text.*

Confirm that using evidence to answer questions about a text allows readers to better understand a writer's opinions. Using text evidence allows readers to reference the text to build understanding.

Explain that now they will practice supporting an opinion with reasons that include details from the text. They will use the evidence organizer to answer a prompt about the natural features. Reinforce that students should look at the pictures in the text to help them form this opinion.

What is your favorite natural feature in Africa? Why?

Divide the class into pairs and distribute copies of the text to each pair. Instruct students to Think-Pair-Share about the prompt. Students verbally share their opinion statement and one reason why that natural feature is their favorite.

Scaffold

Remind students that it is important to think about all the different options before forming an opinion. If needed, model a Think Aloud of this process. Reinforce that one needs to consider more than one option before forming an opinion as to which is their favorite.

✔ Students record their reason sentence in their Response Journals.

EXPERIMENT WITH GIVING AN EXAMPLE TO SHOW UNDERSTANDING
8 MIN.

Whole Group

Post and read the second Craft Question: *How can I show I understand something?*

Ask: "Why is it important to show you understand something?" Volunteers respond.

- *It shows we listened.*
- *It shows we know what we heard.*
- *It means we thought about it, too.*

Ask: "How do we use our ears when we read a text as a class?" Volunteers respond.

- *We listen to the words.*

Ask: "Do we listen to the words and then just forget them? What do we have to make sure we do?" Volunteers respond.

- *We have to remember what we read.*
- *We have to think about them, too.*
- *We need to keep them in our head.*

Reinforce that one way to help them understand what they hear is by "listening to remember."

Display the Speaking and Listening Anchor Chart. Add the line "Listen to remember" to the column "When I listen, I."

Ask: "When we answer a question, why is it important to use text evidence?" Volunteers respond.

- *It helps us answer the question.*
- *It shows what we are trying to say.*
- *It helps people understand our answer.*

Confirm that using text evidence, or giving an example from the text, is a great way to show someone that you understand what you read or heard. Add "Give an example" to the column "When I speak, I".

When I listen, I	When I speak, I
• Listen with my senses.	• Use one voice at a time.
• Use active listening.	• Have conversations.
• Listen for order.	• Speak with a strong voice.
• Listen to remember.	• Ask and answer questions.
	• Use drawings to add detail.
	• Give an example.

Explain that students are going to practice these skills of "listening to remember" and "give an example" to show that they understand something that they hear. Divide the class into pairs to share copies of the text. Distribute a copy of the text to each pair.

Prompt students to turn to page 28 in their texts. Read the "Modern Marvels" page aloud. Reread the third bullet point on that page.

Ask: "What does it mean to <u>hold up</u> something? What happens if you don't hold up something?" Volunteers respond.

- *It means you hold it so it won't fall down.*
- *It will fall down.*
- *It means to lift it up.*

Confirm that columns in the Library of Alexandria are important because they hold up the different parts of the building so it doesn't fall down.

Practice this concept using an object from the classroom. Ask students to hold the object a little off their table and then let go. Ask: "What happened?" Volunteers respond. Then, ask students to use their hand and arm like a column to hold up the object like they are carrying a pizza box. Ask: "What happened when we held up our object?"

Instruct students to look at the image on page 29 with their partner and ask: "What is a column? What does a column look like? Point to and describe an example in the picture." Students point to the columns in the picture, or an example of something being held up by a column. Give students thirty seconds to consider the picture. Use Equity Sticks to call on a few students to share their examples.

Point to the entry "Give an example" on the Speaking and Listening Anchor Chart. Ask: "Why is it important to give an example?" Volunteers respond.

- *It shows we understand something.*
- *It shows we were listening.*
- *It shows we remember what we read.*

TEACHER NOTE

The purpose of this lesson is to practice SL.K.2 by articulating examples from the text to show that they understand a concept. Students have worked with the concept of using text evidence often over the course of the year. This Speaking and Listening mini-lesson provides additional context as to why it is important to show you understand something. Students practice the tools of "listening to remember" and "give an example" as ways to express this understanding when speaking and listening.

Land 5 MIN.

ANSWER THE CONTENT FRAMING QUESTION

Access the link of "Storm-Proofing the World's Biggest Mud Building" (**http://witeng.link/0396**) and play the video for the class.

Display and read the Content Framing Question. Ask: "What have we learned about the natural features in Africa? How are they affected by the weather?" Volunteers respond.

Ask: "What have you noticed about the importance of rain in Africa? Why is rain important?" Volunteers respond.

Wrap 1 MIN.

ASSIGN HOMEWORK

Continue the class home-reading routine.

> **Analyze**
>
> ### Context and Alignment
>
> Students use the words and pictures in *Africa* to learn more about the continent and collect evidence on the different natural features in Africa (RI.K.1, RI.K.7). Each student:
>
> - Annotates examples of natural features in the text.
> - Records one piece of evidence on a sticky note.
>
> ### Next Steps
>
> If students have difficulty understanding what evidence qualifies as natural features, consider the root of the problem. Does the student understand what the category means? If not, redefine the category and provide concrete examples from the text. Does the student have trouble locating evidence in the text? If so, go back through the text slowly, focusing largely on the photographs. Ask: "Is this part of the land? Was it made by people?"

⬇ LESSON 11 DEEP DIVE: VOCABULARY

Opposite Verbs: *Africa*

- **Time:** 15 min.

- **Text:** *Africa*, Rebecca Hirsch

- **Vocabulary Learning Goal:** Demonstrate understanding of *work*, *grow*, and *climb* by acting out their opposites. (L.K.5.b)

Launch

Display the cover of the text. Remind students that Rebecca Hirsch uses a lot of interesting words to help readers learn about the continents in her books. In *Africa* she uses action words to help readers understand what the people, plants, and animals of Africa do.

Instruct students to Think-Pair-Share and then tell an example of an action word. Call on volunteers to share their examples. Use student responses to reinforce that action words are the words that tell what a person, place, or thing does.

Explain that students are going to find and act out opposite action words from *Africa*.

Learn

Explain that students will listen closely as you read sentences from the story. Create and display a chart to record student responses.

Action Word	Illustration	Opposite	Illustration

Display pages 10–11 and read: "Some Africans <u>work</u> on farms." Students stand when they hear the action word in the sentence. Call on a standing student to identify the action word and act it out. Record the response on the chart, using the action to sketch a simple illustration that represents the meaning of the word. Call on a different standing student to act out the opposite of *work*. Use the student response to identify the opposite as *play*. Record the response on the chart, using the action to sketch a simple illustration that represents the meaning of the word.

Repeat the above activity for the following action words:

Grow: Display pages 18–19 and read: "Many kinds of plants <u>grow</u> there." The opposite of *grow* is *shrink*.

Climb: Display pages 26–27 and read: "People climb this mountain." The opposite of *climb* is *go down.*

Ensure that all student responses are recorded on the chart.

Action Word	Illustration	Opposite	Illustration
Work		Play	
Grow		Shrink	
Climb		Go down	

Have students Echo Read the opposite pairs as you point to each word on the chart.

✔ Instruct students to Mix and Mingle. As you call out "action," students find a partner. Read a pair of opposite action words from the chart. One student takes a turn acting out one word from the pair. The other student acts out the opposite. Repeat for all opposite pairs. Circulate to provide support and to ensure accurate portrayal of opposites.

Land

Ask: "What did you learn about Africa by exploring these opposite action words from the text?" Volunteers respond.

- *That the people in Africa work and play.*
- *That many plants grow in Africa.*
- *That people climb the mountains in Africa.*

What interesting natural features can people see in Africa and Antarctica?

1 2 3 4 5 6 7 8 9 10 11 **12** 13 14 15 16 17 18 19 20 21 22 23 24 25 26 27 28 29 30 31 32 33 34 35 36

Lesson 12

TEXTS

- "Penguin Song," *Preschool Education* (**http://witeng.link/0393**)
- *Antarctica*, Rebecca Hirsch

Lesson 12: At a Glance

AGENDA

Welcome (5 min.)

Practice Fluency

Launch (4 min.)

Learn (55 min.)

Analyze Words and Photographs (15 min.)

Collect Evidence for Focusing Question Task 2 (20 min.)

Experiment with Supporting an Opinion (20 min.)

Land (10 min.)

Answer the Content Framing Question

Wrap (1 min.)

Assign Homework

Vocabulary Deep Dive: Shades of Meaning: *Blow, swirl*, and *flow* (15 min.)

STANDARDS ADDRESSED

The full text of ELA Standards can be found in the Module Overview.

Reading

- RI.K.1, RI.K.4, RI.K.7

Writing

- W.K.1, W.K.8

Speaking and Listening

- SL.K.1, SL.K.2

Language

- L.K.1.f, L.K.2.b, L.K.5.c
- ⬇ L.K.5.d

MATERIALS

- Repeated Language Chart
- Evidence Organizer for *Antarctica*
- Sticky notes
- Labeled index cards (see lesson for details)
- Document camera (if available)

Learning Goals

Use photographs and details from the text to describe natural features in Antarctica. (RI.K.7, L.K.5.c)

✔ Record evidence for the Focusing Question Task.

Use details from the words and illustrations to support an opinion statement. (RI.K.1, W.K.1, W.K.8)

✔ After verbally sharing an opinion statement, write one supporting reason sentence.

⬇ Distinguish shades of meaning between *blow, swirl*, and *flow* by acting out their meanings. (L.K.5.d)

✔ Complete sentences by acting out the missing opposite verb.

✔ Checks for Understanding

Prepare

FOCUSING QUESTION: Lessons 9–15

What interesting natural features can people see in Africa and Antarctica?

CONTENT FRAMING QUESTION: Lesson 12

Reveal: *What does a deeper exploration of the words and illustrations reveal in* Antarctica?

CRAFT QUESTION: Lesson 12

Experiment: *How do I support an opinion with reasons from the text?*

In this lesson, students complete their evidence collection for the Focusing Question Task by analyzing the words and pictures in *Antarctica*. Students use the pictures to understand key descriptive words in the text, ultimately helping them understand the natural features in Antarctica. Students strengthen their opinion writing by crafting a reason sentence to support their opinion using details from the text.

Welcome 5 MIN.

PRACTICE FLUENCY

Display the Repeated Language Chart with the third line of the poem added. Read the line aloud. Students Echo Read the line.

Repeated Language
↻
Song: "Penguin Song," Original author unknown ▪ I'm a little penguin ▪ In the sea. ▪ I can swim as fast as can be!

Use Equity Sticks to call on students to approach the chart and point to the words from the high-frequency word list.

191

Point to the punctuation mark at the end of the third line. Call on a volunteer to identify this mark. Confirm that it is an exclamation point. Ask: "What does that tell us about this sentence? How should we read a sentence that ends with a punctuation mark?" Volunteers respond.

- *It means you are excited.*
- *You have to read it in a happy voice.*
- *Maybe you read it a little louder, too.*

Read the line aloud, emphasizing the feeling in your voice. It may also be helpful to increase your volume as you read the line. Students Echo Read the line, emphasizing the feeling in their voices.

Reread the first three lines again. Create a movement for the third line. For example, moving your arms in a swimming motion.

Reread the first three lines of the poem aloud. Students Echo Read the song while incorporating the movements for each line.

Launch 4 MIN.

Instruct students to Mix and Mingle, and ask: "Have you ever been to a desert or rainforest? What do you think it would be like to visit those places?" Use Equity Sticks to call on students to share.

Ask: "How did the words and pictures in *Africa* help us understand these natural features?" Volunteers respond. If needed, call on a volunteer to redefine natural features for the class.

- *The words told us about them but then the pictures showed us.*
- *Sometimes the pictures show us more.*
- *The pictures helped us understand the words.*

Display and read aloud the Content Framing Question. Tell students that today they will use prior experiences to explore the words and pictures in *Antarctica*. This will help them better understand the natural features in Antarctica, and collect evidence for the Focusing Question Task.

Learn 55 MIN.

ANALYZE WORDS AND PHOTOGRAPHS 15 MIN.

Whole Group

Explain that students will take a closer look at the words and illustrations in *Antarctica* to better understand key information about natural features. They will think about how the words and pictures work together to add to their knowledge about the continent Antarctica.

💬 If possible, use a document camera to display the pages of the text in front of the class. Prompt students to sit in "listening position" and look at the copy of the text in front of the class.

> ### Alternate Activity
>
> Divide the class into small groups and distribute a copy of the text to each group. Explain that students will share responsibility for the text with their group as they respond to TDQs about the words and pictures in the text.

Turn to pages 18–19 in the text. Read the heading on the top of page 19. Students Echo Read the heading. Ask: "What do we learn about Antarctica from this heading? Does Antarctica seem like a warm place, or like a cold place?" Volunteers respond. Confirm that the words in the heading reinforce that Antarctica is an extremely cold continent.

Explain that now students will read through this section of the text as a class and respond to questions about how the words and pictures work together to communicate key details about the topic.

Instruct students to Think-Pair-Share about the following TDQs. Use Equity Sticks to call on students to answer.

Read page 19, displaying the picture on page 18.

1 **How does the picture on page 18 help us understand what life is like in Antarctica?**

   ▪ *People wear jackets because it is cold.*

   ▪ *There is a lot of white so people wear colors.*

   ▪ *There is a lot of snow there.*

Ask: "The picture is still and not moving, but how can you tell there are 'fierce winds'?" Volunteers respond.

   ▪ *It looks cloudy.*

   ▪ *You can't see the people's faces because they are bundled up.*

> ▣ *Things are really white because of the snow.*
> ▣ *The wind is blowing the snow all over so it is hard to see the people.*

Use responses to confirm that they can't see the details of the people in the picture because the blowing snow is making it look cloudy. Highlight the fact that people are wearing bright jackets. When the fierce winds blow the snow around it can be hard to see. If people wore white, it would be even harder to see them in a snowstorm.

Read page 23, displaying the picture on page 22.

2 How does this picture help us understand what *giant* and *thick* mean?

> ▣ *The icebergs are really big.*
> ▣ *The icebergs are bigger than the people; they are giant.*
> ▣ Giant *means really big—bigger than a person.*
> ▣ *The icebergs look like walls.*
> ▣ *They are like buildings.*
> ▣ *I think* thick *means big and not skinny.*

Confirm the definitions of *giant* and *thick*. Explain that much of the land in Antarctica is made up of ice. This ice is very thick, like the walls of buildings; people can walk on it, drive on it, and even land planes on it without it breaking! And where most ice usually melts in a season that is not winter, this ice is solid all of the time.

Instruct students to Think-Pair-Share, and ask: "How did the pictures help you understand the words we read about the different characteristics of Antarctica?" Volunteers respond.

> ▣ *They show us how much snow there is!*
> ▣ *We could see how big things were.*
> ▣ *We could see what it would be like to be there.*

Use responses to reinforce that these photographs play a big role in helping a reader understand the text. They provide real-life examples of what the words are describing and help the reader picture what they would see if they visited these places.

Explain that now they will use this understanding help them collect evidence for the Focusing Question Task.

COLLECT EVIDENCE FOR FOCUSING QUESTION TASK 2 20 MIN.

Small Groups

Post and read the Focusing Question. Students Echo Read the question.

Display the blank Evidence Organizer for *Antarctica*.

| TEACHER NOTE | Prepare this evidence organizer beforehand. Consider covering the other two columns on the chart to minimize confusion. Students will revisit the text in Lessons 14 and 15 to collect evidence for the "Things to Do" column. This is preparation for the EOM Task, but not crucial to the completion of Focusing Question Task 2. |

Point to the second column. Call on volunteers to define *natural features*.

- *They are the different parts that make up the land.*
- *They are the different parts of the continent.*
- *They aren't made by people.*

Divide the class into small groups and give each group three sticky notes. Explain that now groups will go back through the text to look for examples of natural features in Antarctica. They will use sticky notes to annotate the photographs in the text showing examples of natural features.

Read aloud the sections "Amazing Animals," "Ice, Wind, and Snow," and "Learning from Antarctica" one at a time, stopping after each section. Groups use sticky notes to annotate photographs showing natural features.

After the read, groups go back to their annotated pages and discuss the following question: "What natural features did you see?"

✔ Give each student a large sticky note. Students choose one natural feature the group annotated in the text to record using drawing and labeling. Allow five minutes for students to choose and record evidence.

Use Equity Sticks to call on students to share their evidence. Once a student names a natural feature, poll the class to see which students recorded the same natural feature. Group similar responses together to add to the evidence organizer.

| TEACHER NOTE | Pair pieces of evidence with a labeled photograph to help students easily access the evidence organizer independently. Consider using the example below to prerecord or print out images to include on the evidence organizer. |

Point to the evidence recorded on the evidence organizer. Ask: "Is there more information we could add? What did we use from the text to add more detail to our evidence collection in the previous lesson?" Volunteers respond.

Confirm that the text did not just list the natural features, but used descriptive words to give more detail. Explain that now they will go back through the text as a class and add more detail to the evidence collected.

Display the text in front of the class using a document camera. Prompt students to stand up and follow along with the text displayed in front of the class. Instruct students to listen closely for descriptive words used to describe these natural features in the text.

Read pages 16–17, 20–21, and 22–23 aloud. Instruct students to make a Nonverbal Signal, such as pointing to their nose, when they hear a descriptive word. Call on students who signal to answer the following questions:

- "What descriptive word did you hear in the text?"

- "What natural feature does this word tell us more about?"

Record the descriptive words students hear on the Evidence Organizer for *Antarctica* next to the corresponding natural feature.

TEACHER NOTE	Descriptive words are seen in bold below. This is to note which information should be collected in the first half of the evidence collection and which words should be added in the second half of the evidence collection.

SAMPLE EVIDENCE ORGANIZER FOR *ANTARCTICA*

Evidence Organizer for *Antarctica*		
Things to Do	**Natural Features**	**Animals**
	▪ **icy** *ocean* ▪ **tall, icy, snowy** *mountains* ▪ **giant, thick** *icebergs*	

EXPERIMENT WITH SUPPORTING AN OPINION 20 MIN.

Individuals

Explain that now students will reflect upon the text and use it to form an opinion about information presented in the text.

Post and read the Craft Question: *How do I support an opinion with reasons from the text?*

Reinforce that supporting an opinion with reason sentences helps the reader understand why you formed that opinion. If needed, display the Opinion Sandwich Anchor Chart to reinforce the order of the sentences.

Explain that now they will use the following prompt to practice supporting an opinion with details or reasons from the text. They will use the text to form an opinion about Antarctica. Reinforce that students can look at the pictures in the text to help them form this opinion.

Would you like to visit Antarctica? Why or why not?

Divide the class into small groups of four and distribute copies of the text to each group. Instruct students to Think-Pair-Share about the prompt. Students verbally share their opinion statement and two reasons why they would want, or would not want, to visit Antarctica.

Scaffold

Remind students that one needs to consider more than one option before forming an opinion. Consider modeling a Think Aloud of reasons why you would or why you would not want to visit Antarctica to demonstrate that there is more than one opinion that can be supported.

✔ Students record one reason sentence in their Response Journals. Students include a drawing to support their reason sentence.

Land 10 MIN.

ANSWER THE CONTENT FRAMING QUESTION

Display and read the Content Framing Question. Ask: "What have we learned about the natural features in Antarctica?" Volunteers respond.

Divide the class into small groups and distribute copies of the text to each group. Give each group one index card with one of the following natural features written on it: ocean, iceberg, or mountain. Support groups in reading the word on their card. Instruct groups to look through the photographs in the text and locate a picture that matches the label on their index card.

Use Equity Sticks to call on groups to share the picture they located in the text. Ask: "How did you know it was a [natural feature]?" Encourage students to use descriptive words to provide detail about their natural feature. Instruct one member from the group to approach the evidence organizer and match their label to a piece of evidence on the chart.

TEACHER NOTE	Engaging in authentic activities to work with the evidence on the evidence organizer fosters student independence with reading and understanding the information on the chart. Prepare these index cards prior to the lesson to save time.

Extension

Ask: "What do you notice about the land in Antarctica? How is it different from where you live? Why do you think it is so different?" Volunteers respond.

Wrap <small>1 MIN.</small>

ASSIGN HOMEWORK

Continue the class home-reading routine.

Analyze

Context and Alignment

Students use the words and pictures in *Antarctica* to learn more about the continent and collect evidence on the different natural features in Africa (RI.K.1, RI.K.7). Each student:

- Annotates examples of natural features in the text.
- Records one piece of evidence on a sticky note.

Next Steps

If students have difficulty understanding which evidence qualifies as natural features, consider the root of the problem. Does the student understand what the category means? If not, redefine the category and provide concrete examples from the text. Does the student have trouble locating evidence in the text? If so, focus students' attention on pages 16–23, which discuss the natural features. Reinforce that the land in Antarctica is made of ice, therefore the natural features will be different than other continents. Scaffold learning by defining *icebergs* and providing additional images of the landscape of Antarctica.

⬇ LESSON 12 DEEP DIVE: VOCABULARY

Shades of Meaning: *Blow*, *swirl*, and *flow*

- **Time:** 15 min.

- **Text:** *Antarctica*, Rebecca Hirsch

- **Vocabulary Learning Goal:** Distinguish shades of meaning between *blow*, *swirl*, and *flow* by acting out their meanings. (L.K.5.d)

Launch

Reinforce that in the book *Antarctica* the author uses many interesting words and photographs to help readers understand what Antarctica feels and looks like

Display page 19 of the text. Remind students that during Lesson 12 they analyzed this illustration and described what life is like on Antarctica.

Instruct students to Think-Pair-Share, and ask: "What do you notice about Antarctica in this picture?" Volunteers respond.

- *It looks very cold.*

- *There is a lot of snow there.*

- *The wind blows a lot in Antarctica.*

Remind students that they can use clues in the illustration to "see" that the wind blows fiercely. Post the word *blow* and describe *blow* as, "to move air quickly and strongly." Call on a student volunteer to create an action for *blow*. Students mimic the action and say, "*blow.*"

Explain that they are going to learn other words that describe how air and water move in Antarctica and all over the world.

Learn

Instruct students to listen as you read for a word that describes the movement of the wind. Students should stand when they hear the word.

Display page 20 of the text and read: "The air <u>swirls</u> down the mountain." Ask: "What word describes how the air moves?" Call on a standing student to answer.

- *Swirls.*

Post the word *swirl* and explain that *swirl* means, "to move in a spinning or twirling motion." Call on another standing student to create an action for *swirl*. Students mimic the action and say, "swirl."

Instruct students to sit down and listen for another word that describes the way air or water moves. Students should stand when they hear the word.

Display and read page 24 in *Antarctica*. Say the following sentence: "The water <u>flows</u> through the ice." Ask: "What word describes how the water moves?" Call on a standing student to answer.

- *Flows.*

Post the word *flows* and explain that *flows* means "to move in a smooth, steady stream." Call on another standing student to create an action for *flows*. Encourage the student to create an action that is distinct from the action for *swirls*. Students mimic the action and say, "flows."

Echo Read *blow, swirl,* and *flow*. Explain that students are going to finish sentences by saying and acting out the correct vocabulary word.

Land

✔ Students stand and find an open space in the classroom. As you read the following sentences, students say and act out the correct missing vocabulary word:

The icy river _____ straight to the sea. (flows)

The strong wind _____ hard in Antarctica. (blows)

The river _____ around the icebergs. (swirls)

Ask: "What are some things that <u>blow</u>, <u>swirl</u>, or <u>flow</u>?" Volunteers respond.

- *The air.*
- *The wind.*
- *Rivers.*
- *Snow.*

■ FOCUSING QUESTION: LESSONS 9–15

What interesting natural features can people see in Africa and Antarctica?

1 2 3 4 5 6 7 8 **9 10 11 12 13 14 15** 16 17 18 19 20 21 22 23 24 25 26 27 28 29 30 31 32 33 34 35 36

Lesson 13

TEXTS

- "Penguin Song," *Preschool Education* (**http://witeng.link/0393**)

- *Africa*, Rebecca Hirsch

- "5 Reasons Why Animal Moms Are Awesome," April Capochino Myers
  (**http://witeng.link/0406**)

Lesson 13: At a Glance

AGENDA

Welcome (5 min.)

Practice Fluency

Launch (4 min.)

Learn (57 min.)

Identify the Reasons That Support a Point in the Text (19 min.)

Engage in New-Read Assessment 1 (19 min.)

Execute Focusing Question Task 2 (19 min.)

Land (8 min.)

Answer the Content Framing Question

Wrap (1 min.)

Assign Homework

Style and Conventions Deep Dive: Experiment with Expanding a Sentence (15 min.)

STANDARDS ADDRESSED

The full text of ELA Standards can be found in the Module Overview.

Reading

- RI.K.1, RI.K.4, RI.K.8

Writing

- W.K.1, W.K.7, W.K.8

Speaking and Listening

- SL.K.1, SL.K.2

Language

- L.K.1.f
- ⬇ L.K.1.f

MATERIALS

- Assessment 13A: New-Read Assessment 1
- Assessment 13B: Focusing Question Task 2
- Repeated Language Chart
- Sticky notes
- Opinion Sandwich Anchor Chart
- Evidence Organizer for *Africa*
- Evidence Organizer for *Antarctica*
- Labeled index cards (see lesson for details)
- Document camera (if available)

Learning Goals

Identify reasons the author gives to support a point in *Africa*. (RI.K.8)

✔ Annotate three reasons that support the author's point.

Identify reasons the author gives to support the point "African elephant moms are awesome!" (RI.K.8)

✔ Complete New-Read Assessment 1.

⬇ Create a complete sentence and expand it by adding a describing word. (L.K.1.f)

✔ Write a complete sentence caption, including a describing word.

✔ Checks for Understanding

Prepare

FOCUSING QUESTION: Lessons 9–15

What interesting natural features can people see in Africa and Antarctica?

CONTENT FRAMING QUESTION: Lesson 13

Reveal: *What does a deeper exploration of Africa reveal about a point the author makes?*

CRAFT QUESTION: Lesson 13

Execute: *How do I write an opinion statement for my Focusing Question Task?*

In this lesson, students demonstrate understanding and independence in identifying the reasons an author gives to support a point in the text. After finding the author's point, they use the words and photographs in the text to deepen their understanding. This prepares them to demonstrate their independence in their first New-Read Assessment. Finally, students reflect on the evidence they collected on the natural features in Africa and Antarctica and form an opinion to begin their Focusing Question Task.

Welcome 5 MIN.

PRACTICE FLUENCY

Display the Repeated Language Chart with the fourth line of the poem added. Read the line aloud. Students Echo Read the line.

Repeated Language
Song: "Penguin Song," Original author unknown   • I'm a little penguin   • In the sea.   • I can swim as fast as can be!   • When I catch a fish, just look at me.

Highlight the comma and the period in the fourth line and ask: "What do marks in a text mean?" Volunteers respond.

- *They tell us to slow down or stop.*
- *They can show that someone is excited too.*

Point to the comma in the middle of the line, and ask: "What does this mark tell us?" Volunteers respond.

- *We should take a breath.*
- *It means we should pause.*

Confirm that the mark tells readers to pause, and reinforce that is called a comma. Remind students that when speakers pause for commas, it helps listeners understand what they are saying. This makes reading or listening less confusing and more fun.

Students Echo Read the line, being sure to pause for the comma.

Reread the first four lines again. Create a movement for the fourth line. For example, put your hands up to your face like a beak and pretend to reach out and catch a fish with your beak.

Reread the first four lines of the poem aloud. Students Echo Read the song while incorporating the movements for each line.

Launch 4 MIN.

Ask: "What do we mean when we ask 'what is the author's point'? What is an author's point?" Volunteers respond.

- *It is like the author's opinion.*
- *It is something they are telling us in the text.*

Confirm that an author's point is like their opinion. It is something that the author is telling the reader.

Ask: "Why does an author give reasons to support their point? Why do you give reasons to support your opinion?" Volunteers respond.

- *It helps people know why we think it.*
- *The reasons help us understand.*
- *The reasons give us information to understand.*

Confirm that, just like with an opinion, an author will support their point with reasons. The reasons are the answer to the question: "Why do you think that?"

Post and read the Content Framing Question. Students Echo Read the question.

Explain that in this lesson they will work together with a partner to identify the reasons the author gives to support her point. They will use their knowledge and understanding of the relationship between the words and the pictures to help them do this. Then, students will demonstrate this skill on their own in a New-Read Assessment.

Learn 57 MIN.

IDENTIFY THE REASONS THAT SUPPORT A POINT IN THE TEXT 19 MIN.

Pairs

Divide the class into pairs to share the text. Explain that students will go back through the text as a class to identify the point the author is trying to make in this text.

Instruct students to Think-Pair-Share, and ask: "What is the author teaching us in this text? What does the author want us to learn about Africa?" Use Equity Sticks to call on students to answer.

- *We are learning about the continent Africa.*
- *We learned about the animals and places.*
- *We learned about the natural features.*
- *We learned about people, too.*

💬 Prompt students to listen to the words they hear and think about how the author feels about the continent Africa. Read the text on page 27 aloud.

Reread the last sentence on page 27, emphasizing the word *amazing*. Instruct students to Think-Pair-Share, and ask: "Thinking about all that you have read about Africa's people, places, and animals, what do you think *amazing* means?" Use Equity Sticks to call on students to answer.

- *I think it means they are really cool.*
- *I think it means they are interesting and different.*
- *I think it means awesome.*

Reinforce that when something is <u>amazing</u>, it causes people to be happily surprised and want to learn more about it.

Confirm that the point the author is making in this text is that Africa has amazing people, places, and animals. On a large sheet of chart paper or on the board write the sentence: Africa has amazing people, places, and animals.

205

Explain that now students are going to go back through sections in the text to identify the different reasons the author gives to support the point: Africa has amazing people, places, and animals.

Prompt students to turn to the section "People of Africa." As a class, turn through the section one page at a time. Prompt pairs to look at each photograph in the section and ask: "What about the people in this photograph seems amazing?" Use Equity Sticks to call on students to answer. Record their responses underneath the author's point.

> ### Scaffold
>
> Model this with pages 10–11. Think Aloud as you look at the photograph and consider what about the people in the photograph seems amazing. Confirm that a mother farming while carrying a baby on her back supports the author's point that Africa has amazing people.

Explain that students will work together in pairs to locate additional reasons in the text to support the author's point. Divide students into pairs and distribute two sticky notes to each pair. Tell students they will read through two additional sections of the text: "Wild Places" and "Amazing Animals." After reading a section, instruct students to Think-Pair-Share about the question, "What information in this section tells us that the [places/animals] are amazing?" Pairs place one sticky note on a page that supports the author's point by providing an example of an amazing place or animal. Students use only one sticky note per section.

✔ Read the remaining two sections noted above aloud, one at a time. Pairs reflect upon the section just read and use one sticky note per section to annotate reasons they hear to support the author's point that Africa has amazing people, places, and animals.

After the read, use Equity Sticks to call on pairs to share their annotations. Record student responses underneath the author's point.

SAMPLE RESPONSE

Africa has amazing people, places, and animals.		
People farm with babies on their backs. People play soccer on the beach.	It has the largest desert. It rains almost every day in the rainforest.	The gorilla lives in the rainforest. The zebras have lots of stripes. Lots of animals live in savannas.

Extension

Remind students that people from around the world have different ways of doing things. Read aloud the research question introduced in Lesson 2: "How do people around the world dance?" Tell students they will now learn about a different style of dancing by watching a dance from one country in Africa: Ethiopia.

Display the questions: "What do I see in this dance performance? What do I hear in this dance performance?" Tell students they can focus their video observations either on what they see or hear, which will help the class learn about different aspects of the dance. Individual students raise their hands to indicate whether they choose to focus on what they see, or what they hear.

Play the video of "Ethiopian Crazy Head Shake Dance" (**http://witeng.link/0408**).

Instruct students to Mix and Mingle, and ask: "What did you see or hear in the Ethiopian dance?"

ENGAGE IN NEW-READ ASSESSMENT 1   19 MIN.

Individuals

TEACHER NOTE	Use New-Read Assessments as an opportunity to reinforce the importance of orienting oneself to a text. Give students an independent, brief routine to support them in locating reasons in the text. For example, you might reread the title of the text and encourage students to silently reflect on what they notice about the photograph in the text. Remember to give young students sufficient time to answer questions and struggle productively with a New-Read text.

Congratulate students on all the great work they have done using the words and pictures to help identify the reasons an author gives to support a point in the text. Explain that they will now demonstrate this skill themselves.

Use a document camera or projector to display the following article in front of the class: "5 Reasons Why Animal Moms Are Awesome" (**http://witeng.link/0406**).

Read the title of the article aloud. Students Echo Read the title. Ask: "What do you think this article is about?" Volunteers respond.

- *It is about animal moms.*
- *It is about how they are awesome.*
- *The point is animal moms are awesome.*

Scroll down in the article to example 5. Read this portion of the text aloud. Instruct students to silently reflect on the question: "What is happening in this text?"

Reread the heading aloud. Reinforce that the point the author is making is that "African elephant moms are awesome!"

Read the text under "African Elephant" aloud, but do not discuss it with the class.

Reread the section aloud and prompt students to think about the following question as they listen a second time: *Why are African elephant moms awesome?*

Distribute copies of Assessment 13A. Point to the author's point at the top and read this aloud: *African elephant moms are awesome!* Explain that this is the point the author is making in the text.

Explain that now they will reread the text multiple times as they identify the reasons to support the author's point.

Engage in the following sequence to administer New-Read Assessment 1:

- Read the section aloud. In the first box provided, students draw and label one reason given to support the author's point in the text.

- Reread the section aloud. In the second box provided, students draw and label a second reason given to support the author's point in the text.

✔ Students complete New-Read Assessment 1.

Name:
Assessment 13A: New-Read Assessment 1
Directions: In the first box, draw and label one reason given to support the author's point. In the second box, draw and label a second reason given to support the author's point.
Author's Point
African elephant moms are awesome!
Supporting Reason 1
Supporting Reason 2

Scaffold

Rereading the text numerous times allows students multiple opportunities to process the information. There is no limit on how many times they can listen to the text. For the integrity of the assessment, do not allow students to discuss the article before answering.

EXECUTE FOCUSING QUESTION TASK 2 19 MIN.

Individuals

Explain that now students will use the evidence they collected over the past few lessons on the natural features in Africa and Antarctica to answer the Focusing Question.

Post and read the Focusing Question. Students Echo Read the question. Call on a volunteer to define *interesting*.

Explain that students will be writing a paragraph to answer the following prompt.

> Which continent do you think has the most interesting natural features?

Ask: "How do we write an opinion sentence? How can we make sure our reader knows we are giving our opinion?" Volunteers respond.

- *We tell them what we feel or think.*
- *We can use words from the question so they know that we are answering it.*
- *We tell them our opinion, then we tell them why.*

Display the Evidence Organizers for *Africa* and *Antarctica*. Explain that students will write an opinion paragraph, like their cookie sandwich, to answer the Focusing Question. They will think about the different evidence they have collected and form an opinion about which continent has the most interesting natural features.

Scaffold

Display the Opinion Sandwich Anchor Chart to support students in understanding what writing an opinion paragraph entails.

Divide the class into pairs. Provide copies of each text around the room for students to look through. Explain that they will now use the evidence they collected on the different natural features in Africa and Antarctica. Instruct students to Think-Pair-Share about the following questions as a verbal rehearsal for Focusing Question Task 2. Encourage students to approach the evidence organizers to help them answer.

- If you visited Africa, what natural feature would you like to see?
- If you visit Antarctica, what natural feature would you like to see?
- Which continent do you think has the most interesting natural features? Why?

Scaffold

Encourage students to discuss the evidence before forming an opinion. It is good practice to consider both sides of a topic before forming an opinion about the evidence collected. If needed, model a Think Aloud as you process the evidence from both continents and explain why you think one continent has the most interesting natural features.

Display Assessment 13B. Explain that they will write their opinion statement on the line provided at the top of page 1.

Students begin Focusing Question Task 2 by writing their opinion statement on Assessment 13B.

TEACHER NOTE   As students write their opinion sentence, encourage them to reference their classroom resources, such as the evidence organizers or the texts, to help them spell the name of the continent they are writing about.

Land 8 MIN.

ANSWER THE CONTENT FRAMING QUESTION

Display and read aloud the Content Framing Question. Reinforce that the author's point was that Africa has amazing people, places, and animals. Remind students that for Focusing Question Task 2 they have formed their opinion and will be supporting their point with evidence, just as the author did in Africa.

Divide the class into five small groups and distribute two or three copies of the text to each group. Give each group one index card with one of the following natural features written on it: desert, savanna, rainforest, river, or mountain. Support groups in reading the word on their card. Instruct groups to look through the photographs in the text and locate a picture that matches the label on their index card.

Use Equity Sticks to call on groups to share the picture they located in the text. Ask: "How did you know it was a [natural feature]?" Encourage students to use descriptive words to provide detail about their natural feature. If time allows, instruct one member from the group to approach the evidence organizer and match their label to a piece of evidence on the chart.

TEACHER NOTE	Engaging in authentic activities to work with the evidence on the evidence organizer fosters student independence with reading and understanding the information on the chart. Prepare these index cards prior to the lesson to save time.

Wrap 1 MIN.

ASSIGN HOMEWORK

Continue the class home-reading routine.

Analyze

Context and Alignment

Students use the words in "5 Reasons Why Animal Moms Are Awesome" to identify the reasons an author gives to support the point in the text (RI.K.8). Each student:

- Draws and labels two reasons the author gives to support the point "African elephant moms are awesome!"

Next Steps

If students have difficulty identifying the reasons the author gives to support the point, read the text slowly, pausing at each comma (or breaking the text into different sentences) to aid students in processing the information. The text is one long sentence and students may become overwhelmed by hearing all of the supporting reasons at once. Reread the text a few times to allow students to process the information differently each time. If students need more practice with this skill, consider using a different animal from the article and identifying the reasons as a class.

⬇ LESSON 13 DEEP DIVE: STYLE AND CONVENTIONS

Experiment with Expanding a Sentence

- **Time:** 15 min.

- **Text:** *Africa*, Rebecca Hirsch

- **Style and Conventions Learning Goal:** Create a complete sentence and expand it by adding a describing word. (L.K.1.f)

> **STYLE AND CONVENTIONS CRAFT QUESTION: Lesson 13**
> Experiment: *How does writing and expanding sentences by adding describing words work?*

Launch

Post and read the Style and Conventions Craft Question.

Ask: "How do authors make complete sentences?" Volunteers respond.

- *They tell who does what.*

Remind students that in Deep Dive Lesson 8, students learned one way authors expand sentences. Ask: "How can you add details to your sentences?"

- *By telling where or when something happens.*

- *By using prepositions.*

Explain that another way authors expand sentences is by adding describing words.

Display page 9 of *Africa* and read the first sentence. Point out that Rebecca Hirsch describes the number of people that live in Africa by writing "<u>Many</u> people."

Students are going to practice making and expanding sentences by adding describing words, as Rebecca Hirsch does in her books.

Learn

Display the cover of *Africa*. Instruct students to Think-Pair-Share, and ask: "What is happening in this photograph? Who is doing what?" Volunteers respond.

- *The child hides.*

- *The child carries.*

- *The child smiles.*

Record two student responses on the board to use for examples. Reinforce that students created complete sentences about the photograph.

Remind students they can expand their sentences by adding a describing word to tell more information about the photograph.

Ask: "How would you describe the child? What descriptive word could you add to give more detail about the child?" Volunteers respond.

- *The child is happy.*
- *The child is strong.*

Use a student response to model how to expand the first example sentence by describing the child. For example, "The happy child hides." Record the sentence on the board and underline the describing word *happy*.

Ask: "How would you describe the plant?" Volunteers respond.

- *The plant is big.*
- *The plant is green.*

Use a student response to model how to expand the second example sentence by describing the plant. For example, "The child carries a big plant." Record the sentence on the board and underline the describing word *big*.

Explain that students are going to work with a partner to practice making a complete sentence and expanding it by adding describing words.

Organize the class into pairs. Distribute a copy of *Africa* and a sticky note to each pair.

✔ Pairs choose a photograph in the text and write a caption for it on the sticky note. They tell "who, is doing what" to make a complete sentence and add a describing word to expand the sentence. Circulate to provide support as needed.

Use Equity Sticks to call on pairs to share their sentences with the class.

Land

Reorganize the class into a whole-group setting. Direct student attention to the Style and Conventions Craft Question. Ask: "How did you make complete sentences?" Volunteers respond.

- *By telling who did what.*

Ask: "How did you expand your sentences with describing words?" Volunteers respond.

- *By adding words that describe the who or their action in our sentence.*

Scaffold

If you have students who are still learning appropriate English syntax, consider pointing out the location of the describing words in the sentence. Ask: "Where did you put the describing word in your sentence?"

- *I put the describing word before the "who." (if students used adjectives)*
- *I put the describing word after the "did what." (if students used adverbs)*

■ FOCUSING QUESTION: LESSONS 9–15

What interesting natural features can people see in Africa and Antarctica?

1 2 3 4 5 6 7 8 **9 10 11 12 13 14 15** 16 17 18 19 20 21 22 23 24 25 26 27 28 29 30 31 32 33 34 35 36

Lesson 14

TEXTS

- "Penguin Song," *Preschool Education* (**http://witeng.link/0393**)

- *Africa*, Rebecca Hirsch

- *World Atlas*, Nick Crane; Illustrations, David Dean

- "5 Reasons Why Animal Moms Are Awesome," April Capochino Myers (**http://witeng.link/0406**)

Lesson 14: At a Glance

AGENDA

Welcome (5 min.)

Practice Fluency

Launch (5 min.)

Learn (60 min.)

Record Knowledge (15 min.)

Execute Focusing Question Task 2 (15 min.)

Compare Africa with World Atlas (15 min.)

Record Evidence for the EOM Task (15 min.)

Land (4 min.)

Answer the Content Framing Question

Wrap (1 min.)

Assign Homework

Vocabulary Deep Dive: Describing Africa with *–ful* (15 min.)

STANDARDS ADDRESSED

The full text of ELA Standards can be found in the Module Overview.

Reading

- RI.K.1, RI.K.9

Writing

- W.K.1, W.K.8, W.10*

Speaking and Listening

- SL.K.1, SL.K.2

Language

- ⬇ LK.4.b

MATERIALS

- Assessment 13B: Focusing Question Task 2

- Repeated Language Chart

- Handout 8A: Passport Journals

- Stamps or stickers (see lesson for details)

- Evidence Organizer for *Africa*

- Evidence Organizer for *Antarctica*

- Document camera (if available)

Learning Goals

Use information gathered from *Africa* and *Antarctica* to provide supporting reasons for an opinion statement. (RI.K.1, W.K.1, W.K.8)

✔ Continue Focusing Question Task 2.

Identify basic similarities in and differences between *Africa* and *World Atlas*. (RI.K.9)

✔ Identify one detail that appears in the map of southern Africa in *World Atlas* that does not appear in *Africa*.

⬇ Use the meaning of the word ending *–ful* as a clue to find the meaning of a new describing word. (L.K.4.b)

✔ Use the word ending *–ful* and a photograph to find the meaning of a new word.

In alignment with the CCSS, W.10 formally begins in Grade 3. However, K–2 students write routinely for a variety of time frames, tasks, purposes, and audiences. As a result, this lesson contains instruction related to W.10 in an effort to familiarize students with a range of writing.

✔ Checks for Understanding

Prepare

FOCUSING QUESTION: Lessons 9–15

What interesting natural features can people see in Africa and Antarctica?

CONTENT FRAMING QUESTION: Lesson 14

Know: *How does Africa build my knowledge of the continents?*

CRAFT QUESTION: Lesson 14

Execute: *How do I support my opinion statement in my Focusing Question Task?*

In this lesson students reflect on important learning from *Africa* and record it in individual Passport Journals. They use text evidence to write a supporting reason sentence for Focusing Question Task 2. In addition, students explore the *World Atlas* text and compare it with *Africa*. Finally, students come back to *Africa* to collect evidence about things to do for the EOM Task.

Welcome   5 MIN.

PRACTICE FLUENCY

Display the Repeated Language Chart with the last line of the song added. Read the line aloud. Students Echo Read.

Repeated Language
Song: "Penguin Song," Original author unknown ▪ I'm a little penguin ▪ In the sea. ▪ I can swim as fast as can be! ▪ When I catch a fish, just look at me. ▪ I'm as proud as I can be!

Ask: "What does *proud* mean? How do you think you would feel if you were able to catch a fish?" Volunteers respond. Prompt students to use the punctuation mark at the end of the sentence to help them think about their answer.

- *He isn't hungry anymore.*
- *He is happy that he caught a fish.*
- *I think he is excited.*

Confirm that *proud* means the penguin is happy with himself because he was able to catch a fish in the big sea!

Create a movement for the last line. For example, stand up tall with your chest out as if you were proud.

Reread the song aloud. Students Echo Read the song while incorporating the movements for each line.

Launch 5 MIN.

Hold up a copy of a Passport Journal in front of the class. Remind students that a passport is a type of book that keeps track of where a person has traveled. It is an important document that shows who you are and where you have been. You must show your passport when you enter and leave a new country.

Post and read aloud the Content Framing Question. Students Echo Read the question. Tell students that today they will think about their learning and add to their Passport Journals.

Instruct students to Think-Pair-Share, and ask: "What did you learn about Africa that surprised you?" Use Equity Sticks to call on a few students to share their answers.

Learn 60 MIN.

RECORD KNOWLEDGE 15 MIN.

Individuals

Remind students that thinking about the knowledge and skills they gain with each text is an important part of learning. Talking about new knowledge helps them remember what they learned, and makes it easier to use and build on that knowledge in the future.

Display a copy of *Africa*. Provide time for students to think about the important knowledge they learned while exploring the text. Instruct students to Mix and Mingle, and ask: "What important knowledge did you learn about Africa?" Encourage students to use the Evidence Organizer for *Africa* as a reference.

Instruct students to take out their Passport Journals and open to page 4 for Africa. Explain that students will draw and label an illustration to share the knowledge they gained from reading *Africa*.

Students draw and label an illustration to share one thing they learned about Africa in their Passport Journals. Make copies of the text available for students to reference as needed. After students complete their journal page, place a stamp or sticker on each section to mark their visit to the continent.

> #### Alternate Activity
>
> Depending on the needs of the class, students may write and illustrate sentences in their Passport Journals instead of drawing and labeling illustrations.

Use Equity Sticks to call on several students to share the sentences and drawings from their Passport Journals with the class.

EXECUTE FOCUSING QUESTION TASK 2 15 MIN.

Individuals

Tell students that the knowledge and skills they have gained over the past several weeks will help them answer the Focusing Question. Students Choral Read the Focusing Question.

Remind students that they will be writing an opinion paragraph to respond to the following prompt.

> Which continent do you think has the most interesting natural features?

Explain that in this lesson, students will write one reason sentence to support their opinion statement.

Scaffold

If students find the visual of the Opinion Sandwich Anchor Chart useful, reference the chart here to confirm that reason sentences support the opinion statement.

Reference the prompt as you instruct students to Think-Pair-Share, and ask: "Does this question have one right answer or could there be different answers? What makes you say that?" Call on several students to respond.

- *There could be different answers.*
- *People could have different ideas.*
- *Someone might think Africa has the most interesting features. Someone else might think Antarctica does.*
- *Maybe people have different opinions.*

Use responses to reinforce that the prompt is asking what students think, or their opinion, about the continents of Africa and Antarctica. Ask: "What role do the reasons sentences play? Why are they important, especially when people might have different opinions?" Volunteers respond.

Place the Evidence Organizer for *Africa* on one side of the room and the Evidence Organizer for *Antarctica* on the other.

Instruct students to take out the first page of Assessment 13B. Direct students to "fly" to the organizer showing the continent they think has the most interesting natural features.

Instruct students to Think-Pair-Share, and ask: "What reasons do you have to support your opinion? What interesting natural features can people see on [continent name]?" Encourage students to reference the pictures on the evidence organizers to help form their reason sentence.

Name:

Assessment 13B: Focusing Question Task 2

Directions: On the lines provided in box 1, write your opinion statement. Write your first supporting reason sentence and create an illustration in box 2. Write and illustrate your second supporting reason sentence in box 3. Write your opinion conclusion by completing the sentence frame in box 4.

Extension

Ask: "What type of words did we add to our evidence? How did we add detail to our evidence?" Volunteers respond.

- *We added the colors.*

- *We added what the places were like.*

- *We added descriptive words.*

Reinforce that adding adjectives, or descriptive words, provides more detail for the reader. Encourage students to use a descriptive word in their reason sentences to provide more information about the natural features.

TEACHER NOTE	Students are not required to use adjectives in their writing for this task. For students who are ready, encourage them to include the descriptive words on the evidence organizer to provide more detail and expand their sentences.

Students verbally practice their sentences with a partner.

Display and read aloud the Craft Question: *How do I support my opinion statement in my Focusing Question Task?*

Explain that now students will write their first reason sentence for the Focusing Question Task.

✔ Students write one reason sentence and include one drawing to complete page 1 of Assessment 13B. Encourage students as they write their sentence to insert a descriptive word about the natural features to add more detail to their sentence.

COMPARE *AFRICA* WITH *WORLD ATLAS* 15 MIN.

Small Groups

Display the front cover of *World Atlas* and read the title, author, and illustrator aloud. Ask: "What is an <u>atlas</u>? How did we use this *World Atlas* to learn more about Europe?" Volunteers respond.

Reinforce that an atlas is a book of maps. This atlas contains maps of the different continents all over the world. Confirm that previously students used the *World Atlas* to learn more about Europe. Explain that in this lesson, they will use the maps of Africa to learn more about Africa.

Display pages 34–37 in *World Atlas*, reading the heading at the top of each page spread and turning slowly back and forth between the two maps. Ask: "Why do you think the maps of Africa are on two different pages and what does that tell us about the continent?" Volunteers respond.

- *It doesn't fit on one page.*

- *Africa is really big.*

Confirm that Africa is spread out onto two pages because the continent is too big and has too much information to put on just one page.

Groups open the atlas to the map of northern Africa on page 34. Allow students to observe the map for thirty seconds. Ask: "What do you notice about this map?" Students take turns sharing their observations in their small groups. Call on several students to share their response with the whole class.

Distribute copies of *Africa* to small groups and prompt students to locate the section "Wild Places."

Point to the desert at the top of part of the map of northern Africa in *World Atlas*, but do not identify what natural feature this is. Ask: "What wild place in *Africa* does this part of the map remind you of? What natural feature might the orange on the map show us?" Instruct groups to point to a picture in *Africa* that they think is similar. Call on a volunteer to share their picture with the class. Confirm that when students see orange on the map this shows them where the desert is located.

Point to the light green area at the bottom of the map of northern Africa. Ask: "What wild place does this part of the map remind you of? What natural feature has a few trees as well as grassy parts?" Instruct groups to point to a picture in the "Wild Places" section in *Africa* that they think is similar. Call on a volunteer to share their picture with the class. Confirm that when students see light green on the map this shows them where the savanna is located.

Turn to the map of southern Africa. Point to the large area of trees at the top of the map of southern Africa. Ask: "What wild place does this part of the map remind you of? What makes you think that?" Instruct groups to point to a picture in the "Wild Places" section in *Africa* that they think is similar. Call on a volunteer to share their picture with the class. Confirm that when students see dark green on the map this shows them where the rainforest is located.

Extension

Ask: "What do you think the blue lines on the map of north Africa are? What natural feature could those be?" Volunteers respond.

Instruct students to Think-Pair-Share, and ask: "How do the colors help us read this map?" Use Equity Sticks to call on students to answer.

- *We know where the natural features are.*
- *We can see which is the desert and the rainforest.*
- *If we are looking for the desert we can just look for the color.*

Confirm that the colors in this map play an important role in communicating information about the natural features in Africa. Remind students that this map also contains much more information.

Extension

Turn back to the map of northern Africa in *World Atlas*. Direct groups to think about the information in *Africa*, and ask: "Can you find an illustration on the northern Africa map that shows one of the same details you read about in *Africa*?" Encourage groups to use their copies of *Africa* as a guide. Use Equity Sticks to call on students to share the matching detail they found with the whole class.

Explain that the *World Atlas* not only shows information they learned about in *Africa*, it also shows additional information. Reinforce that this is why it is important to look at multiple texts when researching a topic; you might learn new information!

Model locating a difference on the map and then demonstrating that it cannot be found in *Africa*. Instruct groups to discuss: "What details can you find on the northern Africa map in *World Atlas* that cannot be found in *Africa*?" Use Equity Sticks to call on three students to share a new detail found only in *World Atlas*.

Scaffold

Students have not yet worked with locating difference. Ask supporting question such as "Is there an animal in *World Atlas* that you did not see in *Africa*? Is there a natural feature or place that you did not see in *Africa*?" If needed, locate new details on the map of north Africa as a class.

Explain that now students will practice finding things that are different in the southern Africa map of Africa. Prompt groups to turn to the map of southern Africa in *World Atlas*. Instruct groups to discuss the following question: "What information do you see on this map that you did not learn about in *Africa*?"

✔ Groups identify a detail that appears on the map of southern Africa in *World Atlas* but not in *Africa*. Students point to the new detail on the map of southern Africa. Use Equity Sticks to call on groups to share the new detail they found with the whole class.

Extension

If time allows, encourage students to locate more details that only appear in the *World Atlas* text.

RECORD EVIDENCE FOR THE EOM TASK 15 MIN.

Whole Group

Post and read the Essential Question. Students Echo Read the question. Explain that understanding different aspects of the continents will help them expand their knowledge and fascination with the world.

Briefly introduce the EOM Task. Explain that after learning about all seven continents, students will be making their own travel brochures to explain why they think someone should visit a continent. Students will choose which continent they would most like to visit and explain why in their brochure. To be able to do this, they need to learn more about the different continents and be able to talk about their different features.

Ask: "Do you like learning new things about the continents? Why?" Volunteers respond. Reinforce that new learning brings new excitement, new questions, and invites them on even more adventures! When they reach their EOM Task, they will want to provide information that will get others excited about the world, too.

Reference the Evidence Organizers for *Europe* and *Asia*, and ask: "What type of information did we collect from *Europe* and *Asia*?" Volunteers respond.

Confirm that they collected evidence on the different things to do in Europe and Asia. Explain that as they continue to build their knowledge of the continents, they will add to their evidence organizers by collecting evidence for the EOM Task.

Display the Evidence Organizer for *Africa* in front of the class. Reveal the title of the first column, "Things to Do." Read this title aloud. Explain that they will now go back through the text to find evidence about different things to do in Africa.

Distribute copies of the text to pairs. Prompt pairs to follow along in their copies of the text as you read. Instruct students to make a Nonverbal Signal, such as pounding their chest lightly like a gorilla, when they hear an example of a thing to do in Africa.

Read the sections "People of Africa" and "Water and Land" in *Africa* aloud. Students make a Nonverbal Signal when they hear evidence in the text. Use Equity Sticks to call on students who signal to share their evidence.

After each response, students consider whether or not that is a piece of evidence. They indicate a level of agreement by holding up anywhere from one to five fingers, with one finger showing the lowest level of agreement and five fingers showing the strongest level of agreement.

Use votes to choose one or two refined responses to record in the "Things to Do" column on the Evidence Organizer for *Africa*.

SAMPLE EVIDENCE ORGANIZER FOR *AFRICA*

Evidence Organizer for *Africa*		
Things to Do	**Natural Features**	**Animals**
▪ *play soccer on the beach* ▪ *hike a tall mountain*	▪ **hot and dry** *deserts* ▪ **grassy** *savannas* ▪ **green** *rainforests* ▪ **long** *Nile River* ▪ **tall** *mountains*	

Land <small>4 MIN.</small>

ANSWER THE CONTENT FRAMING QUESTION

Post and read the Content Framing Question. Ask: "What is a fascinating piece of information that you learned about Africa?" Volunteers respond.

Use a document camera or projector to display the following article in front of the class: "5 Reasons Why Animal Moms Are Awesome" (**http://witeng.link/0406**).

Reread the "African Elephant" section aloud. Instruct students to Think-Pair-Share, and ask: "How does this text build your knowledge of Africa? Did this article teach you something you did not read about in our texts?"

Wrap 1 MIN.

ASSIGN HOMEWORK

Continue the class home-reading routine.

Analyze

Context and Alignment

Students use the illustrations on the map of southern Africa in *World Atlas* and the photographs in *Africa* to locate information presented in only one text (RI.K.9). Each student:

- Identifies one piece of information that appears in only *World Atlas*.

Next Steps

If students struggle with identifying different information, consider focusing on specific images in each text. Point to images that appear in both texts and ask students to locate the matching images. For details that only appear in *World Atlas*, point to the image and ask students to locate a similar image in *Africa*. Reinforce that there is no matching image and therefore this is an example of a different piece of information.

↓ LESSON 14 DEEP DIVE: VOCABULARY

Describing Africa with *-ful*

- **Time:** 15 min.

- **Text:** *Africa*, Rebecca Hirsch

- **Vocabulary Learning Goal:** Use the meaning of the word ending *–ful* as a clue to find the meaning of a new describing word. (L.K.4.b)

TEACHER NOTE	Rebecca Hirsch's books contain vivid illustrations that are great for helping students explore adjectives, or describing words. As students are continuing to work with affixes in this module, the illustrations in *Africa* and *Antarctica* provide an opportunity to use *–ful* and *–less* to describe the continents. As the text in the books is simple, it is helpful to include describing words for the purpose of this lesson. In order to maximize instructional time, it would be helpful to prepare the copies of *Africa* ahead of time by labeling the following pages with sticky notes with these describing words:
	Cover: *wonderful*
	Page 4: *colorful*
	Page 12: *playful*
	Page 20: *harmful*
	Page 22: *beautiful*
	Page 26: *skillful*

Launch

Remind students that, as in previous modules, they can use word parts as a clue to help them figure out the meaning of a new word. Instruct students to Think-Pair-Share, and ask: "What other strategies can you use to find the meaning of a new word?" Volunteers respond.

- *We can look at pictures for clues.*
- *We can use the words around the word to figure it out.*

Explain that students are going to look at illustrations in *Africa*, as well as the word ending *–ful*, to help them find the meaning of new describing words.

Learn

Remind students that they have previously learned the meaning of the ending *–ful*. Ask: "What does the ending *–ful* mean?" Volunteers respond. Use student responses to confirm that *–ful* means "full of." Record the word ending and definition on the board and underline both.

Direct student attention to the illustration on the cover and point out that *wonder* is "a feeling of amazement." Adding *–ful* to the end of *wonder* makes a new describing word—*wonderful*. Instruct students to Think-Pair-Share, and say: "Use these clues to figure out the meaning of the word *wonderful*." Volunteers respond.

- *The picture looks amazing, so it could mean that!*
- *It could mean Africa is full of amazing things.*

Use student responses to reinforce that *wonderful* means "full of amazement." Record *wonderful* and the definition underneath *–ful* on the board.

Organize the class into five small groups. Distribute a text to each group. As you hand the text to the group, present the page and Echo Read the describing word written on the sticky note to ensure students know the word they are working with.

✔ Explain that students will work together to find the meaning of the describing word on the sticky note. Encourage students to use the illustration and the meaning of *–ful* to figure out the meaning of their describing word. Use Equity Sticks to call on each group to share their findings.

Record each word and its meaning on the board. Consider adding a drawing next to each meaning to support understanding.

Land

Reorganize the class into a whole-group setting. Display the given pages and read the following sentences about *Africa*. Students complete each sentence by responding chorally with one of the new describing words. After each sentence, ask students to describe the meaning of the sentence in their own words.

Page 20: **If bothered, gorillas can be _____ to others.**

Page 12: **The _____ children enjoyed soccer on the beach.**

Page 26: **The climbers must be _____ to get to the top of the mountain.**

■ FOCUSING QUESTION: LESSONS 9–15

What interesting natural features can people see in Africa and Antarctica?

1 | 2 | 3 | 4 | 5 | 6 | 7 | 8 | **9** | **10** | **11** | **12** | **13** | **14** | **15** | 16 | 17 | 18 | 19 | 20 | 21 | 22 | 23 | 24 | 25 | 26 | 27 | 28 | 29 | 30 | 31 | 32 | 33 | 34 | 35 | 36

Lesson 15

TEXTS

- "Penguin Song," *Preschool Education* (**http://witeng.link/0393**)
- *Africa*, Rebecca Hirsch
- *Antarctica*, Rebecca Hirsch

Lesson 15: At a Glance

AGENDA

Welcome (7 min.)

Perform Fluency

Launch (5 min.)

Learn (60 min.)

Record Knowledge (20 min.)

Execute Focusing Question Task 2 (15 min.)

Participate in a Socratic Seminar (15 min.)

Record Evidence for the EOM Task (10 min.)

Land (2 min.)

Answer the Content Framing Question

Wrap (1 min.)

Assign Homework

Vocabulary Deep Dive: Describing Antarctica with *-less* (15 min.)

STANDARDS ADDRESSED

The full text of ELA Standards can be found in the Module Overview.

Reading

- RI.K.1

Writing

- W.K.1, W.K.8

Speaking and Listening

- SL.K.1, SL.K.2, SL.K.6

Language

- ⬇ L.K.4.b

MATERIALS

- Assessment 13B: Focusing Question Task 2

- Repeated Language Chart

- Passport Journal (introduced in Lesson 8)

- Stamps or stickers (see lesson for details)

- Knowledge Journal

- Evidence Organizer for *Antarctica*

- Evidence Organizer for *Africa*

- Speaking and Listening Anchor Chart

- Talking chips

- Speaking and Listening Rubric

- Sticky notes

Learning Goals

Use information gathered from *Africa* and *Antarctica* to provide supporting reasons for an opinion statement. (RI.K.1, W.K.1, W.K.8)

✔ Complete Focusing Question Task 2.

Confirm understanding of a text read aloud by answering questions during a group discussion. (RI.K.1, SL.K.1, SL.K.2, SL.K.6)

✔ Participate in a Socratic Seminar to discuss learning gained from *Antarctica*.

⬇ Use the meaning of the word ending *-less* as a clue to figure out the meaning of an unknown describing word. (L.K.4.b)

✔ Use the word ending *-less* and a photograph to figure out the meaning of a new word.

✔ Checks for Understanding

Prepare

FOCUSING QUESTION: Lessons 9–15

What interesting natural features can people see in Africa and Antarctica?

CONTENT FRAMING QUESTION: Lesson 15

Know: *How does Antarctica build my knowledge of the continents?*

CRAFT QUESTIONS: Lesson 15

Execute: *How do I support my opinion statement in my Focusing Question Task?*
Execute: *How can I show my understanding in a Socratic Seminar?*

In this lesson students reflect on important learning from *Antarctica* and record it in Passport Journals. They complete Focusing Question Task 2 by writing a second supporting reason sentence and completing the conclusion frame. Students participate in a Socratic Seminar to apply new speaking and listening skills. Finally, students collect evidence about things to do in Antarctica for the EOM Task.

Welcome 7 MIN.

PERFORM FLUENCY

Display the Repeated Language Chart. Explain that students will conclude work with this song by performing for each other.

The class conducts a rehearsal by Choral Reading the Repeated Language Chart and incorporating the agreed-upon movements.

Divide the class into two groups. Each group takes a turn performing the poem and movements for their peers.

Extension

This poem can be sung to the tune of "I'm a Little Teapot." If students are comfortable with the poem, consider having students perform the poem to this tune.

Launch <small>5 MIN.</small>

Use Equity Sticks to select several students to share their Passport Journal entries from the previous lesson.

Remind students that talking and writing about new knowledge and skills help them own their learning and share their learning with others.

Display and read aloud the Content Framing Question. Students Echo Read the question. Explain that students will reflect on their learning by completing a Passport Journal entry for Antarctica.

Learn <small>60 MIN.</small>

RECORD KNOWLEDGE <small>20 MIN.</small>

Individuals

Display a copy of *Antarctica*. Provide time for students to think about the important knowledge they learned while exploring the text. Instruct students to Mix and Mingle, and ask: "What important knowledge did you learn about Antarctica?" Encourage students to use the Evidence Organizer for *Antarctica* as a reference.

Instruct students to take out their Passport Journals and open to page 5 for Antarctica. Explain that students draw and label an illustration to share the knowledge they gained from reading *Antarctica*.

Students draw and label an illustration to share one thing they learned about Antarctica in their Passport Journals. Make copies of the text available for students to reference as needed. After students complete their journal page, place a stamp or sticker on each section to mark their visit to the continent.

> **Alternate Activity**
>
> Depending on the needs of the class, students may write and illustrate sentences in their Passport Journals instead of drawing and labeling illustrations.

Display the class Knowledge Journal. Point to the left column of the journal and explain that students have already completed this part by writing important learning in their Passport Journals.

Tell students that they will add new items to the "What I Can Do" column by thinking about the new skills they learned as readers and writers.

Instruct students to Think-Pair-Share, and ask: "What did you learn to do as a reader? What did you learn to do as a writer?"

Scaffold

Ask: "What did you learn about points in a text? What did you learn about opinion writing?"

Use Equity Sticks to call on pairs to share responses. After each response, students consider whether or not the piece of learning is something important that they want to remember and include in the Knowledge Journal. They indicate a level of agreement by holding up anywhere from one to five fingers, with one finger showing the lowest level of agreement and five fingers showing the strongest level of agreement.

Use votes to choose one or two refined responses to record in the Knowledge Journal.

SAMPLE KNOWLEDGE JOURNAL

What I Know	What I Can Do
	• I can state an opinion.
	• I can support my opinion.
	• I can find reasons to support a point.

TEACHER NOTE

Students record important learning individually in their Passport Journals instead of on the "What I Know" section of the class Knowledge Journal. If time permits, consider selecting several strong responses from the individual journals to add to the class journal.

Extension

Remind students that another tool that helps them keep track of learning is the Word Wall. Revisit the words added to the Word Wall since the start of the module. Students Echo Read the words. Choose three to five words to highlight based on your knowledge of students' vocabulary and call on volunteers to use the words in context.

EXECUTE FOCUSING QUESTION TASK 2 15 MIN.

Individuals

Explain that working on the Focusing Question Task is another way students can think about what they learned from *Antarctica* and *Africa*.

Remind students that they are writing an opinion paragraph to answer the Focusing Question Task prompt.

> Which continent do you think has the most interesting natural features?

Distribute the completed page 1 of Assessment 13B. Instruct students to Think-Pair-Share, and ask: "Think about the writing you did yesterday for Focusing Question Task 2. How did you support the opinion statement?" Use Equity Sticks to call on students to respond.

- ▧ *I said why I picked Antarctica.*
- ▧ *I wrote a reason.*
- ▧ *I wrote about the desert in Africa.*

Name:

Assessment 13B: Focusing Question Task 2

Directions: On the lines provided in box 1, write your opinion statement. Write your first supporting reason sentence and create an illustration in box 2. Write and illustrate your second supporting reason sentence in box 3. Write your opinion conclusion by completing the sentence frame in box 4.

Extension

Ask: "How did you include more detail in your reason sentences?" Volunteers respond.

- ▪ *I added words like* green.
- ▪ *I added words to describe it.*
- ▪ *I added descriptive words.*

Confirm that using descriptive words provides a reader with more detail. If needed, reread the descriptive words on the evidence organizers to remind students. Encourage students to use descriptive words to expand their sentences.

Explain that students will complete their Focusing Question Task today by writing and illustrating one more reason sentence to support their opinion statement. They will also complete the conclusion sentence by retelling their opinion.

Divide the class into pairs. Partners take turns reading their opinion statement and first reason sentence to each other and sharing their illustrations from page 1 of Assessment 13B.

Display the Evidence Organizers for *Africa* and *Antarctica* and remind students to use them as a reference for creating their next reason sentence. Instruct students to Think-Pair-Share, and ask: "Which reason will you write about next to support your opinion? What other interesting natural feature can people see on [continent name]?"

> **Scaffold**
>
> If needed, review the evidence on each chart to support student understanding.

Remind students to use a different piece of evidence than they wrote about in the previous lesson. Students share another supporting reason with their partner and verbally rehearse the sentence they will write.

✔ Distribute page 2 of Assessment 13B. Students complete Focusing Question Task 2 by writing their second reason sentence to support the opinion statement. Encourage students as they write their sentence to insert a descriptive word about the natural features to add more detail to their sentence.

Students complete the conclusion sentence for their opinion writing piece by writing the name of their chosen continent in the provided sentence frame: **I like the natural features in _____.**

PARTICIPATE IN A SOCRATIC SEMINAR 15 MIN.

Small Groups

Ask: "Which continents have we explored so far?" Volunteers respond.

Confirm that students have explored Europe, Asia, Africa, and Antarctica. Explain that they are about halfway through their world adventure!

Tell students they will reflect on their learning about Antarctica through a Socratic Seminar.

Display and read aloud the second Craft Question: *How can I show my understanding in a Socratic Seminar?*

Ask: "What are some ways you can show that you understand something?" Use Equity Sticks to call on students to respond.

- *I can explain it.*
- *I can give an example.*
- *I can talk about an example.*

Use responses to explain that students will use examples from the text to show their understanding during today's Socratic Seminar.

Display the Speaking and Listening Anchor Chart and highlight the speaking skill students will focus on during the Socratic Seminar. Give an example.

As needed, model how to use talking chips to aid discussion:

- Sit in a semicircle with several volunteers, and model how to take turns speaking and listening.
- Each person has one talking chip in front of them.
- When a student is ready to share, they pick up a chip.
- After sharing, the student places the chip in the middle of the circle.
- Only one person can be holding a chip at a time.
- All students use their chips before the process starts again.

| TEACHER NOTE | Encourage students to use words from the Word Wall in their discussions. |

Write the Socratic Seminar opening question on the board: Imagine you are visiting Antarctica. Which natural feature would you explore? Why?

Students Echo Read the question.

✔ Groups of four to six form circles around the room. Groups use talking chips to have conversations about the text and continent. Place one copy of *Antarctica* in the center of each circle to support students with naming an example. Students point to their example in the text as they describe it.

Circulate and record anecdotal notes using the Speaking and Listening Rubric as a guide (see Appendix C).

Midway through the seminar, stop to call attention to the next discussion question: What would you pack in your suitcase to take on your trip to Antarctica? Why?

Small groups use talking chips to discuss the question.

Reread the speaking goal from the Speaking and Listening Anchor Chart. Students use Nonverbal Signals (thumbs-up, thumbs-sideways, thumbs-down) to self-assess the conversations they had. Use anecdotal notes to share notable discussions from the small groups.

RECORD EVIDENCE FOR THE EOM TASK 10 MIN.

Whole Group

Remind students that as they learn about the continents they can think about different aspects of each continent that make it fascinating and unique.

Display the Evidence Organizer for *Antarctica*. Explain that students have already recorded interesting natural features in Antarctica and will now go back to look at a different aspect of the continent: things to do.

Reveal the title of the first column of the Evidence Organizer for *Antarctica*, "Things to Do." Read this title aloud. Explain that they will now go back through the text to find evidence on the different things to do in Antarctica.

Read the sections "People of Antarctica" and "Learning from Antarctica" in *Antarctica* aloud. Instruct students to make a Nonverbal Signal, such as giving a thumbs-up, when they hear an example of a thing to do in Antarctica. Use Equity Sticks to call on students who signal to share their evidence.

After each response, students consider whether or not that is a piece of evidence. They indicate a level of agreement by holding up anywhere from one to five fingers, with one finger showing the lowest level of agreement and five fingers showing the strongest level of agreement.

Use votes to choose several refined responses to record in the "Things to Do" column on the Evidence Organizer for *Antarctica*.

SAMPLE EVIDENCE ORGANIZER FOR *ANTARCTICA*

Evidence Organizer for *Antarctica*		
Things to Do	**Natural Features**	**Animals**
▪ ski ▪ watch animals ▪ study the ice and animals	▪ **icy** ocean ▪ **tall, icy, snowy** mountains ▪ **giant, thick** icebergs	

Explain that students will continue to add more information to this chart as they go through the module. Then students will share their learning with others by creating a travel brochure for their EOM Task.

Land 2 MIN.

ANSWER THE CONTENT FRAMING QUESTION

Congratulate students on the learning and exploration they have done with *Africa* and *Antarctica*. Instruct students to Mix and Mingle and ask, "We haven't yet traveled to South America, North America, or Australia. Which continent do you hope to explore next? Why?"

Wrap 1 MIN.

ASSIGN HOMEWORK

Continue the class home-reading routine.

Analyze

Context and Alignment

Students use evidence from *Africa* or *Antarctica* to write an opinion paragraph about the continent they believe has the most interesting natural features (RI.K.1, W.K.1, W.K.8). Each student:

- Writes an opinion statement, choosing between Africa and Antarctica.

- Writes and illustrates two sentences to support their opinion with details from the text.

- Creates a conclusion sentence by naming their chosen continent in a sentence frame.

Next Steps

If students have difficulty supporting their opinion, consider the root of the problem. Are they struggling with the concept of supporting an opinion with reasons? Provide verbal practice with the sentence frame: **I think** _____ **because** _____ and emphasize the relationship between stating what you think and why you think it. Are they struggling to write supporting sentences? Provide additional practice with the evidence organizer. Ask: "Why does [continent] have the most interesting natural features? Which natural feature is interesting to you?" Direct students to point to an interesting natural feature listed on the evidence organizer. Support students with verbally stating their supporting reason, then with transferring that thinking into writing.

Group students with similar needs and plan small group support for these skills to set students up for success with their next Focusing Question Task.

⬇ LESSON 15 DEEP DIVE: VOCABULARY

Describing Antarctica with -*less*

- **Time:** 15 min.

- **Text:** *Antarctica*, Rebecca Hirsch

- **Vocabulary Learning Goal:** Use the meaning of the word ending –*less* as a clue to figure out the meaning of an unknown describing word. (L.K.4.b)

TEACHER NOTE

Rebecca Hirsch's books contain vivid illustrations that are great for helping students explore adjectives, or describing words. As students are continuing to work with affixes in this module, the illustrations in *Africa* and *Antarctica* provide an opportunity to use –*ful* and –*less* to describe the continents. As the text in the books is simple, it is helpful to include describing words for the purpose of this lesson. To maximize instructional time, it would be helpful to prepare the copies of *Antarctica* ahead of time by labeling the following pages with sticky notes with these describing words:

- Cover: *grassless*

- Page 10: *lifeless*

- Page 12: *fearless*

- Page 18: *helpless*

- Page 20: *colorless*

- Page 24: *endless*

Launch

Remind students that in the previous Deep Dive they used illustrations and the ending –*ful* as a clue to help them figure out the meaning of a new word. Reinforce that –*ful* means "full of."

Explain that students are going to use a different word ending as a clue to find the meaning of new words describing *Antarctica*. Write –*less* on the board and have students Echo Read it. Point out that –*less* is the opposite of –*ful*. Ask: "What do you think the ending –*less* means?" Volunteers respond.

- It could mean "not full of."

- It might mean "having less of something."

- It could mean "to not have something."

Use student responses to identify the meaning of the word ending –*less* as "not having."

Learn

Display the cover of *Antarctica*. Read the sticky note and explain that *grassless* is an example of a word ending with –*less*, which means "not having." Direct student attention to the picture on the cover and ask: "What does Antarctica NOT have?" Volunteers respond.

- *Grass!*

Use student responses to reinforce that *grassless* means "not having grass."

Explain that students are going to look at the illustrations and use the word ending –*less* as clues to figure out the meaning of new describing words.

Organize the class into five small groups. Distribute a text to each group. As you hand the text to the group, present the page and Echo Read the describing word written on the sticky note to ensure students know the word they are working with.

✔ Explain that students will work together to find the meaning of the describing word on the sticky note. Encourage students to use the illustration and the meaning of –*less* to figure out the meaning of their describing word. Circulate to provide prompts as needed and to ensure understanding.

Use Equity Sticks to call on each group to share their findings. Record each word and its meaning on the board. Consider adding a drawing next to each meaning to support understanding.

Land

Reorganize the class into a whole-group setting. Display the given pages and read the following sentence frames about *Antarctica*. Students complete each sentence by responding chorally with one of the new describing words. After each sentence, ask students to describe the sentences in their own words.

Page 12: **Felicity Aston was _____ to ski across Antarctica.**

Page 20: **Antarctica is _____ because it is covered with white snow.**

Page 24: **Antarctica is an _____ landscape of ice.**

■ FOCUSING QUESTION: LESSONS 16–21

How can a story transport you to a different place?

Lesson 16

TEXTS

- *Why Mosquitoes Buzz in People's Ears: A West African Tale*, Verna Aardema; Illustrations, Leo and Diane Dillon

- *Carta Marina*, Olaus Magnus, (**http://witeng.link/0409**)

Lesson 16: At a Glance

AGENDA

Welcome (7 min.)

Explore the Focusing Question

Launch (3 min.)

Learn (62 min.)

Share Observations and Questions about Why Mosquitoes Buzz in People's Ears *(25 min.)*

Answer Questions about Unknown Words (16 min.)

Examine the Importance of Sharing Writing (8 min.)

Share Observations and Questions about Carta Marina *(13 min.)*

Land (2 min.)

Answer the Content Framing Question

Wrap (1 min.)

Assign Homework

Vocabulary Deep Dive: Multiple-Meaning Words: *Bear* **and** *lumber* **(15 min.)**

STANDARDS ADDRESSED

The full text of ELA Standards can be found in the Module Overview.

Reading

- RL.K.1, RL.K.4

Writing

- W.10*

Speaking and Listening

- SL.K.1.a, SL.K.2

Language

- L.K.1.d, L.K.5.d
- ⬇ L.K.4.a

MATERIALS

- Question Grab Bag (one for the class)
- Wonder Chart for *Why Mosquitoes Buzz in People's Ears*
- Question Cubes
- World map
- Compass rose

Learning Goals

Use familiar words in *Why Mosquitoes Buzz in People's Ears* to determine the meaning of unknown words. (RL.K.4, L.K.5.d)

✔ Think-Pair-Share to define *burrow*.

Use a variety of question words to ask questions about *Carta Marina*. (RL.K.1, L.K.1.d)

✔ Generate questions using Question Cubes.

⬇ Apply both meanings of the words *bear* and *lumber*. (L.K.4.a)

✔ Mix and Mingle, sharing a sentence that uses each word correctly.

In alignment with the CCSS, W.10 formally begins in Grade 3. However, K–2 students write routinely for a variety of time frames, tasks, purposes, and audiences. As a result, this lesson contains instruction related to W.10 in an effort to familiarize students with a range of writing.

✔ Checks for Understanding

Prepare

FOCUSING QUESTION: Lessons 16–21

How can a story transport you to a different place?

CONTENT FRAMING QUESTION: Lesson 16

Wonder: *What do I notice and wonder about* Why Mosquitoes Buzz in People's Ears?

CRAFT QUESTION: Lesson 16

Examine: *Why is it important to share your writing?*

In this lesson, students step back from their study of informational texts to begin exploring a West African folktale, *Why Mosquitoes Buzz in People's Ears*. Students make observations about and generate questions for the text. They learn to use familiar words in the text as clues to define unknown words, adding to their understanding of the text. In addition, students examine the importance of sharing their writing as they prepare to respond to questions and suggestions from their peers. Finally, students begin their study of *Carta Marina* by sharing observations and questions.

Welcome 7 MIN.

EXPLORE THE FOCUSING QUESTION

Display and read aloud the Focusing Question. Students Echo Read the question. Ask: "What does it mean to *transport*? Have you ever heard this word before?" Volunteers respond.

Define *transporting* as "carrying someone or something from one place to another." When you transport something, you carry something from one place to another. If needed, provide an example by moving something in the classroom from one place to another.

Ask students to close their eyes. Describe a scene very different from the classroom. For example,

Pretend you are somewhere very warm and sunny. You hear the waves crashing all around you; you hear a bird chirping; and you feel a warm breeze on your skin.

Ask: "How did that make you feel? What did you imagine?" Volunteers respond.

Ask: "How did the words make you feel like you were really there?" Volunteers respond.

243

Explain that another way to think of the word *transport* is to feel as if you traveled from one place to another. Ask: "When you read a story, are you really standing next to the characters and watching the story?" Reinforce that the words and pictures in a story <u>transport</u> readers in their minds, to help them feel as if they are part of the story.

Ask: "What part of the story tells us where the story is taking place?" Volunteers respond.

- *The setting.*

Post the world map in front of the class. Explain to students that the story they are going to read over the next few lessons takes place in West Africa. Call on a volunteer to approach the map and locate Africa.

Reference the compass rose and point to the W to indicate which direction is west. Explain that West Africa is not a country in Africa, but refers to the western side of the continent where there are a lot of small countries close together. West Africa is the setting of this story.

Explain that over the next few lessons they will explore how the words and pictures in a story can help readers imagine they are in a different place.

Launch 3 MIN.

Post and read aloud the Content Framing Question.

Display the front cover of *Why Mosquitoes Buzz in People's Ears*, and read the title, author's name, and illustrators' names aloud. Ask: "What do you notice about the title of this text? What type of word does the title start with?" Volunteers respond.

Ask: "How do we know if a sentence is a question?" Volunteers respond.

- *It has a question word at the front.*
- *It has a question mark.*

Confirm that for a sentence to be a question, it must end in a question mark. Ask: "Is there a question mark at the end of the title?" Volunteer responds.

Reinforce that this title is not asking a question, but instead giving an answer. Explain that in this lesson they will share what they notice and wonder about the text to learn more about the story.

Learn 62 MIN.

SHARE OBSERVATIONS AND QUESTIONS ABOUT *WHY MOSQUITOES BUZZ IN PEOPLE'S EARS* 25 MIN.

Whole Group

Display the front cover of *Why Mosquitoes Buzz in People's Ears,* and reread the title aloud. Ask: "What is a mosquito? Have you ever had one buzzing around your ear? How did it make you feel?" Volunteers respond.

Explain that now they will listen to the text read aloud to share what they notice and wonder about the text. Prompt students to listen to the words that they hear and use the pictures to guide their understanding.

💬 Read the book aloud with minimal interruptions. Students sit in "listening position," focusing their eyes and ears ahead as you read.

TEACHER NOTE	Because there is only one copy of the text, consider having students sit together on the ground or in a meeting area to get a better view of the illustrations.

Extension

For increased student involvement during the Read Aloud, invite students to echo back the repeated sounds as they are read in the story.

Instruct students to Mix and Mingle, and ask: "What did you notice about the text?" Students use the sentence frame, **I notice** _____ and share their observations with at least two peers. Use Equity Sticks to call on students to share.

Prompt students to come back together. Ask: "What do good readers do after thinking about things they notice in the text?" Volunteers respond. Confirm that good readers ask themselves good questions to help think deeply about the text. Explain that now they will use a Question Grab Bag as a class to think of questions about the text.

Use Equity Sticks to call on four to six students to approach the Question Grab Bag. Students pull out a question word and generate a question about the text using that word.

Post a blank Wonder Chart for *Why Mosquitoes Buzz in People's Ears.* Add students' questions.

SAMPLE WONDER CHART FOR *WHY MOSQUITOES BUZZ IN PEOPLE'S EARS*

Wonders for *Why Mosquitoes Buzz in People's Ears*		
Questions **?**	Answers in Progress ⟷	Complete Answers ✓
▪ *Why didn't the iguana believe the mosquito?* ▪ *How did the monkey hurt the owl?* ▪ *What wakes up the sun?* ▪ *Who are the other animals?*		

Working with one question at a time, have students Echo Read the question and then Think-Pair-Share about details they remember from the text. Pairs use the following Nonverbal Signals to indicate whether they are able to answer the question:

- Thumbs-up: we remember the answer from the text.

- Thumbs-sideways: we remember part of the answer from the text.

- Thumbs-down: we don't remember the answer.

Call on pairs to share their thinking. Return to the text to confirm and clarify students' thinking. Move sticky notes along the progression to indicate the extent to which each question has been answered.

ANSWER QUESTIONS ABOUT UNKNOWN WORDS 16 MIN.

Whole Group

Remind students that when good readers read a text, they pay attention to unfamiliar or new words. They notice when they read a word that they do not know, and try to figure out what the unknown word means to better understand the text. This helps them dive deeper into a text because they are no longer confused by words they don't know.

Explain that students will practice thinking about the words in *Why Mosquitoes Buzz in People's Ears* to help them better understand the text they are reading. Tell students that they will listen to part of the text read aloud and identify words that they do not know the meaning of by making a Nonverbal Signal. Demonstrate a Nonverbal Signal, such as raising one finger, that students should use to indicate unknown words.

Read the third sentence on page 4 aloud. Students use the Nonverbal Signal to indicate unknown words they hear in the text. Possible unfamiliar words include *lumbered*, *bobbing*, and *badamin*.

Define *lumbered* as "moving slowly with heavy steps."

Ask: "What do you think *badamin* means? Have you ever heard this word before?" Volunteers respond. Explain that this is not actually a word! The author is not trying to trick the readers, but instead is using letter sounds to help readers understand the meaning of another word in the text. Explain that *badamin* is meant to help readers understand the word *bobbing*.

Explain that they will think about how the word *badamin* sounds, and move their bodies to that sound. Instruct students to stand up and, as you repeat the word, move their bodies around the room to the way the word sounds.

TEACHER NOTE	*Badamin* is paired with the motion of the iguana bobbing his head. As you repeat the word emphasize the up and down sounds of the syllables and fluctuate the tone of your voice to mimic this up and down sound. Give each syllable equal time as you say the word so students get a sense that this is a slow measured movement.

Foundational Skills Connection

If students need additional practice counting and pronouncing syllables in spoken words, use the author-created words that represent animal movements (e.g., *badamin, wasawusu, purup, kaa*) to practice. As you read the movement words, encourage students to clap out, count, and pronounce the syllables in these nonsense words. If some students need help blending syllables, practice with continent names. Say the syllables in a word, pausing for a second between each syllable. After saying all the syllables, signal students to say the full word.

Ask: "What did you notice about the sound of my voice? Were my sounds all the same? Were they fast or slow?" Volunteers respond.

- *It wasn't fast.*
- *The sounds go up and down.*

Confirm that the sounds in the word *badamin* go up and down and help readers understand what *bobbing* means. Ask: "What does 'bobbing his head' mean?" Volunteers respond.

- *It means moving up and down.*

Extension

Repeat the word *bobbing* a few times, moving your voice up and down as you speak the syllables of the word. Ask: "What did you notice about my voice when I said that word?" Volunteers respond. Confirm that the sounds in the word *bobbing* go up and down, much like the word is meant to describe! Sometimes the sounds in real words can help readers understand their meanings.

Reinforce that as they continue reading through this text, they can use the other words on the page as clues to help them find the meaning of unknown words.

Explain that now they will practice using the words they know on the page to help them understand the words they do not know.

Read the second-to-last paragraph on page 4, but do not have students signal for unknown words yet. Ask: "Where did the python go to hide?" Volunteers respond.

- *He went into the rabbit hole.*

Ask: "What is a rabbit hole?" Volunteers respond.

- *It is where the rabbit lives, I think.*
- *It is a hole in the ground.*
- *The rabbit made a hole in the ground.*

Confirm that the python went to hide from the iguana in a hole in the ground. Explain that now they will continue reading the rest of the page to look for unknown words.

Read the next sentence, starting with "When the rabbit saw…" Students use the Nonverbal Signal to indicate unknown words they hear in the text. Possible unfamiliar words include *burrow* and *terrified*.

Ask: "What do you think *terrified* means? Look at the picture of the rabbit's face to help you." Volunteers respond.

- *It means "really scared."*

Confirm the meaning of *terrified*.

✔ Instruct students to Think-Pair-Share, and ask: "What do you think *burrow* means? How can we use the words we read about the python to understand the meaning of this word?" Use Equity Sticks to call on students to share.

- *The python hides in a rabbit hole.*
- *I think it means rabbit hole!*

Confirm that *burrow* is another name for a rabbit hole, or a hole under the ground where small animals can live.

Congratulate students on using the words in the text that they know to help them understand unfamiliar words in the text. Reinforce that students should always ask questions about words they do not know. It is possible that others do not know that word as well and it would help everyone to know its meaning. They can work together as a class to find the meaning of unknown words. They will continue to look for and define unknown words as they read this text to understand the story.

After defining the unknown words, reread page 4. Ask: "How did thinking about the words help you better understand these pages?" Volunteers respond.

EXAMINE THE IMPORTANCE OF SHARING WRITING 8 MIN.

Whole Group

Ask: "What does it mean to share your writing?" Volunteers respond.

- *It means to show someone else.*

Post and read the Craft Question aloud: *Why is it important to share your writing?*

Explain that in this lesson students will explore why it is important to share your writing with your classmates and others.

Ask: "Why do we read texts many times?" Volunteers respond.

- *We learn more and more.*
- *Because we think about it in different ways.*

Explain that just like readers revisit texts many times, writers also revisit their writing many times. Writers reread their writing to look for mistakes or improve their writing. Reinforce that making mistakes in writing is not a bad thing! Writers make changes to their writing all the time as they learn new information or decide they want to say something a different way.

Explain that when writers are writing something for the first time they are writing a draft. A draft is their practice. Good writers always come back to their writing or drafts and add to them to make them better, or to include new information that they have learned.

Ask: "Why do we talk about our ideas with our peers? Why not just keep all our thoughts or ideas to ourselves?" Volunteers respond.

- *We can learn from them.*
- *Because maybe they know something we don't know.*
- *Maybe they have a different idea and its good.*
- *Maybe we have a good idea, too.*

Confirm that sharing ideas with others, both teachers and classmates, is important because we can all learn from each other. Explain that over the next few lessons they will explore different ways to share their writing with classmates and how to help each other become better writers.

SHARE OBSERVATIONS AND QUESTIONS ABOUT *CARTA MARINA* 13 MIN.

Small Groups

TEACHER NOTE

This large-scale map of Scandinavia, a twelve-year endeavor, was created by woodblock print on nine sheets of paper (3 x 3). The cartographer Olaus Magnus was a Catholic priest who left Sweden after the Reformation and that country's conversion to Lutheranism. He created the map in Rome between 1527-1539. His key to the sea animals on the map was widely used and copied for centuries. While the animals depicted on the map were actually decorative elements, at the time they were believed to be true creatures that lived in other parts of the world.

To promote close observation, do not relay background information about this painting to students at this point. Rather, let them develop and share their own observations and questions. Students revisit this painting over the next few lessons and learn more about its history and purpose.

Remind students that artists create stories with pictures, and that with careful consideration students can learn to "read" works of art as they will learn to read books. Explain that they will "read" a drawing over the next few lessons, as they practice the skills of asking themselves questions and analyzing the details to find answers.

Display the *Carta Marina* (**http://witeng.link/0409**) in front of the class without telling them the title.

Instruct students to turn and talk to remind one another what to do when they first encounter a work of art.

- *We look at the art silently.*
- *We notice and describe what we see.*
- *We wonder and ask questions.*

Provide time for silent observation of the map. Display the whole map for about twenty seconds, then zoom in and pan slowly across the map to allow closer examination of the sea monsters, humans, buildings, mountains, trees, and other map features such as the keys and the numeric system along the borders.

Instruct students to Mix and Mingle, and ask: "What do you notice when you look at this image?"

- I see monsters!
- I see trees and mountains.
- I see people battling on horses.
- I see a serpent attacking a ship.
- I see water with sea creatures.
- I see numbers on the edges.

Alternate Activity

Divide the class into small groups and give each group a small portion of the painting, either on a screen or on paper. Instruct students to share their observations with their groups. Ask: "What kind of details are shown on the painting?" If time allows, consider having students draw one thing they notice from the painting in their Response Journals.

Divide the class into small groups. Distribute a copy of the image, or display the image for students to easily see, and give each group a Question Cube. Explain that now they will think about the painting with their groups and use the Question Cube to generate questions about the image.

✔ Groups use the Question Cube to generate questions about *Carta Marina* using the designated question word.

Circulate to support students in reading the question words as needed, calling attention to key letters and sounds. Encourage them to return to the image to develop their questions, and listen in on questions.

After a few minutes, come back together and use Equity Sticks to call on students to share their questions with the class.

- Is this a map of the world?
- Are those real animals or made up?
- Why are there numbers around the edges?
- Who made this?
- Is this old?
- Why are there so many animals and people in this picture?
- What do all those words say?

Explain that they will revisit this painting in the next lesson to learn more about what is happening in the image.

Land 2 MIN.

ANSWER THE CONTENT FRAMING QUESTION

Display and read aloud the Content Framing Question. Ask: "Why is it important for readers to notice and wonder about texts? How did noticing and wondering about unknown words in the text help us?" Call on several students to respond.

- ▪ *It helps us think about the text.*
- ▪ *It makes us interested to learn more.*
- ▪ *We noticed things we didn't know and asked questions.*
- ▪ *We could wonder about words we don't know and find the answers.*

Remind students that sharing their observations and questions helps everyone learn because not every person sees a text in the same way. They can all work together and learn from each other.

Wrap 1 MIN.

ASSIGN HOMEWORK

Continue the class home-reading routine.

Analyze

Context and Alignment

Students utilize use familiar words in *Why Mosquitoes Buzz in People's Ears* to help define unknown words in the text (RL.K.4). Each student:

- • Makes a Nonverbal Signal to identify an unknown word.
- • Defines the word *burrow* using familiar words around it in the text.

Next Steps

If students have difficulty defining the word *burrow*, revisit the illustration to provide more context. The purpose of this lesson is to help students develop a strategy for understanding and determining the meaning of unknown words in the text. If needed, reread the sentences in the second-to-last paragraph again to remind students of what is happening in the text.

↓ LESSON 16 DEEP DIVE: VOCABULARY

Multiple-Meaning Words: *Bear* and *lumber*

- **Time:** 15 min.

- **Text:** *Why Mosquitoes Buzz in People's Ears: A West African Tale*, Verna Aardema; Illustrations, Leo and Diane Dillon

- **Vocabulary Learning Goal:** Apply both meanings of the words *bear* and *lumber*. (L.K.4.a)

Launch

Remind students that in *Ferdinand*, they learned words that have multiple meanings: *horns* and *stick*.

Display the illustration on pages 1–2 and read the last sentence on page 2, emphasizing the word *sticks*. Instruct students to Think-Pair-Share, and ask: "What does *sticks* mean in this sentence? Is this same meaning as in *Ferdinand* or is it different?" Volunteers respond.

- *They are sticks that come from trees.*
- *This is a different meaning than in Ferdinand.*
- *In Ferdinand,* stick *means "to poke with something sharp."*

Explain that Verna Aardema uses other interesting words with multiple meanings in *Why Mosquitoes Buzz in People's Ears*. Students are going to explore these words.

Learn

Post the words:

- *bear*
- *lumber*

Point to and read the word *bear*. Ask: "What is a bear?" Volunteers respond.

- *A large, furry animal.*
- *A big animal that can be brown, black, or white.*
- *A bear lives in the woods.*

Use student responses to draw a picture of a bear next to the word.

| bear | [bear image] | |

Reinforce that this story takes place in Africa and has lots of animals but no bears, so this word must have a different meaning. Display pages 8–9 of the text and read the second and third paragraphs, emphasizing the word *bear*. Ask: "What does the owl mean when she says 'I cannot <u>bear</u> to wake the sun'?" Volunteers respond.

- *She means it is too hard.*
- *Owl is feeling too sad.*
- *She means she cannot do it.*

Use student responses to reinforce that *bear* also means "to live with something even if it is hard or difficult." Draw a picture representing the verb *bear* next to the word.

| bear | [bear image] | [person image] |

Point to and read the word *lumber*. Explain that people build with lumber. Ask: "What is lumber?" Volunteers respond.

- *It's a lot of wood.*
- *Trees that are cut into big pieces to build with.*
- *Lincoln logs are like lumber.*

Use student responses to draw a picture of *lumber* next to the word.

| lumber | [lumber image] | |

Reinforce that this story is not about trees or wood so *lumber* has a different meaning in the book. Display pages 3–4 of the text and read the second and third paragraphs, emphasizing the word *lumbered*. Instruct students to Think-Pair-Share, and ask: "What does *lumbered* mean in the story? What is the iguana doing?" Volunteers respond.

- *The iguana is moving or walking.*
- *The iguana is going slowly.*
- *The iguana is bobbing his head.*

Use student responses to reinforce that *lumbered* means "to move in a slow, clumsy way." Draw a picture representing the verb *lumber* next to the word.

lumber		

Explain that students are going to use the words in sentences to show they understand both meanings of the words. Model making a sentence using the word *bear*. First, point to the picture of the animal *bear* and say, "A <u>bear</u> sleeps in winter." Then, point to the verb *bear* and say, "I can't <u>bear</u> cold weather." Call on a student volunteer to give an example for each meaning of *bear*.

Scaffold

If you feel students would benefit with additional practice, repeat the above activity for the word *lumber*. First, point to the picture of wood *lumber* and say, "We built a house with <u>lumber</u>." Then, point to the verb *lumber* and say, "The elephants <u>lumber</u> through the jungle." Call on a student volunteer to give an example or each meaning of *lumber*.

✔ Call out a word from the chart and point to a picture representing one meaning. Instruct students to Mix and Mingle and share a sentence using that word correctly. Circulate to provide support as needed and to ensure that students are using the words correctly in their sentences. Repeat this sequence for each meaning of the words *lumber* and *bear*.

Land

Reorganize students back into a whole group. Review each word and its meanings.

Use Equity Sticks to call on several students to share their sentences for each word and meaning.

■ FOCUSING QUESTION: LESSONS 16–21

How can a story transport you to a different place?

1 | 2 | 3 | 4 | 5 | 6 | 7 | 8 | 9 | 10 | 11 | 12 | 13 | 14 | 15 | **16** | **17** | **18** | **19** | **20** | **21** | 22 | 23 | 24 | 25 | 26 | 27 | 28 | 29 | 30 | 31 | 32 | 33 | 34 | 35 | 36

Lesson 17

TEXTS

- "Lions Roar," *CanTeach* (**http://witeng.link/0410**)

- *Why Mosquitoes Buzz in People's Ears: A West African Tale*, Verna Aardema; Illustrations, Leo and Diane Dillon

- *Carta Marina*, Olaus Magnus (**http://witeng.link/0409**)

- "Burkina Faso: Music," *Our Africa* (video) (**http://witeng.link/0411**)

Lesson 17: At a Glance

AGENDA

Welcome (5 min.)

Practice Fluency

Launch (7 min.)

Learn (57 min.)

Use Illustrations to Understand Events (30 min.)

Experiment with Sharing a Piece of Writing (15 min.)

Explore Carta Marina (12 min.)

Land (5 min.)

Answer the Content Framing Question

Wrap (1 min.)

Assign Homework

Vocabulary Deep Dive: Finding Meaning with the Prefix *re-* (15 min.)

STANDARDS ADDRESSED

The full text of ELA Standards can be found in the Module Overview.

Reading

- RL.K.1, RL.K.2, RL.K.7

Writing

- W.K.5, W.K.7

Speaking and Listening

- SL.K.1.a, SL.K.2

Language

- ↓ L.K.4.b

MATERIALS

- Repeated Language Chart (see lesson for details; retain for future lessons)
- Sharing Our Writing Anchor Chart
- Index cards
- Chart paper

Learning Goals

Use illustrations from *Why Mosquitoes Buzz in People's Ears* to better understand the events in the story. (RL.K.2, RL.K.7)

✔ Think-Pair-Share about how illustrations show events in the story.

Follow agreed-upon rules for discussion when sharing writing with a peer. (W.K.5, SL.K.1.a)

✔ Share a Response Journal entry with a peer.

↓ Use the meaning of the prefix *re-* as a clue to find the meaning of an unknown word (L.K.4.b)

✔ Use the word part *re-* and an illustration to determine the meaning of *reappears*.

✔ Checks for Understanding

Prepare

FOCUSING QUESTION: Lessons 16–21

How can a story transport you to a different place?

CONTENT FRAMING QUESTION: Lesson 17

Organize: *What is happening in* Why Mosquitoes Buzz in People's Ears?

CRAFT QUESTION: Lesson 17

Experiment: *How can I share my writing with others?*

In this lesson students reread *Why Mosquitoes Buzz in People's Ears* to focus on what is happening. Students explore the award-winning artwork created by Leo and Diane Dillon and consider how the illustrations add to the telling of the story. In addition, students build their ability to share their writing and consider the writing of others by sharing a Response Journal entry with a peer. Finally, students transfer habits of mind from the analysis of books to the analysis of art by considering what is happening in *Carta Marina*.

Welcome 5 MIN.

PRACTICE FLUENCY

Ask: "What kind of characters did you read about in *Why Mosquitoes Buzz in People's Ears?*" Volunteers respond.

- *There was an iguana.*
- *I remember the monkey.*
- *We read about a snake.*

Use responses to confirm that the characters in the story are animals. Explain that the fluency passage students will practice as they explore *Why Mosquitoes Buzz in People's Ears* is also about African animals.

TEACHER NOTE	The fluency passage, "Lions Roar," can be found at the following link: (**http://witeng.link/0410**). This webpage contains a collection of African songs and chants. In Lessons 17–21 students will be using "Lions Roar" for their fluency practice. This chant is the fifth title listed under "Songs & Chants."

Display the Repeated Language Chart with the first two lines of the poem added and read the lines aloud. Students Echo Read the lines.

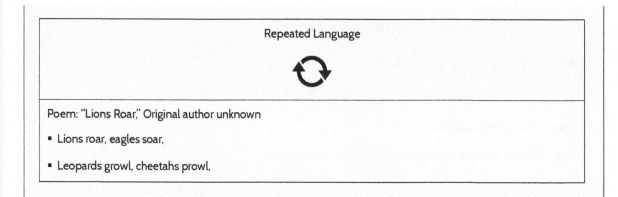

Ask: "What do you notice about these lines? What is the poem about?" Volunteers respond.

- *There are lots of animals in the poem.*
- *It says how the animals sound.*
- *It's about animals and what they do.*

Extension

Provide background knowledge and context by sharing images and information about the animals in the poem with students.

Point to and read aloud the word *prowl* and explain that when an animal prowls it moves around slowly and secretly, like it is sneaking up on something. Invite students to practice prowling.

Create hand movements for the last verb in each line to help students internalize the definitions. For example:

- Soar: extend your arms to indicate coasting while flying.
- Prowl: holding your hands out flat and parallel to the ground, move them slowly forward, one at a time.

TEACHER NOTE
As you add each line of the poem, consider adding pictures of each animal to accompany the words. This will help students reference the poem independently and use the pictures to guide their fluent reading.

Reread the first two lines of the poem aloud. Students Echo Read the poem while incorporating the movements for each line.

Launch 7 MIN.

Ask: "What's your opinion: do you think a picture can tell a story? Why or why not?" Designate one side of the room as "yes" and the other as "no." Students show their opinion by moving to the side of the room that corresponds with their opinion. Ask several students from each side to share their reasons.

Extension

Point out the Caldecott Medal on the front cover of *Why Mosquitoes Buzz in People's Ears* and explain that the illustrators, Leo and Diane Dillon, won an award for their beautiful artwork in the book.

Students move back to the whole-group gathering area. Display the front cover of *Why Mosquitoes Buzz in People's Ears*, and ask: "Think about what happens in *Why Mosquitoes Buzz in People's Ears*. How does this illustration tell the story?" Volunteers respond.

- *The mosquito is really big. That shows he's an important character.*
- *The mosquito looks like he is whispering a question to the man. That shows he is still wondering if people are mad at him.*
- *The man doesn't look happy with the mosquito. That shows that he is still mad at the mosquito for causing problems.*

Display and read aloud the Content Framing Question. Students Echo Read the question.

Explain that today students will examine other illustrations from the book, and from *Carta Marina*, to explore how pictures can help tell stories.

Learn 57 MIN.

USE ILLUSTRATIONS TO UNDERSTAND EVENTS 30 MIN.

Whole Group

Read aloud pages 1–2 of the text and ask the following TDQ. Use Equity Sticks to call on students to respond.

1   Why did the iguana put sticks in his ears? What did the mosquito tell him?

- *The iguana didn't want to hear the mosquito anymore.*
- *The iguana thought the mosquito was talking "nonsense."*
- *The mosquito said he saw a farmer digging yams that were almost as big as the mosquito.*

Provide context by displaying the illustration on the title page and pointing out the yam in the farmer's hand. Ask: "What do you notice about the size of a yam? How does that make the mosquito's statement seem silly?" Volunteers respond.

- *The yam is bigger than the farmer's hand.*
- *It's way bigger than a mosquito!*
- *The mosquito was telling a lie, because yams are way bigger than mosquitoes.*

Display the illustration on pages 1–2 of the text. Ask: "How does this illustration show what's happening in this part of the story?" Volunteers respond. As students respond, point to the moment in the illustration to highlight the sequence of events on the page.

- *I see the mosquito talking to the iguana.*
- *I see the iguana covering his ears.*
- *I can see the iguana walking away with sticks in his ears.*

Direct pairs of students to use their hands to act out what is happening in the illustration. One student acts out the part of the mosquito, pretending to fly with their hands. The other student acts out the part of the iguana, pretending to walk away.

Alternate Activity

Create character puppets by attaching images of the animals in the story to popsicle sticks. Students use the puppets to act out events from the story.

Display the illustration on pages 3–4 of the text. Prompt students to think about how the illustration shows what is happening in the story as you read the pages aloud. Read pages 3–4 aloud.

Ask: "What is happening on these pages?" Volunteers respond. As students respond, point to the moment in the illustration to highlight the sequence of events on the page.

- *The iguana scares the snake.*
- *The snake goes into hole.*
- *The rabbit gets scared of the snake and runs away.*

Point out the two python heads and the two rabbits in the illustration. Ask: "I see two snakes and two rabbits in this picture. Are there two snakes and rabbits in the story?" Students chorally respond.

- *No!*

Instruct students to Think-Pair-Share, and ask: "Why do you think the illustrators drew two snakes and rabbits? How does that help tell the story?" Encourage students to remember the sequence of events in the story to help interpret the two images of the python and rabbit. Use Equity Sticks to call on students to respond.

- It helps show what happened.
- The first picture of the python shows when he talked to the iguana. The second picture shows what happened next.
- The first picture of the rabbit shows when she was scared to see the python. The second picture shows how she ran out of her burrow.

Direct pairs of students to use their hands to act out what is happening in the illustration. One student acts out the part of the snake, making a slithering motion with their hands. The other student acts out the part of the rabbit, making a hopping motion with their hands.

Read aloud pages 5–6 of the text and ask the following TDQ. Use Equity Sticks to call on students to respond.

2   Why was the monkey leaping through the trees?

- He heard the crow calling and warning of danger.
- He thought that there must be a dangerous animal nearby.
- The monkey was warning other animals about the danger.

Display the illustration on pages 5–6 of the text. Ask: "How does this illustration show what's happening in this part of the story?" Volunteers respond.

- I see the crow watching the rabbit.
- I see the monkey listening to the crow.
- I can see the branch falling on the baby owl.

Direct pairs of students to use their hands to act out what is happening in the illustration. One student acts out the part of the crow, pretending to fly with their hands. The other student acts out the part of the monkey, pretending to leap through the trees and breaking a branch.

Read pages 9–16. Display the illustration on pages 15–16 of the text. Direct students to think about how the illustration shows what is happening in the story as you read page 15 aloud. Ask: "How does this illustration show what's happening in this part of the story?" Volunteers respond.

- I see the lion calling the rabbit to the meeting.
- The rabbit looks scared, just like it said in the words.
- I see the python looking mean, like the rabbit said to King Lion.

Scaffold

Ask: "What color is the sky in this illustration? Why is it dark?" Confirm that the sky is dark because Mother Owl will not wake the sun. Reinforce that the background on these pages helps readers understand at what point in the story these events are taking place.

Ask: "Why is there a python on this page? Is the python actually chasing the rabbit in this part of the story?" Use Equity Sticks to call on students to respond.

- *No, the python isn't chasing the rabbit now.*
- *But the rabbit is remembering what happened.*

Ask: "Is the rabbit remembering correctly what actually happened? How do you know?" Use Equity Sticks to call on students to respond.

- *No, rabbit isn't remembering how it really happened.*
- *The python was going into the rabbit's hole because he was scared. He wasn't trying to hurt the rabbit.*

✔ Flip back and forth between the illustration on pages 3–4 and 15–16. Instruct students to Think-Pair-Share, and ask: "How do the illustrations show the difference between what really happened and what the rabbit remembers?" Call on several students to respond.

- *In the first illustration the python's mouth is closed. He doesn't look scary.*
- *At first the python is looking back at iguana. He's not thinking about the rabbit.*
- *In the second illustration the python has huge teeth. He looks very scary!*
- *The rabbit remembers the python being very scary, but that wasn't true.*

Read the remainder of the text aloud, inviting students to join in saying the repeated lines in the text, as they are able.

Ask: "What made Mother Owl feel good enough to wake the sun?" Volunteers respond.

- *They figured out it was the mosquito's fault.*
- *The animals decided to punish the mosquito.*

Display the illustration on page 27. Instruct students to Mix and Mingle, and ask: "Is everyone still mad at the mosquito? How do you know?"

EXPERIMENT WITH SHARING A PIECE OF WRITING 15 MIN.

Pairs

TEACHER NOTE	Lessons 16–21 build towards understanding of W.K.5. Students are learning about the different processes of writing, such as drafting, sharing, and revising based on input. Students start by learning the process of sharing writing and learning how to respond to their peers by offering a compliment and a suggestion. The best application of the skill for this age group is sharing drawings. Students will not be revising their writing in these lessons, as the purpose is to build towards this skill, which students will address in Lessons 22–27.

Remind students that writers share their writing with others to become better writers. Their classmates, teachers, and other people might be able to help them improve their writing. Reinforce this idea by explaining that Verna Aardema showed her story *Why Mosquitoes Buzz in People's Ears* to many, many people before the book was published and sold.

Display and read aloud the Craft Question: *How can I share my writing with others?*

Explain that students will share their Response Journal entries from the previous lesson with a classmate. Ask: "How could you share your writing with someone? How would they know what you wrote?" Volunteers respond.

- *I could show them my journal.*
- *They could read my writing themselves.*
- *I could read it to them.*
- *I could show them my drawing.*

Display a blank piece of chart paper for the Sharing Our Writing Anchor Chart. Read the title of the chart aloud. Use responses to explain the sharing process:

- One student shares their writing by reading it aloud and explaining the accompanying illustration.
- The other student actively listens and says one thing they notice about the writing or drawing.
- Students switch roles.

Emphasize that while one student shares, their partner actively listens. Invite two volunteers to the front of the room to model the sharing process outlined above. Add "Share and listen" as the first step on the Sharing Our Writing Anchor Chart. Explain that they will add to this chart over the next two lessons as they experiment with this process.

Sharing Our Writing Anchor Chart
1. Share and listen

TEACHER NOTE

Encourage students to share something they notice about their partner's writing by using the **I notice** _____ sentence frame. The goal in this lesson is for students to be attentive to one another's writing and to practice responding to a specific aspect of someone's writing. Instruction on how to give compliments and suggestions about a peer's writing will appear in subsequent lessons.

✔ Divide class into pairs and distribute Response Journals. Students take turns sharing their most recent Response Journal entries with each other, following the process outlined above.

Ask: "How did it feel to share your writing with a classmate? How did it feel to listen to a classmate's writing?" Volunteers respond.

EXPLORE *CARTA MARINA* 12 MIN.

Whole Group

Explain that the habit of considering what is happening is not only an important part of understanding text, it is also an important part of understanding art. Tell students they will explore what is happening in the piece of art they looked at in the previous lesson to better understand and enjoy the artwork.

Display *Carta Marina* (**http://witeng.link/0409**) and explain that it is a map showing part of Europe. Instruct students to Think-Pair-Share, and ask: "When have you seen or used a map?" Call on several students to respond.

- *My mom checks a map on her phone when we need to drive somewhere.*
- *We looked at a map of a mall to figure out where the food court was.*
- *We used a map to find our favorite ride at an amusement park.*
- *I look at the subway/bus map at the station to know where to get off.*
- *We looked at a globe in our classroom last week.*
- *We use a map of the school for our fire drill exits.*

Students consider the map silently for thirty seconds, holding questions and comments. Ask: "When do you think this map was made? Is it from the past or the present? What makes you think that?" Volunteers respond.

Use responses to explain that this map was made close to 500 years ago. It is called the *Carta Marina.* Explain that the words are written in a different language, and tell the names of the places on the map.

Tell students that the *Carta Marina* was created by a *cartographer* named Olaus Magnus. Explain that a *cartographer* is an artist who uses information to make maps. Students repeat the word *cartographer.* Share that Olaus Magnus was a cartographer and also a priest. It took him nearly twelve years to research and draw this map!

Explain that the map shows both the sea and the land and point out a few areas of each. Ask a few students to come up and point to the water and land in different parts of the map. Zoom in on these areas.

Ask: "How did the cartographer show the difference between the land and the water?" Use Equity Sticks to call on students to respond.

- *The water is blue.*
- *The land is white with colors around the edges.*

- *There are sea creatures and boats in the water.*
- *There are mountains, trees, and people on the land.*

Ask: "What are some things you see in the water?" Students respond by pointing to a detail they notice. Use Equity Sticks to call on several students to share what they see.

- *I see a strange animal. It looks like a monster.*
- *There are ships.*
- *I can see logs floating in the water.*

Ask: "Do you think anything on this map might be imaginary, or pretend? How can you tell?" Volunteers respond.

- *Yes, I think the sea creatures are not real.*
- *Many of them look like made-up monsters from storybooks.*
- *I can see dragons, and I know they are not real!*
- *The creatures are much larger than the ships. That's not real.*

Confirm that while there are many real animals and places depicted on this map, many of the creatures shown on this map are imaginary. At the time this map was made, people believed sea monsters like the ones shown on the map really existed. Now scientists know more about the real animals in the ocean and on land.

Scroll slowly over the land areas of the map, and ask: "What details do you see on the land?" Students respond by pointing to a detail they notice. Use Equity Sticks to call on several students to share what they see.

- *I see mountains.*
- *There are trees.*
- *I can see houses and tents.*
- *There are animals, too.*

Ask: "Why might cartographers include details such as animals, mountains, houses, and trees on their maps?" Volunteers respond.

- *To show people where different animals live in the world.*
- *To warn people about areas where dangerous animals are.*
- *So people will know how to get to the mountains.*
- *To show parts of the world where there are cities and towns, or forests and mountains.*

Land   5 MIN.

ANSWER THE CONTENT FRAMING QUESTION

Read aloud the Content Framing Question.

Instruct students to Mix and Mingle, and ask: "Do you think the illustrations in *Why Mosquitoes Buzz in People's Ears* are important to the story? Why or why not?"

Extension

Read aloud the names of the illustrators and ask: "Do these names sound familiar? Where have you heard them before?" Confirm that Leo and Diane Dillon were also the illustrators for the Module 1 text, *Rap a Tap Tap*. Display illustrations from both texts and ask students to look for similarities and differences between the artwork.

Explain that like folktales, the music and dance of different places are often passed down from grandparents and parents to their children. Read aloud the research question introduced in Lesson 2: "How do people around the world dance?" Tell students that now they will learn about a different style of dancing by watching a dance from a West African nation: Burkina Faso. Display the questions: "What do I see in this dance performance? What do I hear in this dance performance?" Tell students they can focus their video observations either on what they see or hear, which will help the class learn about different aspects of the dance. Individual students raise their hands to indicate whether they choose to focus on what they see, or what they hear.

Play the video "Burkina Faso: Music" (**http://witeng.link/0411**).

Ask: "What did you see or hear in the music and dance from West Africa?" Use Equity Sticks to call on students to respond.

Wrap 1 MIN.

ASSIGN HOMEWORK

Continue the class home-reading routine.

Analyze

Context and Alignment

Students identify the relationship between events depicted in the written text and in the illustrations of *Why Mosquitoes Buzz in People's Ears* (RL.K.2, RL.K.7). Each student:

- Considers how an illustration shows a character's memory of an event.
- Shares their thinking with a partner.

Next Steps

If students have difficulty describing the relationship between the written text and the illustrations, reread portions of the story, one page spread at a time. After reading about an event in the text, pause to ask: "Where do you see this happening in the illustration?" Students point to the place in the illustration where they see the event and share their thinking.

↓ LESSON 17 DEEP DIVE: VOCABULARY

Finding Meaning with the Prefix *re-*

- **Time:** 15 min.

- **Text:** *Why Mosquitoes Buzz in People's Ears: A West African Tale*, Verna Aardema; Illustrations, Leo and Diane Dillon

- **Vocabulary Learning Goal:** Use the meaning of the prefix *re-* as a clue to find the meaning of an unknown word. (L.K.4.b)

Launch

Remind students that in Deep Dive Lessons 14 and 15, they used the word endings *–ful* and *–less* as clues to figure out the meanings of new words.

Explain that students are going to use a new word beginning as a clue to figure out the meanings of new words that describe the actions of characters from the story.

Post and Echo Read the following words: *retell*, *return*, and *reappear*.

Ask: "What word beginning do these words have in common?" Students respond chorally.

- *Re!*

Redirect student attention to the list of posted words and underline *re-* in each word. Explain that the word beginning *re-* means "doing something again."

Reinforce that students are going to use this information as a clue to figure out the meaning of these words.

Learn

Instruct students to listen closely as you read a sentence about the story and to give a thumbs-up signal when they hear a word that starts with the word beginning *re-*.

Display pages 5–6 of the text and read: "The monkey retells the crow's warning." Call on a student with a thumbs-up to identify the word starting with *re-*.

- *Retells.*

Reinforce that since the word starts with *re-*, it must mean the monkey was "doing something again." Model how to use the illustration and other words in the sentence to determine what the monkey is doing. For example, point out that the monkey is sharing the crow's message. Ask: "What do you think *retell* means?" Volunteers respond.

- *It means the monkey is warning the animals again.*
- *It means the monkey says the same thing as the crow.*

Use student responses to determine the meaning of *retell* as "to share a story again." Record this definition next to *retell* on the board.

Display pages 7–8 of the text and read: "Mother owl <u>returned</u> to her nest after hunting." Call on a student with a thumbs-up to identify the word starting with *re–*.

- *Returned.*

Reinforce that because the word starts with *re–*, it must mean the owl was "doing something again." Encourage students to use the illustration and other words in the sentence to determine what the Mother Owl is doing. Instruct students to Think-Pair-Share and ask: "What do you think *return* means?" Volunteers respond.

- *Since Mother Owl came home, it could mean "come home again."*
- *Since Mother Owl came back to her babies, it could mean "come back again."*

Use student responses to determine the meaning of *return* as "to come back again." Record this definition next to *return* on the board.

Display pages 25–26 of the text and read: "The mosquito <u>reappears</u> at the end of the story." Call on a student with a thumbs-up to identify the word starting with *re–*.

- *Reappears*

Organize students into pairs. Explain that students are going to work with their partner to figure out the meaning of the word *reappears*. Reinforce that students should use the meaning of the word beginning *re–*, the illustration, and the other words in the sentence as clues to help them.

Land

✔ Distribute an index card to each pair. Display pages 25–26 and read the sentence again. Students work together to determine the meaning of the word *reappears*. They discuss their ideas with each other. Encourage students to write or draw their ideas on the index card. Circulate to provide support and ensure understanding of the word beginning *re–*.

Use Equity Sticks to call on pairs to share their ideas.

- *The mosquito shows up again at the end of the story.*
- *The mosquito is seen again by people.*

Use student responses to determine the meaning of *reappears* as "to be seen again." Record the definition on the board.

Ask: "Why did the mosquito *reappear* at the end of the story?" Volunteers respond.

- *Because she felt bad.*

■ FOCUSING QUESTION: LESSONS 16–21

How can a story transport you to a different place?

1 | 2 | 3 | 4 | 5 | 6 | 7 | 8 | 9 | 10 | 11 | 12 | 13 | 14 | 15 | **16** | **17** | **18** | **19** | **20** | **21** | 22 | 23 | 24 | 25 | 26 | 27 | 28 | 29 | 30 | 31 | 32 | 33 | 34 | 35 | 36

Lesson 18

TEXTS

- "Lions Roar," *CanTeach* (**http://witeng.link/0410**)

- *Why Mosquitoes Buzz in People's Ears: A West African Tale*, Verna Aardema; Illustrations, Leo and Diane Dillon

- *Carta Marina*, Olaus Magnus (**http://witeng.link/0409**)

Lesson 18: At a Glance

AGENDA

Welcome (5 min.)

Practice Fluency

Launch (6 min.)

Learn (61 min.)

Define Unknown Words (20 min.)

Collect Evidence for Focusing Question Task 3 (12 min.)

Experiment with Responding to a Peer's Writing (15 min.)

Analyze Scale in Carta Marina (14 min.)

Land (2 min.)

Answer the Content Framing Question

Wrap (1 min.)

Assign Homework

Vocabulary Deep Dive: Opposite Verbs in a Narrative (15 min.)

STANDARDS ADDRESSED

The full text of ELA Standards can be found in the Module Overview.

Reading

- RL.K.1, RL.K.4. RL.K.7

Writing

- W.K.5, W.10*

Speaking and Listening

- SL.K.1

Language

- ↓ L.K.5.b

MATERIALS

- Repeated Language Chart
- Evidence Organizer for *Why Mosquitoes Buzz in People's Ears* (see lesson for details)
- Sticky notes
- Puppet
- Sharing Our Writing Anchor Chart
- Document camera (if available)

Learning Goals

Use context clues from the words and illustrations to define unknown words in *Why Mosquitoes Buzz in People's Ears.* (RL.K.4, RL.K.7)

✔ Think-Pair-Share about the meaning of the word *timid*.

Provide feedback to a peer about their writing. (W.K.5)

✔ Respond to a peer's Response Journal entry by giving a compliment.

↓ Demonstrate understanding of *lumbered, scurried, returned,* and *left* by acting out their opposites. (L.K.5.b)

✔ Mix and Mingle, acting out opposite pairs.

*In alignment with the CCSS, W.10 formally begins in Grade 3. However, K–2 students write routinely for a variety of time frames, tasks, purposes, and audiences. As a result, this lesson contains instruction related to W.10 in an effort to familiarize students with a range of writing.

✔ Checks for Understanding

Prepare

FOCUSING QUESTION: Lessons 16–21

How can a story transport you to a different place?

CONTENT FRAMING QUESTION: Lesson 18

Reveal: *What does a deeper exploration of the words and illustrations reveal about unknown words in* Why Mosquitoes Buzz in People's Ears?

CRAFT QUESTION: Lesson 18

Experiment: *How do I respond to someone's writing?*

In this lesson, students practice using clues from the written text and illustrations to determine the meaning of unknown words in *Why Mosquitoes Buzz in People's Ears*. They also build capacity for responding to a peer's writing by complimenting a partner's Response Journal entry. Finally, students analyze scale in *Carta Marina* to explore the way artists and illustrators use scale to communicate through paintings and drawings.

Welcome 5 MIN.

PRACTICE FLUENCY

Display the Repeated Language Chart with the third and fourth lines of the poem added. Read the lines aloud. Students Echo Read the lines.

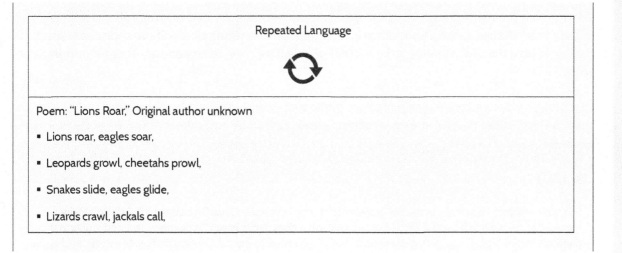

Repeated Language

Poem: "Lions Roar," Original author unknown

- Lions roar, eagles soar,

- Leopards growl, cheetahs prowl,

- Snakes slide, eagles glide,

- Lizards crawl, jackals call,

Reread the third and fourth lines again, prompting students to point to their ears when they hear a rhyming pair. Use Equity Sticks to call on students to share the rhyming words they hear.

Ask: "What does it mean to <u>slide</u> and <u>glide</u>? Are these movements smooth or choppy?" Volunteers respond. Encourage those who answer to stand up and act out the movements.

Ask: "What does it mean to <u>crawl</u>? Is this a fast movement or a slow movement?" Volunteers respond. Prompt the class to stand up and act out the word *crawl*.

Create hand movements for the last verb in each line to help students internalize the definitions. For example:

- Glide: spread arms out wide and glide like an eagle through the air.
- Call: hold hands up to both sides of your mouth as if you were amplifying your voice.

Reread all four lines of the poem aloud. Students Echo Read the poem while incorporating the movements for each line.

Launch 6 MIN.

Display the front cover of *Why Mosquitoes Buzz in People's Ears*. Instruct students to Think-Pair-Share, and ask: "Is this a storybook or an informational text? What makes you say that?" Use Equity Sticks to call on students to respond.

- *It's a storybook because it's not real.*
- *I think it's a storybook because it has talking animals.*
- *It's a storybook because it's telling a story, not giving information.*

Confirm that the text is a storybook and explain that it is a special kind of story called a <u>folktale</u>. Explain that folktales are stories that have been told for a very long time. Different places around the world have their own unique folktales that people have been telling one another for hundreds of years.

Open *Why Mosquitoes Buzz in People's Ears* to the title page and point out the words "A West African Tale" in the subtitle. Remind students that the story is a folktale from West Africa, retold by Verna Aardema.

Scaffold

Reactivate student knowledge of the prefix *re–*, which they discussed in Deep Dive Lesson 18. Ask: "What does *re–* mean when we put it in front of a word? For example, what does *reread* mean?" Volunteers respond. Confirm that the prefix *re–* means "again." Ask: "What does *retold* mean?" Volunteers respond. Confirm that *retold* means "told again." Emphasize that the author did not create the story herself, she <u>retold</u> a story that was created in the past. Verna Aardema wrote down a tale that has been told orally many times in West Africa.

Display and read aloud the Content Framing Question. Students Echo Read the question.

Tell students that understanding the words in a text is an important part of understanding the story. Remind students that good readers stop and think when they read a word they do not understand. They often look for clues in the words and pictures to help them figure out the unknown word.

Explain that *Why Mosquitoes Buzz in People's Ears* contains some challenging words that readers may not know. Students will practice thinking about the meaning of unknown words today as they reread portions of the story.

Learn 61 MIN.

DEFINE UNKNOWN WORDS 20 MIN.

Whole Group

Explain that now students will look for unknown words in *Why Mosquitoes Buzz in People's Ears*, and use the words and illustrations to help understand the meanings.

Extension

Write the word *unknown* on the board. Ask: "What happens to a word when the sound *un-* is put in front it?" Volunteers respond. Confirm that it means the opposite of the word it is in front of. Provide students with additional examples such as *unsafe, unfair, unreal, unhook,* etc. Reinforce that *unknown* means "not known."

Students will engage further with this prefix during Deep Dive Lesson 19.

Read aloud pages 1–4. Model the process of using context clues to define unknown words by engaging in a Think Aloud to determine the meaning of *mischief* on page 4. For example, say:

In the text it says, "Iguana must be angry about something. I'm afraid he is plotting some mischief against me." Hmm, *mischief*. I'm not sure what that word means. Let me go back to the text to see if there are any clues in the story to help me. Well, it says the iguana was plotting something and I know that *plotting* usually means planning something bad. So that gives me a clue that *mischief* is something that might be bad. It also said the python was afraid of the mischief Iguana might be planning, so he hid in the rabbit's hole. That tells me that *mischief* is probably something bad that someone might be afraid of. Maybe *mischief* is like a trap or a trick?

Emphasize that the illustrations in the story can also help explain unknown words. Ask: "Look at the illustration of the python. How could the illustration help you understand what *mischief* means?" Volunteers respond.

- *The python is trying to get away from the iguana.*
- *The python is looking back at the Iguana with a worried look.*

277

Use responses to confirm that readers can tell by the python's movement down the rabbit's hole, and his worried expression, that he is concerned about the mischief Iguana might have planned. Emphasize that the illustration can help confirm that *mischief* is something like a trap or trick that someone might try to get away from.

Explain that students will practice looking for clues to define unknown words in another part of the story, right after King Lion calls a meeting of the animals. Read aloud pages 9–10. Instruct students to Think-Pair-Share, and ask: "In the story it says, 'Mother Owl did not come, so the antelope was sent to fetch her.' What do you think *fetch* might mean? What clues from the words help you know what it means?" Volunteers respond.

- *I think it means he went to look for the owl.*
- *The antelope went to find Mother Owl and bring her to the meeting.*
- *The clue from the story is that Mother Owl wasn't there. So they had to go get her, or fetch her.*
- *At first Mother Owl wasn't there, then he went to fetch her, and she was there. So I know it means he went to get her.*

Read aloud pages 11–16. Pause and reread the following sentences from page 15: "Then King Lion called the rabbit. The timid little creature stood before him, one trembling paw drawn up uncertainly."

Instruct students to Think-Pair-Share, and ask: "What do you think *timid* might mean? How do you know?" Encourage students to think about clues from the words and the illustrations, rereading the sentence as needed. Use Equity Sticks to call on several students to share their thinking.

- *Maybe it means shy or scared.*
- *I heard it say the rabbit was trembling. That's a clue that timid might mean "scared." I know because you might tremble if you're scared.*
- *The rabbit looks scared in the illustration.*
- *The rabbit looks shy. She's trying to hide behind her paws.*

Emphasize that the illustrations in the story are helpful for readers in many ways. Ask: "How have you used the illustrations to help you understand and enjoy *Why Mosquitoes Buzz in People's Ears?*" Volunteers respond.

- *I used them to figure out what fetch means.*
- *I used them to understand words in the story.*
- *The illustrations help show what is happening.*
- *The illustrations are beautiful to look at!*
- *They help me know what the animals look like.*

Distribute Response Journals and display the illustration on pages 15–16 of the text. If possible, use a document camera to project the illustration in front of the class to allow for easier reference. Students write and illustrate a response to the following prompt.

What do you like most about this illustration?

COLLECT EVIDENCE FOR FOCUSING QUESTION TASK 3 12 MIN.

Pairs

Explain that students will now use the illustrations in the story for a different purpose: to collect evidence for Focusing Question Task 3.

Display and read aloud the Focusing Question: *How can a story transport you to a different place?* Remind students that their thinking and learning during the week is preparing them to answer this question.

Ask: "How do the illustrations in *Why Mosquitoes Buzz in People's Ears* help you imagine the forest in Africa? What helps you understand what it might be like there?" Volunteers respond.

- *I can imagine what the animals look like.*
- *The pictures help me imagine the trees.*
- *The colors help me feel like I'm there.*
- *The pictures look like they're from a different place.*

Tell students that they will be writing about their favorite character for their Focusing Question Task. Explain that to form an opinion, students first need to collect evidence on the characters in the text.

Display the Evidence Organizer for *Why Mosquitoes Buzz in People's Ears* in front of the class. Tell students that they will collect evidence about five characters from the text. Read aloud the character names, pointing to the associated column headings.

Read aloud the following question from the chart: "What do they look like?" Explain that now students will work together to record evidence from the illustrations that describes what each character looks like.

Divide the class into pairs and distribute sticky notes to each pair. Assign each pair one animal from the evidence organizer.

Give groups two minutes to discuss the following question: "What does your character look like?" Remind students that descriptive words are very helpful in adding detail and helping readers understand more about a topic. Encourage students to use descriptive words as they describe their character. If needed, briefly model this for the class using the mosquito as an example.

Circulate with the text or use a document camera to project its pages to allow students to reference the illustrations as they discuss. Consider displaying the illustrations on pages 3–4 and 5–6 because they show several characters on one page.

Using the illustrations as a guide, students draw an illustration of what their character looks like and label it with descriptive words.

After student record their evidence, ask pairs to share their evidence aloud with the class. Choose two or three drawings for each animal to represent on the evidence organizer. Write legible descriptive words on the chart to ensure readability.

SAMPLE EVIDENCE ORGANIZER FOR *WHY MOSQUITOES BUZZ IN PEOPLE'S EARS*

Evidence Organizer for *Why Mosquitoes Buzz in People's Ears*					
Characters	Iguana	Python	Rabbit	Crow	Monkey
What do they look like?	▪ green ▪ sticks in ears ▪ short	▪ purple ▪ no legs ▪ long	▪ gray ▪ big ears ▪ big eyes	▪ black ▪ wings ▪ beak	▪ brown ▪ long tail ▪ long arms
How do they move?					

TEACHER NOTE	Pair headings with corresponding images to increase independent readability of the chart. Cover the bottom row of the evidence organizer to focus students' attention on the portion of the chart completed in this lesson.

EXPERIMENT WITH RESPONDING TO A PEER'S WRITING 15 MIN.

Pairs

Tell students that today they will learn more about sharing their writing with others and will have the opportunity to share their Response Journal entries with a partner.

Display and read aloud the Craft Question: *How do I respond to someone's writing?* Highlight or underline the word *respond* and explain that when you respond to someone's writing you say something about it.

Scaffold

Foster a connection to previous learning by holding up a Response Journal. Remind students that when they wrote their Response Journal entry earlier in the lesson they were responding to an illustration in the text by writing something about the illustration.

Explain that when someone responds to an author's writing, it can help the author become a better writer. Hearing what someone else says about a piece of writing can help the author know what they did well, and how they can improve their writing to make it even better.

Tell students to watch as a friend (puppet) responds to your writing.

TEACHER NOTE	Create a sample Response Journal entry to use as an example.

Use a puppet to model the process of responding to someone's writing by giving a compliment. For example, say:

TEACHER: Here is my Response Journal. It says, "I like the rabbit most." And I drew this picture of the rabbit. [Show the drawing to the class.]

PUPPET: I like the colors you used to draw the rabbit! [Puppet points to a part of the drawing.] It looks just like the rabbit in the story.

TEACHER: Thank you, [puppet's name]!

Ask: "What did you notice about the way [puppet's name] responded to my writing?" Volunteers respond.

- *She said something nice.*
- *She said what she liked about the drawing.*
- *She pointed to it in the drawing.*

Use responses to confirm that the puppet gave a compliment, or said what she liked about the writing.

Display the Sharing Our Writing Anchor Chart and add "Give a compliment" to the sequence on the chart.

Sharing Our Writing Anchor Chart
1. Share and listen
2. Give a compliment

Students Echo Read the steps on the chart to review the process for sharing writing with a peer. Explain that students will practice sharing their writing with a partner and will give each other one compliment about something good they notice.

✔ Divide the class into pairs. Students share their Response Journal entries, giving one compliment to their peer.

After partners share their Response Journal entries and receive feedback, instruct students to Mix and Mingle, and ask: "How did it feel to hear a compliment from your partner? How did it help your writing?" Use Equity Sticks to call on several students to share.

ANALYZE SCALE IN *CARTA MARINA* 14 MIN.

Whole Group

Explain that students will continue to think about artwork as they take a closer look at images in *Carta Marina*. Tell that one tool artists use to help their artwork tell a story is scale. Ask: "What do you already know about scale?" Volunteers respond.

- *I get on a scale when I go to the doctor's office.*
- *I think a scale tells how much you weigh.*

Use responses to affirm that a scale can be a tool people use to find the weight of something. Explain that in art, *scale* has something to do with size, too, but it means something a little different. In art, *scale* means how large or small something seems when it is compared to something else. Place the word *scale* on the Word Wall as a yearlong word.

Use the illustration on the cover of *Why Mosquitoes Buzz in People's Ears* to provide an example of scale. Point out that the scale, or size, of the mosquito in the picture is much larger than a mosquito is in real life. He's almost as big as the man's head! The illustrators drew the mosquito in a larger scale to show the importance of the mosquito character to the story.

Display *Carta Marina* (**http://witeng.link/0409**) and explain that cartographers also use scale when they create maps. Zoom in on the land areas at the top right corner of the map. Focus on a few scenes where the humans and animals are out of proportion with their surroundings, such as the archer standing in a forest or the birds nested in the treetops near the number 79 along the right side.

Instruct students to Think-Pair-Share, and ask: "Remember that *scale* means how large or small an object seems when compared to something else. What do you notice about the size or scale of the animals, ships, and land features?" Call on several students to respond.

- *Many of the people are bigger than the trees, mountains, and houses.*
- *The birds in the trees look almost as big as the trees.*
- *Many of the sea creatures are larger than the boats.*
- *The trees are larger than the mountains. That's not right!*

Ask: "Why would a cartographer show land features, animals, plants, buildings, and people with a scale that doesn't match their sizes in real life?"

- *He might make the people bigger because they are more important.*
- *He might make the animals bigger to show how scary they are.*
- *He might draw the animals bigger to make them easier to see.*

Distribute a blank piece of paper to each student. Ask them to draw a picture of an elephant and a picture of a mouse. Students share their drawing with a partner and discuss the scale of their animals in relation to each other. Instruct pairs to discuss the following questions: "How are your drawings the same? How are they different?"

Use Equity Sticks to call on students to respond to the following questions:

- Did you draw your mouse the same size as your elephant?
- How big would a mouse look, compared to an elephant in real life?
- Did you draw your mouse in a larger scale than you would see in real life?

Extension

Compare *Carta Marina* to the map of Europe from *World Atlas*. Ask:

- "What similarities do you notice between the two maps?" (Both show land and water areas; both show pictures of plants, animals, and people that can be found in a country; both use scale that is inaccurate.)

- "What differences do you notice between the two maps?" (Each country is a different color in the *World Atlas*; language is in English; *Carta Marina* shows imaginary animals and this one does not; areas next to the main part of the map are left one color, without illustrations; no delicate lines drawn in the ocean, etc.)

Land 2 MIN.

ANSWER THE CONTENT FRAMING QUESTION

Display and read aloud the Content Framing Question. Instruct students to Mix and Mingle, and ask: "How did you use the words and pictures to help you understand unknown words?" Call on several students to share their responses with the class.

- *I listened for clues in the words to help the word make sense.*
- *I looked for clues in the pictures.*

Wrap 1 MIN.

ASSIGN HOMEWORK

Continue the class home-reading routine.

Analyze

Context and Alignment

Students use context clues from the words and illustrations to define unknown words in *Why Mosquitoes Buzz in People's Ears* (RL.K.4, RL.K.7). Each student:

- Determines meaning of the word *timid* from the text.
- Shares the clues from the text and illustration that informed their thinking.

Next Steps

If students have difficulty using clues from the text to define unknown words, practice defining words from the text that have a direct connection to an illustration. For example, read the last paragraph on page 2 and support students with defining the word *reeds*. Ask students to identify the reeds in the illustration and use the picture as a clue for defining the word.

⬇ LESSON 18 DEEP DIVE: VOCABULARY

Opposite Verbs in a Narrative

- **Time:** 15 min.

- **Text:** *Why Mosquitoes Buzz in People's Ears: A West African Tale*, Verna Aardema; Illustrations, Leo and Diane Dillon

- **Vocabulary Learning Goal:** Demonstrate understanding of *lumbered, scurried, returned,* and *left* by acting out their opposites. (L.K.5.b)

Launch

Display the cover of the text. Point out that Verna Aardema uses a lot of interesting words to tell this story. She uses action words to help readers imagine what the animals in the story do.

Students Think-Pair-Share and describe an action of an animal in the story. Call on volunteers to share their examples. Use student responses to reinforce that action words are the words that tell what a person, place, or thing does.

Explain that students are going to find and act out opposite action words from *Why Mosquitoes Buzz in People's Ears.*

Learn

Explain that students will listen closely as you read sentences from the story. Create a chart on the board to record student responses.

Action Word	Illustration	Opposite	Illustration

Display pages 3–4 and read: "The iguana lumbered on." Students stand when they hear the action word in the sentence. Remind students that they learned the meaning of the word in Deep Dive 16. Call on a standing student to identify the action word and act it out. Encourage the student to describe their action to define the word. All students sit.

Continue displaying pages 3–4 and read: "The rabbit scurried out of her hole." Call on a different standing student to identify the action word and act it out. Encourage the student to describe their action to define the word.

Ask: "What do you notice about the action words *lumbered* and *scurried*?" Volunteers respond.

- *They are both action words.*
- *They both tell how animals move.*
- *They describe ways to move that are very different.*
- *They are opposite movement words.*

Use student responses to reinforce that *lumbered* and *scurried* are opposite action words. Record the words on the chart, using the student actions and descriptions to sketch a simple illustration that represents the meaning of the word.

Action Word	Illustration	Opposite	Illustration
lumbered		scurried	

Display pages 7–8 and read: "The Mother Owl returned to her nest." Students stand when they hear the action word in the sentence. Remind the students that they learned the meaning of the word in Deep Dive 17. Call on a standing student to identify the action word and act it out. Encourage the student to describe their action to define the word. All students sit.

Display pages 25–26 and read: "The mosquito left the animal council." Call on a different standing student to identify the action word and act it out. Ask: "What do you notice about the action words *returned* and *left*?" Volunteers respond.

- *They are both action words.*
- *They both tell where an animal went.*
- *They describe animals doing very different things.*
- *They are opposite of each other.*

Use student responses to reinforce that *returned* and *left* are opposite action words. Record the words on the chart, using the student actions and descriptions to sketch a simple illustration that represents the meaning of the word.

Action Word	Illustration	Opposite	Illustration
lumbered		scurried	
returned		left	

✔ Instruct students to Mix and Mingle. As you call out "action," students find a partner. Read a pair of opposite action words from the board. One student takes a turn acting out one word from the pair. The other student acts out the opposite. Repeat for both opposite pairs. Circulate to provide support and to ensure accurate portrayal of opposites.

Land

Explain that these opposite action words help readers better understand the story.

Ask: "What did you learn about the animals in the story by exploring opposite movement words?"

- *Different animals move in different ways.*
- *Some animals are slow and some are fast.*

Ask: "What did you learn about the Mother Owl and the mosquito by exploring their opposite actions?"

- *The Mother Owl was a good mom since she came back to take care of her owlets.*
- *The Mother Owl was brave for coming home again.*
- *The mosquito was scared to face the other animals.*
- *The mosquito felt bad and worried the animals were mad at her.*

How can a story transport you to a different place?

1 | 2 | 3 | 4 | 5 | 6 | 7 | 8 | 9 | 10 | 11 | 12 | 13 | 14 | 15 | **16** | **17** | **18** | **19** | **20** | **21** | 22 | 23 | 24 | 25 | 26 | 27 | 28 | 29 | 30 | 31 | 32 | 33 | 34 | 35 | 36

Lesson 19

TEXTS

- "Lions Roar," *CanTeach* (**http://witeng.link/0410**)

- *Why Mosquitoes Buzz in People's Ears: A West African Tale*, Verna Aardema; Illustrations, Leo and Diane Dillon

Lesson 19: At a Glance

AGENDA

Welcome (7 min.)

Practice Fluency

Launch (2 min.)

Learn (62 min.)

Analyze Words and Illustrations (18 min.)

Collect Evidence for Focusing Question Task 3 (14 min.)

Execute Part 1 of Focusing Question Task 3 (15 min.)

Experiment with Responding to a Peer's Writing (15 min.)

Land (3 min.)

Answer the Content Framing Question

Wrap (1 min.)

Assign Homework

Vocabulary Deep Dive: Finding Meaning with the Prefix *un-* (15 min.)

STANDARDS ADDRESSED

The full text of ELA Standards can be found in the Module Overview.

Reading

- RL.K.1, RL.K.4, RL.K.7

Writing

- W.K.2, W.K.5

Speaking and Listening

- SL.K.1.a, SL.K.2

Language

- L.K.5.c
- ⬇ L.K.4.b

MATERIALS

- Assessment 19A: Focusing Question Task 3
- Repeated Language Chart
- Evidence Organizer for *Why Mosquitoes Buzz in People's Ears*
- Sticky notes
- Sharing Our Writing Anchor Chart
- Sample response to Focusing Question Task 3, Part 1
- Index cards
- Document camera (if available)
- Puppet

Learning Goals

Use the words and illustrations in the text to describe the characters' actions. (RLK.4, RL.K.7)

✔ Collect evidence for the Focusing Question Task.

Use the illustrations to determine what is happening in one scene of the text. (RL.K.7, W.K.2)

✔ Complete Part 1 of the Focusing Question Task.

⬇ Use the meaning of the prefix *un-* as a clue to find the meaning of an unknown word. (L.K.4.b)

✔ Use the word part *un-* and an illustration to figure out the meaning of the word *unwilling*.

✔ Checks for Understanding

Prepare

FOCUSING QUESTION: Lessons 16–21

How can a story transport you to a different place?

CONTENT FRAMING QUESTION: Lesson 19

Reveal: *What does a deeper exploration of the words and illustrations reveal in* Why Mosquitoes Buzz in People's Ears?

CRAFT QUESTION: Lesson 19

Experiment: *How do I respond to someone's writing?*

In this lesson, students rely heavily on illustrations in the text to guide learning. They use them to define new verbs as well as to collect evidence on the characters' actions for the Focusing Question Task. Students begin the first part of their Focusing Question Task by analyzing an illustration to determine whether it depicts a specific moment in the story, or is instead a moment from a character's memory.

Welcome 7 MIN.

PRACTICE FLUENCY

Display the Repeated Language Chart with the fifth and sixth lines of the poem added. Read the lines aloud. Students Echo Read the lines.

Repeated Language
Poem: "Lions Roar," Original author unknown • Lions roar, eagles soar, • Leopards growl, cheetahs prowl, • Snakes slide, eagles glide, • Lizards crawl, jackals call, • Monkeys leap, snails creep, • Ants heap, fledglings cheep,

Reread the fifth and sixth lines again, prompting students to point to their ears when they hear a rhyming pair. Use Equity Sticks to call on students to share the rhyming words they hear.

Ask: "How is a monkey different from the snail? Do they move in the same ways?" Volunteers respond.

Ask: "Thinking about monkeys and snails and how they move, what kind of movements are <u>leap</u> and <u>creep</u>? Are they the same or different?" Volunteers respond. Encourage students to stand up and act out these contrast movements.

Explain that animals move in many different ways. Snails do not have legs or arms like a monkey so they can only creep or glide slowly a little bit at a time.

Ask: "What do ants do? What does it mean to <u>heap</u>? Think of the way ants move and where they live to help you answer." Volunteers respond.

- *They move things around.*
- *They carry things back to their hole.*
- *They make hills in the ground.*

Reinforce that ants carry things on their back to the anthill. They <u>heap</u> or make a pile at the anthill. Define *fledglings* as young birds that are just learning to fly.

Create movements for the last verb in each line to help students internalize the definitions. For example:

- Creep: hunch shoulders and move slowly forward.
- Cheep: flutter your hands like little wings and say "cheep."

Reread all six lines of the poem aloud. Students Echo Read the poem while incorporating the movements for each line.

Launch 2 MIN.

Post and read aloud the Content Framing Question.

Ask: "How did we use the illustrations in the previous lesson? How did they help us understand the story and the characters?" Volunteers respond.

- *They helped show what was happening in the story.*
- *They helped tell the story.*
- *They showed what the characters looked like.*

Explain that in this lesson students use illustrations from *Why Mosquitoes Buzz in People's Ears* to understand the actions and movements of the characters. This will help them collect evidence for Focusing Question Task 3.

Learn 62 MIN.

ANALYZE WORDS AND ILLUSTRATIONS 18 MIN.

Whole Group

Remind students that in the previous lesson, they collected evidence about different characters in the text and what those characters look like. Explain that in this lesson they will use the words and illustrations to understand how the characters act or move.

Ask: "Do the illustrations in a text move? How can we figure out how the animals are moving in this text?" Volunteers respond.

- *They don't move! It's not TV.*
- *We can look at the pictures and pretend.*
- *Sometimes the illustration shows two pictures of the animal. We see how it moved from one place to another.*
- *We can listen to the words and maybe that tells us.*

Confirm that the pictures in a text do not move, but there are ways for the author and illustrator to help readers imagine how the characters move.

💬 Explain that now students will read through portions of the text and use the words and illustrations to learn more about the characters' movements. Prompt students to sit in "listening position" and to follow along with the copy of the text in your hands.

Display pages 3–4 and read the first three sentences on page 4. Prompt students to listen closely to the words the author uses to describe the way the iguana moves.

Ask: "What words did you hear to describe how the iguana moves?" Volunteers respond.

- *He bobs his head.*
- *He lumbers.*

Extension

Remind students of how the author created words such as *badamin* to help readers understand how the characters move. The way the sound moves through the word gives you a good picture of how the character is moving its body. For example, say, "badamin," emphasizing the up and down sounds of the syllables. Explain that the up and down sound in the word mimics the up and down movements of the iguana's head.

Confirm that the words in the text tell readers how the iguana is moving in the text. The picture does not move so readers need to use the words to help them understand.

Read the next paragraph on page 4. Explain that the author does not use any action words to describe how the python moves. Ask: "If the words do not tell us, how can we use the illustration? What do you notice about the python's body that will help us understand how it moves?" Volunteers respond.

- *He doesn't have legs or arms.*
- *He needs to slide.*
- *He slides down the hole.*
- *He moves like an* S.

Reinforce that the illustrator shows how the python is moving. Confirm that the way a python moves is by slithering. Define *slithering* as "moving by sliding along the ground." Instruct students to place their hand on the ground and mimic slithering like a snake.

Use Equity Sticks to call on a volunteer to approach the text and point to the part in the illustration that shows the python <u>slithering</u> away.

Read the selected portions of the text below. Instruct students to Think-Pair-Share about the following questions. Use Equity Sticks to call on students to approach the text and point to the moment in the text where a character demonstrates a specific action. Students use the following Nonverbal Signal to indicate their level of agreement:

- Thumbs-up: we agree.
- Thumbs-sideways: we are not sure.
- Thumbs-down: we don't agree.

Read the last paragraph on page 4. If needed, briefly define *scurried* as moving quickly with short steps, and *bounded* as hopping fast.

1   **How do the words help us understand how the rabbit moves?**

- *She moves away fast.*
- *She hops away.*
- *The words tell us she hops away really fast.*

Use Equity Sticks to call on a student to approach the text and point to the rabbit in the illustration that is <u>scurrying</u> out of the burrow. Students indicate their level of agreement.

Read the first paragraph on page 5.

2 How do the words help us understand what the crow does?

- *The crow flies away.*
- *He says, "Kaa, kaa."*
- *He wants to tell people there is danger.*

> **Scaffold**
>
> Define *crying* as making a loud yell or shout, not having tears come down from the eyes.

Use Equity Sticks to call on a student to approach the text and point to the crow in the illustration that is flying and <u>crying</u> out. Students indicate their level of agreement.

Read the second paragraph on pages 5–6. If needed, define *leaping* as "jumping a long distance."

3 How do the words help us understand what the monkey does?

- *He screeches.*
- *He jumps far in the trees.*
- *He wants to tell people there is danger.*

Use Equity Sticks to call on a student to approach the text and point to the monkey in the illustration that is <u>leaping</u>. Students indicate their level of agreement.

COLLECT EVIDENCE FOR FOCUSING QUESTION TASK 3 14 MIN.

Small Groups

Explain that now students will use their understanding of the characters' movements to record evidence for the Focusing Question Task.

Display the Evidence Organizer for *Why Mosquitoes Buzz in People's Ears* in front of the class. Point to the second row on the chart and read aloud the following question from the chart: "How do they move?" Students Echo Read the question. Explain that now students will work together to record evidence from the words and illustrations that describes the movements of each character.

Divide the class into small groups of five. Assign each member of the group one animal from the evidence organizer. Explain that they will record the evidence for this animal.

Alternate Activity

Locate images of each animal on the evidence organizer and put them in a bag. Allow each group member to reach into the bag and pull out one image. Students collect evidence on the animal they pulled from the bag.

Give groups two minutes to discuss the following questions:

- What does that animal do in the story?

- How does that animal move in the story?

As students discuss, circulate with the text, or use a document camera to project pages of the text, to allow students to reference the illustration.

✔ Using the illustrations as a guide, students draw and label a picture of the characters acting out their movements.

After students record their evidence, ask each group to share their evidence aloud with the class. Choose two to three drawings of each animal to represent on the evidence organizer.

TEACHER NOTE	Consider creating a second chart near the evidence organizer to display the drawings not being used. This helps build students' confidence and ensures that no feelings are hurt.

SAMPLE EVIDENCE ORGANIZER FOR *WHY MOSQUITOES BUZZ IN PEOPLE'S EARS*

Evidence Organizer for *Why Mosquitoes Buzz in People's Ears*					
Characters	**Iguana**	**Python**	**Rabbit**	**Crow**	**Monkey**
What do they look like?	• green • sticks in ears • short	• purple • no legs • long	• gray • big ears • big eyes	• black • wings • beak	• brown • long tail • long arms
How do they move?	• walks slow • bobs head	• slithers • slides	• runs out • hops away	• flies away • says "kaa"	• jumps on branches

EXECUTE PART 1 OF FOCUSING QUESTION TASK 3   15 MIN.

Individuals

Acknowledge the work students have done with the illustrations in *Why Mosquitoes Buzz in People's Ears*. Remind them that they have used the illustrations to understand key events, define new words, and even figure out which part of the story is in a character's imagination.

Explain that now they will use this knowledge to write a sentence about one of the illustrations as the first part of the Focusing Question Task. Remind students that they have learned a lot about the different characters, specifically their actions and movements. For the first part of the Focusing Question Task they will look at an illustration in the text and respond to the following prompt about that illustration. Emphasize that students should use their knowledge of the illustrations as well as the characters to help them answer this question.

Post and read aloud pages 17–18. If possible, use a document camera to project the image to allow students to easily see the illustration.

> What is happening in this picture? Does this picture show a real moment from the story, or is it an imaginary moment?

Ask: "What do we mean by *imaginary*?" Volunteers respond.

- *It is something that isn't real.*
- *It is something you make up.*
- *It is something that happens in your mind but not real life.*

Instruct students to Think-Pair-Share about the prompt. Students discuss why they believe it is an imaginary or a real moment from the story. Encourage students to use the evidence organizer and the description of the characters as a guide.

Distribute page 1 of Assessment 19A. Explain that students will now write a sentence and draw a picture to answer the prompt.

✔ Students write and illustrate one sentence about what part of the story the illustration on pages 17–18 depicts.

Name:

Assessment 19A: Focusing Question Task 3

Part 1
Directions: Write your sentence on the lines provided below and add a drawing to illustrate your sentence.

TEACHER
NOTE
While students complete Part 1 or prior to the lesson, prepare your own sample response to Focusing Question Task 3, Part 1, using the sample response in Appendix C as a guide. This sample response will be used later in this lesson as students experiment with responding to peer's writing. You will use this sample response to model giving a suggestion to another's writing or drawing.

EXPERIMENT WITH RESPONDING TO A PEER'S WRITING 15 MIN.

Pairs

Post and read the Craft Question aloud: *How do I respond to someone's writing?*

Instruct students to Think-Pair-Share, and ask: "How did we answer this same question in the previous lesson? What is one way that we can respond to another's writing?" Use Equity Sticks to call on students to share.

- *We can tell them what we like about it.*
- *We can tell them what they did a good job at.*
- *We can point to what is our favorite part.*

Display the Sharing Our Writing Anchor Chart. Ask: "How do we share our writing with each other? What do we do?" Use Equity Sticks to call on students to remind the class of the sequence for sharing writing with one another.

- *First we have to read our sentence to our partner. Our partner listens.*
- *Then, we tell them what we like about their sentence.*
- *Then we switch.*

Explain that in this lesson students will learn about another step in this sequence: giving a suggestion.

Define *suggestion* as "a piece of advice or an idea to add to one's writing." Explain that suggestions are meant to help, provide encouragement, and show ways to make a piece of writing better, not to say something mean about someone's writing or make them feel bad.

Use a puppet to model the process of providing a suggestion about one's writing. For example,

TEACHER: Here is my sentence: *The python remembers the iguana.* It is a memory so I drew the iguana making a mean face, because it didn't really happen like that in the story.

PUPPET: I really like the iguana's mean face. I have one suggestion. You can make bigger teeth so the iguana looks scary! The real iguana doesn't show his teeth.

TEACHER: Thank you for your suggestion! That is a really great idea.

Ask: "Why do we share our writing with others? Should we get angry or upset if someone has a suggestion or an idea that changes our writing?" Volunteers respond.

- *We share because we can learn more.*

- *Maybe someone has a good idea.*

- *We shouldn't get upset. They are trying to help.*

Ask: "Does sharing our writing and hearing a suggestion mean our work is wrong?" Volunteers respond. Confirm that when someone suggests adding to your writing or drawing, this doesn't mean the work is bad or wrong. The person is just suggesting something to make the writing or drawing even better.

Reinforce that all writers get feedback from others. No one's writing is perfect the first time–even teachers'! Sharing with a partner and giving a suggestion is a great way to learn from one another. Suggestions are helpful because they help writers improve their writing. Revising can also help writers feel more confident about their work.

Add "Give a suggestion" to the Sharing Our Writing Anchor Chart. Read this line aloud. Students Echo Read the line.

Sharing Our Writing Anchor Chart
1. Share and listen
2. Give a compliment
3. Give a suggestion

Explain that now they will practice responding to another's writing by sharing one suggestion with their partner. Review the sharing sequence established in the previous lesson. Explain that after students share a compliment, they will offer one suggestion to their partner about how to make their drawing even better. Then, students switch roles.

Divide the class into pairs. Pairs share the sentences and drawings from page 1 of Assessment 19A. Partners offer one compliment and one suggestion with their peer.

TEACHER NOTE	Students will not respond to suggestions from peers and add to their writing at this time. Adding to their writing will be addressed in Lessons 22–27. Students' work with W.K.5 is broken down into these two parts in order to gradually introduce the concept of responding to feedback.

After partners share their sentences and receive feedback, instruct students to Mix and Mingle, and ask: "How did it feel to hear an idea from your partner? Do you think it could help your drawing?" Use Equity Sticks to call on four students to share.

Land 3 MIN.

ANSWER THE CONTENT FRAMING QUESTION

Display and read aloud the Content Framing Question. Ask: "Why are the illustrations so important in a story? How can they help readers better understand a story?" Call on several students to respond.

- *They show us what is happening.*
- *They tell us more about the characters.*
- *We can see the animals act out the words.*
- *The pictures show us the events.*
- *The illustrator puts hints in the pictures to remind us what is a memory.*

Wrap 1 MIN.

ASSIGN HOMEWORK

Continue the class home-reading routine.

Analyze

Context and Alignment

Students use the words and illustrations in the text to determine a moment in the text an illustration depicts (RL.K.7, W.K.2). Each student:

- Writes one sentence about what is happening in the illustration.
- Includes a drawing to support their response.

Next Steps

If students have difficulty identifying what moment the illustration on pages 17–18 depicts, consider turning back to pages 3–4. Reread these pages aloud and compare and contrast the characterizations of the python. Revisit the evidence organizer to discuss how the python moves in the story and compare that to the depiction of the python in pages 17–18. Ask: "Does this show the python going down the rabbit hole? Does the python in the story have such big teeth as this?"

⬇ LESSON 19 DEEP DIVE: VOCABULARY

Finding Meaning with the Prefix *un-*

- **Time:** 15 min.

- **Text:** *Why Mosquitoes Buzz in People's Ears: A West African Tale*, Verna Aardema; Illustrations, Leo and Diane Dillon

- **Vocabulary Learning Goal:** Use the meaning of the prefix *un-* as a clue to find the meaning of an unknown word. (L.K.4.b)

Launch

Remind students that in Deep Dive Lesson 17, they used the word beginning *re-* to find the meaning of new words.

Explain that students are going to use a different word beginning as a clue to figure out the meanings of more words describing the animals in the story.

Post and Echo Read the following words: *uncertainly, unkind,* and *unwilling.*

Ask: "What word beginning do these words have in common?" Students respond chorally.

  ▪ *Un!*

Redirect student attention to the list of posted words and underline *un-* in each word. Explain that the word beginning *un-* means "not." Point out that, as such, when you add *un-* to a word it changes it to mean the opposite.

Reinforce that students are going to use this information as a clue to figure out the meaning of these words.

Learn

Instruct students to listen closely as you read and to give a thumbs-up signal when they hear a word that starts with the word beginning *un-*.

Display page 14 of the text and read the first paragraph, emphasizing the word *uncertainly.* Call on a student with a thumbs-up to identify the word starting with *un-*.

  ▪ *Uncertainly.*

Direct student attention to *uncertainly* on the board. Draw a box around the root word, *certain*, and point out that this is the main word part in the word. Reinforce that because *un–* means "not" the new word is the opposite of this word.

Ask: "When someone says, 'I am certain,' what do they mean?" Volunteers respond.

- *They mean they are sure.*
- *They mean they feel 100% about it.*

Reinforce that now students know that this new word means the opposite of *certain* or "not for sure."

Model how to use the illustration to figure out how the rabbit is feeling and acting. For example, point out that the rabbit looks scared, nervous, or shy. Ask: "If the rabbit is scared, what is the rabbit not?" Volunteers respond.

- *The rabbit is not being brave.*
- *The rabbit is not confident.*
- *The rabbit looks like he is not sure of himself.*

Use student responses to determine the meaning of *uncertainly* as "to not know for sure."

Display pages 1–2 of the text and read: "The iguana was <u>unkind</u> to the mosquito." Call on a student with a thumbs-up to identify the word starting with *un–*.

- *Unkind.*

Direct student attention to *unkind* on the board. Draw a box around the root word *kind* and ask: "What is the main word part?" Volunteers respond.

- *Kind!*

Reinforce that because *un–* means "not" the new word is the opposite of the main word part: *kind*. Encourage students to use the illustration and knowledge of both word parts to determine the meaning of *unkind*. Instruct students to Think-Pair-Share, and ask: "What does *unkind* mean?" Volunteers respond.

- *Because the iguana is being mean to the mosquito, it could mean, "mean."*
- *It could mean "not kind" or "not nice."*

Use student responses to determine the meaning of *unkind* as "not nice." Record this definition next to *unkind* on the board.

Display pages 9–10 of the text and read: "The owl was <u>unwilling</u> to call the sun." Call on a student with a thumbs-up to identify the word starting with *un–*.

- *Unwilling.*

Organize students into pairs. Explain that students are going to work with their partner to figure out the meaning of the word *unwilling*. Reinforce that students should use the meaning of the word beginning *un–* and the main word part *willing*, and the illustration of the owl as clues to help them.

Land

✔ Distribute an index card to each pair. Display pages 9–10 and read the sentence again. Students work together to determine the meaning of the word *unwilling*. Allow time for students to discuss their ideas. Encourage students to write or draw their ideas on the index card. Circulate to provide support and ensure understanding of the word beginning *un–*.

Use Equity Sticks to call on pairs to share their ideas.

- *Mother Owl could not bear to call the sun.*
- *Mother Owl would not wake the sun.*
- *Mother Owl did not want day to come.*

Use student responses to determine the meaning of *unwilling* as "not wanting to do something." Record this definition on the board.

Ask: "Why was Mother Owl <u>unwilling</u> to call the sun?" Volunteers respond.

- *Because she was so sad one of her babies had died.*

■ FOCUSING QUESTION: LESSONS 16–21

How can a story transport you to a different place?

1 | 2 | 3 | 4 | 5 | 6 | 7 | 8 | 9 | 10 | 11 | 12 | 13 | 14 | 15 | **16** | **17** | **18** | **19** | **20** | **21** | 22 | 23 | 24 | 25 | 26 | 27 | 28 | 29 | 30 | 31 | 32 | 33 | 34 | 35 | 36

Lesson 20

TEXTS

- "Lions Roar," *CanTeach* (**http://witeng.link/0410**)

- *Why Mosquitoes Buzz in People's Ears: A West African Tale*, Verna Aardema; Illustrations, Leo and Diane Dillon

- *Carta Marina*, Olaus Magnus, (**http://witeng.link/0409**)

- *Earth from Space*, Stöckli, Reto, et al. (**http://witeng.link/0373**)

- "Burkina Faso: Music," *Our Africa* (**http://witeng.link/0411**)

Lesson 20: At a Glance

AGENDA

Welcome (5 min.)

Practice Fluency

Launch (3 min.)

Learn (63 min.)

Determine the Essential Meaning of Why Mosquitoes Buzz in People's Ears *(20 min.)*

Explore Sound Effect Words (10 min.)

Execute Focusing Question Task 3 (25 min.)

Interpret the Essential Meaning of Carta Marina *and* Earth from Space *(8 min.)*

Land (3 min.)

Answer the Content Framing Question

Wrap (1 min.)

Assign Homework

Vocabulary Deep Dive: Multiple-Meaning Words: *Snap* and *mind* (15 min.)

STANDARDS ADDRESSED

The full text of ELA Standards can be found in the Module Overview.

Reading

- RL.K.1, RL.K.2, RL.K.4

Writing

- W.K.1, W.K.8

Speaking and Listening

- SL.K.1

Language

- ⬇ L.K.4.a

MATERIALS

- Assessment 19A: Focusing Question Task 3
- Repeated Language Chart
- Dominoes
- Sound Effects Words Chart (see lesson for details)
- Evidence Organizer for *Why Mosquitoes Buzz in People's Ears*
- Evidence organizer matching cards (see lesson for details)
- Chart paper or large sheets of paper

Learning Goals

Determine essential meanings of *Why Mosquitoes Buzz in People's Ears.* (RL.K.1)

✔ Select an essential meaning from the story that resonates most personally.

Express understanding of the characters in *Why Mosquitoes Buzz in People's Ears* by writing an opinion piece about a favorite character. (RL.K.1, W.K.1, W.K.8)

✔ Begin the written portion of Focusing Question Task 3.

⬇ Describe multiple meanings of the words *snap* and *mind*. (L.K.4.a)

✔ Mix and Mingle, explaining the meanings of each word and sharing a sentence using each word correctly.

✔ Checks for Understanding

Prepare

FOCUSING QUESTION: Lessons 16–21

How can a story transport you to a different place?

CONTENT FRAMING QUESTION: Lesson 20

Distill: *What is the essential meaning of* Why Mosquitoes Buzz in People's Ears?

CRAFT QUESTION: Lesson 20

Execute: *How do I execute my Focusing Question Task?*

Students explore essential meanings in *Why Mosquitoes Buzz in People's Ears* by thinking about the life lessons readers can learn from the story. They apply this habit of mind to artwork as they consider the essential meanings of *Carta Marina* and *Earth from Space*. Students also examine the storytelling craft by considering the words the author chose to evoke the sight and sounds of the African jungle. In addition, students synthesize their learning about the characters in the text as they form an opinion about their favorite character and begin writing an opinion piece for their Focusing Question Task.

Welcome 5 MIN.

PRACTICE FLUENCY

Display the Repeated Language Chart with the last two lines of the poem added. Read the lines aloud. Students Echo Read the lines.

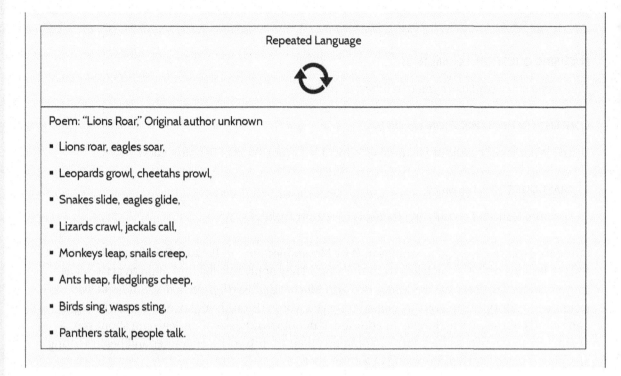

Repeated Language

Poem: "Lions Roar," Original author unknown

- Lions roar, eagles soar,

- Leopards growl, cheetahs prowl,

- Snakes slide, eagles glide,

- Lizards crawl, jackals call,

- Monkeys leap, snails creep,

- Ants heap, fledglings cheep,

- Birds sing, wasps sting,

- Panthers stalk, people talk.

Reread the last two lines again, prompting students to point to their ears when they hear a rhyming pair. Use Equity Sticks to call on students to share the rhyming words they hear.

Define *stalk* as walking in a sneaky way like you are hunting something. Ask students to stand up and act out *stalk*.

Ask: "How are people different from animals? How does this poem give us one example of a difference?" Volunteers respond.

Create movements for the last verb in each line to help students internalize the definitions. For example:

- Sting: Put your hands behind you like a stinger and shake your hips.

- Talk: Place one hand near your mouth and open and close your fingers as if they were a mouth talking.

Reread the entire poem aloud. Students Echo Read the poem while incorporating the movements for each line.

Launch 3 MIN.

Display the front cover of *Why Mosquitoes Buzz in People's Ears*. Remind students that over the past few lessons they have explored the text in different ways. They started by noticing interesting things and asking good questions. Then they thought about what was happening in the text and looked more deeply at the illustrations.

Explain that building a strong understanding of what is happening in the story has prepared them to go deeper and think about the essential meaning of the text.

Display and read aloud the Content Framing Question. Students Echo Read the question.

Ask: "What do we look for when we think about the essential meaning of a text?" Volunteers respond.

- *We look for the important message of the story.*
- *We think about what the author is trying to tell us.*
- *We find out what the story means.*

Learn 63 MIN.

DETERMINE THE ESSENTIAL MEANING OF *WHY MOSQUITOES BUZZ IN PEOPLE'S EARS* 20 MIN.

Whole Group

Remind students that *Why Mosquitoes Buzz in People's Ears* is a folktale. Explain that folktales, like the one shared in this text, are stories that have been told over and over for a very long time. Long ago, folktales were stories that were told and retold out loud; they were not written down at first.

Tell students that folktales were often created to explain something about the world, or to teach a lesson about life. Ask: "What does the story in *Why Mosquitoes Buzz in People's Ears* explain about the world?" Volunteers respond.

- *It explains why mosquitoes buzz in people's ears.*
- *It explains why mosquitoes are annoying.*
- *It explains why people don't like mosquitoes.*

💬 Tell students that *Why Mosquitoes Buzz in People's Ears* explains something about the world and teaches a lesson about life. Ask students to think about the life lesson the story teaches as they read the story one more time.

309

Read the text aloud. After the reading, ask the following TDQs.

1 How did King Lion use questions to learn why the night was lasting so long?

- *He called a meeting of the animals.*
- *He asked each animal a question.*
- *He kept asking questions until he figured out what really happened.*

2 What might have happened if King Lion only listened to Mother Owl and didn't continue to ask more questions?

- *He might have punished the monkey because Mother Owl said it was the monkey's fault.*
- *The animals might not learn the whole story.*
- *Maybe the animals would stay mad at each other.*

3 At the end of the story, it says the mosquito had a "guilty conscience." What is a guilty conscience? Why might the mosquito feel guilty?

- *A guilty conscience is when you feel bad about something you did.*
- *You have a guilty conscience when you did something wrong and you feel bad.*
- *Maybe the mosquito feels bad because she knows she lied.*
- *Maybe the mosquito feels guilty because she lied and then the baby owl died.*

4 What lines do you hear repeated over and over in the text? Why do you think the author repeated those lines?

- *I hear King Lion telling what happened.*
- *I hear the events repeated, step by step.*
- *I think the author is showing those lines are important.*
- *I think the repeated lines show how King Lion is figuring out what really happened.*
- *Maybe the author is showing how each event made something else happen.*

Reread the chain of events from page 21. As you read each event, place one domino in a line, in a place easily visible to students. After reading the final event, knock down the domino chain.

Extension

Prior to the lesson, locate images of the animals in *Why Mosquitoes Buzz in People's Ears* and attach a character image to each domino. This will provide a visual reinforcement for the cause and effect nature of the story.

Ask: "How is this domino chain similar to what happens in the story?" Volunteers respond.

- *It's like how the python was scared, and then he scared the rabbit, and the rabbit scared the crow, and then it kept going.*
- *Little things happened and led up to a big thing happening.*

■ *All the animals' actions led up to the night lasting too long. Each one played a part.*

Instruct students to Think-Pair-Share, and ask: "What is the essential meaning of the story? What life lesson does it teach you?" Call on several students to respond.

■ *Don't lie.*

■ *A small lie can turn into a big problem.*

■ *Ask questions to get to the bottom of a problem.*

■ *Things aren't always the way they seem.*

Select three or four strong responses and write each essential meaning on a large piece of paper. Post each poster in a different area of the room.

✔ Students select the essential meaning that stands out the most to them from the story. They walk to the area of the room with the poster showing their selected essential meaning. Use Equity Sticks to call on at least two students from each area to explain their thinking.

EXPLORE SOUND EFFECT WORDS 10 MIN.

Whole Group

Tell students that Verna Aardema not only explained something about the world and taught a lesson about life with *Why Mosquitoes Buzz in People's Ears*, she also made the book really fun to read! Explain that students will look at some words from the text that make the story interesting and fun to read.

Ask students: "What does a mosquito say?" Students chorally respond.

■ *Buzz!*

Invite students to make a buzzing sound like a mosquito. Point to the word *Buzz* in the title on the front cover of the text. Explain that the word *buzz* is a special kind of word because it names something by trying to copy its sound. The word *buzz* actually sounds like the buzzing noise a mosquito makes. It's like a sound effect!

Begin a simple chart to record sound effect words from the text (see example below).

Tell students they will look in the text for more sound effect words. Read page 2 aloud and ask: "Did you hear any words that tried to copy the real sound? What did you hear?" Volunteers respond.

■ *I heard "mek, mek, mek."*

Confirm that *mek, mek, mek* is a sound effect word. Reread the last sentence on page 2 and ask: "What is *mek, mek, mek* trying to sound like from the story?"

■ *It sounds like the iguana walking.*

Add *mek, mek* to the chart. Invite students to pretend to walk like an iguana while saying, "mek, mek, mek."

As time permits, continue to read through sections of the story and discuss sound effect words in the text, using the questioning procedure outlined above. Possible pages to explore include:

- Page 4: *wasawusu, krik*

- Page 5: *kaa*

- Page 12: *taaa*

- Page 24: *hoooo!*

SAMPLE SOUND EFFECTS WORDS CHART

Words	Sounds like
buzz	Mosquito
mek, mek	Iguana
wasuwusu	Python
krik, krik	Rabbit
kaa	Crow
taa	Falling branch
Hooo!	Owl

Instruct students to Mix and Mingle, and ask: "How do these sound effect words help transport you to the African forest?"

Foundational Skills Connection

If students need additional practice blending and segmenting onsets and rimes, use the author-created words that represent animal movements (e.g., *krik*, *rim*, *pem*, *mek*) to practice. Students can also use these words to add or substitute sounds to make new words. As you read the movement words, invite students to blend and/or segment the onset (beginning sound) and rime (ending sounds) in each word and encourage students to change sounds to make other new nonsense words. For example, you might point out that the author used a nonsense word to describe how the crowd gathered–*pem*. Ask: "What sound do you hear at the beginning of this word? What sounds do you hear at the end?" or Ask: "What new word would you make if I changed the beginning sound to a 'v' (or any consonant)?"

EXECUTE FOCUSING QUESTION TASK 3 25 MIN.

Individuals

Explain that now students will use the evidence they have collected over the past few lessons to answer the Focusing Question.

Display and read aloud the Focusing Question: *How can a story transport you to a different place?* Students Echo Read the question.

Explain that different elements of the story work together to help transport readers to a different place. The story can help readers imagine what it might look like, sound like, and feel like in a different place.

Instruct students to Think-Pair-Share, and ask: "What parts of *Why Mosquitoes Buzz in People's Ears* help transport you to the West African forest? How does the story take you there in your imagination?" Use Equity Sticks to call on students to respond.

- *The pictures help me imagine what it looks like.*
- *The funny words help me imagine what it sounds like.*
- *The characters help me imagine the animals.*

Use responses to explain that they will be writing about one of the elements from the text that can help transport them into the story: the characters.

Tell students that they will respond to the following prompt for their Focusing Question Task.

Who is your favorite character in *Why Mosquitoes Buzz in People's Ears*? Why?

Display the Evidence Organizer for *Why Mosquitoes Buzz in People's Ears*. Explain that students will write an opinion paragraph. They will think about the different evidence they have collected and form an opinion about which character is their favorite.

Ask: "What do we need to do before we make our opinion?" Volunteers respond.

- *We need to think about it.*
- *We need to look at the evidence.*
- *We need to think about the different characters and what makes them special.*

Use responses to confirm that students need to consider the evidence they collected about the character before they decide which character is their favorite.

TEACHER NOTE | Use index cards to create evidence organizer matching cards prior to the lesson. Write one phrase describing physical characteristics or movement from the evidence organizer on each card. Add visual cues as needed.

Use a matching game to support students in reading the evidence organizer. Give each student a card with a different descriptive word or phrase from the evidence organizer. Students identify the character associated with the word on their card. Call out each character and instruct students with words matching that character to stand up. Students share the word on their cards.

Divide the class into pairs. Students Think-Pair-Share about the following questions as their verbal rehearsal for Focusing Question Task 3.

- Think about the way the characters look. Which character stands out to you? Why?

- Think about the way the characters move. Which character stands out to you? Why?

- Which character is your favorite? Why?

Display page 2 of Assessment 19A: Focusing Question Task 3. Introduce the parts of the assessment students will complete in this lesson, pointing to each section of the handout as you explain where students record their sentences:

- Students write their opinion statement on the line provided at the top of page 2.

- Students write their first reason sentence on the lines provided at the bottom of page 2 and begin creating a drawing in the box provided.

TEACHER NOTE	Students work at different paces. Consider introducing the different steps one at time, leaving time for students to write their sentences before introducing the next step. It is not necessary that students memorize the structure of this piece to be successful at this task.

Ask: "How do we write an opinion statement? How can we make sure our reader knows we are giving our opinion?" Volunteers respond.

- *We tell them what we feel or think.*

- *We can use words from the question so they know that we are answering it.*

- *We tell them and then we tell them why.*

✔ Students begin Focusing Question Task 3 by writing their opinion statement and first supporting reason on page 2 of Assessment 19A. As time permits, students begin creating a drawing to accompany their first supporting reason.

INTERPRET THE ESSENTIAL MEANING OF *CARTA MARINA* AND *EARTH FROM SPACE* 8 MIN.

Whole Group

Remind students that they can think about the essential meanings of artwork, like they think about the essential meanings of texts. Explain that students will think about the essential meaning of the *Carta Marina* and the *Earth from Space* image they looked at earlier in the module.

Display *Carta Marina* (**http://witeng.link/0409**) and *Earth from Space* (**http://witeng.link/0373**).

Ask: "What is similar/different about these images?" Use Equity Sticks to call on students to respond.

- *The Carta Marina map shows what people thought the world looked like a long time ago. The photo shows what Earth looks like now.*

- *The Carta Marina shows details like animals, trees, houses, and ships. We can't see any of these things in the Earth photo.*

- *In both images we can see areas with mountains, water, and forests or greenery.*

- *The water is blue in both images. The land is different colors in both images.*

Ask: "How might people have used the *Carta Marina* map?" Volunteers respond.

- *To be able to travel from place to place safely.*

- *To know where people lived and where countries were.*

- *To learn about all the amazing and interesting things in the world.*

- *To imagine all the beautiful and frightening places in the world.*

Ask: "How might people use the *Earth from Space* photo? Volunteers respond.

- *To understand what Earth looks like from outer space.*

- *To know where different parts of the world are.*

- *To see how beautiful Earth is from far away.*

Instruct students to Think-Pair-Share, and ask: "How do these images help transport you to a different place or time? How does the art take you there in your imagination?" Use Equity Sticks to call on students to respond.

- *The Earth picture transports me to outer space.*

- *The Earth picture shows me what the world looks like from outer space.*

- *The map transports me to Europe.*

- *The map transports me to the past.*

- *The map helps me imagine sea monsters that people once thought were real.*

Land 3 MIN.

ANSWER THE CONTENT FRAMING QUESTION

Play the first 38 seconds of the "Burkina Faso: Music" video (**http://witeng.link/0411**) and ask students to pay attention to the rhythm of the music.

Ask: "Do you think the rhythm of the music is similar to any of the words in *Why Mosquitoes Buzz in People's Ears*? How so?" Volunteers respond.

Use responses to draw a correlation between the repetition in the drumming on the video and the repeating lines in the text. Ask: "How might the rhythm of the text transport you to Africa?" Volunteers respond.

Wrap 1 MIN.

ASSIGN HOMEWORK

Continue the class home-reading routine.

Analyze

Context and Alignment

Students write an opinion paragraph about their favorite character in *Why Mosquitoes Buzz in People's Ears* (RL.K.1, W.K.1, W.K.8). Each student:

- Writes an opinion statement.

- Writes and illustrates one reason sentence.

Next Steps

If students have difficulty writing an opinion statement, work with small groups and provide additional opportunities for verbal rehearsal. Using a copy of the text, direct students to locate an image of their favorite character. Students take turns showing the group their favorite character and verbally rehearsing their opinion statement. If needed, provide a sentence frame such as: **In *Why Mosquitoes Buzz in People's Ears*, my favorite character is _____.**

↓ **LESSON 20 DEEP DIVE: VOCABULARY**

Multiple-Meaning Words: *Snap* and *mind*

- **Time:** 15 min.
- **Text:** *Why Mosquitoes Buzz in People's Ears: A West African Tale*, Verna Aardema; Illustrations, Leo and Diane Dillon
- **Vocabulary Learning Goal:** Describe multiple meanings of the words *snap* and *mind*. (L.K.4.a)

Launch

Remind students that in *Why Mosquitoes Buzz in People's Ears*, they learned that Verna Aardema used interesting words to tell the story. Some of these words have more than one meaning.

Ask: "If we didn't learn the new meanings of multiple-meaning words in the text, would we understand the book? Why or why not?" Volunteers respond.

- *No, because the other meanings wouldn't make sense.*
- *No, because then the story would be confusing.*

Reinforce that it is important to explore multiple-meaning words so students can better understand the story. Explain that students are going to learn the multiple meanings of other words from the book.

Learn

Post the words:

- *snap*
- *mind*

Point to and read the word *snap*. Explain that many jackets close with snaps. Ask: "What is a snap?" Volunteers respond.

- *They are the buttons on my jacket.*
- *They are metal and click together.*
- *I can snap my fingers!*

Use student responses to reinforce that some words have lots of meanings. Explain that they are going to focus on two of the meanings in this Deep Dive. Draw a picture of a button <u>snap</u> next to the picture.

Reinforce that this story is not about clothing or jackets so *snap* must have a different meaning in the book. Display pages 1–2 of the text and read the final paragraph, emphasizing the word *snapped*. Ask: "What does *snapped* mean in this story? How did the iguana respond to the mosquito?" Volunteers respond.

- *The iguana yelled at the mosquito.*
- *He used a grumpy voice.*

Use student responses to reinforce the *snap* means "to speak in a short, sharp, or grumpy way." Draw a picture representing the verb *snap* next to the word.

Point to and read the word *mind*. Explain that people think with their <u>mind</u>. Ask: "What is a <u>mind</u>?" Volunteers respond.

- *It's like your brain.*
- *It helps you remember stuff.*
- *A mind helps you get smart.*

Use student responses to draw a picture of *mind* next to the word.

Reinforce that this story is not about brains so *mind* has a different meaning in the book. Display page 25 of the text and read the last paragraph, emphasizing the word *minding*. Instruct students to Think-Pair-Share, and ask: "What does *minding* mean in the story? What did the rabbit do?" Volunteers respond.

- *The rabbit was minding his own business.*
- *The rabbit was paying attention to himself.*
- *He was ignoring the other animals.*

Use student responses to reinforce that *mind* means "to pay attention to." Draw a picture representing the verb *mind* next to the word.

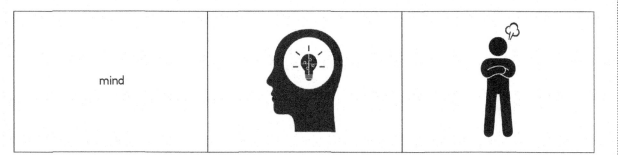

Explain that students are going to describe the meaning of each word and create a new sentence as you call out each word and point to the corresponding picture.

✔ Call out each word, pointing to an illustration to indicate the correct meaning. Students Mix and Mingle, explaining the meaning of the vocabulary word and sharing a sentence using the word. Circulate to provide support as needed and to ensure students are describing word meanings correctly.

Land

Reorganize students back into a whole group setting. Review each word and its meanings.

Ask: "How did learning the new meanings of interesting words help you to better understand the story?" Volunteers respond.

- *It helped us know better what the animals were doing.*
- *It helped us understand how the animals were feeling.*
- *The other meanings would have made the story confusing!*

■ FOCUSING QUESTION: LESSONS 16–21

How can a story transport you to a different place?

1 2 3 4 5 6 7 8 9 10 11 12 13 14 15 **16 17 18 19 20 21** 22 23 24 25 26 27 28 29 30 31 32 33 34 35 36

Lesson 21

TEXTS

- "Lions Roar," *CanTeach* (**http://witeng.link/0410**)

- *Why Mosquitoes Buzz in People's Ears: A West African Tale*, Verna Aardema; Illustrations, Leo and Diane Dillon

- *Carta Marina*, Olaus Magnus, (**http://witeng.link/0409**)

- *Earth from Space*, Stöckli, Reto, et al. (**http://witeng.link/0373**)

Lesson 21: At a Glance

AGENDA

Welcome (7 min.)

Perform Fluency

Launch (3 min.)

Learn (61 min.)

Execute Focusing Question Task 3 (21 min.)

Execute Responding to a Peer's Writing   (10 min.)

Act Out Verbs in the Text (15 min.)

Record Knowledge (15 min.)

Land (3 min.)

Answer the Content Framing Question

Wrap (1 min.)

Assign Homework

Style and Conventions Deep Dive: Execute Expanding a Sentence (15 min.)

STANDARDS ADDRESSED

The full text of ELA Standards can be found in the Module Overview.

Reading

- RL.K.1

Writing

- W.K.1, W.K.5, W.10*

Speaking and Listening

- SL.K.1.a, SL.K.2,

Language

- L.K.5.d
- ⬇ L.K.1.f

MATERIALS

- Assessment 19A: Focusing Question Task 3

- Evidence Organizer for *Why Mosquitoes Buzz in People's Ears*

- Sharing Our Writing Anchor Chart

- Handout 21A: Sentence Expansion

- Repeated Language Chart

- Knowledge Journal

Learning Goals

Express understanding of the characters in *Why Mosquitoes Buzz in People's Ears* by writing an opinion piece about a favorite character. (RL.K.1, W.K.1, W.K.8)

✔ Complete Part 2 of Focusing Question Task 3.

Distinguish the different shades of meaning between verbs of movement. (L.K.5.d)

✔ Act out the verbs *tiptoe*, *walk*, *lumber*, and *scurry* to complete Part 3 of Focusing Question Task 3.

⬇ Write a complete sentence and expand it by adding an adjective and preposition. (L.K.1.f)

✔ Complete Handout 21A.

*In alignment with the CCSS, W.10 formally begins in Grade 3. However, K–2 students write routinely for a variety of time frames, tasks, purposes, and audiences. As a result, this lesson contains instruction related to W.10 in an effort to familiarize students with a range of writing.

✔ Checks for Understanding

Prepare

FOCUSING QUESTION: Lessons 16–21

How can a story transport you to a different place?

CONTENT FRAMING QUESTION: Lesson 21

Know: *How does* Why Mosquitoes Buzz in People's Ears *build my knowledge?*

CRAFT QUESTIONS: Lesson 21

Execute: *How do I execute my Focusing Question Task?*
Execute: *How do I respond to my peer's Focusing Question Task?*

In this lesson students complete Focusing Question Task 3 by finishing an opinion paragraph. They demonstrate understanding of the evidence collected from the words and illustrations in the text, and use this information to write a second supporting reason sentence. They continue their work responding to a peer's writing and demonstrating their abilities to give both a compliment and a suggestion. In addition, students use their whole bodies to act out verbs related to movement in the text, demonstrating knowledge of shades of meaning. Finally, students conclude the lesson by cataloging their knowledge from the text, as well as from *Carta Marina* and *Earth from Space*, in the class's Knowledge Journal.

Welcome 7 MIN.

PERFORM FLUENCY

Display the Repeated Language Chart with the complete poem. Read through the whole poem, using the hand gestures or movements. Students Echo Read the poem.

Explain that now students will demonstrate their ability to fluently read the poem. Divide the class into five small groups, and give them one minute to practice.

Call groups to the front of the room one at a time to perform.

Alternate Activity

If students are not comfortable performing in small groups, consider performing the song as a large group. Record the performance and allow students to watch themselves perform and reflect upon their fluent reading skills.

Launch 3 MIN.

Post and read the Focusing Question. Students Echo Read the question. Ask: "Did we go anywhere when we read this story? What do we mean by <u>transport</u>?" Volunteers respond.

Confirm that the Focusing Question is asking about their imagination, not really where their bodies are moving.

Instruct students to Think-Pair-Share, and ask: "How did the author and illustrator work together to transport us? How did they make us feel part of the story and setting?" Volunteers respond.

- *They used the words to tell us what they did.*
- *The pictures show us what happens.*
- *The pictures also show us what the animals are thinking.*
- *We could pretend we were there because we could picture things in our mind.*

Post and read the Content Framing Question. Praise students on thoughtful work. Explain that in this lesson students show story knowledge by completing the Focusing Question Task and adding to the Knowledge Journal.

Learn 61 MIN.

EXECUTE FOCUSING QUESTION TASK 3 21 MIN.

Individuals

Explain that students will continue to think about their understanding of the text as they complete the Focusing Question Task.

Explain that in this lesson, students complete an opinion paragraph by writing a second reason sentence and restating their opinions in a sentence frame. Display page 3 of Assessment 19A. Explain where to record sentences and drawings as well as where to complete the sentence frame.

Name: _____

Assessment 19A: Focusing Question Task 3

Part 1
Directions: Write your sentence on the lines provided below and add a drawing to illustrate your sentence.

TEACHER NOTE	See Appendix C for a full listing of the criteria for the Focusing Question Task.

Students respond in writing to the following prompt.

> Who is your favorite character in *Why Mosquitoes Buzz in People's Ears*? Why?

Instruct students to take out their first two sentences recorded on Assessment 19A. Students turn to a partner and share their first two sentences.

Display the Evidence Organizer for *Why Mosquitoes Buzz in People's Ears*. Explain that students will add another supporting reason sentence to their paragraphs to help support their opinion statement and explain why that character is their favorite.

Students turn to a partner and verbally rehearse a second reason sentence. Students point to the blank space in the conclusion sentence frame and insert the name of their chosen animal to verbally restate their opinions.

TEACHER NOTE	Students work at different paces. Consider introducing the conclusion sentence frame after students complete their second supporting reason sentence. Students are not expected to remember the full paragraph structure as they are writing.

✔ Each student completes Focusing Question Task 3 by writing a second detail sentence and restating their opinion by completing a sentence frame. Each student includes drawings to support their reason sentences.

TEACHER NOTE	Have students keep their Focusing Question Tasks; they will use them in the next section of the lesson.

EXECUTE RESPONDING TO A PEER'S WRITING 10 MIN.

Pairs

Post and read the second Craft Question. Ask: "How do we share our writing with our peers? How do we respond to our peer's writing?" Volunteers respond.

- *We read our writing to them.*

■ *We can show them our drawings.*

■ *We listen to our friends.*

■ *We tell them what we like.*

■ *We tell them what they can add to their drawing.*

Display the Sharing Our Writing Anchor Chart and point to each step as students respond.

Explain that now students will demonstrate their understanding of how to respond to one another's writing. Students will share one of their reason sentences and drawings with a partner. The partners will listen to their peer and offer one compliment and one suggestion. Then, they will switch.

Ask: "How do I give a compliment? How do I give a suggestion?" Volunteers respond.

■ *I give a compliment by saying what I like.*

■ *I give a suggestion by saying maybe they could add something to their drawing.*

Scaffold

Use puppets or figurines to model how to give and receive suggestions. Reinforce the tone peers should use as well as the appropriate reaction to a suggestion.

Students share one reason sentence and a supporting drawing with a partner from Focusing Question Task 3. Partners offer one compliment and one suggestion about something that could be added to the drawing. Students switch roles.

TEACHER NOTE	Students will not respond to suggestions from peers and add to their writing at this time. Adding to their writing will be addressed in Lessons 22–27. Students' work with W.K.5 is broken down into these two parts to gradually introduce the concept of responding to feedback.

Ask: "How did it feel to share your writing and drawing with a partner? How did it feel to respond to your partner's writing?" Volunteers respond.

Ask: "How did your partner's suggestion help your writing?" Volunteers respond.

Explain that sharing one's writing and receiving suggestions is all part of being a great writer! Offer praise for being thoughtful partners and for helping their peers improve. Explain to the class that as they continue to build their writing skills, they will learn ways to revisit and add to their writing.

ACT OUT VERBS IN THE TEXT 15 MIN.

Small Groups

Display the evidence organizer. Point to the second row and read the title aloud. Ask: "What words in the text did we use to help us collect evidence on how the characters move?" Volunteers respond.

- *We read the words about how they move.*
- *We read the action words.*

Reinforce that action words help readers better understand what is happening in the text, and how the characters move in different ways. Explain that it is important to understand the meaning of different action words because they help readers recognize the differences between different types of movement.

Scaffold

Reactivate students' knowledge of verbs and their different shades of meaning. Ask: "What is the difference between walking and running? How are they the same and how are they different?" Volunteers respond. Call on a volunteer to act out each movement. Explain that they are the same type of movement, except one is fast and one is slow.

Explain that to complete their Focusing Question Task, students will express their understanding of specific action words in the text by acting them out in small groups. They listen to the word read aloud, then act out that movement.

Divide the class into small groups of five or six students. Call groups up one at a time to act out the different verbs. Say the words *tiptoe, walk, lumber,* and *scurry* in no particular order. Instruct groups to think about the word they hear and act out the action with their bodies. Call each word at least two times.

✔ Students demonstrate the meaning of the words *tiptoe, walk, lumber,* and *scurry* by acting them out with their whole bodies to complete Part 3 of Focusing Question Task 3.

TEACHER NOTE	See Appendix C for a full listing of the criteria and an anecdotal checklist for Part 3 of Focusing Question Task 3.

As groups engage in Part 3 of Focusing Question Task 3, use knowledge of students' needs and interests to design classroom stations where other students can quietly engage while waiting to act out the verbs. For example:

- If computers or tablets are available, locate websites that allow students to explore facts about African animals. For example, *Go Wild* (**http://witeng.link/0416**)

- Distribute copies of the *World Atlas* to each group. Assign each group one of the following maps from *World Atlas*: "The Pacific Ocean," "The Atlantic Ocean," "The Indian Ocean," or "The Arctic Ocean." Groups record one thing they notice in their Response Journals.

- Distribute Question Cubes to small groups and have them generate questions about a new map in *World Atlas*.

- Distribute copies of *Carta Marina* and *World Atlas* to small groups. Assign each group one of the following maps from *World Atlas*: "The Pacific Ocean," "The Atlantic Ocean," "The Indian Ocean," or "The Arctic Ocean." Instruct groups to discuss the following questions: "How are these two maps similar? How are they different?"

RECORD KNOWLEDGE 15 MIN.

Whole Group

Display the Knowledge Journal. Ask: "Where do we write down important things we learned from our texts?" Students respond by pointing to the left side of the Knowledge Journal. Students Echo Read the title at the top of the column.

Ask: "Is *Why Mosquitoes Buzz in People's Ears* a storybook or an informational text? How do you know?" Volunteers respond.

Confirm that *Why Mosquitoes Buzz in People's Ears* is a storybook. Ask: "What story does this text tell us? What do we learn from reading this story?" Volunteers respond.

- *It tells us about mosquitoes.*
- *It tells us why they buzz in ears.*
- *We learn why.*

Reinforce that *Why Mosquitoes Buzz in People's Ears* is an <u>origin story</u>. Origin stories attempt to explain why something is the way it is. Add this to the "What I know" column of the Knowledge Journal.

Display *Carta Marina* and *Earth from Space*. Instruct students to Think-Pair-Share, and ask: "What can maps teach us about the world? Why did we study *Carta Marina* and *Earth from Space* in this module?" Use Equity Sticks to call on students to share.

- *They can tell us about where places are.*
- *They can give us directions on how to get from one place to another safely.*
- *We can pretend we are looking at it from far away.*
- *They can tell us where different types of animals might live.*
- *They can give us information about how people understood the world a long time ago.*
- *We can see Earth from a different place.*

Instruct students to Think-Pair-Share, and ask: "What important knowledge did you learn from our lessons with *Carta Marina*?"

- *We know that people can make maps with photographs or by drawing.*

- *We know that maps can include real or imaginary things.*

- *We know that some maps do not have the right scale.*

- *We know that cartographers make maps.*

- *Maps can make you feel like you are there.*

Use Equity Sticks to call on pairs to share responses. After each response, students consider whether or not that piece of learning is something important that they want to remember and include in the Knowledge Journal. They indicate a level of agreement by holding up anywhere from one to five fingers, with one finger showing the lowest level of agreement and five fingers showing the strongest level of agreement.

Use votes to choose several refined responses to record in the Knowledge Journal.

Ask: "Where do we write down important things we learned how to do?" Students respond by pointing to the right side of the Knowledge Journal. Students Echo Read the title at the top of the column.

Instruct students to Think-Pair-Share, and ask: "What did you learn to do as a writer? What did you learn to do as a reader?"

Repeat the process detailed above to engage students in a class vote and record refined responses.

SAMPLE KNOWLEDGE JOURNAL

What I Know	What I Can Do
• People use stories to explain why. • Maps can be drawings or photographs.	• I can use the pictures to help me understand the events. • I can give a compliment. • I can give a suggestion.

Land 3 MIN.

ANSWER THE CONTENT FRAMING QUESTION

Post and read the Content Framing Question. Instruct students to Think-Pair-Share, and ask: "Why do you think we read this story as we study the continents? How can we learn from stories just like we learn from informational texts?" Use Equity Sticks to call on students to answer.

Wrap 1 MIN.

ASSIGN HOMEWORK

Continue the class home-reading routine.

Analyze

Context and Alignment

Students write an opinion paragraph about their favorite character in *Why Mosquitoes Buzz in People's Ears* (RL.K.1, W.K.1, W.K.8). Each student:

- Writes an opinion statement.

- Writes and illustrates two reason sentences to support their opinion.

- Completes a sentence frame to restate their opinion in a conclusion statement.

Next Steps

If students have difficulty supporting an opinion, consider the root of the problem. Are they struggling with the concept of supporting an opinion with reasons? Provide verbal practice with a sentence frame such as **I think** _____ **because** _____ and emphasize the relationship between stating what you think and why you think it. Are they struggling to write supporting sentences? Provide additional practice with the evidence organizer. Ask: "Do you like the way the character looks? Do you like the way the character acts and moves?" Direct students to point to a characteristic and movement listed on the evidence organizer. Support students with verbally stating their supporting reason, and then help them transfer that thinking into writing.

Group students with similar needs and plan small group support for these skills to set students up for success with their next Focusing Question Task.

⬇ LESSON 21 DEEP DIVE: STYLE AND CONVENTIONS

Execute Expanding a Sentence

- **Time:** 15 min.

- **Text:** *Why Mosquitoes Buzz in People's Ears: A West African Tale*, Verna Aardema; Illustrations, Leo and Diane Dillon

- **Style and Conventions Learning Goal:** Write a complete sentence and expand it by adding an adjective and preposition. (L.K.1.f)

   STYLE AND CONVENTIONS CRAFT QUESTION: Lesson 21
   Experiment: *How do I create and expand complete sentences?*

Launch

Post and read the Style and Conventions Craft Question.

Remind students that complete sentences tell "who, does what." Reinforce that authors add more details to their sentences to tell even more information.

Ask: "What are the two ways you learned to expand sentences?"

- *We can add describing words to our sentences.*
- *We can tell where or when our sentences happened.*

Explain that students are going to write a complete sentence about an animal from the story. They will expand their sentence by adding describing words and telling where or when the action happened.

Learn

Display the cover of *Why Mosquitoes Buzz in People's Ears*. Ask: "What animal is this story about?" Students respond chorally.

- *A mosquito!*

Point out that the mosquito is buzzing in the picture. Ask: "What is a complete sentence that tells about the mosquito? Who, does what?" Volunteers respond.

- *The mosquito buzzes.*

Record the sentence on the board.

Reinforce that students can expand the sentence by describing the mosquito and telling where or when she buzzes. Instruct students to Think-Pair-Share, and ask: "How would you describe the mosquito? Where is she buzzing?" Volunteers respond.

◦ *The mosquito is annoying.*

◦ *It is a big, blue mosquito.*

◦ *The mosquito is buzzing in the person's ear.*

◦ *The mosquito is buzzing in the jungle.*

Use student responses to expand the sentence. Record the sentence on the board.

The annoying mosquito buzzes in the person's ear.

Reinforce that the expanded sentence gives more information and is more interesting to read.

Explain that students are going to write a complete sentence about another animal from the story. They will expand the sentence by describing the animal and telling where or when the action happens.

✔ Distribute Handout 21A. Read the directions at the top of the handout. Repeat a second time if needed. Allow students time to draw and write to complete the handout. Circulate to provide support.

Extension

If time allows, use Equity Sticks to call on students to share their expanded sentences.

Collect completed handouts to assess for student understanding.

Land

Direct student attention to the Style and Conventions Craft Question. Ask: "How did you create and expand complete sentences?" Volunteers respond.

◦ *We told about an animal from the story.*

◦ *We told who, did what.*

◦ *We added describing words to our sentences.*

◦ *We told where or when our sentences happened.*

Name: _____

Handout 21A: Sentence Expansion

Directions: In the top box, draw a picture of an animal from the story. In the middle box, write a complete sentence. Tell the animal's name and what it is doing. In the bottom box, expand the sentence by adding a describing word and telling where or when it happened.

■ FOCUSING QUESTION: LESSONS 22-27

What amazing animals can people see in South America and Australia?

1 2 3 4 5 6 7 8 9 10 11 12 13 14 15 16 17 18 19 20 21 **22 23 24 25 26 27** 28 29 30 31 32 33 34 35 36

Lesson 22

TEXTS

- *"Where in the World Is Carmen Sandiego? from Smithsonian Folkways,"* Smithsonian Folkways (**http://witeng.link/0375**)

- *South America*, Rebecca Hirsch

- *Australia*, Rebecca Hirsch

Lesson 22: At a Glance

AGENDA

Welcome (6 min.)

Explore the Focusing Question

Launch (4 min.)

Learn (60 min.)

Listen Actively and Share Observations about South America (20 min.)

Share Questions about South America (10 min.)

Listen Actively and Share Observations about Australia (12 min.)

Share Questions about Australia (10 min.)

Examine the Importance of Revising Writing (8 min.)

Land (4 min.)

Answer the Content Framing Question

Wrap (1 min.)

Assign Homework

Vocabulary Deep Dive: Finding Meaning with the Prefix *un*– (15 min.)

STANDARDS ADDRESSED

The full text of ELA Standards can be found in the Module Overview.

Reading

- RI.K.1

Writing

- W.K.5, W.10*

Speaking and Listening

- SL.K.1, SL.K.2

Language

- L.K.1.d
- ⬇ L.K.4.b

MATERIALS

- Suitcase containing items related to South America (see lesson for details)
- World map
- Question Grab Bags
- Question Corner signs
- Wonder Chart for *South America* and *Australia*
- Sharing Our Writing Anchor Chart
- Sample Response Journal entry (see lesson for details)
- Sticky notes
- Document camera (if available)

Learning Goals

Represent learning through writing and drawing. (W.10*)

✔ Record an observation about *South America* in Response Journals.

Use a variety of question words to ask questions about *Australia*. (RI.K.1, L.K.1.d)

✔ Generate questions using Question Grab Bags.

⬇ Use the meaning of the prefix *un*– as a clue to figure out the meaning of an unknown word. (L.K.4.b)

✔ Use the word part *un*– and illustrations to figure out the meaning of an unknown word.

In alignment with the CCSS, W.10 formally begins in Grade 3. However, K–2 students write routinely for a variety of time frames, tasks, purposes, and audiences. As a result, this lesson contains instruction related to W.10 in an effort to familiarize students with a range of writing.

✔ Checks for Understanding

Prepare

FOCUSING QUESTION: Lessons 22–27

What amazing animals can people see in South America and Australia?

CONTENT FRAMING QUESTION: Lesson 22

Wonder: *What do I notice and wonder about South America and Australia?*

CRAFT QUESTION: Lesson 22

Examine: *Why do writers add to their writing?*

Students resume their exploration of the continents by reading the informational texts *South America* and *Australia*. The familiar text structure allows for increased independence throughout Lessons 22–27. Students make observations about and generate questions for each text. In addition, they continue to revise as they examine the importance of adding details to a piece of writing.

Welcome 6 MIN.

EXPLORE THE FOCUSING QUESTION

TEACHER NOTE	Use a "mystery suitcase" to build anticipation and excitement about new texts and continents. Prior to the lesson, gather materials that provide hints about South America, and place them in a suitcase. For example, pack sunglasses, an umbrella, hiking boots, a stuffed parrot (or image of a parrot), and an image of a compass with the S highlighted to indicate south.

Scaffold

To reactivate previous knowledge of the continents, direct students' attention to the world map and label the different continents.

Display the closed suitcase, explaining that it's time to travel to a new continent for more exploration and adventure. The suitcase contains clues about where the class will travel next.

Direct students to observe each item as it is pulled out of the suitcase. Ask: "Which continent do you think we are heading to? What makes you say that?" Volunteers respond.

Confirm that students will explore the continent of South America, home of the largest rainforest in the world.

Display and read aloud the Focusing Question. Students Echo Read the question. Ask: "What other continent will we explore? What did you hear in the Focusing Question?" Volunteers respond.

Confirm that students will also explore Australia, which has rainforests as well.

Highlight or underline the words *amazing animals* in the Focusing Question. Explain that as students learn about South America and Australia, they will focus on the amazing, unique animals that live on the continents.

Ask: "What amazing animals do you remember from other continents we have explored?" Volunteers respond.

Launch 4 MIN.

Tell students they will explore South America and Australia through books, videos, music, and pictures. Post and read aloud the Content Framing Question.

Display the front covers of *South America* and *Australia*, and read the titles and author's name aloud. Ask: "What animals do you see in these photographs? What do you notice about the animals?" Volunteers respond.

- *I see a kangaroo on the cover of* Australia.
- *I see llamas on the cover of* South America.
- *The llamas look like pets. They have leashes around their necks.*
- *The kangaroo has huge feet!*

Instruct students to Mix and Mingle, and ask: "What do you think makes an animal 'amazing'?"

Learn 60 MIN.

LISTEN ACTIVELY AND SHARE OBSERVATIONS ABOUT *SOUTH AMERICA*
20 MIN.

Whole Group

Tell students they will start today's adventure by exploring the continent of South America. Display the world map and direct students to point to where they believe South America might be located. Confirm the location by circling the continent with your finger and placing the image of an airplane on South America.

Invite students to travel to South America by pretending to fly there in an airplane. Students walk around the room, pretending to fly in an airplane. As they "fly," play music from South America using the link "*Where in the World Is Carmen Sandiego?* from Smithsonian Folkways" (**http://witeng. link/0375**). Scroll down for clips of music from a variety of countries in South America. Consider using track 14, "Bolivia - Linda Companerita." Stop the music to indicate that students should "land" at the whole-group gathering area.

TEACHER NOTE	The above link is a suggestion. Substitute different South American music if desired.

Display the front cover of *South America* as you read aloud the title and author's name. Ask: "What do you think you already know about South America? Have you ever been to South America?" Volunteers respond.

💬 Read the book aloud with minimal interruptions. Students sit in "listening position," focusing eyes and ears on you as you read.

TEACHER NOTE	Consider projecting the pages of the book on a document camera. The pages are small and may not easily be seen from where students sit. If your classroom does not have a way to project the book, organize chairs in a way that will allow students to better view the pages.

Instruct students to Think-Pair-Share, and ask: "What did you learn about South America that surprised you?" Use Equity Sticks to call on students to respond.

Distribute copies of the text to pairs of students. Instruct students to take turns sharing what they notice about the text with their partner. Students use the sentence frame **I notice** _____ and point to the relevant illustration in the text to share observations.

✔ Distribute Response Journals to students and ask them to record one of their observations about *South America* in their journals. Students write a sentence about something they noticed in the text and illustrate the sentence as time permits.

SHARE QUESTIONS ABOUT *SOUTH AMERICA* 10 MIN.

Pairs

As students complete their Response Journal entries, join them into pairs and explain that they will use Question Corners to ask questions about the text. Assign pairs a starting Question Corner, reviewing the routine as needed.

Pairs move to assigned Question Corner and generate questions about *South America* using the designated question word. Place a few copies of the text at each corner.

Circulate to support students in reading the question words as needed, calling attention to key letters and sounds. Encourage them to return to the text to develop questions, and listen in on questions. Choose four to six student-generated questions to record on sticky notes, labeling them with students' initials.

Display the Wonder Chart for *South America* and *Australia*. Add students' questions underneath the questions recorded earlier in the lesson.

Working with one question at a time, students Echo Read the question and Think-Pair-Share about details they remember from the text. Pairs use the following Nonverbal Signals to indicate whether they are able to answer the question:

- Thumbs-up: we remember the answer from the text.
- Thumbs-sideways: we remember part of the answer from the text.
- Thumbs-down: we don't remember the answer.

Call on pairs to share their thinking. Return to the text to confirm and clarify students' thinking. Move sticky notes along the progression to indicate the extent to which each question has been answered.

LISTEN ACTIVELY AND SHARE OBSERVATIONS ABOUT *AUSTRALIA* 12 MIN.

Whole Group

Tell students that they will continue their world exploration by traveling to their next continent: Australia. Display the world map and direct students to point to where they believe Australia is located. Confirm the location by circling Australia with your finger.

Direct students to look at Australia on the world map, and ask: "What do you notice about the continent of Australia?" Volunteers respond.

- *There is water all around it.*
- *It looks small.*
- *It's close to Antarctica.*

Use responses to point out that Australia is an island, and the smallest continent in the world.

Mark the destination by moving the airplane image to Australia. Invite students to walk around the room, pretending to fly in an airplane. As they "fly," play music from Australia using the link "Where in the World Is Carmen Sandiego? from Smithsonian Folkways." (**http://witeng.link/0375**) Scroll down for clips of music from Australia. Consider using track 8, "Australia - Djedbang-ari." Stop the music to indicate that students should "land" at the whole-group gathering area.

TEACHER NOTE	The above link is a suggestion. Substitute different Australian music if desired. Continue to use the airplane image daily to note the continent students are exploring. Move the airplane image between the continents as appropriate.

Display the front cover of *Australia* as you read aloud the title and author's name. Ask: "What do you know about Australia? Has anyone in the class ever been to Australia? Do you know anyone who has?" Volunteers respond.

Read the book aloud with minimal interruptions. Instruct students to Think-Pair-Share, and ask: "What did you learn about Australia that surprised you?" Use Equity Sticks to call on students to respond.

Instruct students to Mix and Mingle, and ask: "What else did you notice about the text?" Spread copies of the text around the room for students to reference as needed.

SHARE QUESTIONS ABOUT *AUSTRALIA* 10 MIN.

Small Groups

Remind students that it is important for both readers and explorers to ask good questions. Tell students they will use Question Grab Bags to ask questions about the text.

✔ Divide the class into five small groups and distribute a Question Grab Bag and a copy of the text to each group. Small groups of students take turns pulling a question word from the Question Grab Bag and using the word to ask a question about *Australia*.

Circulate to support groups in reading the question words as needed, calling attention to key letters and sounds. Encourage them to return to the text to develop their questions, and listen in on questions. Choose four to six student-generated questions to record on sticky notes, labeling them with students' initials.

Post a blank Wonder Chart for *South America* and *Australia*. Add students' questions.

Working with one question at a time, students Echo Read the question and Think-Pair-Share about details they remember from the text. Students use the following Nonverbal Signals to indicate whether they are able to answer the question:

- Thumbs-up: we remember the answer from the text.

- Thumbs-sideways: we remember part of the answer from the text.

- Thumbs-down: we don't remember the answer.

Call on students to share their thinking. Return to the text to confirm and clarify students' thinking. Move sticky notes along the progression to indicate the extent to which each question has been answered.

SAMPLE WONDER CHART FOR *SOUTH AMERICA* AND *AUSTRALIA*

Questions ?	Answers in Progress ⟷	Complete Answers ✓
▪ *What do llamas eat?* ▪ *Why is the ground in the desert cracked?* ▪ *Who lives in the rainforest?* ▪ *Where is the coral reef?* ▪ *How big is Uluru Rock?* ▪ *When was the opera house built?*		

EXAMINE THE IMPORTANCE OF REVISING WRITING 8 MIN.

Whole Group

TEACHER NOTE	In Lessons 22–27 students explore the purpose and process of revising one's writing. Instruction focuses on improving a piece of writing by adding descriptive labels and details to drawings, as most Kindergarten students are not developmentally ready to use carets and other revision tools within written text. The purpose of this instruction is for students to understand and embrace the process of returning to their writing and improving their work through revision.

Display the Sharing Our Writing Anchor Chart, and ask: "How can sharing our writing with others help make our writing better?" Volunteers respond.

- *Talking about our writing helps us think about it more.*
- *We know what is good when someone says what they like.*
- *Someone can give me a suggestion to make my writing better.*

Explain that students will continue to think about sharing and responding to one another's writing. Display and read aloud the Craft Question: *Why do writers add to their writing?*

Ask: "What might it mean to *add* something to a piece of writing?" Volunteers respond.

- *It means you write more.*
- *Maybe you put something in that wasn't there before.*

Uses responses to explain that one way writers make a piece of writing better is by adding labels to their drawings to provide more detail. Labels or captions give readers more information and details about the topic, connecting the pictures to the written ideas, ultimately making writing more meaningful and easier to understand.

TEACHER NOTE	Prior to the lesson, create a sample Response Journal entry about *South America* to use as an example. Create a drawing to accompany the sentence. This is what the class will be adding to.

Model the process of adding details to a piece of writing by engaging in a Think-Aloud about a prewritten Response Journal entry. For example, say:

My sentence says, "I notice waterfalls," and I drew a picture of some water. [Display Response Journal entry for students to view.] Hmm, I wonder what details I could add to make this writing better. Let me go back to the picture of the waterfalls in the text. [Display the corresponding page from the text.] I see people in the picture and they look tiny compared to the waterfalls. That must mean the waterfalls are

really big. Maybe I could add details about the size of the waterfalls! I think I should add the label "huge waterfalls" to my drawing. I should also add more water to my drawing, to make the waterfalls look bigger.

Add a descriptive label to the drawing in the sample journal entry. Instruct students to Think-Pair-Share, and ask: "What did I add to my writing? How did it make the writing better?" Use Equity Sticks to call on students to respond.

- *You added the label "huge waterfalls."*
- *You added more water to the picture, too.*
- *You added details.*
- *The details gave more information.*
- *The details made your writing more interesting.*

Point to the Sharing Our Writing Anchor Chart. Add "Add details" to the chart. Briefly review all the steps on the chart.

Sharing Our Writing Anchor Chart
1. Share and listen
2. Give a compliment
3. Give a suggestion
4. Add details

Land 4 MIN.

ANSWER THE CONTENT FRAMING QUESTION

Instruct students to Mix and Mingle, and ask: "Do you think *South America* and *Australia* are storybooks or informational texts? What are the reasons for your response?" Call on several students to share with the class.

As time permits, invite several students to share their Response Journal entries with the class.

Extension

Use the following websites to explore more information about animals from South America and Australia.

Jaguar: http://witeng.link/0418

Duck-billed platypus: http://witeng.link/0419

Wrap <small>1 MIN.</small>

ASSIGN HOMEWORK

Continue the class home-reading routine.

Analyze

Context and Alignment

Students utilize Question Grab Bags to generate questions about *Australia*. This questioning tool supports students in developing the habit of wondering as they read a text (RI.K.1, L.K.1.d). Each student:

- Generates text-based questions.
- Correctly uses the question word presented on the Question Card.

Next Steps

If students struggle to generate questions, focus on one question word, such as *how* or *why*. Work with small groups and go through the text together, one page spread at a time. Support students in generating one question per page spread.

⬇ LESSON 22 DEEP DIVE: VOCABULARY

Finding Meaning with the Prefix *un–*

- **Time:** 15 min.

- **Text:** *Australia*, Rebecca Hirsch

- **Vocabulary Learning Goal:** Use the meaning of the prefix *un–* as a clue to find the meaning of an unknown word. (L.K.4.b)

Launch

TEACHER NOTE	Students are building on previous knowledge of the prefix *un–* in this lesson as they prepare to be assessed on this standard later in the module. Once again, Rebecca Hirsch's book *Australia* provides great illustrations and information to practice this prefix, even though very few words beginning with *un–* appear in the text. Therefore, to maximize instructional time, it would be helpful to prepare four copies of *Australia* ahead of time by labeling the following pages with sticky notes with these sentences, making sure to underline the word beginning with the prefix *un–*:
	Page 4: Australia is unlike any other place.
	Page 12: Many traditions in Australia are unchanged.
	Page 20: Uluru rock is very uneven.
	Page 24: Many uncommon fish live in the reef.
	Additionally, prepare a teacher copy of the text by labeling *all* of the pages above with sticky notes with these sentences.

Remind students that in Deep Dive Lesson 19, the class worked together and used the word beginning *un–* to find the meaning of new words.

Instruct students to Think-Pair-Share and ask: "What does the word beginning *un–* mean? How does it change the main word part?" Volunteers respond.

- *Un– means "not."*

- *The word with* un– *is the opposite of the main word part without* un–.

Explain that students are going to work in small groups to find the meaning of new words that start with the word beginning *un–*.

Learn

Instruct students to listen closely as you read and to give a thumbs-up signal when they hear a word that starts with the word beginning *un–*.

Display pages 14–15 of the text and read the first sentence, emphasizing the word *unusual*. Call on a student with a thumbs-up to identify the word starting with *un–*.

   ▪ *Unusual.*

Write *unusual* on the board. Underline *un–* and draw a squiggly line under the root word, *usual*, and point out that this is the main word part in the word. Reinforce that because *un–* means "not" the new word is the opposite of this word.

Model how to use the illustration to figure out the meaning of *unusual*. For example, point out that kangaroos are not seen in most places. Ask: "If a kangaroo is unusual, what is it not?" Volunteers respond.

   ▪ *The kangaroo is not common.*
   ▪ *The kangaroo is not normally seen anywhere else.*
   ▪ *The kangaroo is special or unique.*

Use student responses to determine the meaning of *unusual* as "not common or not normal."

Post and Echo Read the list of *un–* words: *unlike, unchanged, uneven,* and *uncommon.*

Explain that these words are describing words that tell about illustrations in *Australia*. Display your previously prepared teacher copy of the text. Turn to the illustrations marked with sticky notes and read the sentences, emphasizing the *un–* word in each.

Redirect student attention to the list of posted words and underline *un–* in each word. Reinforce that the word beginning *un–* means "not." Point out that as such, when you add *un–* to a word it changes it to mean the opposite.

Explain that students are going to use this information as a clue to figure out the meaning of these words.

Organize the class into four small groups. Distribute a text with a sticky note to each group. As you hand the text to the group, present the page and read the sentence on the sticky note. Echo Read the word beginning with *un–* to ensure students know the word they are working with.

✔ Explain that students will work together to find the meaning of the describing word on the sticky note. Encourage students to use the illustration and the meaning of *un–* to figure out the meaning of their describing word. Circulate to provide support as needed. Use Equity Sticks to call on each group to share their findings.

If time allows, record each word's meaning next to it on the board. Consider adding simple illustrations to each definition to facilitate understanding.

Land

Reorganize students in a whole group setting. Explain that you are going to ask them "Yes" or "No" questions about the new words. If they think the answer is yes, they should give a thumbs-up signal and if they think the answer is no, they should give a thumbs-down signal.

Ask: "If an animal is <u>unusual</u>, do you see it everywhere?" Students give a thumbs-down signal.

Ask: "If Uluru rock is bumpy, is it <u>uneven</u>?" Students give a thumbs-up signal.

Ask: "If the fish of the Great Barrier Reef are special and unique, are they <u>uncommon</u>?" Students give a thumbs-up signal.

■ FOCUSING QUESTION: LESSONS 22–27

What amazing animals can people see in South America and Australia?

1 | 2 | 3 | 4 | 5 | 6 | 7 | 8 | 9 | 10 | 11 | 12 | 13 | 14 | 15 | 16 | 17 | 18 | 19 | 20 | 21 | **22** | **23** | **24** | **25** | **26** | **27** | 28 | 29 | 30 | 31 | 32 | 33 | 34 | 35 | 36

Lesson 23

TEXTS

- "Americas—Fact Files," *Go Wild* (**http://witeng.link/0420**)
- *Moon Rope*, Lois Ehlert
- *South America*, Rebecca Hirsch
- "Moles," *DK Find Out!* (**http://witeng.link/0421**)

Lesson 23: At a Glance

AGENDA

Welcome (5 min.)

Explore South American Animals

Launch (6 min.)

Learn (56 min.)

Identify the Main Topic and Key Details in South America *(18 min.)*

Listen Actively to Moon Rope *(15 min.)*

Engage in New-Read Assessment 2 (18 min.)

Practice Fluency (5 min.)

Land (7 min.)

Answer the Content Framing Question

Wrap (1 min.)

Assign Homework

Vocabulary Deep Dive: Shades of Meaning: *Hitch* and *hang* (15 min.)

STANDARDS ADDRESSED

The full text of ELA Standards can be found in the Module Overview.

Reading

- RL.K.4, RI.K.1, RI.K.2,

Speaking and Listening

- SL.K.1, SL.K.2

Language

- L.K.4.a, L.K.4.b, L.K.5.b
- ⬇ L.K.5.d

MATERIALS

- Assessment 23A: New-Read Assessment 2
- Repeated Language Chart (see lesson for details; retain for future lessons)
- World map

Learning Goals

Use text features to identify the main topic and key details in sections of *South America*. (RI.K.2)

✔ Use Nonverbal Signals to identify and retell the main topic and key details of a section in the text.

Use knowledge of word relationships and the illustrations in *Moon Rope* to define key vocabulary. (RL.K.4, L.K.4.a, L.K.4.b, L.K.5.b)

✔ Complete New-Read Assessment 2.

⬇ Distinguish shades of meaning between *hitch* and *hang* by acting out their meanings and analyzing how the meaning of the words change the meaning of the story. (L.K.5.d)

✔ Mix and Mingle to complete sentences with missing word and action.

✔ Checks for Understanding

Prepare

FOCUSING QUESTION: Lessons 22–27

What amazing animals can people see in South America and Australia?

CONTENT FRAMING QUESTION: Lesson 23

Organize: *What is happening in* South America?

In this lesson students develop a solid understanding of the structure and content of *South America*. They practice locating a particular section of the text with the table of contents, using headings to identify the main idea and key details of the "People and Places" section. In addition, students read *Moon Rope* for the first time and display their vocabulary knowledge and skills through the completion of New-Read Assessment 2.

Welcome 5 MIN.

EXPLORE SOUTH AMERICAN ANIMALS

Ask: "Which continents are we exploring this week?" Volunteers respond.

Confirm correct answers. Explain that today students will focus on South America. Invite a student to move the airplane on the world map to South America.

Display the interactive "Americas–Fact Files" website (**http://witeng.link/0420**). Read aloud the topic headings for the Americas Fact Files and conduct a class vote to decide which topic to explore. Use the website to look at facts, pictures, and videos of the selected South American animals (or the Amazon Rainforest).

Alternate Activity

Use questions from the Wonders Chart to guide topic selection while exploring the Fact Files website.

Launch 6 MIN.

Display and read aloud the Content Framing Question. Explain that after reading, noticing, and wondering about *South America* in the previous lesson, students are now ready to read more closely and learn more about the texts and the continent.

Distribute copies of *South America* to pairs of students and direct them to open their books to the table of contents page. Instruct students to Think-Pair-Share, and ask: "What is a table of contents? How can a table of contents help readers?" Use Equity Sticks to call on students to respond.

- *It is like a list of the headings.*
- *It tells you where to find things in the book.*
- *It tells readers the page number for the topics.*

Ask students to place a finger on the second section listed in the table of contents. Read the name of the section aloud. Instruct students to trace their fingers across the page to find the starting page number for the "People and Places" section. Ask: "Which page can you turn to for the 'People and Places' section?" Volunteers respond.

- *Page 9.*

Students turn to the "People and Places" section in the text.

Learn 56 MIN.

IDENTIFY THE MAIN TOPIC AND KEY DETAILS IN *SOUTH AMERICA* 18 MIN.

Whole Group

Direct students to place a finger on the heading of page 9. Read the heading aloud. Explain that students will use this heading to help them find the main topic and key details of this section of *South America*.

Instruct students to Think-Pair-Share, and ask: "Think about the heading of this section: 'People and Places.' What is the main topic of this section? What will this part of the text tell us about?" Use Equity Sticks to call on students to respond.

- *The main topic is the people and places of South America.*
- *It will tell us about people who live in South America.*
- *It will tell us about places in South America.*

Remind students that the heading of a section is often the same as the section's main topic because they are both explaining what the section is mostly about.

Explain again that key details about a main topic are in the section that follows the heading. Instruct students to listen for key details about the people and places of South America while you read the "People and Places" section.

Read pages 8–9 aloud as students follow along in their copies. Instruct students to Think-Pair-Share, and ask: "What key details did you hear on this page about people and places in South America?" Use Equity Sticks to call on students to respond.

- *There is a big rainforest in South America.*
- *People use plants from the rainforest for food.*
- *People use plants for medicine, too.*

Use responses to confirm the key details that the Amazon Rainforest is located in South America, and people use its plants for food and medicine.

Read pages 10–11 aloud. Instruct students to Think-Pair-Share, and ask: "What key detail did you hear on this page about people and places in South America?" Use Equity Sticks to call on students to respond.

- *People live in the rainforest.*
- *They hunt and fish in the rainforest.*
- *They have farms in the rainforest, too.*

Use responses to confirm the key details that people live, hunt, and farm in the rainforest.

Emphasize that this section of the text is full of key details and important information about the people and places of South America. Explain that students will pause and retell the main topic and key details they have discovered thus far before continuing with the section.

As needed, remind students how to use Nonverbal Signals to retell the main topic (placing one hand on top of your head) and key details (waving arms or hands).

Pairs take turns using Nonverbal Signals to retell the main topic and key details of pages 8–11 of the "People and Places" section, using the text for reference.

Read pages 12–15 aloud. Instruct students to Think-Pair-Share, and ask: "What key details did you hear on these pages about people and places in South America?" Use Equity Sticks to call on students to respond.

- *There are mountains in South America.*
- *Llamas help people carry things down the mountains.*
- *There are deserts in South America, too.*

Use responses to confirm the key details are that there are mountains and deserts in South America.

Pairs take turns using Nonverbal Signals to retell the main topic and key details of pages 12–15 of the "People and Places" section, using the text for reference.

TEACHER NOTE	If students have difficulty speaking and moving at the same time, instruct students to say the key detail aloud, then wave their hand or arm. This will allow students to focus on retelling the key details first, which is the main purpose of this lesson.

LISTEN ACTIVELY TO *MOON ROPE* 15 MIN.

Whole Group

Reference South America on the world map and remind students that the continent is made up of twelve countries, each with their own languages and ways of living. Explain that students will read a story that comes from one country in South America: Peru. Identify Peru on the world map.

Emphasize that reading a story from a different country can help transport readers to a new place as they imagine what it might be like to visit or live in that country.

Display the front cover of *Moon Rope* and read aloud the title and author's name. Instruct students to Mix and Mingle, and ask: "What do you think this story might be about? What makes you think that?"

After completing the Mix and Mingle routine, students sit in the whole-group gathering area. Read the text aloud with minimal interruptions.

TEACHER NOTE	Limit the amount of discussion about the text at this point to acquire accurate student data from the New-Read Assessment.

Instruct students to think quietly to themselves for a minute about the following question: "What did you notice about *Moon Rope*?"

Explain that now they will follow along as you read through the text a second time to think about the problem and resolution in the story. Read the text aloud a second time with minimal interruptions.

Distribute Response Journals. Students write a sentence to respond to the following prompt and include supporting illustrations as time permits.

What is the problem the characters face in *Moon Rope*?

Foundational Skills Connection

If students need practice identifying vowel sounds, use key words from the text to support building this skill. As you read key words, students identify the vowel sound they hear and the common spelling for the sound. Display and read the words from the following pages:

Page 1: Mole /o-e/ = long o

Page 1: Fox /o/ = short o

Page 5: tip /i/ = short i

Page 7: us /u/ = short u

Page 10: braided /ai/ = long a

Page 10: grass /a/ = short a

Page 13: beaks /ea/ = long e

Page 18: fell /e/= short e

ENGAGE IN NEW-READ ASSESSMENT 2 18 MIN.

Individuals

TEACHER NOTE

Use New-Read Assessments to reinforce the importance of orienting oneself to a text. Give students an independent, brief routine to support them in responding to the following vocabulary questions. For example, you might encourage them to silently use Story Stones to think about the story elements in the text. Remember to give young students sufficient time to answer questions and struggle productively with a New-Read Assessment text.

Distribute Assessment 23A and explain that students will think about words from *Moon Rope* as they complete New-Read Assessment 2.

Point out that students have seen a similar assessment format during Direct Vocabulary Assessments. Explain that you will read each question aloud. If students think the answer to the question is "yes," they draw a circle around the smiley face. If they think the answer is "no," they draw a circle around the frowning face.

Name:

Assessment 23A: New-Read Assessment 2

Directions: Circle 😊 Yes or 😞 No to answer each question.

Example: Is Moon Rope the title of the story?	😊 Yes	😞 No
1. Did Fox want to travel to the moon?	😊 Yes	😞 No
2. Did Fox want to stay home?	😊 Yes	😞 No
3. Did Mole want others to notice him?	😊 Yes	😞 No
4. If someone is <u>unkind</u>, are they nice to others?	😊 Yes	😞 No
5. If a place is <u>unsafe</u>, should you play there?	😊 Yes	😞 No
6. Fox was <u>mad</u>. Was he upset?	😊 Yes	😞 No
7. Fox was <u>mad</u>. Was he happy?	😊 Yes	😞 No

TEACHER NOTE	The pages in *Moon Rope* are not numbered. Consider writing small page numbers at the bottom of each page to make it easier to reference. Page 1 begins with "Mole was taking a break from digging worms…"

Use the teacher-facing version (with key) in Appendix C to administer the assessment.

✔ Students complete New-Read Assessment 2. Read each question twice before students fill in answers. Circulate to ensure students follow directions and mark the correct question. Give oral cues as necessary to help students locate the proper row where they should be marking answers.

PRACTICE FLUENCY 5 MIN.

Whole Group

Explain that students will use part of *Moon Rope* for their fluency passage. Ask: "Who are the main characters in *Moon Rope*?" Volunteers respond.

Confirm that Fox and Mole are the main characters in the story. Tell students that the fluency passage is a conversation between Fox and Mole from *Moon Rope*. Display the Repeated Language Chart and read aloud the title and the first line of the text, tracking the words with your finger. Students Echo Read the line.

Repeated Language
⟳

Text: *Moon Rope*

- Mole," he said, "if you could have anything in the world, what would it be?"

Point to the question mark at the end of the sentence and ask: "What is this punctuation mark in the text? What does it tell us as readers? As speakers?" Volunteers respond.

- *It's a question mark.*
- *It tells us that the sentence is asking a question.*
- *We should make it sound like a question when we read it.*

Confirm that the end punctuation is a question mark and ask: "Which character from the story is asking this question?" Volunteers respond

- *Fox.*

Students Echo Read the line several times.

Instruct students to Mix and Mingle, and ask: "How would you answer Fox's question? If you could have anything in the world, what would it be? Why?"

Land 7 MIN.

ANSWER THE CONTENT FRAMING QUESTION

Explain that students will return to *Moon Rope* later to explore the story more. Ask: "Have you ever heard of an animal called a mole? What do you already know about moles?" Volunteers respond.

Display and read aloud the web page "Moles" (**http://witeng.link/0421**) to provide background information about moles.

Display and read aloud the Content Framing Question. Instruct students to Think-Pair-Share, and ask: "What did you learn about South America today?" Use Equity Sticks to call on students to respond.

Wrap 1 MIN.

ASSIGN HOMEWORK

Continue the class home-reading routine.

Analyze

Context and Alignment

Students use knowledge of word relationships and the illustrations in *Moon Rope* to define key vocabulary. (RL.K.4, L.K.4.a, L.K.4.b, L.K.5.b) Each student:

- Demonstrates understanding of the meaning of the verb *go* by relating it to its opposite.

- Demonstrates understanding of the meaning of the adjective *mad* by relating it to its opposite.

- Uses the prefix *un–* to determine the meaning of the word *unnoticed*.

- Demonstrates understanding of the multiple meanings of the word *land*.

- Demonstrates understanding of a *crescent moon* using the illustration as a guide.

Next Steps

If students have difficulty completing New-Read Assessment 2, provide support by revisiting specific pages in the text. While this assessment should be done without prior discussion about the text, rereading portions of the story will help students gain a better understanding of the vocabulary in the text. After the assessment, determine the vocabulary and skills with which students require additional support. Group students with similar needs and plan small group support for these skills to set students up for success with these concepts.

⬇ **LESSON 23 DEEP DIVE: VOCABULARY**

Shades of Meaning: *Hitch* and *hang*

- **Time:** 15 min.

- **Text:** *Moon Rope*, Lois Ehlert

- **Vocabulary Learning Goal:** Distinguish shades of meaning between *hitch* and *hang* by acting out their meanings and analyzing how the words change the meaning of the story. (L.K.5.d)

Launch

Remind students that authors of fiction books also use interesting words to tell their stories. Explain that authors do this so readers better understand the story and can imagine the story's events in their mind like a movie.

Explain that students are going to listen to a part of *Moon Rope* and try to imagine the scene. Instruct students to close their eyes as you read, so they can make a movie of the story in their mind. Read page 5 of the text slowly.

After finishing the page, ask students to open their eyes. Ask: "What did you see as you imagined the scene from the story?" Volunteers respond.

- *I saw a fox running in grass.*

- *I saw grass tickling Fox's fur.*

- *I saw a long, green rope made from grass.*

- *I saw the green rope hanging off the moon.*

- *I saw a moon-shape that has a tip.*

Ask: "In your imagination, how was the rope connected to the moon?"

- *It was tied around it.*

- *It was hanging off the edge.*

- *It was glued to the side.*

Explain that students are going to explore the word *hitch* so they can better understand how the rope was connected to the moon. They will also explore other words that mean similar things to see if Lois Ehlert could have used a different word to describe the event in the story.

Learn

Display pages 5–6 of the text and read the last sentence on page 5, emphasizing the word *hitch*. Record *hitch* on the board. Model using the other words in the sentence to figure out the meaning of the word *hitch*. For example, say, "The rope has a loop on one end, so that means Fox tied a big circle at the end of the rope. The moon has a tip, so it must be a crescent shape so that the rope can attach by hanging the loop around the pointy end."

As you model, draw a simple illustration on the board to show how the loop of the rope *hitches* by hanging tightly around the tip of a crescent moon.

> ### Scaffold
>
> If available, model hitching a real rope to something in the classroom by tying a loop at one end and hanging it off a tip or point of something.

Ask: "Using this information, what do you think *hitch* means?" Volunteers respond.

- *It means that you connect something with a rope.*
- *It means that the loop is tied around the tip of the moon.*

Use student responses to determine the meaning of *hitch* as "to attach tightly with a rope." Record the definition next to the word on the board. Use Equity Sticks to call on a student to create an action for *hitch*. Invite students to mimic the action as they say the word, "hitch."

Explain that another way to attach with rope is to <u>hang</u>. Display the illustration on page 3 and point out that worm <u>hangs</u> from the Mole's claw. Encourage students to use their previous knowledge and the illustration to determine the meaning of *hang*. Ask: "Using this information, what do you think *hang* means?"

- *It means he is holding it loosely.*
- *The worm is attached to the Mole's claw.*

Use student responses to determine the meaning of *hang* as "to attach loosely without support." Record the definition next to the word on the board. Ask: "What is the difference between *hitch* and *hang*?

- Hitch *means a rope is tied tightly and* hang *means the rope is loose.*
- Hitch *means you are using a rope, but anything can hang!*

Use Equity Sticks to call on a student to create an action for *hang*. Encourage the student to develop an action that is distinct from *hitch*. Invite students to mimic the action as they say the word, "hang."

Extension

If time allows, consider expanding student knowledge by exploring other actions words that describing attaching something with rope, such as *knot*, *tie*, or *buckle*. Repeat the activity above by labeling an illustration in the story with the action word and encouraging students to develop the definition of the word and a matching action.

Land

✔ As you the read the following sentences, students Mix and Mingle to complete the sentence by saying and acting out the missing word:

The worms _____ loosely from Moles' mouth.

The birds _____ the rope tightly to the crescent moon.

Students Mix and Mingle to answer the follow-up question: "Why did the birds <u>hitch</u> the rope to the moon instead of just <u>hanging</u> it?"

- *Because the rope needed to be tied tightly or Fox and Mole would fall.*
- *Because if it was hanging loosely, it might not stay there long enough for them to climb.*

■ FOCUSING QUESTION: LESSONS 22–27

What amazing animals can people see in South America and Australia?

1 2 3 4 5 6 7 8 9 10 11 12 13 14 15 16 17 18 19 20 21 **22 23 24 25 26 27** 28 29 30 31 32 33 34 35 36

Lesson 24

TEXTS

- *Moon Rope*, Lois Ehlert

- *Australia*, Rebecca Hirsch

Lesson 24: At a Glance

AGENDA

Welcome (5 min.)

Practice Fluency

Launch (5 min.)

Learn (60 min.)

Identify the Main Topic and Key Details in Australia (25 min.)

Explore Captions (15 min.)

Experiment with Revising Writing (20 min.)

Land (4 min.)

Answer the Content Framing Question

Wrap (1 min.)

Assign Homework

Style and Conventions Deep Dive: Examine Beginning a Sentence with a Capital Letter (15 min.)

STANDARDS ADDRESSED

The full text of ELA Standards can be found in the Module Overview.

Reading

- RI.K.1, RI.K.2, RI.K.3, RI.K.4, RI.K.7

Writing

- W.K.5

Speaking and Listening

- SL.K.1

Language

- ⬇ L.K.1.f, L.K.2.a

MATERIALS

- Repeated Language Chart
- Sharing Our Writing Anchor Chart
- Sample Response Journal entry (see lesson for details)
- Document camera (if available)
- World map
- Compass rose
- Chart paper

Learning Goals

Use text features to identify the main topic and key details in a section of *Australia*. (RI.K.2)

✔ Use Nonverbal Signals to identify and retell the main topic and key details of a section of the text.

Add details to strengthen a piece of writing. (W.K.5)

✔ Think-Pair-Share about details to add to a Response Journal entry.

⬇ Distinguish between a phrase and a complete sentence and identify the letter that should be capitalized in a complete sentence. (L.K.1.f, L.K.2.a)

✔ Use Nonverbal Signals to identify a complete sentence and the correct capital letter in a sentence.

✔ Checks for Understanding

Prepare

FOCUSING QUESTION: Lessons 22–27

What amazing animals can people see in South America and Australia?

CONTENT FRAMING QUESTION: Lesson 24

Organize: *What is happening in Australia?*

CRAFT QUESTION: Lesson 24

Experiment: *How do writers add to their writing?*

In this lesson students continue to deepen their understanding of the structure of informational texts. They apply their skills with identifying the main topic and key details in the text to a more complex section of *Australia*. Students also identify and explore the function of captions in the text. Finally, students experiment with revising a piece of writing by adding details.

Welcome 5 MIN.

PRACTICE FLUENCY

Display the Repeated Language Chart, with the next line of text added. Read the first two lines of the passage. Students Echo Read the lines.

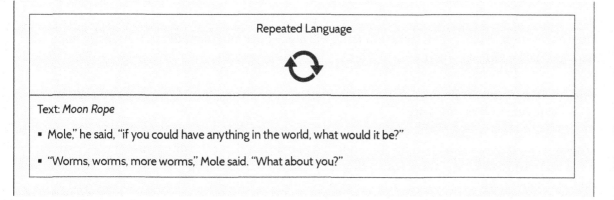

Repeated Language

Text: *Moon Rope*

- Mole," he said, "if you could have anything in the world, what would it be?"

- "Worms, worms, more worms," Mole said. "What about you?"

Ask: "What does Mole want, more than anything in the world?" Students chorally respond.

- *Worms!*

Ask: "Why might Mole want worms?" Volunteers respond.

- *Because moles eat worms.*
- *Maybe that's his favorite food.*

Scaffold

As needed, return to the web page "Moles" (**http://witeng.link/0421**) to reinforce background information about moles.

Remind students that moles cannot see well. Ask: "How can moles find worms without being able to see them?" Volunteers respond.

- *They can smell them.*
- *They can feel them.*

Invite students to pretend they are moles and mimic hunting for worms with their noses and hands. Instruct students to do this from their seats and keeping their hands to themselves.

Students Echo Read both lines of text several times.

Launch 5 MIN.

Display and read aloud the Content Framing Question. Ask: "What do you notice about today's question?" Volunteers respond.

- *It's the same question we had yesterday about South America.*
- *Today's question is about Australia.*

Use responses to confirm that today students will dig deeper into *Australia* to learn more about the text and the continent.

Display the world map and ask: "Where is the continent called Australia?" Students respond by pointing to Australia on the map.

Display a compass rose and remind students that people often use the directions of north, south, west, and east to describe where something is in relation to something else. Highlight the directions on the compass rose.

Reference the locations of South America and Australia on the world map, and ask: "To travel to Australia from South America, which direction do we need to go?" Volunteers respond.

- *West.*
- *East.*

TEACHER NOTE	Affirm both "west" and "east" as correct responses to the previous question. Consider using a globe to demonstrate how traveling in either direction would enable one to arrive in Australia.

Invite a student to approach the map and move the airplane to Australia.

Learn 60 MIN.

IDENTIFY THE MAIN TOPIC AND KEY DETAILS IN *AUSTRALIA* 25 MIN.

Whole Group

Display the front cover of *Australia* and explain that students will continue to use headings to think about the main topic and key details of each section in the text.

Use a document camera or projector to display the table of contents page from the text. Point to the "Land and Water" section and read the heading aloud. Ask, "Where can readers find the 'Land and Water' section?" Volunteers respond.

- *Page 19.*

Scaffold

This is an introduction to a text feature: the table of contents. If students have difficulty grasping how the table of contents works or how to locate the appropriate pages, model this for them and direct them to the correct pages. Students are not expected to be able to use the table of contents at this stage in their learning.

Display page 19 of *Australia*. Instruct students to Think-Pair-Share, and ask: "Think about the heading of this section: 'Land and Water.' What is the main topic of this section? What will this part of the text tell us about? How do you know?" Use Equity Sticks to call on students to respond.

- *The main topic is the land and water of Australia.*
- *It will tell us about the land in Australia.*
- *It will tell us about the water in Australia.*

Confirm that the main topic of the section is the land and water in Australia. Remind students that a continent's land and water are part of its natural features.

Remind students that readers can find key details about the main topic in the section that follows the heading. Ask students to listen for key details about the land and water in Australia while you read the "Land and Water" section.

Read pages 18–21 aloud. Instruct students to Think-Pair-Share, and ask: "What key details did you hear on these pages about the land and water in Australia?" Use Equity Sticks to call on students to respond.

- *Australia has something called the outback.*
- *The outback is dry.*
- *It's hot during the day and cold at night.*
- *The world's largest rock is in the outback.*

Use responses to confirm the key details that Australia has a dry place called the outback. Display the photograph on page 18 and ask: "What do you notice about the outback from the photograph?" Volunteers respond.

- *The dirt looks red.*
- *There aren't any houses or buildings.*
- *I don't see any trees, there are only bushes.*

Read pages 22–27 aloud. Instruct students to Think-Pair-Share, and ask: "What key details did you hear on these pages about the land and water in Australia?" Use Equity Sticks to call on students to respond.

- *Australia has forests with tall trees.*
- *Australia has the biggest coral reef in the world.*
- *There are waterfalls in Australia.*

Display the photograph on page 24 and ask: "What is a coral reef? What clues can you use from the photograph to help you understand what a coral reef might be?" Volunteers respond.

- *I think it's something under the water.*
- *Maybe it's a place where fish live.*
- *I see a lot of fish in the photo.*
- *The picture looks like it's underwater.*

Use responses to define *coral reef* as "an underwater mound of coral rock." Explain that coral reefs make great homes for fish and many other sea creatures.

Ask: "How are all the key details in this section connected? What do they all tell readers about?" Use Equity Sticks to call on students to respond.

- *They are all telling about the land and water in Australia.*
- *They all tell about the main topic.*
- *Each detail gives more information about the land or water.*

As needed, remind students how to use Nonverbal Signals to retell the main topic (placing one hand on top of your head) and key details (waving arms or hands).

✔ Assign each student a partner. Pairs take turns using Nonverbal Signals to retell the main topic and key details of the "Land and Water" section to each other. Display pages from the section in the text for students to use as reference.

TEACHER NOTE	If students have difficulty speaking and moving at the same time, instruct students to say the key detail aloud, then wave their hand or arm. This will allow students to focus on retelling the key details first, which is the main purpose of this lesson.

Extension

Select one or two students to demonstrate their retelling of the main topic and key details for the whole class.

Instruct students to Mix and Mingle, and ask: "Think about the natural features in Australia that you read about in the 'Land and Water' section. Which natural feature in Australia is your favorite? Why?" Make copies of the text available for students to reference.

Distribute Response Journals. Students write a sentence to share their favorite natural feature. As time permits, they draw an illustration to support their sentence.

EXPLORE CAPTIONS 15 MIN.

Small Groups

Remind students that text features help them better understand informational texts. Ask: "What text features have we used to help us understand our books about the continents?" Volunteers respond.

- *The headings.*
- *We used the table of contents.*
- *We looked at photographs.*

Explain that students will use a new text feature to help them better understand the text: captions. Explain that captions are words underneath or next to a photograph that give information about the picture. Students repeat the word *captions*.

Use a document camera or projector to display page 4 from *Australia*. Ask: "What does this picture show readers?" Volunteers respond.

- *It shows people walking.*
- *I see trees.*
- *There are hills, too.*

Point to the sentence underneath the photograph and identify it as a caption. Ask: "What do you notice about the way the words look in the caption? How are they different from the other words in the text?" Volunteers respond.

- *The words in the caption are smaller.*

Read the caption aloud. Ask: "What did you learn from the caption? What does this picture show readers?" Volunteers respond.

- *It shows people hiking.*
- *It shows Uluru Park.*

Use responses to reinforce that captions help explain what's happening in the picture. They give more information to help readers better understand the text. The caption on page 4 helps readers better understand where the people are and what they are doing.

Remind students that the caption looks different from the other words on the page. Explain that captions are made to stand out from the rest of the text. The words in a caption could be smaller than the other words or they could be written in fancy or bold print. Sometimes captions are placed in special boxes near the picture they describe.

Tell students that they will go on a scavenger hunt through the text to find more captions. Divide students into small groups and distribute a copy of the text to each group. Have students sit in a circle to take turns holding the book and looking through the book for a caption. When they find a caption they show it to the group and share how they know it's a caption. They then pass it to the next person in the group and the pattern repeats.

As time permits, use Equity Sticks to call on students to share a caption they found during the scavenger hunt. Display the associated photograph for the class and ask the following questions.

- What do you see in this picture?

- [Read the caption aloud to the class.] How does the caption help you understand the picture?

EXPERIMENT WITH REVISING WRITING 20 MIN.

Whole Group

Display the Sharing Our Writing Anchor Chart and remind students that sharing one's writing is an important part of becoming a better writer. Read the steps on the chart, emphasizing the last step: Add details. Explain that today students will focus on adding details to a piece of writing to make it better.

Display the Craft Question: *How do writers add to their writing?* Students Echo Read the question.

TEACHER NOTE	Prior to the lesson, write a sample Response Journal entry responding to the question "What natural feature in Australia is your favorite? Why?" on chart paper to use as an example. Draw a simple illustration to support the response.

Explain that students will help you add a detail to a Response Journal entry. Read the sample journal entry aloud and display the supporting illustration.

I like the outback.

Instruct students to Think-Pair-Share, and ask: "What compliment would you give about this journal entry?" Use Equity Sticks to call on students to respond.

✔ Instruct students to Think-Pair-Share, and ask: "What suggestion would you give about this journal entry? What descriptive word could I use to label my drawing? What detail could I add to my drawing to make it better?" Use Equity Sticks to call on students to respond. Reread pages 19–21 as needed.

  ▪ *You could say it is really dry.*
  ▪ *You could say that the outback is hot.*
  ▪ *You could draw the really big rock and put its name on it.*

Use responses to model the process of adding details to the Response Journal entry. For example, label the drawing with words such as "hot" and "dry," or add details to the illustration, such as including and labeling Uluru Rock.

Reread the sample Response Journal entry, with the new details added. Ask: "How did I add details to my writing piece?" Volunteers respond.

  ▪ *You added descriptive words.*
  ▪ *You added labels to the picture.*
  ▪ *You added more detail to the drawing.*

Distribute Response Journals. Instruct students to think about a descriptive label or detail they could add to their drawing. Students practice revising their writing by adding details such as descriptive labels or additional details to their drawing, as modeled in the lesson.

Land 4 MIN.

ANSWER THE CONTENT FRAMING QUESTION

Display and read aloud the Content Framing Question. Ask: "What did you learn about Australia today?" Volunteers respond.

Instruct students to Mix and Mingle, and ask: "Imagine that you are taking a trip to Australia. What would you pack in your suitcase? Why?"

Wrap 1 MIN.

ASSIGN HOMEWORK

Continue the class home-reading routine.

Analyze

Context and Alignment

Students use the heading of a section in *Australia* to identify the main topic. After reading the section they retell key details (RI.K.2). Each student:

- Uses the heading to identify the main topic.
- Uses Nonverbal Signals to retell the main topic and key details.

Next Steps

If students have difficulty retelling key details in the text, work with small groups and reread the section. Stop after each page spread and ask: "What details did you learn about the main topic from this page?" After students gain confidence with the key details of the section, support them in using the Nonverbal Signals to retell the main topic and key details of the section as a whole.

⬇ **LESSON 24 DEEP DIVE: STYLE AND CONVENTIONS**

Examine Beginning a Sentence with a Capital Letter

- **Time:** 15 min.

- **Text:** *Australia*, Rebecca Hirsch

- **Style and Conventions Learning Goal:** Distinguish between a phrase and a complete sentence and identify the letter that should be capitalized in a complete sentence. (L.K.1.f, L.K.2.a)

   STYLE AND CONVENTIONS CRAFT QUESTION: Lesson 24
   Examine: *Why is it important write a complete sentence that begins with a capital letter?*

Launch

TEACHER NOTE	The purpose of this arc is to for students to write a complete sentence and to start the sentence correctly with a capital letter. Students can be encouraged to continue to expand their sentences as practiced in the previous Style and Conventions arc, but it is not necessary for the purpose of meeting standard L.K.2.a at this time. Throughout the course of this module, students are working towards writing and expanding complete sentences that start with a capital letter.

Post and read the Style and Conventions Craft Question.

Explain that in the previous module they learned a rule about capital letters. Ask: "What is the rule about how to begin a sentence?" Volunteers respond.

- *The first letter of the beginning word needs to be capitalized.*

Remind students that they determined that authors capitalize the first letter in a sentence because it lets the reader know they are starting to tell a new thought or idea. It is also important for authors to follow the rules of writing.

Reinforce that students have also been learning more about complete sentences in this module. In Deep Dive Lesson 21, they wrote and expanded a complete sentence.

Ask: "What are the parts of a complete sentence?" Volunteers respond.

- *Who.*
- *Does what.*

371

Extension

Ask: "How did you expand your sentences?" Volunteers respond.

- *We added describing words to give more details.*

- *We told where or when our sentences happened.*

Remind students that during today's lesson, they learned about captions. Explain that students are going to explore captions to determine if they are complete sentences or not. They will also show which letter needs to be capitalized if it is a complete sentence.

Learn

Instruct students to listen closely to determine if the information from the book is a complete sentence or not. If it is a complete sentence, students give a thumbs-up signal and if it is not, students give a thumbs-down signal.

Display page 20, point out the illustration and read the caption: "Uluru Rock." Students give a thumbs-down signal.

Ask: "Is this a complete sentence? Why or why not?"

- *No, because it only tells who.*

- *No, because it doesn't tell what the rock does.*

Display page 4, point out the illustration and read the caption: "People hike in Uluru National Park." Students give a thumbs-up signal.

Ask: "Why is this a complete sentence?"

- *Because it tells who, does what.*

- *Because it tells that people hike.*

- *Because it tells more information about where the people hike.*

Write the caption from page 4 on the board in all lowercase letters and remind students that a letter needs to be capitalized since it is a complete sentence. Instruct students to Think-Pair-Share and ask, "What letter needs to be capitalized?" Students identify which letter needs to be capitalized by standing and making the letter with their whole body. Students stand and make a capital P.

TEACHER NOTE	To maximize instructional time, write the following captions on sentence strips prior to the lesson. Begin both with lowercase letters. the outback in Australia. (page 18) eucalyptus trees grow in Australia. (page 22)

✔ Students give a thumbs-up signal if they hear a complete sentence or a thumbs-down signal if not. Display page 18 and read the caption. Post the phrase on the board. Students respond with the correct signal. Display page 22 and read the caption. Post the phrase on the board. Students respond with the correct signal. Instruct students to look at the complete sentence to determine which letter needs to be capitalized. Students stand and make the correct capital letter with their whole body.

Use Equity Sticks to call on a student to state the letter and edit the sentence appropriately.

Land

Redirect student attention back to the Style and Conventions Craft Question.

Ask: "Why do authors write complete sentences?" Volunteers respond.

- *So the story or information they are sharing is clear.*
- *So readers can understand what they are writing about.*

Ask: "Why is it important that authors start each sentence with a capital letter?"

- *Because that is the rule they need to follow.*
- *So they let readers know when they are starting to tell a new thought or idea.*

■ FOCUSING QUESTION: LESSONS 22-27

What amazing animals can people see in South America and Australia?

1 | 2 | 3 | 4 | 5 | 6 | 7 | 8 | 9 | 10 | 11 | 12 | 13 | 14 | 15 | 16 | 17 | 18 | 19 | 20 | 21 | 22 | 23 | 24 | 25 | 26 | 27 | 28 | 29 | 30 | 31 | 32 | 33 | 34 | 35 | 36

Lesson 25

TEXTS

- *Moon Rope*, Lois Ehlert
- *Earth from Space*, Stöckli, Reto, et al. (**http://witeng.link/0373**)
- *South America*, Rebecca Hirsch
- "Patterns of Chinchero," *Descendants of the Incas* (**http://witeng.link/0435**)

Lesson 25: At a Glance

AGENDA

Welcome (5 min.)

Practice Fluency

Launch (3 min.)

Learn (62 min.)

Analyze Words and Photographs in South America (15 min.)

Collect Evidence for Focusing Question Task 4 (14 min.)

Experiment with Adding to Writing (15 min.)

Analyze Illustrations in Moon Rope (18 min.)

Land (4 min.)

Answer the Content Framing Question

Wrap (1 min.)

Assign Homework

Style and Conventions Deep Dive: Experiment with Beginning a Sentence with a Capital Letter (15 min.)

STANDARDS ADDRESSED

The full text of ELA Standards can be found in the Module Overview.

Reading

- RL.K.1, RL.K.7, RI.K.1, RI.K.4, RI.K.7

Writing

- W.K.1, W.K.5, W.K.8

Speaking and Listening

- SL.K.1, SL.K.2

Language

- L.K.1.f
- ⬇ L.K.1.f, L.K.2.a

MATERIALS

- Repeated Language Chart
- Evidence Organizer for *South America*
- Sticky notes

Learning Goals

Use photographs and details from the text to describe animals in *South America*. (RI.K.7)

✔ Record evidence for the Focusing Question Task.

Respond to suggestions from a peer to improve writing. (W.K.5)

✔ Add a descriptive label or detail to a drawing based on peer feedback.

⬇ Write a complete sentence caption that begins with a capital letter. (L.K.1.f, L.K.2.a)

✔ With a partner, write a complete sentence caption that begins with a capital letter.

✔ Checks for Understanding

Prepare

FOCUSING QUESTION: Lessons 22–27

What amazing animals can people see in South America and Australia?

CONTENT FRAMING QUESTION: Lesson 25

Reveal: *What does a deeper exploration of the words and illustrations reveal in* South America?

CRAFT QUESTION: Lesson 25

Experiment: *How do I add to my writing?*

In this lesson, students continue exploring *South America* by looking closely at text pictures to understand key descriptive words. Students use the words and pictures in the text to collect evidence for the Focusing Question Task. Familiarity with similar texts and routines allows them to demonstrate increasing independence. Students express learning by writing an opinion statement about the text. They then share this sentence and drawing and practice giving, receiving, and implementing feedback from peers. Finally, students revisit *Moon Rope* and look closely at the illustrations to make connections between the illustrations and Peruvian textiles.

Welcome 5 MIN.

PRACTICE FLUENCY

Display the Repeated Language Chart, with the next line of text added. Read the first three lines of the passage. Students Echo Read the lines.

Repeated Language
Text: *Moon Rope*

- Mole," he said, "if you could have anything in the world, what would it be?"

- "Worms, worms, more worms," Mole said. "What about you?"

- "I want to go to the moon."

Display *Earth from Space* (**http://witeng.link/0373**). Call on a volunteer to approach the image and point to Earth. Confirm that it is Earth and highlight that South America is shown on the lower right-hand side of Earth.

Call on a volunteer to approach the image and point to the moon.

Ask: "Is the moon close to Earth? How do you think a person—or fox!—gets to the moon?" Volunteers respond. Use responses to reinforce that the moon is located outside Earth in outer space.

Reread the three lines of the passage aloud. Students Echo Read the lines of text several times.

Launch 3 MIN.

Direct students' attention to the cover of *South America*. Ask: "What animal is this? How did the words and pictures in a previous lesson help you understand key details about this animal?" If needed, refer back to pages 12–13. Volunteers respond.

- *We learned it is a llama.*
- *They help people who live in the mountains.*
- *They carry things up the mountain. The words told us.*
- *We saw them in the pictures with kids.*

Confirm that the words and the pictures in this text helped them learn that the llama is an animal in South America that lives in the mountains. People of South America use llamas to carry things up and down the mountains there.

Read the Focusing Question and the Content Framing Question aloud. Tell students that today they will explore the words and pictures in *South America* to help them better understand more amazing animals in South America and collect evidence for the Focusing Question Task.

Learn 62 MIN.

ANALYZE WORDS AND PHOTOGRAPHS IN *SOUTH AMERICA* 15 MIN.

Whole Group

💬 Divide the class into pairs and distribute a copy of the text to each. Explain that students will now engage in Partner Reading, sharing responsibility for the text as they respond to TDQs about the words and pictures.

Prompt students to turn to pages 16–17. Read the heading on the top of page 17. Students Echo Read. Explain that now they will read through this section as a class and respond to questions about how the words and pictures work together to communicate key details and information about the animals.

Instruct students to Think-Pair-Share about the following TDQs. Use Equity Sticks to call on students to answer.

Display the picture on page 16 but do not read the text on page 17.

1   How does the picture on page 16 help us understand where monkeys live? What makes you think so?

-   *They live in trees. They are hanging from the tree.*

-   *They live in the rainforest.*

-   *I see green leaves so it is the rainforest not the mountains.*

Scaffold

Encourage students to think about natural features that exist in South America. If needed, refer back to pages 10–13 and ask: "Using these illustrations as a guide, do you think monkeys live in the mountains or the rainforest?"

Read the text on page 17. Confirm that monkeys live in the trees in the rainforest. Remind students that pictures can tell them about the animals, as well as other details about where they live or what they do.

Read page 19, then the caption underneath the photo on page 18.

2   If you did not know what a parrot was, what details can you learn about them from the photograph?

-   *They are birds!*

-   *They have bright feathers.*

-   *They have wings and stand on the branches.*

Extension

3   How does this picture help us understand what a "pair" is?

-   *I think it means two.*

-   *I only see two parrots.*

Confirm the definition of *pair.*

Read pages 20–21.

4 How does this picture show us the details we just read? Are there details in the words that you do not see in this picture?

- ▪ *I see the dolphin swimming.*
- ▪ *I see that it is pink, too.*
- ▪ *I don't see them catching fish.*
- ▪ *His mouth is open though, so maybe he is trying to catch a fish.*

Remind students that good readers use both words and the pictures to form a deeper understanding of what they are reading.

Explain that now they will use this understanding help them collect evidence for the Focusing Question Task.

COLLECT EVIDENCE FOR FOCUSING QUESTION TASK 4 14 MIN.

Pairs

Post and read the Focusing Question. Students Echo Read the question.

Display the blank Evidence Organizer for *South America*.

TEACHER NOTE	Prepare this evidence organizer beforehand (see example below). In Lessons 25 and 26 students will focus their evidence collection on "Animals." Consider covering the other two columns on the chart to focus students' attention.

Point to the third column on the chart. Read the title aloud. Students Echo Read the title. Explain that now they will go back through the whole text to look for examples of amazing animals in South America. As they listen, pairs use sticky notes to annotate their text for examples of animals in South America.

Divide the class into pairs, giving each pair four sticky notes.

✔ Read pages 16–21 and page 30 aloud. Pairs use sticky notes to annotate picture evidence of amazing animals in the text. After they read, pairs go back to the photographs they marked and choose two animals to record, using drawing and labeling, as the evidence on the sticky note provided. Use Equity Sticks to call on pairs share the animals they recorded.

Group similar responses together to add to the evidence organizer.

TEACHER NOTE	Pair pieces of evidence with a photograph to help students access the evidence organizer independently. Consider using the example below to prerecord or print out images to include on the evidence organizer.

SAMPLE EVIDENCE ORGANIZER FOR *SOUTH AMERICA*

Evidence Organizer for *South America*		
Things to Do	**Natural Features**	**Animals**
		▪ *monkey* ▪ *pink dolphin* ▪ *parrot* ▪ *jaguar*

EXPERIMENT WITH ADDING TO WRITING   15 MIN.

Pairs

Explain that now students will reflect upon the evidence they have collected and use it to form an opinion and write a sentence in their Response Journals using the following prompt.

> What is your favorite animal in South America? Why?

Instruct students to Think-Pair-Share about the prompt. Students write a sentence stating their opinion in their Response Journals. Students include a drawing to support their sentence.

Scaffold

Consider giving students the sentence frame **My favorite animal in South America is _____** to save time. The purpose of this lesson is to practice adding descriptive labels or details to their drawing based on peer feedback, not to craft an opinion statement.

Post and read the Craft Question: *How do I add to my writing?*

Explain that now they will practice sharing their writing with a partner and adding to their writing based on what their partner suggests.

Display the Sharing Our Writing Anchor Chart. Ask: "How do we respond to another's writing?" Volunteers respond. Confirm the sharing and response sequence established by the class.

Students take out their Response Journal entries and share their sentences and drawings with a partner. Partners offer one compliment. Then, students switch roles.

Ask: "What are some ways we can add to our writing and drawing? What types of words can we add that give more detail?" Volunteers respond.

- *We can add words to tell about the animal.*
- *We can add to our drawings.*

Reinforce that one way to improve one's writing and provide more detail is by adding descriptive labels to a drawing or adding more details to the drawing itself.

Explain that now students are going to share their journal entries again. Students will offer one suggestion to their partner about a descriptive label or additional detail they could add to their drawings to improve the writing.

Distribute copies of the text to pairs. Ask students to turn to the animal they wrote about in their sentence. Instruct students to Think-Pair-Share, and ask: "What words can we use to describe this animal?"

✔ Instruct students to share their journal entries again with a partner. Partners suggest one descriptive label or additional detail to add to the drawing. Students switch roles and repeat the sequence. Students add a descriptive word or detail to their drawing in their Response Journals.

ANALYZE ILLUSTRATIONS IN *MOON ROPE*   18 MIN.

Whole Group

Hold up a copy of *Moon Rope* in front of the class. Read the title aloud in both English and Spanish. Explain that the title is written in two languages. Ask: "Why do you think that is?" Volunteers respond.

Explain that *Moon Rope* is based on a story from Peru, a country in South America. Locate Peru on the world map. Reinforce that in Peru, most people speak Spanish; Spanish is their main language. Writing the book in Spanish means that those who do not speak or read English will still be able to enjoy it!

> ### Extension
>
> Ask: "Does anyone in the class speak Spanish? Do you know a friend or family member who speaks Spanish?" Volunteers respond.

Explain that today they will read through the text and focus on the illustrations in the text. Prompt students to sit in "listening position" in front of the book. Read the book aloud with minimal interruptions.

Instruct students to Think-Pair-Share, and ask: "What do you notice about the illustrations? How are they different from ones we have seen in other books?" Use Equity Sticks to call on students to answer.

- *It is hard to see the animals' faces.*
- *They have lots of different colors.*
- *I don't think a fox is really silver though.*
- *They don't look like other pictures.*
- *There are a lot of shapes.*

Display pages 1–2. Ask: "Which animal is the fox and which is the mole? How do you know?" Volunteers respond. Ask a student who answers to come up and identify the animals by pointing to them in the illustration.

Display pages 15–16. Ask: "What animal do you see in this picture? What makes you think that?" Volunteers respond.

Ask: "Do they look like birds you have seen in real life or in other stories? How are they the same? How are they different?" Volunteers respond.

Reinforce that the illustrations are not typical drawings or photographs. These are made by putting different shapes together. Turn through the pages of the text. Ask: "What shapes do you recognize in the illustrations?" Instruct students to make a Nonverbal Signal, such as putting a finger on their nose when they recognize a shape in the text. Call on students who signal to identify the shapes they see.

Scaffold

Consider focusing on specific pages in *Moon Rope*. For example, pages 13-16 and 21-26 display the most diverse shapes.

TEACHER NOTE	For background information on the illustrations, reference the second paragraph on the back of the title page.

Access the following link "Patterns of Chinchero" (**http://witeng.link/0435**) and project one of the images of Peruvian textiles in front of the class. If possible, zoom in on the details of the fabric allowing students to see the different shapes.

Explain that these are examples of textiles from Peru. Define *textile* as "pieces of cloth woven together."

Scaffold

Define *weave* as twisting or looping long threads of fabric together. Consider using the video "Traditional Weaving, Chincheros Peru" (**http://witeng.link/0436**) to provide a visual of how someone weaves fabric together.

TEACHER NOTE	Consider looking at "Some patterns of Chinchero, side by side" from the "Patterns of Chinchero" link. This shows a wide array of patterns and shapes.

Ask: "What do you notice that is the same about the pictures in *Moon Rope* and these pictures of real textiles?" Volunteers respond.

- I see zig-zag lines.
- I see circles and loops.
- I see crisscross lines.
- They have different shapes.

Extension

Give students a sheet of paper and a collection of shapes cut out from construction paper. Students create their own illustration for *Moon Rope* using the shapes.

Turn to page 12 in *South America*. Ask: "What do you see in this picture?" Volunteers respond. If possible, zoom in on the details on the children's clothing. Confirm that these are examples of children wearing woven textiles.

Explain that many people who live in South America make their own clothing by weaving fabric together, and that textiles are a large part of South American culture, just as certain kinds of art, music, and dance help define other continents and countries.

Land 4 MIN.

ANSWER THE CONTENT FRAMING QUESTION

Post and read the Content Framing Question. Instruct students to Mix and Mingle, and ask: "How did we use our knowledge of the pictures to learn more about South America?"

Display the picture on page 12 of *South America*. Ask: "While the text does not talk about textiles, what can we learn about them from this picture? Do you think they are used to keep people warm? Where do people live who are creating textiles? Use the picture to help you answer."

Wrap 1 MIN.

ASSIGN HOMEWORK

Continue the class home-reading routine.

Analyze

Context and Alignment

Students share their writing with a peer and add details to their writing based on feedback (W.K.5). Each student:

- Adds a descriptive label or additional details to a drawing.

Next Steps

If students have difficulty adding to their writing based on peer feedback, consider the root of the problem. Do students understand what their peer is suggesting? Circulate around the room as students share their journal entries to provide support where you see miscommunications. Do students have difficulty determining a descriptive word to suggest? If so, focus their attention on the photograph in the text. Work with them to describe the animal and generate adjectives.

Group students with similar needs and plan small group support for these skills to set students up for success with their Focusing Question Task.

LESSON 25 DEEP DIVE: STYLE AND CONVENTIONS

Experiment with Beginning a Sentence with a Capital Letter

- **Time:** 15 min.

- **Text:** *South America*, Rebecca Hirsch

- **Style and Conventions Learning Goal:** Write a complete sentence caption that begins with a capital letter. (L.K.1.f, L.K.2.a)

> **STYLE AND CONVENTIONS CRAFT QUESTION: Lesson 25**
> Experiment: *How does writing a complete sentence that begins with a capital letter work?*

Launch

Post and read the Style and Conventions Craft Question.

Explain that students are going to continue practicing how to create complete sentences that begin with a capital letter. Ask: "Why is it important to start a sentence with a capital letter?" Volunteers respond.

- *Because it is an important rule to follow.*
- *Because it shows a new thought or idea is starting.*

Explain that students are going to create complete sentence captions for photographs in *South America*. They will begin their complete sentences with capital letters.

Learn

Display the cover of *South America*. Ask: "Who is in this photograph?" Volunteers respond.

- *A girl.*
- *Llamas.*

Ask: "What are they doing?" Volunteers respond.

- *The girl is holding the llamas.*
- *The llamas are standing.*

Use student responses to record two examples of complete sentences on the board. Write the first sentence correctly. Ask: "Which letter is capitalized?" Use student responses to reinforce that the first letter is capitalized.

Write the second sentence in all lowercase letters, avoiding proper nouns if possible. Ask: "Which letter needs to be capitalized in this sentence?" Use student responses to correctly edit the sentence.

Display page 8 of the text. Instruct students to Mix and Mingle, and ask: "Who is doing what in this photograph?" Call on several students to share their complete sentences. After each student shares, ask him or her to identify which letter needs to be capitalized. Provide prompts as needed.

Scaffold

If students need additional support identify the correct capital letter, consider recording their sentence in all lowercase letters on the board to provide a visual cue.

Organize the class into pairs. Distribute a copy of the text and a sticky note to each pair. Instruct students to choose a photograph in the text. Allow pairs two minutes to choose before assigning a page number to undecided groups.

✔ Students work together to write a complete sentence caption for the photograph they chose from the text. One partner writes the "who" part of the sentence. The other partner writes the "does what" part of the sentence. Both partners make sure that their sentence begins with the correct capital letter. Circulate to provide support as needed.

Use Equity Sticks to call on pairs to share their complete sentences. Ask each pair to identify which letter they capitalized in their sentence.

Land

Redirect student attention back to the Style and Conventions Craft Question.

Ask: "How did you write complete sentences?" Volunteers respond.

- *We looked at a photograph from the book.*
- *We told who was in the photograph.*
- *We told what they did in the photograph.*

Ask: "How did you know which letter to capitalize?" Volunteers respond.

- *We followed the rule to capitalize the first letter of the beginning word.*

■ FOCUSING QUESTION: LESSONS 22–27

What amazing animals can people see in South America and Australia?

Lesson 26

TEXTS

- *Moon Rope*, Lois Ehlert
- *Australia*, Rebecca Hirsch
- *South America*, Rebecca Hirsch

Lesson 26: At a Glance

AGENDA

Welcome (5 min.)

Practice Fluency

Launch (3 min.)

Learn (64 min.)

Analyze Words and Photographs (15 min.)

Collect Evidence for Focusing Question Task 4 (10 min.)

Demonstrate Understanding of the Photographs (14 min.)

Execute Focusing Question Task 4 (25 min.)

Land (2 min.)

Answer the Content Framing Question

Wrap (1 min.)

Assign Homework

Vocabulary Deep Dive: Direct Vocabulary Assessment 1 (15 min.)

STANDARDS ADDRESSED

The full text of ELA Standards can be found in the Module Overview.

Reading

- RI.K.1, RI.K.4, RI.K.7

Writing

- W.K.1, W.K.8

Speaking and Listening

- SL.K.1, SL.K.2

Language

- ⬇ L.K.6

MATERIALS

- Assessment 26A: Focusing Question Task 4
- Assessment 26B: Direct Vocabulary Assessment 1
- Repeated Language Chart
- Evidence Organizers for *Australia* and *South America*
- Sticky notes with preprinted images of a koala, kangaroo, and platypus (see lesson for details)
- World map
- Opinion Sandwich Anchor Chart
- Document camera (if available)

Learning Goals

Use illustrations and details from the text to respond to questions about *South America*. (RI.K.7)

✔ Complete Part 1 of Focusing Question Task 4.

Use information gathered from *South America* and *Australia* to form an opinion about the animals on those continents. (RI.K.1, W.K.1, W.K.8)

✔ Begin Part 2 of Focusing Question Task 4.

⬇ Demonstrate understanding of grade-level vocabulary. (L.K.6)

✔ Complete Direct Vocabulary Assessment 1.

✔ Checks for Understanding

Prepare

FOCUSING QUESTION: Lessons 22–27

What amazing animals can people see in South America and Australia?

CONTENT FRAMING QUESTION: Lesson 26

Reveal: *What does a deeper exploration of the words and illustrations reveal in* Australia?

CRAFT QUESTION: Lesson 26

Execute: *How do I execute my Focusing Question Task?*

In this lesson, students continue to progress towards answering the Focusing Question by using words and photographs together to understand key details about Australian animals and by recording evidence for the Focusing Question Task. Students prepare for the task by reviewing the evidence organizers and forming an opinion about the animals in *Australia* and *South America*. They demonstrate their understanding of the relationship between the words and photographs in the text by responding to questions about the photographs, completing Part 1 of Focusing Question Task 4. Finally, they write an opinion statement and a supporting reason sentence to begin Part 2 of the task.

Welcome 5 MIN.

PRACTICE FLUENCY

Display the Repeated Language Chart. Read each line one a time. Students Echo Read each line.

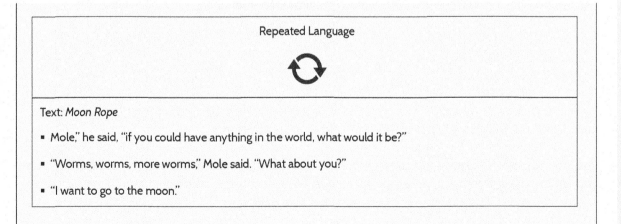

Repeated Language
Text: *Moon Rope*   ▪ Mole," he said, "if you could have anything in the world, what would it be?"   ▪ "Worms, worms, more worms," Mole said. "What about you?"   ▪ "I want to go to the moon."

Reinforce that this is a conversation between two characters. Remind students that they learned this speaking and listening skill earlier in the year. Ask: "How do we have conversations? What do we do with our eyes, our ears, and our voices?" Volunteers respond.

- *We look at who is talking.*
- *We listen with our ears and whole bodies.*
- *We are quiet until it is our turn.*

Divide the class in half, assigning one group the role of Mole and the other group the role of Fox.

Reread the three lines of the passage aloud one at a time while pointing to the corresponding group for that character. Groups Echo Read the line of their character. Switch roles so each group gets to read for Fox and Mole.

Launch 3 MIN.

Direct students' attention to the world map. Point to Australia on the map. Ask: "What do you notice about this continent? How is it different from the other continents?" Volunteers respond.

- *It looks smaller.*
- *It's all by itself over there.*
- *It's not very close to the others.*
- *It has blue all around it.*

Reinforce that Australia is an *island*, which means it is surrounded by water on all sides. Reference Africa, Europe, and Asia to demonstrate that other continents are connected to each other by land. While it would be far, people can actually walk from one of those continents to another.

Ask: "How could a person travel to Australia?" Volunteers respond.

- *They could fly in a plane.*
- *They could take a boat.*
- *They could swim but it's really far!*

Explain that because Australia is an island, it has a lot of features that are unique, because animals and plants and people could not travel over land to other continents.

Read the Focusing Question and the Content Framing Question aloud. Tell students that today they will explore the words and pictures in *Australia* to help them better understand the unique animals in Australia and collect evidence for Focusing Question Task 4.

Learn 64 MIN.

ANALYZE WORDS AND PHOTOGRAPHS 15MIN.

Whole Group

Explain that students will take a closer look at the words and illustrations in *Australia* to better understand key information about the animals. They will think about how the words and pictures work together add to their knowledge about the continent Australia.

💬 If possible, use a document camera to display the pages of the text in front of the class. Prompt students to sit in "listening position" and look at the copy of the text in front of the class.

> *Alternate Activity*
>
> Divide the class into small groups and distribute a copy of the text to each group. Explain to students that they will share responsibility for the text with their group as they respond to TDQs about the words and pictures in the text.

Prompt students to turn to pages 14–15. Read the heading on the top of page 15. Students Echo Read.

Read the first sentence on page 15. Define *usual* as something not surprising, that you see a lot. Read the word "unusual" aloud, emphasizing the prefix *un–*. Ask: "How do the letters *un* at the start of the word change its meaning?" Volunteers respond.

- *It means it's the opposite.*

Reinforce that *unusual* means something that you do not see often and that is different from normal. Reread the first sentence again. Ask: "What is this sentence telling us? How does it help us prepare to learn about the animals?" Volunteers respond.

- *It says the animals are unusual.*

- *The animals are different than normal animals.*

- *It is telling us that we will read about different animals.*

Reinforce that as they read through the text, students can use the words and pictures to learn more about the animals and understand how they are "unusual."

Display and read the following pages aloud. Instruct students to Think-Pair-Share about the associated TDQs. Use Equity Sticks to call on students to answer.

Read page 15 and the caption on page 14.

1 **How does this picture help us understand what a "pouch" is?**

- *It is on their bellies.*

- *It is something on their tummy that the baby sits in.*
- *Maybe it's like a little seat or bag.*

Ask: "How are kangaroos unusual?" Volunteers respond.

- *They carry babies in a pouch.*
- *They hop really fast.*

Scaffold

Encourage students to look closely at the picture of the kangaroo and describe its physical traits.

Read page 17, then the caption on page 16.

2 **What does this tell us about the type of food that koalas eat?**

- *They eat leaves.*
- *They don't drink anything but their food has water.*
- *The leaves have water in them.*

Scaffold

Ask students to think about foods they eat that have a lot of water or juice in them, such as fruit or lettuce.

Ask: "What does this tell us about where koalas live? Do you think they live in a dry desert? Why or why not?" Volunteers respond.

- *I think it rains there.*
- *They live in forests because there are trees.*
- *They need to live where it rains so the leaves have water.*
- *I think they live in the forest.*

Ask: "How are koalas unusual?" Volunteers respond.

- *They don't drink any water.*
- *They sleep a lot.*
- *They have funny ears and noses.*

Turn to page 30 and, if possible, zoom in on the photograph of the platypus. Read the first three bullets on page 30 aloud. Explain that when there is a thin layer of skin between fingers and toes that this is called "webbed feet." Point out the platypus. Instruct students to hold out their hands in front of them and spread their fingers wide. Ask: "Do you think water could get in between your fingers?" Volunteers respond.

Instruct students to close their fingers together, keeping your hand open. Ask: "Do you think water would be able to get in between your fingers now? Why not?" Volunteers respond.

Reinforce that platypuses have webbed feet in order to be better swimmers! Explain that many animals that live on the water, such as ducks and frogs, have webbed feet in order to swim easily.

Ask: "How else is this animal like a duck?" Volunteers respond.

- *It has a nose like a duck.*
- *It lives near the water.*

Ask: "What makes the platypus unusual?" Volunteers respond.

- *It has a duck nose and feet but no wings.*
- *It has fur.*
- *It has webbed feet and a bill.*

Instruct students to Mix and Mingle, and ask: "Which unusual animal from Australia is your favorite? Why?" Use Equity Sticks to call on students to share their answers.

COLLECT EVIDENCE FOR FOCUSING QUESTION TASK 4 10 MIN.

Small Groups

Explain that students can use this knowledge of the animals in Australia to collect evidence for the Focusing Question Task. Post and read the Focusing Question. Students Echo Read the question.

Display the blank Evidence Organizer for *Australia*.

TEACHER NOTE	Prepare this evidence organizer beforehand (see example below). In this first part of the lesson, students will focus their evidence collection on "Animals." Consider covering the other two columns on the chart in order to focus students' attention. Students will revisit the text later in the lesson in order to collect evidence for the "Natural Features" column. This is preparation for the EOM Task, but not crucial to the completion of Focusing Question Task 4.

Point to the third column on the chart. Read the title aloud. Students Echo read the title. Explain that now they will go back through the text to annotate examples of amazing animals in Australia.

Divide the class into three small groups, distributing copies of the text accordingly. Read pages 14–17 and page 30 aloud. Prompt groups to listen closely to the description of the animals.

Assign each group one animal from the text: a koala, kangaroo, or platypus. Give each group a sticky note with the image of their assigned animal on it.

Groups discuss the following questions: "What do we know about this animal? What details did we learn from the text?" Prompt groups to look at the corresponding pages in the text. Instruct students to label their sticky note with the name of the animal. If time allows, students add one descriptive word to describe the animal.

✔ Students label evidence with details from the text.

Call on each group to share the animal evidence they labeled. Choose one image from each group to add to the evidence organizer.

TEACHER NOTE	For student responses not used on the evidence organizer, consider creating a chart near the evidence organizer labeled "Other Great Evidence" and add student responses to the chart. Or, allow students to add these images to their Response Journals.

SAMPLE EVIDENCE ORGANIZER FOR *AUSTRALIA*

Evidence Organizer for *Australia*		
Things to Do	**Natural Features**	**Animals**
		▪ kangaroo ▪ koala ▪ platypus

DEMONSTRATE UNDERSTANDING OF THE PHOTOGRAPHS 14 MIN.

Individuals

Acknowledge students for all the great work they have done with the photographs over the course of this module. Ask: "Do you think of photographs differently now? Why are photographs or illustrations important to a text? How can we use the words and illustrations to understand key details in the text?" Volunteers respond.

Ask: "Why do we pair our own writing with a drawing? How does that help our readers?" Volunteers respond.

Explain that to begin Focusing Question Task 4, students will express understanding of the relationship between the words and photographs in the text. They will use pictures to answer questions about the text. This will prepare them for their Focusing Question Task as they will see how the words and photographs work together to convey information to a reader—something they will do with their own writing.

Display pages 16–17 of *South America* and read the heading on page 17 aloud. Explain that now they will go back through this section of the text and respond to questions about the words and photographs.

Distribute and introduce Part 1 of Assessment 26A: Focusing Question Task 4. Point out that students have seen a similar assessment format during Direct Vocabulary Assessments and New-Read Assessment 2. Explain that you will read each question aloud. If students think the answer to the question is "yes," they draw a circle around the smiley face. If they think the answer is "no," they draw a circle around the frowning face.

> Name:
>
> **Assessment 26A: Focusing Question Task 4**
>
> Part 1
> Directions: Circle 🙂 Yes or 🙁 No to answer each question.
>
> | Example: Is South America the title of the text? | 🙂 Yes | 🙁 No |
> | 1. Does this photograph show us parrots living in trees? | 🙂 Yes | 🙁 No |
> | 2. Does this photograph show us parrots eating fruits and seeds? | 🙂 Yes | 🙁 No |
>
> Directions: Circle the image for words or for photographs.
>
> | 3. Did we learn that parrots eat fruits and seeds from the words or the photographs? Circle the image of where you learned this information. | Words | Photographs |

TEACHER NOTE

Questions 3 and 5 do not follow this format. For question 3 students circle an image to represent the words or an image to represent the photographs in the text. For question 5, students write a sentence, or create and label a drawing, about the photograph in the text. As students approach these questions, explain how students should answer these questions.

Use a document camera to display pages 16–21 as you read the "Amazing Animals" section aloud. Prompt students to listen closely to the words they hear and think about how the pictures help them understand those words.

Use the teacher-facing version (with key) in Appendix C to administer the assessment. Begin by completing the example together. Display the following pages from the book during the assessment.

- Display page 18. Ask questions 1–3.

- Display page 16. Ask questions 4 and 5.

Scaffold

Use a document camera to project the pages of the text as you ask the corresponding questions. If this is not available, distribute copies of the text to pairs. While students will not discuss the text during the assessment, allow pairs to share copies of the text to get a closer look at the photographs.

✔ Students complete Part 1 of Focusing Question Task 4. Read each question twice before students fill in answers. Circulate to ensure students follow directions and mark the correct question. Give oral cues as necessary to help students locate the proper row for marking answers.

EXECUTE FOCUSING QUESTION TASK 4 25 MIN.

Individuals

Explain that now students will use the evidence they collected over the past few lessons on the animals in *South America* and *Australia* to answer the Focusing Question.

Post and read the Focusing Question. Students Echo Read the question. Call on a volunteer to define *amazing*.

Display the Evidence Organizers for *South America* and *Australia*. Explain that students will be writing a paragraph to answer the following prompt. They will think about the different evidence they have collected and form an opinion about which continent has the most amazing animals. They will use examples from the text to support their opinion with reason sentences.

> Which continent do you think has the most amazing animals?

Display the Opinion Sandwich Anchor Chart. Explain that in this lesson they will be using the evidence organizers to form an opinion and write one opinion sentence and one supporting reason sentence for their Focusing Question Task.

Divide the class into pairs. Provide copies of each text around the room for students to look through. Explain that they will now use the evidence they collected on the different animals in South America and Australia. Instruct students to Think-Pair-Share about the following questions as their verbal rehearsal for the Focusing Question Task.

- If you visited South America, what animal would you like to see?

- If you visited Australia, what animal would you like to see?

- Which continent do you think has the most amazing animals? Why?

| **TEACHER NOTE** | Encourage students to discuss the evidence before forming an opinion. It is good practice to consider both sides of a topic before forming an opinion about the evidence collected. If needed, model a Think-Aloud as you process the evidence from both continents and explain why you think one continent has the most amazing animals. |

Display Part 2 of Assessment 26A. Introduce the different parts of the assessment, point to each section of the handout as you explain where students record their sentences.

- Students write their opinion statement on the line provided at the top of page 3.

- Students write their first reason sentence on the lines provided at the bottom of page 3 and add a drawing in the box provided.

TEACHER NOTE	Consider introducing the different parts of the assessment one at time, providing time for students to write their sentence before moving on to the next part of the task. Students do not need to be able to internalize the structure of the opinion paragraph at this time.

✔ Students begin Part 2 of Focusing Question Task 4 by writing their opinion statement and one supporting reason sentence on page 3 of Assessment 26A.

Land 2 MIN.

ANSWER THE CONTENT FRAMING QUESTION

Post and read the Content Framing Question. Instruct students to Mix and Mingle, and ask: "What do you think makes Australia an interesting place? What is one thing someone should see if they visit Australia?"

Wrap 1 MIN.

ASSIGN HOMEWORK

Continue the class home-reading routine.

Analyze

Context and Alignment

Students use their understanding of the words and pictures in *South America* to respond to questions about the text (RI.K.7). Each student:

- Responds to questions by circling *yes* or *no*.

- Writes a sentence about one photograph in the text.

Next Steps

If students have difficulty responding to the questions for Part 1 of the Focusing Question Task, consider rereading the corresponding pages in the text. Prompt students to listen closely to the words they hear and how the photograph on the page supports these words. For example, if students have difficulty responding to question 3, reread page 19 and ask supportive questions such as: "Did the words tell you what parrots eat? Do you see parrots eating in the photograph? Did you learn that parrots eat fruit and seeds from the words or the photograph?" If students have difficulty responding to question 5, encourage them to think about the details they know about the rainforest.

⬇ **LESSON 26 DEEP DIVE: VOCABULARY**

Direct Vocabulary Assessment 1

- **Time:** 15 min.

- **Text:** All Module Texts

- **Vocabulary Learning Goal:** Demonstrate understanding of grade-level vocabulary. (L.K.6)

Launch

Remind students how they completed Direct Vocabulary Assessments in the previous modules. Explain that they will do a similar activity to demonstrate understanding of key words from this module.

TEACHER NOTE	As it has been awhile since students took previous assessments, they may benefit from a visual or additional dialogue to cue their memories.

Learn

Distribute Assessment 26B and pencils (as needed).

Remind students that you will read a question aloud that contains the word listed beside the number. If students think the answer to the question is "yes," they draw a circle around the smiley face. If they think the answer is "no," they draw a circle around the frowning face.

Use the teacher-facing version (with key) located in Appendix C to administer the assessment. Begin by completing the example together.

Read each question twice before students fill in answers, always reading the focus word before reading the question. Circulate to ensure students follow directions and mark the correct question. Give oral cues as necessary to help students locate the proper row where they should be marking answers.

✔ Students complete Direct Vocabulary Assessment 1.

Name: _____

Assessment 26B: Direct Vocabulary Assessment 1

Directions: Circle 😊 yes or 🙁 no to answer each question.

Example: hot	😊 Yes	🙁 No
1. continent	😊 Yes	🙁 No
2. tallest	😊 Yes	🙁 No
3. stick	😊 Yes	🙁 No
4. amazing	😊 Yes	🙁 No
5. giant	😊 Yes	🙁 No
6. continent	😊 Yes	🙁 No

Land

Congratulate students on all their hard work! Explain that they will do this type of assessment once more during the module.

▓ FOCUSING QUESTION: LESSONS 22–27

What amazing animals can people see in South America and Australia?

1 2 3 4 5 6 7 8 9 10 11 12 13 14 15 16 17 18 19 20 21 **22 23 24 25 26 27** 28 29 30 31 32 33 34 35 36

Lesson 27

TEXTS

- *Moon Rope*, Lois Ehlert

- *Australia*, Rebecca Hirsch

- *South America*, Rebecca Hirsch

- *World Atlas*, Nick Crane; Illustrations, David Dean

Lesson 27: At a Glance

AGENDA

Welcome (5 min.)

Perform Fluency

Launch (4 min.)

Learn (63 min.)

Execute Focusing Question Task 4 (20 min.)

Execute Adding to Writing (8 min.)

Collect Evidence for the EOM Task (10 min.)

Compare South America with World Atlas (10 min.)

Record Knowledge (15 min.)

Land (2 min.)

Answer the Content Framing Question

Wrap (1 min.)

Assign Homework

Style and Conventions Deep Dive: Experiment with Beginning a Sentence with a Capital Letter (15 min.)

STANDARDS ADDRESSED

The full text of ELA Standards can be found in the Module Overview.

Reading

- RI.K.1, RI.K.9

Writing

- W.K.1, W.K.5, W.K.8, W.10*

Speaking and Listening

- SL.K.1, SL.K.2

Language

- ⬇ L.K.1.f, L.K.2.a

MATERIALS

- Assessment 26A: Focusing Question Task 4
- Repeated Language Chart
- Evidence Organizers for *Australia* and *South America*
- Opinion Sandwich Anchor Chart
- Sharing Our Writing Anchor Chart
- Knowledge Journal
- Document camera (if available)
- Stamps or stickers (see lesson for details)
- Handout 8A: Passport Journals

Learning Goals

Use information gathered from *South America* and *Australia* to support an opinion about the continent. (RI.K.1, W.K.1, W.K.8)

✔ Continue Part 2 of Focusing Question Task 4.

Respond to suggestions from a peer to improve writing for the Focusing Question Task. (W.K.5)

✔ Add a descriptive label or details to a drawing to complete Part 2 of Focusing Question Task 4.

Identify basic similarities in and differences between *South America* and *World Atlas*. (RI.K.9)

✔ Identify one similarity and one difference between details in *World Atlas* and *South America*.

⬇ Write a complete sentence that begins with a capital letter. (L.K.1.f, L.K.2.a)

✔ Write a complete sentence that begins with a capital letter in Response Journals.

In alignment with the CCSS, W.10 formally begins in Grade 3. However, K–2 students write routinely for a variety of time frames, tasks, purposes, and audiences. As a result, this lesson contains instruction related to W.10 in an effort to familiarize students with a range of writing.

✔ Checks for Understanding

Prepare

FOCUSING QUESTION: Lessons 22–27

What amazing animals can people see in South America and Australia?

CONTENT FRAMING QUESTION: Lesson 27

Know: *How do Australia and South America build my knowledge of the continents?*

CRAFT QUESTION: Lesson 27

Execute: *How do I add to my writing in my Focusing Question Task?*

In this lesson students complete Focusing Question Task 4 by writing a second supporting reason sentence and completing the conclusion frame. They also demonstrate understanding of how to respond to a peer's feedback by adding descriptive labels or details to their writing. Students continue their progress towards the EOM Task by collecting evidence about things to do and natural features in South America for the EOM Task. In addition students compare and contrast information on South American animals found in *South America* and *World Atlas*. Finally, students reflect upon their learning from *Australia* and *South America* and record it in individual Passport Journals.

Welcome 5 MIN.

PERFORM FLUENCY

Display the Repeated Language Chart. Explain that students will conclude work with this passage by performing for each other.

The class conducts a rehearsal by Choral Reading the Repeated Language Chart.

Divide the class into two groups, assigning each group one animal role to perform. Groups take a turn performing the lines of their assigned animal from *Moon Rope*. Switch roles to allow each group to perform the roles of both Fox and Mole.

Launch 4 MIN.

Ask: "Which continents have we explored so far?" Volunteers respond. Confirm that students have learned about Europe, Asia, Africa, Antarctica, Australia, and South America.

Play "Guess the Continent." Provide clues about a continent, one at a time, and invite students to guess the continent you are describing. For example,

> **This continent has lots of museums. There are castles, too. People can ski in the mountains. Which continent is it?**
>
> ▪ *It's Europe!*

Give clues for other continents, as time allows. If students are ready, invite a volunteer to be the clue-giver.

Display and read aloud the Content Framing Question. Students Echo Read the question. Explain that in this lesson each student will reflect upon the information they gathered about South America and Australia and express their opinion about the amazing animals that live there.

Learn 63 MIN.

EXECUTE FOCUSING QUESTION TASK 4 20 MIN.

Individuals

Explain that working on the Focusing Question Task is another way students will think about what they learned from *South America* and *Australia.*

Reintroduce Part 2 of the Focusing Question Task and criteria for success. Explain that they are writing an opinion paragraph to answer the following prompt.

> Which continent do you think has the most amazing animals?

Explain that students will complete their paragraph for the Focusing Question Task today by writing and illustrating one more reason sentence to support the opinion statement. They will also complete the conclusion sentence by retelling their opinion.

Divide the class into pairs and instruct students to take out their completed page 3 of Assessment 26A. Partners take turns reading their opinion statement and first reason sentence to each other and sharing their illustrations.

Display the Evidence Organizers for *South America* and *Australia* and briefly review each piece of evidence recorded in the "Animals" column. Remind students to use them as a reference for creating their next reason sentence.

TEACHER NOTE	For this portion of the task, consider covering the "Things to Do" and "Natural Features" columns on the Evidence Organizer for *Australia* so that students can focus their attention on one column. While students need this information for the EOM Task, they will not use this evidence for Focusing Question Task 4.

Instruct students to Think-Pair-Share, and ask: "Which reason will you write about next to support your opinion? What other amazing animal can people see in [continent name]?"

Students share another supporting reason with their partner and verbally rehearse the sentence they will write.

Distribute page 4 of Assessment 26A.

✔ Students write their second supporting reason sentence and complete a sentence frame for their conclusion sentence on page 4 of Assessment 26A.

EXECUTE ADDING TO WRITING 8 MIN.

Individuals

Explain that to finish Focusing Question Task 4, students will now demonstrate how to share their writing with a peer and add to their writing based on a suggestion from a peer.

Post and read the Craft Question aloud. Students Echo Read the question. Display the Sharing Our Writing Anchor Chart. Call on student volunteers to read each step in the sharing sequence.

Explain that to complete their task, students will share one of their supporting reason sentences and drawings with a partner. The partner will respond to their writing by suggesting one descriptive label or detail about the animal they can use to add to their drawing.

Scaffold

Model a Think Aloud about giving a suggestion using pages 18–19 in *South America*. For example:

> My partner's sentence is "There are parrots" and she drew a picture of a parrot. How can I use the picture of the parrot to make a suggestion? [Display photograph of the parrots.] What do the parrots look like? They have feathers. They have lots of different colors. They are so pretty. That is what I should say! [Mimic turning to a partner.] I think you should add a label that says "colorful feathers" to your drawing.

If needed, model how to add this label to the drawing.

Divide the class into pairs. Students choose one supporting reason sentence and drawing from Assessment 26A to share. Distribute copies of the text to pairs.

TEACHER NOTE	If there are not enough copies of the text to go around, consider grouping pairs together to share certain texts. The important thing is that students get to see the photograph of the animal in their partner's reason sentence to generate a descriptive label or a detail to add to the drawing.

Pairs share one supporting reason sentence and drawing from Assessment 26A. Pairs offer one compliment and, using the photograph from the text, offer one descriptive label or detail for their partner to add to their drawing.

✔ Students add a descriptive label or detail to one supporting reason drawing based on peer feedback.

COLLECT EVIDENCE FOR THE EOM TASK 10 MIN.

Whole Group

Post and read the Essential Question. Students Echo Read the question. Remind them that understanding different aspects of the continents will help them expand their knowledge and fascination with the world.

Scaffold

If needed, briefly revisit the EOM Task and remind students that they will be writing a travel brochure about their favorite continent.

Display the Evidence Organizer for *South America*. Reveal the title of the first column, "Things to Do." Read this title aloud. Explain that they will now go back through the text to find evidence on the different things to do in South America.

If possible, use a document camera to project the pages of the book. Distribute copies of the text to pairs. Prompt pairs to follow along with their copy of the text. Instruct students to make a Nonverbal Signal, such as pointing to their ears, when they hear an example of a thing to do in South America.

Read the section "Visit South America" in *South America* aloud. Students make a Nonverbal Signal when they hear evidence in the text. Use Equity Sticks to call on students who signal to share their evidence.

After each response, students consider whether or not that is a piece of evidence. They indicate a level of agreement by holding up anywhere from one to five fingers, with one finger showing the lowest level of agreement and five fingers showing the strongest level of agreement.

Use votes to choose one or two refined responses to record in the "Things to Do" column on the Evidence Organizer for *South America*.

TEACHER NOTE	Consider preparing sticky notes with this evidence beforehand using the example below. This will save time and allow for the lesson to flow smoothly. Using preprinted photographs will allow students to independently access these notes in future lessons.

Reveal the title of the second column, "Natural Features." Read this title aloud.

Read the section "People and Places" in *South America*. Repeat the sequence above to add evidence to the "Natural Features" column.

Evidence Organizer for *South America*		
Things to Do	**Natural Features**	**Animals**
▪ *ride boats* ▪ *see where people lived long ago* ▪ *visit busy cities*	▪ *rainforest* ▪ *deserts* ▪ *mountains*	▪ *monkey* ▪ *pink dolphin* ▪ *parrot* ▪ *jaguar*

COMPARE *SOUTH AMERICA* WITH *WORLD ATLAS* 10 MIN.

Small Groups

Display the front cover of *World Atlas* and read the title, author, and illustrator aloud. Ask: "How have we used this *World Atlas*? How does it help us learn more about a continent?" Volunteers respond.

- *We saw things that we saw in the little books.*
- *We also saw new information.*
- *We can see the whole continent.*
- *There are different colors to show us different natural features, too.*

Explain that in this lesson, they will use the map of South America to learn more about South America.

Display pages 42–43 in *World Atlas*, reading the heading at the top of the page spread.

Divide the class into six small groups. Distribute one copy of *World Atlas* and two copies of *South America* to each group.

Groups open the atlas to the map of South America on page 43. Allow students to observe the map for thirty seconds. Ask: "What do you notice about this map?" Students take turns sharing their observations in their small groups. Call on several students to share their response with the whole class.

Ask: "How did we locate natural features on this map when studying Africa? What hints does this map give us?" Volunteers respond. Confirm that the colors in this map play an important role in communicating information about the natural features.

Display the Evidence Organizer for *South America*. Call on volunteers to list the evidence recorded in the "Natural Features" column.

Ask: "Does this map of South America have any of these natural features? How do you know?" Volunteers respond.

- *I see the rainforest. It is green.*
- *I see the desert. It is orange.*

Confirm that this map shows both the rainforest and the desert that students learned about in *South America*. That is an example of information that is the same in both texts.

Direct students' attention to the top of the map in *World Atlas*. Point to the waterfall labeled "Angel Falls" but do not identify this feature for students. Ask: "What is this natural feature?" Volunteers respond.

Scaffold

Remind students of the natural features in Australia. Ask: "What natural feature is tall like a mountain and has lots of fast water flowing off of it?" If students still have difficulty, identify this as a waterfall for them. They have only read one text with a waterfall so they may not be familiar with it yet.

Confirm that this is a waterfall. Point to the "Natural Features" on Evidence Organizer for *South America*. Ask: "Did we read about waterfalls in *South America*?" Volunteers respond.

Confirm that this is an example of information that only appears in *World Atlas*. It is something new they learned about South America!

Direct students' attention to the "Animals" column on the Evidence Organizer for *South America*. Call on volunteers to list the animals recorded on the evidence organizer. Explain that now they will look at the map of South America and locate one animal that appears on both the evidence organizer and on the map, as well as one new animal that only appears in *World Atlas*.

✔ Instruct students to Think-Pair-Share, and ask: "What animal do we see in both texts? What animal do we only see in *World Atlas*?" Use Equity Sticks to call on groups to share the new detail they found with the whole class.

RECORD KNOWLEDGE 15 MIN.

Individuals

Display a copy of *Australia*. Provide time for students to think about the important knowledge they learned while exploring the text. Instruct students to Mix and Mingle, and ask: "What important knowledge did you learn about Australia?" Encourage students to use the Evidence Organizer for *Australia* as a reference.

Instruct students to take out their Passport Journals and open to page 6 for Australia. Explain that students will draw and label an illustration to share the knowledge they gained from reading *Australia*.

Students draw and label an illustration to share one thing they learned about Australia in their Passport Journals. Make copies of the text available for students to reference as needed. After students complete their journal pages, place a stamp or sticker on each section to mark their visit to the continent.

Repeat the same sequence above with *South America*. Students draw and label an illustration to share one thing they learned about South America on page 7 in their Passport Journals. Make copies of the text available for students to reference as needed. After students complete their journal pages, place a stamp or sticker on each section to mark their visit to the continent.

411

Alternate Activity

Depending on the needs of the class, students may write and illustrate sentences in their Passport Journals instead of drawing and labeling illustrations.

Display the class Knowledge Journal. Point to the left part of the journal, and explain that students have already completed this part by writing important learning in their Passport Journals.

Tell students that they will add new items to the "What I Can Do" column by thinking about the new skills they learned as readers and writers.

Instruct students to Think-Pair-Share, and ask: "What did you learn to do as a reader? What did you learn to do as a writer?"

Scaffold

Ask: "What did you learn about sharing your writing?"

Use Equity Sticks to call on pairs to share responses. After each response, students consider whether or not that piece of learning is something important that they want to remember and include in the Knowledge Journal. They indicate a level of agreement by holding up anywhere from one to five fingers, with one finger showing the lowest level of agreement and five fingers showing the strongest level of agreement.

Use votes to choose one or two refined responses to record in the Knowledge Journal.

SAMPLE KNOWLEDGE JOURNAL

What I Know	What I Can Do
	• I share my writing.
	• I can give a compliment and a suggestion.
	• I can add to my writing.

<table>
<tr>
<td>TEACHER NOTE</td>
<td>Students record important learning individually in their Passport Journals instead of on the "What I Know" section of the class Knowledge Journal. If time permits, consider selecting several strong responses from the individual journals to add to the class journal.</td>
</tr>
</table>

Extension

Remind students that another tool that helps them keep track of learning is the Word Wall. Revisit the words added to the Word Wall since the start of the module. Students Echo Read the words. Choose three to five words to highlight based on your knowledge of students' vocabulary and call on volunteers to use the words in context.

Land 2 MIN.

ANSWER THE CONTENT FRAMING QUESTION

Congratulate students on the learning and exploration they have done with *South America* and *Australia*. Instruct students to Mix and Mingle, and ask: "What is your favorite continent we have studied so far? Why?"

Wrap 1 MIN.

ASSIGN HOMEWORK

Continue the class home-reading routine.

Analyze

Context and Alignment

Students use evidence from *South America* or *Australia* to write an opinion paragraph about the continent they believe has the most amazing animals (RI.K.1, W.K.1, W.K.5, W.K.8). Each student:

- Writes an opinion statement, making their choice between the continents of South America and Australia.

- Writes and illustrates two sentences to support their opinion with details from the text.

- Creates an opinion conclusion sentence by naming their chosen continent in a sentence frame.

- Shares one supporting reason sentence with a peer.

- Adds a descriptive label or details to a drawing based on feedback.

Next Steps

If students have difficulty adding to their writing based on peer feedback, consider the root of the problem. Do they have difficulty generating a descriptive word? If so, revisit the photographs in the text and support students in describing the physical attributes of the animals. Or, revisit the words in the text and look for descriptions there. Do students understand their peers' suggestions? If not, circulate as students share and revise. Support them in understanding the feedback and finding proper place to add a descriptive word or detail to their drawing.

Group students with similar needs and plan small group support for these skills to set students up for success with their next Focusing Question Task.

⬇ LESSON 27 DEEP DIVE: STYLE AND CONVENTIONS

Experiment with Beginning a Sentence with a Capital Letter

- **Time:** 15 min.

- **Texts:** *South America*, Rebecca Hirsch; *Australia*, Rebecca Hirsch

- **Style and Conventions Learning Goal:** Write a complete sentence that begins with a capital letter. (L.K.1.f, L.K.2.a)

> **STYLE AND CONVENTIONS CRAFT QUESTION: Lesson 27**
> Experiment: *How do I write a complete sentence that begins with a capital letter?*

Launch

Post and read the Style and Conventions Craft Question.

Reinforce that in the previous lesson and this lesson, students wrote a paragraph where they explained their opinion about which continent has the most amazing animals.

Create a chart on the board with two columns. At the top of the left column, write "WHO" in large print. At the top of right column, write "DOES WHAT" in large print.

WHO	DOES WHAT

Display the evidence organizers from Lessons 26 and 27. Ask: "What are some of the amazing animals in *Australia* and *South America*?" Volunteers respond.

- *Kangaroos.*
- *Platypuses.*
- *Koalas.*
- *Pink dolphins.*
- *Parrots.*
- *Monkeys.*
- *Jaguars.*

Use student responses to record the names of the animals in the WHO column.

WHO	DOES WHAT
kangaroos	
platypuses	
koalas	
pink dolphins	
parrots	
monkeys	
jaguars	

Explain that students are going to create a complete sentence about an amazing animal from Australia or South America. They will begin their complete sentences with capital letters.

Learn

Redirect student attention back to the chart. Instruct students to choose one animal from the chart that they are going to write about. Ask: "What does your animal do?" Use Equity Sticks to call on a student to give an example for each animal. Record their responses next to the animal, in the DOES WHAT column.

Students take out their Response Journals. On the next blank page, students draw a picture of the animal they chose doing the action they shared. Encourage students to reference the chart as needed. Allow students three minutes to create their drawings. Instruct students to turn to the student next to them and describe their drawing in a complete sentence by telling "who, does what" in the picture.

Extension

If students are ready for the challenge, encourage them to expand their descriptions of their drawings by adding a describing word or preposition.

Explain that students are going to write this complete sentence under their drawing in their Response Journal. Ask: "Since you described your picture with a complete sentence, what type of letter should you start your sentence with?" Students respond chorally.

- *A capital letter!*

✔ Allow time for students to write their complete sentence under their drawing in their Response Journal. Circulate to provide support as needed and to ensure that students begin their sentences with a capital letter.

If time allows, use Equity Sticks to call on students to share their complete sentences. Ask each student to identify which letter they capitalized in their sentence.

Land

Redirect students' attention to the Style and Conventions Craft Question.

Ask: "What steps did you do to write a complete sentence that begins with a capital letter?" Volunteers respond.

- *First, we chose an amazing animal to write about.*
- *Next, we told what the animal does.*
- *Then, we drew a picture of the animal doing the action.*
- *After, we shared our complete sentence idea with a friend.*
- *Finally, we wrote the complete sentence in our Response Journal and made sure it started with a capital letter.*

■ FOCUSING QUESTION: LESSONS 28–31

Why might people want to visit North America?

1 | 2 | 3 | 4 | 5 | 6 | 7 | 8 | 9 | 10 | 11 | 12 | 13 | 14 | 15 | 16 | 17 | 18 | 19 | 20 | 21 | 22 | 23 | 24 | 25 | 26 | 27 | **28** | **29** | **30** | **31** | 32 | 33 | 34 | 35 | 36

Lesson 28

TEXTS

- "*Where in the World Is Carmen Sandiego?* from Smithsonian Folkways," Smithsonian Folkways (**http://witeng.link/0375**)

- *Introducing North America*, Chris Oxlade

- "What is life?" Crowfoot (**http://witeng.link/0437**)

- "Grand Canyon Scenic Splendor," *National Park Service* (**http://witeng.link/0438**)

Lesson 28: At a Glance

AGENDA

Welcome (7 min.)

Explore the Focusing Question

Launch (4 min.)

Learn (57 min.)

Listen Actively and Share Observations (25 min.)

Share Questions (12 min.)

Examine the Importance of Restating an Opinion (15 min.)

Practice Fluency (5 min.)

Land (6 min.)

Answer the Content Framing Question

Wrap (1 min.)

Assign Homework

Style and Conventions Deep Dive: Examine Using Ending Punctuation (15 min.)

STANDARDS ADDRESSED

The full text of ELA Standards can be found in the Module Overview.

Reading

- RI.K.1

Writing

- W.K.1, W.10*

Speaking and Listening

- SL.K.1, SL.K.2

Language

- L.K.1.d
- ↓ L.K.1.f, L.K.2.b

MATERIALS

- Blow-up globes or soft balls
- Question Grab Bags
- Wonder Chart for *Introducing North America*
- Opinion Sandwich Anchor Chart
- Example opinion paragraph (see lesson for details)
- Repeated Language Chart (see lesson for details; retain for future lessons)
- World map
- Sticky notes
- Document camera (if available)

Learning Goals

Use a variety of question words to ask questions about *Introducing North America*. (RI.K.1, L.K.1.d)

✔ Generate questions using Question Grab Bags. (W.K.10*)

Examine the importance of writing a conclusion sentence in an opinion paragraph. (W.K.1)

✔ Think-Pair-Share about a conclusion sentence.

↓ Identify a complete sentence and describe the end punctuation. (L.K.1.f, L.K.2.b)

✔ Use a Nonverbal Signal to identify a complete sentence and answer questions to describe end punctuation.

In alignment with the CCSS, W.10 formally begins in Grade 3. However, K–2 students write routinely for a variety of time frames, tasks, purposes, and audiences. As a result, this lesson contains instruction related to W.10 in an effort to familiarize students with a range of writing.

✔ Checks for Understanding

Prepare

FOCUSING QUESTION: Lessons 28–31

Why might people want to visit North America?

CONTENT FRAMING QUESTION: Lesson 28

Wonder: *What do I notice and wonder about* Introducing North America?

CRAFT QUESTION: Lesson 28

Examine: *Why is restating an opinion important?*

Students embark on the last leg of their adventure through the continents as they explore North America by using the text *Introducing North America*. The foundational knowledge about informational text structure and the continents that students have built over the course of this module have prepared them to access this more complex text. Students make observations about and generate questions for the text. In addition, they continue their work with opinion writing as they examine the importance of restating an opinion to provide a conclusion.

Welcome 7 MIN.

EXPLORE THE FOCUSING QUESTION

Divide students into small groups and give each group a blow-up globe or soft ball. One student holds the ball and names a continent. They pass the ball to another student in the group and that student names a continent. Students continue to take turns naming continents while passing the ball around the group. Continents may be named multiple times.

Explain that the class's journey around the world is coming to an end. But there is still one more continent left to explore! Ask: "Which continent will we travel to next? Which continent do we still need to explore?" Volunteers respond.

Confirm that students will explore the continent of North America, their home continent.

Display and read aloud the Focusing Question. Students Echo Read the question.

Highlight the word *visit* in the Focusing Question. Ask: "What does it mean to <u>visit</u> a place?" Volunteers respond.

> ▪ *It's like when you take a trip somewhere.*
>
> ▪ *You go see a place for a little while.*

Explain that over the next several lessons students will learn about amazing people, places, and animals that inspire people from around the world to visit North America.

Launch 4 MIN.

Tell students they will explore North America through books, videos, music, and pictures. Post and read aloud the Content Framing Question.

Display the front cover of *Introducing North America*, and read the title and author's name aloud. Ask: "What do you notice about this text from the front cover and the title? How is it different from the other continent books we have read? The same?"

> ▪ *It's bigger.*
>
> ▪ *The title is different.*
>
> ▪ *There's a different author.*
>
> ▪ *It says the name of a continent, like the other continent books.*

Confirm that *Introducing North America* is written by a different author and is not from the same series as the other continent books.

Instruct students to Mix and Mingle, and ask: "What do think you already know about North America?"

Learn 57 MIN.

LISTEN ACTIVELY AND SHARE OBSERVATIONS 25 MIN.

Whole Group

Tell students they will end their world adventure by flying home, to North America. Display the world map and direct students to point to where North America is located. Confirm the location by circling North America with your finger and placing the image of an airplane on the continent.

Invite students travel home to North America by pretending to fly there in an airplane. Students walk around the room, pretending to fly in an airplane. As they "fly," play music from North America using the "*Where in the World Is Carmen Sandiego?* from Smithsonian Folkways" link (**http://witeng. link/0375**). Scroll down for clips of music from a variety of countries in North America. Consider using track 172, "U.S.A. - Rabbit Dance." Stop the music to indicate that students should "land" at the whole-group gathering area.

TEACHER NOTE	The above link is a suggestion. Substitute different North American music if desired.

Display the front cover of *Introducing North America* as you reread the title and author's name aloud. Ask: "What does it mean to <u>introduce</u> something?" Volunteers respond.

Use responses to confirm that *introduce* means "to present something new." Tell students to look for new information about North America as you read the text.

💬 Read the book aloud with minimal interruptions. Students sit in "listening position," focusing eyes and ears on you as you read.

TEACHER NOTE	Due to the length and complexity of *Introducing North America*, consider reading only portions of the text. For example, read aloud pages 4–21, omitting the last three sections of the text. This will reduce the informational load for students while still providing the information needed for students to gain an understanding of North America and be successful with Focusing Question Task 5.

Instruct students to Think-Pair-Share, and ask: "What is something new you learned about North America?" Use Equity Sticks to call on students to respond.

Distribute copies of the text to pairs of students. Instruct students to take turns sharing what they notice about the text with their partner. Students use the sentence frame **I notice** _____ and point to the relevant illustration in the text to share observations.

Distribute Response Journals to students and ask them to record one of their observations about *Introducing North America* in their journals. Students write a sentence about something they noticed in the text and illustrate the sentence as time permits.

SHARE QUESTIONS 12 MIN.

Small Groups

Reference the Content Framing Question, and ask: "Now that we shared what we noticed about *Introducing North America*, what will we do next to help us think about the text?" Volunteers respond. Reinforce that asking questions to wonder about a book is another way to help readers think about the text.

Divide students into small groups, providing a Question Grab Bag and a copy of the text for each group.

✔ Small groups take turns pulling a question word from the Question Grab Bag and using the word to ask a question about *Introducing North America*.

Circulate to support groups in reading the question words as needed, calling attention to key letters and sounds. Encourage them to return to the text to develop their questions, and listen in. Choose four to six student-generated questions to record on sticky notes, labeling with students' initials.

Post a blank Wonder Chart for *Introducing North America*. Add students' questions.

Working with one question at a time, have students Echo Read the question and Think-Pair-Share about details they remember from the text. Students use the following Nonverbal Signals to indicate whether they are able to answer the question:

- Thumbs-up: we remember the answer from the text.
- Thumbs-sideways: we remember part of the answer from the text.
- Thumbs-down: we don't remember the answer.

Call on students to share their thinking. Return to the text to confirm and clarify students' thinking. Move sticky notes along the progression to indicate the extent to which each question has been answered.

SAMPLE WONDER CHART FOR *INTRODUCING NORTH AMERICA*

Questions ?	Answers in Progress ⟷	Complete Answers ✔
• *Where do the really big trees grow?* • *Why is there a fire coming out of the tower in the water?* • *What do alligators eat?* • *How was the canyon made?*		

EXAMINE THE IMPORTANCE OF RESTATING AN OPINION 15 MIN.

Whole Group

Display the Opinion Sandwich Anchor Chart. Ask: "What are the different parts of an opinion paragraph? What do the top and bottom cookies stand for? What does the cream in the middle stand for?" Volunteers respond.

- *The parts are: opinion, reasons, opinion conclusion.*
- *The top and bottom cookies stand for your opinion.*
- *The cream stands for the reasons why.*

Ask: "Why do we begin an opinion paragraph with an opinion statement? What is the job of the opinion statement?" Volunteers respond.

- *It tells my opinion.*
- *It helps me share what I think.*
- *It tells what the writing is about.*

Use responses to reinforce that writers use an opinion statement to begin their opinion paragraphs because it introduces readers to the topic and lets them know the writer's opinion.

Ask: "Why do we include reason sentences? What is the job of the supporting reasons?" Volunteers respond.

- *They explain why I think something.*
- *They give readers more information.*
- *Reason sentences tell why I have my opinion.*

Point to the cookie at the bottom of the Opinion Sandwich. Remind students that the bottom cookie also stands for the writer's opinion. It is the opinion conclusion.

Display and read aloud the Craft Question: *Why is restating an opinion important?* Highlight the word *restating*, and ask: "What does it mean to *restate* something?" Volunteers respond.

Use responses to reinforce that the prefix *re–* means to "do something again." When people restate something, they say (or state) it again. When writers restate their opinion, they tell their opinion again.

Explain that writers restate, or state again, their opinion at the end of an opinion paragraph. This statement, done again, can be their conclusion, or ending. The opinion conclusion provides a satisfying ending, which makes a paragraph feel like it's over. Tell students that providing closure to a piece of writing is important for readers, just like the bottom of a cookie sandwich is important for eaters! Without a bottom cookie, the sandwich would fall apart.

Post and read aloud an example opinion paragraph with the conclusion missing.

| TEACHER NOTE | Prior to the lesson, prepare an example opinion paragraph with the conclusion sentence missing, similar to example below. |

Alligators are the most amazing animals in North America.

They live in the swamp.

They have big, sharp teeth.

Ask: "If we ended our paragraph there, how does that sound? What might the reader think if we leave the paragraph open like that?" Volunteers respond.

- *It doesn't sound over.*
- *They might think we have more to say.*
- *They won't know that we are done.*

Reread the opinion paragraph, and ask: "What is the opinion statement in this paragraph?" Volunteers respond.

Engage in a Think Aloud to model the process of restating the opinion to create a conclusion sentence. For example, say:

The opinion statement says, "Alligators are the most amazing animal in North America." I need to restate the opinion at the end, or tell it again. I could just keep the sentence exactly the same. Or, maybe I could make it sound just a little different to make it more interesting. Hmmm. I know! I can say, "Alligators are amazing!" at the end. That retells my opinion, but I think the exclamation mark makes it exciting.

Add the opinion conclusion sentence to the example opinion paragraph and read the entire paragraph aloud.

✔ Instruct students to Think-Pair-Share, and ask: "Why is it important to restate an opinion? How does it help our reader?" Use Equity Sticks to call on students to answer.

- *It shows that the paragraph is over.*
- *It shows that we are done writing.*
- *It closes our thinking and writing.*

PRACTICE FLUENCY 5 MIN.

Whole Group

TEACHER NOTE

The fluency passage "What is life?" can be found at the following link: (**http://witeng.link/0437**). This web page contains quotations from Crowfoot, a chief of the Blackfoot, or Siksika, tribe. In Lessons 28–31 students will be using the "What is life?" quotation from Crowfoot for their fluency practice. This quotation is the second one listed on the web page.

Explain that students will use words from Crowfoot, a head chief of the Blackfoot tribe in North America, for their fluency passage. Highlight the word *quotation* on the Repeated Language Chart and explain that when you <u>quote</u> someone, you repeat their words, exactly as the person said them. Emphasize that this passage is a <u>quotation</u> because it retells words that Crowfoot spoke.

Scaffold

Display and read aloud page 18 of *Introducing North America* to provide context and additional background information. Explain that the Blackfoot tribe is a North American Indian tribe.

Display the Repeated Language Chart with the first two lines of the quotation added and read the lines aloud, tracking the words with your finger. Students Echo Read the lines.

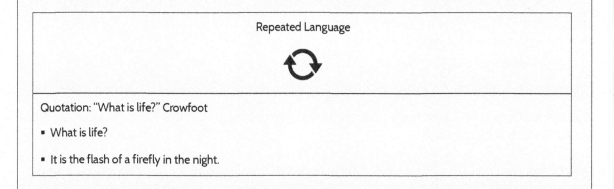

Repeated Language

Quotation: "What is life?" Crowfoot

- What is life?

- It is the flash of a firefly in the night.

Point to the question mark at the end of the first line and ask: "What is this text marking? What kind of sentence is this?" Use Equity Sticks to call on students to respond.

- *It's a question mark.*

- *The sentence is asking a question.*

Use responses to point out that the first sentence is asking a question and the rest of the passage is responding to the question.

Scaffold

Locate and display a video clip of a firefly flying at night to build background knowledge.

Ask: "What is a firefly? How does it flash in the night?" Volunteers respond.

- *It's a flying bug.*
- *It makes a little light shine as it flies at night.*
- *Their lights go off and on, they don't stay lit.*

Explain that Crowfoot's first response to the question, "What is life?" is that life is like the flash of a firefly in the night. Students Echo Read the lines several times.

Land 6 MIN.

ANSWER THE CONTENT FRAMING QUESTION

Display and read aloud the Content Framing Question. Ask: "What helped us answer this question today?" Volunteers respond.

- *We read the book together.*
- *We said what we noticed.*
- *We wrote about what we noticed.*
- *We asked questions about the book.*
- *We talked about our questions.*

Instruct students to Mix and Mingle, and ask: "What places have you visited in North America? What places would you like to visit?"

Explain that the Grand Canyon is a beautiful place in North America that many people visit. Display photographs of different areas of the Grand Canyon from the National Park Service website "Grand Canyon Scenic Splendor" (**http://witeng.link/0438**). After displaying a photo, ask: "What do you see in this picture? What do you notice about the Grand Canyon?"

Wrap 1 MIN.

ASSIGN HOMEWORK

Continue the class home-reading routine.

Analyze

Context and Alignment

Students utilize the Question Grab Bag to generate questions about *Introducing North America* (RL.K.1, L.K.1.d). Each student:

- Generates text-based questions.
- Correctly uses the question word pulled from the Question Grab Bag.

Next Steps

If students have difficulty generating text-based questions, work with small groups of students to focus on selected page spreads. Ask students to share something they notice about the page spread. Then have them ask a question about the detail they noticed. Utilize a Question Grab Bag or Question Cube to support students in asking questions with a variety of question words.

↓ LESSON 28 DEEP DIVE: STYLE AND CONVENTIONS

Examine Using Ending Punctuation

- **Time:** 15 min.

- **Text:** *Introducing North America*, Chris Oxlade

- **Style and Conventions Learning Goal:** Identify a complete sentence and describe the ending punctuation. (L.K.1.f, L.K.2.b)

  STYLE AND CONVENTIONS CRAFT QUESTION: Lesson 28
  Examine: *Why is it important to use a punctuation mark at the end of a complete sentence?*

Launch

Post and read the Style and Conventions Craft Question.

Remind students that they have been learning rules about writing complete sentences. Explain that in the previous module they learned a rule about how to end complete sentences.

Display page 4 of *Introducing North America*, using a document projector if available. Point out the end of each sentence, and ask: "What do you notice about the end of these sentences?" Volunteers respond.

- *There are dots at the end of each sentence.*
- *These sentences end with a period!*

Use student responses to reinforce the rule that complete sentences always end with a punctuation mark, or special symbols that let the reader know that a thought or idea is finished.

Remind students that there are three symbols that end sentences. Explain that students are going to review the names of these symbols and learn why it is important to use them.

Learn

Remind students that the punctuation marks that are used to end a sentence are a period, a question mark, and an exclamation point. Draw and label each symbol on the board. Point to each symbol and Echo Read its name. Reinforce that the different end punctuation symbols tell what type of sentence it is.

Organize students into pairs and distribute a copy of the text to each group. Students turn to page 15 of the text and point to the caption on page 15. Read the caption aloud as students follow along. Invite students to give a thumbs-up signal if the caption is a complete sentence. Reinforce that is a complete sentence because it tells "who, does what," and begins with a capital letter.

Ask: "What do you notice about the end of this sentence?" Volunteers respond.

- *It ends with a dot.*
- *It ends with a period.*

Use student responses to reinforce that this sentence ends with a period because it is a complete sentence that tells information.

Students turn to page 17 of the text and point to the last sentence on page 17. Read the sentence aloud. Invite students to give a thumbs-up signal if it is a complete sentence. Reinforce that is a complete sentence because it tells "who, does what," and begins with a capital letter.

Ask: "What do you notice about the ending of this sentence?" Volunteers respond.

- *It ends with a line with a dot underneath.*
- *It ends with an upside-down lowercase i.*

Use student responses to reinforce that this sentence ends with an exclamation point because it is a complete sentence that is exciting.

Students turn to page 29 of the text and point to question number one on page 29. Read the question aloud. Invite students to give a thumbs-up signal if it is a complete sentence. Reinforce that is a complete sentence because it asks "who, does what," and begins with a capital letter.

Ask: "What do you notice about the ending of this sentence?" Volunteers respond.

- *It ends with a curly line with a dot underneath.*
- *It ends with a question mark.*

Use student responses to reinforce that this sentence ends with a question mark because it is a complete sentence that is asking a question.

TEACHER NOTE	To maximize instructional time, write the following three sentences from *Introducing North America* on sentence strips prior to the lesson: • North America is the third-largest continent. • Giant Redwoods grow 367-feet tall! • Who built pyramids in Mexico?

Collect the copies of the text and reorganize students back into a whole group.

Explain that students are going to listen to parts of the book and tell if they hear a complete sentence or not. They will describe how each complete sentence ends.

✔ Post and read the first sentence. Students identify if it is a complete sentence by giving a thumbs-up signal if so or a thumbs-down signal if not. After reading the sentence, instruct students to Think-Pair-Share and ask: "What punctuation mark did you notice at the end of the sentence? Why do you think the author used this symbol? How do you know?" Call on volunteers to share their ideas. Repeat for all three sentences.

Land

Redirect student attention back to the Style and Conventions Craft Question.

Ask: "Why do you think it is important for authors to use punctuation marks at the end of sentences?" Volunteers respond.

- *Because it lets readers know when a thought or idea is finished.*
- *Because the different punctuation marks tell what kind of complete sentence it is.*

▨ FOCUSING QUESTION: LESSONS 28–31

Why might people want to visit North America?

1 2 3 4 5 6 7 8 9 10 11 12 13 14 15 16 17 18 19 20 21 22 23 24 25 26 27 **28** **29** **30** **31** 32 33 34 35 36

Lesson 29

TEXTS

- "What is life?" Crowfoot (**http://witeng.link/0437**)

- *Introducing North America*, Chris Oxlade

Lesson 29: At a Glance

AGENDA

Welcome (5 min.)

Practice Fluency

Launch (5 min.)

Learn (60 min.)

Explore Text Features (10 min.)

Identify the Main Topic and Key Details (20 min.)

Collect Evidence for Focusing Question Task 5 (12 min.)

Experiment with Restating an Opinion (18 min.)

Land (4 min.)

Answer the Content Framing Question

Wrap (1 min.)

Assign Homework

Style and Conventions Deep Dive: Experiment with Using Ending Punctuation (15 min.)

STANDARDS ADDRESSED

The full text of ELA Standards can be found in the Module Overview.

Reading

- RI.K.1, RI.K.2, RI.K.7

Writing

- W.K.1

Speaking and Listening

- SL.K.1

Language

- ⬇ L.K.1.f, L.K.2.b

MATERIALS

- Repeated Language Chart
- Evidence Organizer for *Introducing North America* (see lesson for details)
- Sticky notes
- Opinion Sandwich Anchor Chart

Learning Goals

Use text features to identify the main topic and key details in sections of *Introducing North America*. (RI.K.2)

✔ Use Nonverbal Signals to identify and retell the main topic and key details of a section in the text.

Restate an opinion to provide a conclusion for an opinion paragraph. (W.K.1)

✔ Think-Pair-Share about ways to restate an opinion from a Response Journal entry.

⬇ Create a complete sentence and describe the end punctuation. (L.K.1.f, L.K.2.b)

✔ Mix and Mingle, sharing complete sentences and describing the punctuation mark needed at the end of the sentence.

✔ Checks for Understanding

Prepare

FOCUSING QUESTION: Lessons 28–31

Why might people want to visit North America?

CONTENT FRAMING QUESTION: Lesson 29

Organize: *What is happening in* Introducing North America?

CRAFT QUESTION: Lesson 29

Experiment: *How can I restate my opinion?*

In this lesson students apply the skills they have developed with identifying main topics and key details in a text with a slightly different structure. This practice supports students with transferring their previous knowledge to new texts. In addition, students practice restating an opinion as they develop strategies for providing closure in an opinion piece.

Welcome 5 MIN.

PRACTICE FLUENCY

Display the Repeated Language Chart with the third line of the quotation added. Read the lines aloud. Students Echo Read the lines.

Repeated Language
Quotation: "What is life?" Crowfoot   ▪ What is life?   ▪ It is the flash of a firefly in the night.   ▪ It is the breath of a buffalo in the wintertime.

Scaffold

Locate and display an image of a buffalo to build background knowledge.

Tell students to imagine playing outside on a cold winter's day. Ask: "What happens when you open your mouth and breathe out on a cold day? What might you see?" Volunteers respond.

- *You can see your breath!*
- *It looks like a little cloud.*

Instruct students to breathe in and out. Ask: "Does taking a breath in and out take a long time or does it happen quickly?" Volunteers respond.

- *It's quick!*

Students Echo Read the lines several times.

Launch　5 MIN.

Display the front cover of *Introducing North America*. Instruct students to Mix and Mingle, and ask: "Is *Introducing North America* a storybook or an informational text? What makes you think that?" Call on several students to share their thoughts with the whole class.

Remind students that they made observations and asked questions about *Introducing North America* in the previous lesson. Ask: "How will we explore the text today? What do we think about after we notice and wonder?" Volunteers respond.

- *We think about what is happening.*
- *We read the text again to understand more.*

Display and read aloud the Content Framing Question. Explain that students will answer this question by thinking about main topics and key details in the text.

Learn 60 MIN.

EXPLORE TEXT FEATURES 10 MIN.

Pairs

Remind students that *Introducing North America* is written by a different author than the other continent books they have read. Emphasize that even though it looks a little different, it has many of the same text features with which students are already familiar.

Ask students to stand up if they can name a text feature. Call on students to share the text features they know.

- *Headings.*
- *Table of contents.*
- *Photographs.*
- *Captions.*

Use responses to review text features as needed. Tell students that they will go on a scavenger hunt to find text features in *Introducing North America*.

Divide students into pairs and distribute a copy of the text and sticky notes to each pair. Students work together to identify text features in *Introducing North America*, marking them with sticky notes. After the scavenger hunt, use Equity Sticks to call on pairs to share a text feature they found.

TEACHER NOTE	After the scavenger hunt, students retain their copies of the text, and continue to work in pairs during the next section of the lesson.

Ask: "Did anyone spot a text feature in *Introducing North America* that you didn't see in the other continent books?" Volunteers respond. Use responses to point out additional text features such as bold words and the glossary.

IDENTIFY THE MAIN TOPIC AND KEY DETAILS 20 MIN.

Whole Group

Ask: "Which text feature have we used to help us think about the main topic of a section in the text?" Volunteers respond.

- *We used the headings.*

Ask: "How do headings help us think about the main topic of a section?" Use Equity Sticks to call on students to respond.

- *They tell us what the section is about.*
- *They help us get ready to learn more information.*
- *Headings tell us the main topic.*

Explain that students will continue to use headings to think about the main topic and key details of sections in *Introducing North America*.

Direct pairs to open their books to the "Contents" page. Read the title of the page and explain that *Contents* is short for *table of contents*.

Ask students to place a finger on the second section listed in the table of contents. Read the name of the section aloud. Instruct students to trace their fingers across the page to find the starting page number for the "Famous Places" section. Ask: "Which page can you turn to for the 'Famous Places' section?" Volunteers respond.

- *Page 6.*

Students turn to the "Famous Places" section (page 6) in the text. Direct students to place a finger on the heading. Instruct students to Think-Pair-Share, and ask: "Think about the heading of this section: 'Famous Places.' What is the main topic of this section? What will this part of the text tell us about?" Use Equity Sticks to call on students to respond.

- *The main topic is the famous places in North America.*
- *It will tell us about special places in North America.*

Confirm that the main topic of the section is famous places in North America.

Remind students that readers can find key details about the main topic in the section that follows the heading. Ask students to listen for key details about famous places in North America while you read the "Famous Places" section.

Read page 6 aloud as students follow along in their copies of the text. Instruct students to Think-Pair-Share, and ask: "What key details did you hear on this page about famous places in North America?" Use Equity Sticks to call on students to respond.

- *The Grand Canyon is a famous place.*
- *Niagara Falls is famous, too.*
- *People visit Yellowstone National Park.*

Extension

Build background knowledge by displaying images of Niagara Falls and Yellowstone National Park. An Internet search will yield images.

Read page 7 aloud. Instruct students to Think-Pair-Share, and ask: "What key detail did you hear on this page about famous places in North America?" Use Equity Sticks to call on students to respond.

- *There are pyramids in Mexico.*

- *There are famous buildings, too.*

Reread the caption on page 7 and ask: "Which famous place does the photograph on page 7 show readers? How do you know? Volunteers respond.

- *It shows a pyramid from Mexico.*

- *I know because it looks like a pyramid.*

- *The caption said it is a pyramid.*

As needed, remind students how to use Nonverbal Signals to retell the main topic (placing one hand on top of your head) and key details (waving arms or hands).

Pairs take turns using Nonverbal Signals to retell the main topic and key details of the "Famous Places" section, using the text for reference.

TEACHER NOTE	If students have difficulty speaking and moving at the same time, instruct students to say the key detail aloud and then wave their hand or arm. This will allow students to focus on retelling the key details first, which is the main purpose of this lesson.

Explain that now students will think about the main topic and key details of another section in the text. Direct pairs to turn to the "Sports and Culture" section on page 20.

Direct students to place a finger on the heading on page 20. Reread the heading and explain that in this text *culture* means "the arts," such as music, artwork, and writing.

Instruct students to Think-Pair-Share, and ask: "Think about the heading of this section: 'Sports and Culture.' What is the main topic of this section? What will this part of the text tell us about?" Use Equity Sticks to call on students to respond.

- *The main topic is the sports and culture of North America.*

- *It will tell us about sports in North America.*

- *We will learn about culture, like music or art.*

Scaffold

Define *culture* as the pastimes, arts, food, and languages of a group of people. Explain that groups of people all over the world have their own specific culture, and it can affect the way people dress, think about life, spend free time, and relate to each other.

Confirm that the main topic of the section is sports and culture in North America.

Read page 20 aloud as students follow along in their copies of the text. Instruct students to Think-Pair-Share, and ask: "What key details did you hear on this page about sports and culture in North America?" Use Equity Sticks to call on students to respond.

- ▪ *People like baseball and football.*
- ▪ *Basketball is popular.*
- ▪ *People like ice hockey, too.*

Reread the caption on page 20 and ask: "Which sport does the photograph on page 20 show readers? How do you know?" Volunteers respond.

- ▪ *It shows baseball.*
- ▪ *I know because I see a baseball field.*
- ▪ *The caption said it is a baseball game.*

Read page 21 aloud. Instruct students to Think-Pair-Share, and ask: "What key detail did you hear on this page about sports and culture in North America?" Use Equity Sticks to call on students to respond.

- ▪ *People make lots of movies.*
- ▪ *Some people like country music.*
- ▪ *Some people like reggae music.*

Extension

Build background knowledge by playing clips of child-friendly country and reggae music.

✔ Pairs take turns using Nonverbal Signals to retell the main topic and key details of the "Sports and Culture" section, using the text for reference.

COLLECT EVIDENCE FOR FOCUSING QUESTION TASK 5 12 MIN.

Pairs

Remind students that the Focusing Question for *Introducing North America* is: *Why might people want to visit North America?* Emphasize that the sections students explored today shared some reasons why people might want to visit North America. Explain that students will collect evidence from the sections they read today that will help them answer the Focusing Question.

Display the Evidence Organizer for *Introducing North America*. Read the headings of each column aloud. Ask: "Think about what we read today. Which column matches best with what you learned about North America? What makes you say that?" Volunteers respond.

Use responses to confirm that students will collect evidence for the "Things to Do" column.

TEACHER NOTE	If students suggest the "Natural Features" category, affirm that the sections contained information about some natural features. Explain that the text emphasized that the natural landmarks are popular places to visit, so they can also be considered as "Things to Do."

Explain that half the class will look for evidence from the "Famous Places" section and the other half will look at the "Sports and Culture" section.

Direct pairs to the either the "Famous Places" section on pages 6–7 or the "Sports and Culture" section on pages 20–21. Instruct students to Think-Pair-Share, and ask: "What interesting things are there to do in North America? What famous places might people want to visit? Which sports or arts events might people want to see?" Encourage partners to use the photographs to help them answer.

Give each pair two sticky notes. Students annotate examples of things to do in North America by placing a sticky note on a photograph. Circulate and provide support, rereading portions of the text as needed.

Use Equity Sticks to call on students to share their answers. As students respond, record their responses on the "Things to Do" column on the evidence organizer.

TEACHER NOTE	Record evidence in short words or phrases and pair pieces of evidence with an image to help students access the evidence organizer independently. Consider using the example below to prerecord or print out images to include on the evidence organizer.

SAMPLE EVIDENCE ORGANIZER FOR *INTRODUCING NORTH AMERICA*

Evidence Organizer for *Introducing North America*		
Things to Do	**Natural Features**	**Animals**
▫ *Grand Canyon* ▫ *pyramids* ▫ *football* ▫ *movies* ▫ *music*		

441

EXPERIMENT WITH RESTATING AN OPINION 18 MIN.

Whole Group

Instruct students to Think-Pair-Share, and ask: "Think about the things to do in North America that we added to the chart. What do you think is the most exciting thing to do on the list? Why?"

Distribute Response Journals. Students write an opinion statement to respond to the following prompt.

What is the most exciting thing to do in North America?

Reference the Opinion Sandwich Anchor Chart and remind students that the sentences they wrote in their Response Journals are opinion statements, represented by the top cookie on the chart.

Point to the other parts of the Opinion Sandwich Anchor Chart, and ask: "What else do writers include in an opinion piece?" Use Equity Sticks to call on students to respond.

- *They tell reasons why they have their opinion.*
- *They say their opinion again.*

Extension

Instruct students to turn to a partner and share their opinion statement and one reason to support that opinion.

Display and read aloud the Craft Question: *How can I restate my opinion?*

Remind students that authors restate their opinion to provide a conclusion to their writing. To restate is to say something, or state it, again. Explain that in their opinion paragraphs, students can rewrite their opinion statement or they can change the words a little to make their writing more interesting. The important thing is to remind the reader what their opinion is!

Display an example opinion statement from the Response Journal prompt and model how to change a descriptive word to alter the sentence. Display an opinion statement, such as: "The Grand Canyon is the most exciting thing to see in North America." Engage in a Think Aloud about altering the opinion statement. For example, say:

I wonder how I could change a word in my opinion statement to make it a little different and interesting. Well, I see the word *"exciting"* in my sentence. Maybe I could change that word! Hmm, what other word could I use to describe how exciting the Grand Canyon is? Maybe, *"amazing"*? Another way I could state my opinion is to say, "The Grand Canyon is amazing!"

Write the restated opinion on a chart or board and reread both the original opinion statement and the altered statement. Ask: "What did I do to restate my opinion?" Volunteers respond.

- *You changed a word.*
- *You put a new descriptive word in.*
- *You added an exclamation point.*

✔ Instruct students to read their Response Journal entries to a partner and think about a word they could change to tell their opinion in a different way. Then pairs verbally share their restated opinion.

As time permits, have several students share their opinion statement and opinion conclusion with the whole class.

Land 4 MIN.

ANSWER THE CONTENT FRAMING QUESTION

Display and read aloud the Content Framing Question. Ask: "What did we do to help us answer this question today?" Volunteers respond.

Instruct students to Mix and Mingle, and ask: "What did you learn about North America today?"

Wrap 1 MIN.

ASSIGN HOMEWORK

Continue the class home-reading routine.

Analyze

Context and Alignment

Students restate an opinion to create an opinion conclusion for an opinion paragraph (W.K.1). Each student:

- Writes an opinion statement about the most exciting thing to do in North America.

- Determines a word from the opinion statement they could change to tell their opinion in a different way.

- Verbally shares their restated opinion with a partner.

Next Steps

If students have difficulty restating their opinion, ask them to return to their original opinion statement and support them in underlining a descriptive word in the sentence. Ask: "What's another word you could use instead of [descriptive word] to describe [the thing to do in North America]?" After students determine an alternate descriptive word, they verbally share their opinion with the alternate word.

↓ **LESSON 29 DEEP DIVE: STYLE AND CONVENTIONS**

Experiment with Using Ending Punctuation

- **Time:** 15 min.

- **Text:** *Introducing North America*, Chris Oxlade

- **Style and Conventions Learning Goal:** Create a complete sentence and describe the end punctuation. (L.K.1.f, L.K.2.b)

   STYLE AND CONVENTIONS CRAFT QUESTION: Lesson 28
   Experiment: *How does using a punctuation mark at the end of a complete sentence work?*

Launch

Post and read the Style and Conventions Craft Question.

Remind students that in the previous Deep Dive, they learned more about how to end complete sentences with the correct punctuation mark.

Draw a period, an exclamation point, and a question mark on the board. As you point to each symbol, invite students to "air write" the symbol and state its name. Use student responses to label each punctuation mark correctly.

Explain that students are going to learn when to use each punctuation mark to end a complete sentence correctly.

Learn

Post and read the following sentence from page 19 of *Introducing North America*: "People from many different groups live in New York City_," leaving off the end punctuation mark. Ask: "Is this a telling sentence, an exciting sentence, or an asking sentence?" Students respond chorally.

   ▪ *It is a telling sentence.*

TEACHER NOTE	Consider altering the tone of your voice as you read the various sentences. This will allow students to use cues from your voice to identify the appropriate punctuation.

Reinforce that a telling sentence ends with a period. Instruct students to "air write" a period as you add it to the end of the complete sentence.

Post and read the following sentence derived from page 6 of *Introducing North America*: "North America's landmarks are amazing_," leaving off the end punctuation mark. Ask: "Is this a telling sentence, an exciting sentence, or an asking sentence?" Students respond chorally.

- *It is an exciting sentence.*

Reinforce that an exciting sentence ends with an exclamation point. Instruct students to "air write" an exclamation point as you add it to the end of the complete sentence.

Post and read the following sentence from page 29 of *Introducing North America*: "What is the world's largest fresh water lake_," leaving off the end punctuation mark. Ask: "Is this a telling sentence, an exciting sentence, or an asking sentence?" Students respond chorally.

- *It is an asking sentence.*

Reinforce that an asking sentence ends with a question mark. Instruct students to "air write" a question mark as you add it to the end of the complete sentence.

Explain that students are going to create a sentence about North America. Reinforce that they can create a telling sentence, an exciting sentence, or an asking sentence.

Display the evidence organizer from today's lesson. Echo Read the items listed. Explain that students are going to create complete sentences using these things from North America. Reinforce that these things will tell the "who" in their sentence and they need to add what the "who" does.

✔ Instruct students to Mix and Mingle and share their complete sentences. Students also identify the punctuation mark they would use to end their sentence and explain why. Use Equity Sticks to call on students to share their complete sentences. Encourage students to identify the end punctuation mark they used and explain how they chose it.

Land

Redirect student attention back to the Style and Conventions Craft Question.

Ask: "How did you know which punctuation mark to use at the end of your complete sentence?" Volunteers respond.

- *By the type of information I was telling in my sentence.*
- *If it was a telling sentence, it should end with a period.*
- *If it was an exciting sentence, it should end with an exclamation point.*
- *If it was an asking sentence, it should end with a question mark.*

■ FOCUSING QUESTION: LESSONS 28–31

Why might people want to visit North America?

1 2 3 4 5 6 7 8 9 10 11 12 13 14 15 16 17 18 19 20 21 22 23 24 25 26 27 **28 29 30 31** 32 33 34 35 36

Lesson 30

TEXTS

- "What is life?" Crowfoot (**http://witeng.link/0437**)
- *Introducing North America*, Chris Oxlade

Lesson 30: At a Glance

AGENDA

Welcome (5 min.)

Practice Fluency

Launch (3 min.)

Learn (64 min.)

Analyze Words and Photographs (20 min.)

Collect Evidence for Focusing Question Task 5 (10 min.)

Sort Evidence (10 min.)

Execute Focusing Question Task 5 (24 min.)

Land (2 min.)

Answer the Content Framing Question

Wrap (1 min.)

Assign Homework

Style and Conventions Deep Dive: Experiment with Using Ending Punctuation (15 min.)

STANDARDS ADDRESSED

The full text of ELA Standards can be found in the Module Overview.

Reading

- RI.K.1, RI.K.4, RI.K.7

Writing

- W.K.1, W.K.8

Speaking and Listening

- SL.K.1, SL.K.2

Language

- L.K.1.f, L.K.2.a
- ⬇ L.K.1.f, L.K.2.b

MATERIALS

- Assessment 30A: Focusing Question Task 5
- Repeated Language Chart
- Evidence Organizer for *Introducing North America*
- Sticky notes
- Index cards with text evidence (see lesson for details)
- Opinion Sandwich Anchor Chart
- Document camera (if available)
- World map

Learning Goals

Use photographs and details from the text to describe natural features and animals in North America. (RI.K.7)

✔ Record evidence for the Focusing Question Task.

Use information gathered from *Introducing North America* to form an opinion about the continent. (W.K.1, W.K.8, L.K.2.a)

✔ Begin Focusing Question Task 5.

⬇ Write a complete sentence that ends with the correct punctuation mark. (L.K.1.f, L.K.2.b)

✔ Write a complete sentence and end it with correct punctuation mark in Response Journals.

✔ Checks for Understanding

Prepare

FOCUSING QUESTION: Lessons 28–31

Why might people want to visit North America?

CONTENT FRAMING QUESTION: Lesson 30

Reveal: *What does a deeper exploration of the words and illustrations reveal in* Introducing North America?

CRAFT QUESTION: Lesson 30

Execute: *How do I execute my Focusing Question Task?*

In this lesson, students finish collecting evidence for the Focusing Question by using the words and photographs in the text. Students sort the collected evidence to demonstrate increased understanding of the different categories of evidence. This prepares them well to form an opinion about what makes North America an interesting place to visit and verbally rehearse their opinion statements. Students begin work on Focusing Question Task 5 by writing this opinion statement and a supporting reason sentence using complete sentences.

Welcome 5 MIN.

PRACTICE FLUENCY

Display the Repeated Language Chart with the next line of the quotation added. Read the line aloud. Students Echo Read the line.

Repeated Language
↻
Quotation: "What is life?" Crowfoot • What is life? • It is the flash of a firefly in the night. • It is the breath of a buffalo in the wintertime. • It is the little shadow which runs across the grass and loses itself in the sunset.

Ask: "What is a shadow?" Volunteers respond. Reinforce that a shadow is a dark shape that appears when you put something in front of a light. Model this by holding your hand or an object from the classroom near a light and directing students' attention to the shape it makes on the floor or wall.

Ask: "What happens when the sun sets? What happens to the sky?" Volunteers respond.

- *It gets dark.*
- *There is no more sunlight.*

Turn off the light in the classroom. Ask: "What happened to my shadow?" Volunteers respond. Confirm that when the light goes off, or the sun goes down, then the shadows disappear.

Reread the lines of the quotation aloud. Students Echo Read the lines.

Extension

As a class, create a hand gesture to demonstrate something running away, such as wiggling your fingers in a running motion as you move your hand away from your body. Students Echo Read the lines using the agreed-upon hand gestures.

Launch 3 MIN.

Ask: "What does it mean to *visit* a place? What is the difference between visiting and living in a place?" Volunteers respond.

Direct students' attention to the world map. Point to North America on the map. Instruct students to Mix and Mingle, and ask: "What is your favorite thing about living in North America?" Volunteers respond. Encourage students to think about things that are a part of their daily life such as what they like to do at home, at school, places they like to see, etc.

Post and read the Content Framing Question and the Focusing Question. Remind students that they have visited six other continents around the world. Now it is time for someone to visit them! They will use the words and pictures in the text to learn more about their home continent and gather information that will help them understand why someone might want to visit North America.

Learn 61 MIN.

ANALYZE WORDS AND PHOTOGRAPHS 20 MIN.

Whole Group

Explain that students will take a closer look at the words and photographs in *Introducing North America* to better understand key information about the continent, specifically its natural features. They will think about how the words and pictures work together to add to their knowledge about the continent North America.

💬 Distribute copies of the text to pairs. Explain that students will share responsibility for the text with their partner as they respond to questions about the words and pictures in the text.

Prompt students to turn to pages 8–9. Read the heading on the top of page 8. Students Echo Read. Define *geography* as the study of places. Explain that geographers study the natural features of a certain place. Call on a volunteer to list a few different types of natural features they have learned about in this module. Reinforce that geography is the study of these natural features.

Point to the photograph on page 8. Ask: "What natural feature do you see in this photograph? What makes you think that?" Volunteers respond.

- *It is a mountain because it goes up high to the sky.*
- *It looks like a triangle, like a mountain.*
- *Mountains are pointy at the top like that.*

Read the photo caption on page 8 aloud to confirm that this is a photograph of a mountain; not just any mountain, but the tallest mountain in North America.

Extension

Read page 8 aloud. If possible, use a document camera to zoom in on the small map on page 8. Explain that this map shows all the different mountains throughout North America. The dark colors on the map show where the groups of mountains are located. Instruct students to Think-Pair-Share, and ask: "Looking at this map, which group of mountains do you think is the Rocky Mountains, or the largest group of mountains?" Use Equity Sticks to call on a student to point to their answer in the text. Reinforce that the Rocky Mountains are the largest group of mountains and reach almost the whole length of North America!

Read page 9 aloud. Ask: "What does *flat* mean? Can you find something in the room that is flat?" Use Equity Sticks to call on two students to answer and point to something in the classroom that is flat. Use responses to reinforce that *flat* describes something that is smooth or doesn't have any bumps.

Point to the photograph on page 9. Instruct students to Think-Pair-Share, and ask: "Do you think this is a picture of the flat plains? What makes you think that?" Use Equity Sticks to call on students to answer.

- *It is not the plains because I see mountains.*
- *I see hills of sand. It is not flat.*

Ask: "What natural feature do you see in this picture? What makes you think that?" Volunteers respond.

- *I see a mountain high in the sky.*
- *I see lots of sand. I think it is a desert.*
- *There are not a lot of plants. I think it's a dry desert.*

Read the photo caption on page 9 to confirm that this is a photograph of a desert in North America.

Display pages 10–11. Ask: "What natural feature do you see on these pages? What makes you think that?" Volunteers respond.

- *I see water. I think it is a river.*
- *I see a boat on a river.*

Read the photo caption on page 11 to reinforce that North America does have rivers. Read page 10 aloud. Explain that North America also has lakes. Define *lakes* as "huge areas of water that are surrounded by land on all sides."

If possible, use a document camera to zoom in on the small map on page 10. Explain that this map shows some of the rivers and lakes in North America. Instruct students to Think-Pair-Share, and ask: "Which part of this map is a river? Which part of the map is a lake? What makes you think that?" Use Equity Sticks to call on students to share their answers and point to their example in the map.

- *I think the rivers are the squiggly lines.*
- *A lake looks like a big pool on the map.*
- *The lake is big and has lots of water.*

Use responses to reinforce that lakes and rivers are both natural features that are similar in that they contain water, but they also have differences. Rivers can be very long and carry water to the ocean. Lakes are big areas enclosed areas of water—more like a giant pool!—in the middle of the land. Point to the two examples on the small map to reinforce the differences.

Extension

Ask: "What do you think *freshwater* means? What two words do you hear in that word that could help you figure it out?" Volunteers respond. If needed, remind students of the word *saltwater* and ask them to define this word. Use student responses to reinforce that lakes and rivers have freshwater, which means they are not salty like the salt water in oceans.

Display the Evidence Organizer for *Introducing North America*. Explain that students can catalog the learning they just did on the evidence organizer. Ask: "What information did we just read about? What evidence can we add to the evidence organizer?" Volunteers respond.

- *We can add to the natural features.*

Instruct students to Think-Pair-Share, and ask: "What natural features did we just read about in this lesson?" Encourage partners to turn back through pages 8–11 to help them answer.

✔ Give each pair two sticky notes. Students record one example of a natural feature from North America on each sticky note.

Use Equity Sticks to call on students to share their answers. As students respond, record their answers on a sticky note and add them to the "Natural Features" column on the evidence organizer.

TEACHER NOTE	Pair pieces of evidence with a drawing or photograph to help students access the evidence organizer independently. Consider using the example below to prerecord or print out images to include on the evidence organizer.

COLLECT EVIDENCE FOR FOCUSING QUESTION TASK 5 10 MIN.

Whole Group

Explain that students can use their knowledge of the words and photographs in this text to finish collecting evidence for the Focusing Question Task. Point to the blank column in the evidence organizer. Call on a volunteer to identify the last blank column on the evidence organizer. Confirm that to complete their evidence collection they will use the words and pictures to collect evidence on the animals in North America.

Display pages 14–15. Ask: "What two animals do we see on these pages?" Volunteers respond. Confirm that there is a bear and an alligator. Ask students to use their hands to mimic the action of the alligator in the photograph on page 15.

Explain that now they will read through these pages in the text to identify more animals in North America. Instruct students to make a Nonverbal Signal, such as using their hands to snap like an alligator when they hear another animal mentioned in the text.

Read pages 14–15 aloud. Students make a Nonverbal Signal when they hear another animal mentioned in the text. Call on students who signal to name the animal they heard. Record students' answers on a sticky note and add them to the "Animals" column.

<table>
<tr><td>TEACHER NOTE</td><td>Consider preparing these sticky notes ahead of time using the example below as a guide. Using preprinted photographs will allow students to read back the notes independently. This will allow for easier transitions and less wait time between each answer.</td></tr>
</table>

SAMPLE EVIDENCE ORGANIZER FOR *INTRODUCING NORTH AMERICA*

Evidence Organizer for *Introducing North America*		
Things to Do	**Natural Features**	**Animals**
▪ *Grand Canyon*	▪ *mountains*	▪ *bears*
▪ *pyramids*	▪ *deserts*	▪ *alligators*
▪ *football*	▪ *plains*	▪ *polar bears*
▪ *movies*	▪ *lakes*	▪ *bison*
▪ *music*	▪ *rivers*	

SORT EVIDENCE 10 MIN.

Whole Group

Post and read aloud the Focusing Question. Students Echo Read the question. Explain that now students will use the evidence they have collected over the past few lessons to prepare for the Focusing Question Task.

Tell students that they will respond to the following prompt for their Focusing Question Task.

Why should someone visit North America? What amazing animal, fun thing to do, or interesting natural feature would make North America an interesting place to visit?

Display the Evidence Organizer for *Introducing North America*. Explain that before they write, they will think about the different evidence they have collected and form an opinion about why they think North America is an interesting place to visit.

<table>
<tr><td>TEACHER NOTE</td><td>Use index cards to create cards for the matching game prior to the lesson. Write one piece of evidence from the evidence organizer on each card. Add visual cues as needed.</td></tr>
</table>

Use a matching game to support students in reading the evidence organizer. Give each student a card with a different piece of evidence on it. Students turn to a partner and verbally identify the evidence on their card.

Point to one corner of the room. Instruct students with words from the category "Things to Do" to stand up and fly like an airplane to that corner of the room. Students share the words on their cards. After each response, students consider whether or not that piece of evidence is an example of things to do in North America. They indicate a level of agreement by holding up anywhere from one to five fingers, with one finger showing the lowest level of agreement and five fingers showing the strongest level of agreement.

Repeat this same sequence for the "Natural Features" and "Animals" columns on the evidence organizer until each student is standing and in a different corner of the room.

EXECUTE FOCUSING QUESTION TASK 5 24 MIN.

Individuals

Post and read the Craft Question. Display the Evidence Organizer for *Introducing North America*. Remind students that they will be writing a paragraph to answer the following prompt.

> Why should someone visit North America? What amazing animal, fun thing to do, or interesting natural feature would make North America an interesting place to visit?

Display the Opinion Sandwich Anchor Chart. Explain that students will be writing an opinion paragraph in the form of a letter. They will write a letter to someone of their choice to explain why they think that person should visit North America.

Scaffold

While students wrote a letter in Module 3, they may need a reminder of the structure. For example, remind them that **Dear** _____ is where they name who they are writing the letter to. Then, students write their own name at the bottom to let others know who the letter is from.

Divide the class into pairs. Students Think-Pair-Share about the following questions as their verbal rehearsal for the Focusing Question Task.

- Who do you think should visit North America? Who will you write your letter to?

- If they visit, what should they do? Why?

- If they visit, what natural feature should they see? Why?

- If they visit, what animal should they see? Why?

Distribute page 1 of Assessment 30A. Point to the blank line at the top of the page. Ask: "Who will you write your letter to?" Instruct students to write the name on the blank line.

Introduce the remaining parts of the assessment students will complete in this lesson, pointing to each section of the handout as you explain where students record their sentences:

- Students will write their opinion statement on the second line provided at the top of page 1.

- Students will write their first reason sentence on the lines provided at the bottom of page 1 and create a drawing in the box provided.

<table>
<tr><td></td><td>Name:</td></tr>
<tr><td></td><td>**Assessment 30A: Focusing Question Task 5**
Part 1
Directions: On the lines provided in box 1, write the name of the person to whom you are writing your letter and your opinion statement. Write your first supporting reason sentence and create an illustration in box 2. Write and illustrate your second supporting reason sentence in box 3. Complete your letter by writing your opinion conclusion and your name on the lines in box 4.</td></tr>
</table>

TEACHER NOTE	Consider introducing the different parts of the assessment one at time, providing time for students to write their sentences before moving on to the next part of the task. Students are not required to internalize the structure of the opinion paragraph at this time.

Ask: "How do we begin our sentences? What type of letter do we put at the beginning to signal to readers that this is the start of a sentence?" Volunteer responds.

- *A capital letter.*

Use responses to reinforce that students need to capitalize the first letter of their sentences.

✔ Students begin Part 1 of Focusing Question Task 5 by writing their opinion statement and one supporting reason sentence on page 1 of Assessment 30A. Students capitalize the first letter in each sentence.

Land 2 MIN.

ANSWER THE CONTENT FRAMING QUESTION

Post and read the Content Framing Question. Instruct students to Mix and Mingle, and ask: "What piece of evidence did you find that is the same as on another continent? What piece of evidence is different?"

Wrap 1 MIN.

ASSIGN HOMEWORK

Continue the class home-reading routine.

Analyze

Context and Alignment

Students use the words and pictures in *Introducing North America* to learn more about the continent and collect evidence for the Focusing Question Task (RI.K.1, RI.K.7). Each student:

- Records one piece of evidence on a sticky note.

Next Steps

If students have difficulty remembering the natural features discussed earlier, consider rereading the pages in the text. Students may need help with the complex vocabulary. In addition, it is not required for students to learn the proper names of each natural feature. Encourage students to use the photographs in the text to guide their understanding.

⬇ LESSON 30 DEEP DIVE: STYLE AND CONVENTIONS

Experiment with Using Ending Punctuation

- **Time:** 15 min.

- **Text:** *Introducing North America*, Chris Oxlade

- **Style and Conventions Learning Goal:** Write a complete sentence that ends with the correct punctuation mark. (L.K.1.f, L.K.2.b)

    STYLE AND CONVENTIONS CRAFT QUESTION: Lesson 30
    Experiment: *How do I end a complete sentence with the correct punctuation mark?*

Launch

Post and read the Style and Conventions Craft Question.

Reinforce that in today's lesson, students began writing a letter telling why someone should visit North America. To plan for their writing, students collected evidence from the text. Explain that students will use this evidence to practice writing a complete sentence that ends with the correct punctuation mark.

Create a chart on the board with two columns. At the top of the left column, write "WHO" in large print. At the top of right column, write "DOES WHAT" in large print.

WHO	DOES WHAT

Display the evidence organizers from Lessons 26 and 27. Ask: "What amazing animals make North America an interesting place to visit?" Volunteers respond.

- *Bears*

- *Alligators*

- *Bison*

- *Polar bears*

Use student responses to record the names of the animals in the "WHO" column.

WHO	DOES WHAT
bears	
alligators	
bison	
polar bears	

Explain that students are going to create a complete sentence about an amazing animal from North America. Encourage students to start their complete sentences with a capital letter. Instruct students to end their sentence with the correct punctuation mark.

Learn

Redirect student attention back to the chart. Instruct students to choose one animal from the chart that they are going to write about. Ask: "What does your animal do?" Use Equity Sticks to call on a student to share an example for each animal. Record their responses next to the animal, in the "DOES WHAT" column.

Instruct students to Think-Pair-Share and tell a complete sentence about the animal they chose. Encourage students to reference the chart as needed.

Extension

If students are ready for the challenge, encourage them to expand their descriptions of their drawings by adding a describing word or preposition.

Students take out their Response Journals. On the next blank page, students draw a picture of the animal they chose doing the action they shared. Allow students three minutes to create their drawings.

Explain that students are going to write this complete sentence under their drawing in their Response Journals. Ask: "Since you described your picture with a complete sentence, how should you end your sentence?" Students respond chorally.

▪ *With a punctuation mark!*

Reinforce that students need to think about the type of sentence they wrote to decide which punctuation mark to use.

Ask: "If you told a telling sentence, what type of punctuation mark will you use?" Students respond chorally.

▪ *A period!*

Draw a large period on the board.

Ask: "If you told a loud, exciting sentence, what type of punctuation mark will you use?" Students respond chorally.

   ▪ *An exclamation point!*

Draw a large exclamation point on the board.

Ask: "If you told an asking sentence, what type of punctuation mark will you use?" Students respond chorally.

   ▪ *A question mark!*

Draw a large question mark on the board.

✔ Allow time for students to write their complete sentence under their drawing in their Response Journal. Circulate to provide support as needed and to ensure that students end their sentences with the correct punctuation mark.

If time allows, use Equity Sticks to call on students to share their complete sentences. Ask each student to identify which letter they capitalized in their sentence.

Land

Redirect students' attention back to the Style and Conventions Craft Question.

Ask: "What steps did you do to write a complete sentence that ends with the correct punctuation mark?" Volunteers respond.

   ▪ *First, we chose an amazing animal and action to write about.*
   ▪ *Next, we shared our complete sentence idea with a friend.*
   ▪ *Then, we drew a picture of the animal doing the action.*
   ▪ *After, we decided if our idea was a telling sentence, a loud and exciting sentence, or an asking sentence.*
   ▪ *Finally, we wrote the complete sentence in our Response Journal and made sure it ended with the correct punctuation mark.*

■ FOCUSING QUESTION: LESSONS 28–31

Why might people want to visit North America?

1 2 3 4 5 6 7 8 9 10 11 12 13 14 15 16 17 18 19 20 21 22 23 24 25 26 27 28 29 30 31 32 33 34 35 36

Lesson 31

TEXTS

- "What is life?" Crowfoot (**http://witeng.link/0437**)
- *Introducing North America*, Chris Oxlade
- *World Atlas*, Nick Crane; Illustrations, David Dean

Lesson 31: At a Glance

AGENDA

Welcome (5 min.)

Perform Fluency

Launch (10 min.)

Learn (57 min.)

Execute Recognizing End Punctuation (10 min.)

Execute Focusing Question Task 5 (22 min.)

Record Knowledge (5 min.)

Complete New-Read Assessment 3 (20 min.)

Land (2 min.)

Answer the Content Framing Question

Wrap (1 min.)

Assign Homework

Vocabulary Deep Dive: Explore Natural Features (15 min.)

STANDARDS ADDRESSED

The full text of ELA Standards can be found in the Module Overview.

Reading

- RI.K.1, RI.K.9

Writing

- W.K.1, W.K.8, W.10*

Speaking and Listening

- SL.K.1, SL.K.2

Language

- L.K.1.f, L.K.2.a, L.K.2.b
- ⬇ L.K.5.a

MATERIALS

- Assessment 30A: Focusing Question Task 5
- Assessment 31A: New-Read Assessment 3
- Handout 31A: Natural Features Map
- Repeated Language Chart
- Handout 8A: Passport Journals
- Stamps or stickers (see lesson for details)
- Blue, yellow, and red crayons
- Evidence Organizer for *Introducing North America*
- Knowledge Journal

Learning Goals

Recognize and annotate end punctuation. (L.K.2.b)

✔ Circle the period, the exclamation point, and the question mark using different colors.

Use information gathered from *Introducing North America* to support an opinion about the continent. (RI.K.1, W.K.1, W.K.8, L.K.1.f, L.K.2.a)

✔ Complete Focusing Question Task 5.

Identify basic similarities in and differences between *Introducing North America* and *World Atlas*. (RI.K.9)

✔ Complete New-Read Assessment 3.

⬇ Sort photographs from the text into categories based on the type of natural feature it depicts. (L.K.5.a)

✔ Complete Handout 31A.

In alignment with the CCSS, W.10 formally begins in Grade 3. However, K–2 students write routinely for a variety of time frames, tasks, purposes, and audiences. As a result, this lesson contains instruction related to W.10 in an effort to familiarize students with a range of writing.

✔ Checks for Understanding

FOCUSING QUESTION: Lessons 28–31

Why might people want to visit North America?

CONTENT FRAMING QUESTION: Lesson 31

Know: *How does* Introducing North America *build my knowledge of the continents?*

CRAFT QUESTION: Lesson 31

Execute: *How do I execute using capital letters in my Focusing Question Task?*

In this lesson students complete their exploration of the continents by finishing their work with *Introducing North America*. Over the course of the module they have built their writing skills and worked towards creating opinion paragraphs and writing complete sentences. Students demonstrate independence with these skills by identifying different types of end punctuation and completing the written portion of their Focusing Question Task. Students also reflect upon their learning by adding to the class Knowledge Journal. Finally, students independently compare and contrast information found in *Introducing North America* and *World Atlas*.

Welcome 5 MIN.

PERFORM FLUENCY

Display the Repeated Language Chart. Explain that students will conclude work with this quotation by performing for each other.

The class conducts a rehearsal by Choral Reading the Repeated Language Chart.

Divide the class into two groups. Each group takes a turn performing the lines from the quotation using the agreed-upon hand gestures.

Launch 10 MIN.

Post and read the Content Framing Question aloud. Students Echo Read the question. Explain that in this lesson students will complete their trip around the world by finishing their exploration of North America.

Display a copy of *Introducing North America*. Provide time for students to think about the important knowledge they learned while exploring the text. Instruct students to Think-Pair-Share, and ask: "What important knowledge did you learn about North America?" Encourage students to use the Evidence Organizer for *Introducing North America* as a reference.

Instruct students to take out their Passport Journals and open up to page 8 for North America. Explain that students will draw and label an illustration to share the knowledge they gained from reading *Introducing North America*.

Students draw and label an illustration to share one thing they learned about North America in their Passport Journals. After students complete their journal page, place a stamp or sticker on the page to mark their visit to the continent.

Learn 57 MIN.

EXECUTE RECOGNIZING END PUNCTUATION 10 MIN.

Individuals

Post and read the Craft Question aloud. Ask: "What are the different parts of a complete sentence? What makes a sentence complete?" Volunteers respond.

- *We say who, did what.*
- *We put a period at the end.*
- *We make the first letter big.*

Confirm the different parts of a complete sentence. Explain to students that in their Focusing Question Task they will demonstrate their ability to write in complete sentences. Before they do this, they need to show they that are able to recognize the different types of end punctuation.

Distribute page 3 of Assessment 30A to each student. Give each student a blue, a yellow, and a red crayon. Explain that they will demonstrate their knowledge of the different punctuation by circling the end punctuation at the end of each sentence.

Read the three sentences on page 3 of Assessment 30A aloud. Instruct students to complete the following tasks one at a time:

Name:

Assessment 30A: Focusing Question Task 5

Part 1
Directions: On the lines provided in box 1, write the name of the person to whom you are writing your letter and your opinion statement. Write your first supporting reason sentence and create an illustration in box 2. Write and illustrate your second supporting reason sentence in box 3. Complete your letter by writing your opinion conclusion and your name on the lines in box 4.

- Circle the question mark with a red crayon.

- Circle the period with a blue crayon.

- Circle the exclamation point with a yellow crayon.

✔ Students complete Part 2 of Focusing Question Task 5 by circling the different punctuation marks in three different colors.

Extension

Collect page 3 of Assessment 30A before moving on to complete the Focusing Question Task. Call on volunteers to identify the different punctuation marks at the end of each sentence and explain why writers use that specific mark.

EXECUTE FOCUSING QUESTION TASK 5   22 MIN.

Individuals

Explain that working on the Focusing Question Task is another way students will use to think about what they learned from *Introducing North America*.

Reintroduce Part 1 of the Focusing Question Task and criteria for success. Explain that they are writing an opinion paragraph to answer the following prompt:

Why should someone visit North America? What amazing animal, fun thing to do, or interesting natural feature would make North America an interesting place to visit?

Explain that students will complete their Focusing Question Task today by writing and illustrating one more reason sentence to support the opinion statement. They will also write their own opinion conclusion sentence.

Ask: "How can we end our opinion paragraph? Why?" Volunteers respond. If needed, refer to the Opinion Sandwich Anchor Chart to remind students of the structure of an opinion paragraph.

- *We say our opinion again.*

- *We can use different words if we want.*

- *We close the sandwich with our opinion conclusion.*

- *It means that we are done with our writing.*

Use responses to reinforce that they end their opinion paragraph by restating their opinion.

Ask: "How can we restate our opinion?" Volunteers respond.

- *We can write the sentence again.*

- *We can use different words.*

- *We can use a descriptive word.*

465

TEACHER NOTE	To succeed in this part of the assessment students only need to restate their opinion, which can mean students recopy their opinion statement recorded in the previous lesson. Depending on students' ability, encourage students to restate their opinion using different words or descriptive words. This can serve as an additional challenge for those students who are ready.

Divide the class into pairs and distribute page 1 of Assessment 30A. Partners take turns reading their opinion statement and first reason sentence to each other and sharing their illustrations. Explain that now they will think about their next supporting reason sentence.

Display the evidence organizer for *Introducing North America*. Divide the class into pairs. Students Think-Pair-Share again about the following questions as their verbal rehearsal for the Focusing Question Task. Prompt students to use different information from the evidence organizer than what they wrote about in the previous lesson.

- If they visit, what should they do? Why?
- If they visit, what natural feature should they see? Why?
- If they visit, what animal should they see? Why?

Introduce the parts of the assessment students will complete in this lesson, pointing to each section of the handout as you explain where students record their sentences:

- Students will write their second reason sentence on the lines provided at the top of page 2 and begin creating a drawing in the box provided.
- Students will restate their opinion in a concluding sentence on the lines provided at the bottom of page 2.

TEACHER NOTE	Consider introducing the different parts of the assessment one at time, providing time for students to write their sentence before moving on to the next part of the task. Students are not required to internalize the structure of the opinion paragraph at this time.

Remind students to capitalize the first letter in each sentence.

Scaffold

If students struggle to reword their opinion statement, consider having them copy their opinion statement or use a sentence frame such as **North America is ___!** Students insert a descriptive word in the blank space.

✔ Distribute page 2 of Assessment 30A. Students complete Focusing Question Task 5 by writing a second supporting reason sentence and a conclusion sentence.

RECORD KNOWLEDGE 5 MIN.

Whole Group

Congratulate students on all the great work they have done over the course of the past few lessons and even the whole module. They have learned many things about the continents as well as become better readers and writers.

Display the class Knowledge Journal. Point to the left part of the journal and explain that students have already completed this part by writing important learning in their Passport Journals.

Tell students that they will add new items to the "What I Can Do" column by thinking about the new skills they learned as readers and writers.

Instruct students to Mix and Mingle, and ask: "What did you learn to do as a reader? What did you learn to do as a writer?"

Use Equity Sticks to call on pairs to share responses. After each response, students continue to stand as they consider whether or not the piece of learning in question is something important enough to remember and include in the Knowledge Journal. They indicate a level of agreement by crouching down low to the floor showing the lowest level of agreement and jumping up high showing the strongest level of agreement.

Use votes to choose one or two refined responses to record in the Knowledge Journal.

SAMPLE KNOWLEDGE JOURNAL

What I Know	What I Can Do
	• I can write in complete sentences.
	• I capitalize the first letter.
	• I recognize end punctuation.
	• I can say my opinion in a different way.

TEACHER NOTE Students record important learning individually in their Passport Journals instead of on the "What I Know" section of the class Knowledge Journal. If time permits, consider selecting several strong responses from the individual journals to add to the class journal.

Extension

Remind students that another tool that helps them keep track of learning is the Word Wall. Revisit the words added to the Word Wall since the start of the module. Students Echo Read the words. Choose three to five words to highlight based on your knowledge of students' vocabulary and call on volunteers to use the words in context.

COMPLETE NEW-READ ASSESSMENT 3 20 MIN.

Individuals

TEACHER NOTE	Use New-Read Assessments as an opportunity to reinforce the importance of orienting oneself to a text. Give students an independent, brief routine to support them in identifying the similarities and differences of the New-Read text. For example, you might encourage them to think quietly about what they notice in the text—prompting them to think about the information they have already learned about the continent. Remember to give young students sufficient time to answer questions and struggle productively with a New-Read text.

Display the front cover of *World Atlas*. Ask students: "How has this text built our knowledge of the continents?" Volunteers respond.

- *We learned new things.*
- *We saw big maps of the continents.*
- *We could see natural features and animals.*

Ask: "Why is it important to use a second text?" Volunteers respond.

- *We can see what is the same, then it is important.*
- *We can learn new things too.*
- *It helps us learn more.*

Explain that in this lesson, they will demonstrate their ability to locate similar and different information in *World Atlas* in a New-Read Assessment.

Ask: "What do we mean by *similar*? What do we mean by *different*?" Volunteers respond.

- Similar *means the same. We need to find details that are the same.*
- *We need to find details that are different. They are not the same in both books.*

Display the evidence organizer for *Introducing North America*. Reinforce that they will find one piece of information that is in both texts and one piece of information that is only in *World Atlas*.

Display Assessment 31A. Introduce the different parts of the assessment:

- In the top box, students draw and label one piece of information that appears in both texts.

- In the bottom box, students draw and label one piece of information that appears only in *World Atlas*.

Distribute Assessment 31A. Divide the class into small groups to share copies of *World Atlas*. Open each text to pages 38–39. Without discussing the text with their peers, students quietly look at the map of North America for two minutes. Encourage students to think quietly about the following questions: "What information is the same? What information is different?"

✔ Students complete New-Read Assessment 3.

Scaffold

If students need help focusing their search, consider prompting students to focus on only one column of the evidence organizer. For example, students locate information about the animals in North America that is the same and that is different.

Land 2 MIN.

ANSWER THE CONTENT FRAMING QUESTION

Post and read the Content Framing Question. Instruct students to Mix and Mingle, and ask: "What are some reasons that it is important to learn about the world? Would you encourage others to learn more about the seven continents?"

Wrap 1 MIN.

ASSIGN HOMEWORK

Continue the class home-reading routine.

Analyze

Context and Alignment

Students use evidence from *Introducing North America* to write an opinion paragraph in the form of a letter, explaining why someone should visit North America (RI.K.1, W.K.1, W.K.8, L.K.1.f, L.K.2.a). Each student:

- Writes an opinion statement.

- Writes and illustrates two sentences to support their opinion with details from the text.

- Creates a conclusion sentence by restating their opinion.

- Capitalizes the first letter in their sentences.

Next Steps

If students have difficulty with their task, consider the root of the problem. Do they have difficulty with the structure of a letter? If so, use the Opinion Sandwich Anchor Chart to remind them of the shape of an opinion paragraph. Consider asking them to just write an opinion paragraph to answer the prompt, and introduce the letter heading after their task is complete. Do they have difficulty locating evidence to support their opinion? If so, provide support by helping them focus on one column of evidence at a time. This is the first writing task where students have had to use multiple columns and they may need help expanding their focus.

Group students with similar needs and plan small-group support for these skills to set students up for success with their EOM Task.

⬇ LESSON 31 DEEP DIVE: VOCABULARY

Explore Natural Features

- **Time:** 15 min.

- **Text:** *Introducing North America*, Chris Oxlade

- **Vocabulary Learning Goal:** Sort photographs from the text into categories based on the type of natural feature it depicts. (L.K.5.a)

Launch

Reinforce that students have been exploring natural features. Ask: "What are the natural features found in North America?" Reference the previously created evidence organizer to prompt students as needed. Volunteers respond.

- *Mountains.*

- *Deserts.*

- *Plains.*

- *Lakes.*

- *Rivers.*

Use student responses to record *mountains, desert, lakes,* and *rivers.* Explain that students are going to sort photographs from the text into these natural feature categories.

Learn

Organize students into pairs and distribute a text to each group.

Remind students that a mountain is an area of land that rises very high. Instruct students to look through the book to find a photograph of a mountain. Students raise a hand when they successfully find a mountain. Ask: "What page has a photograph of a mountain on it?" Call on a student with a raised hand. Students share the page number so rest of class can see the photograph as well.

- *Page 8 (Mount McKinley).*

- *Page 14 (Rocky Mountains).*

Remind students that a desert is an area of very dry land usually covered by sand. Instruct students to look through the book to find a photograph of a desert. Students raise a hand when they successfully find a desert. Ask: "What page has a photograph of a desert on it?" Call on a student with a raised hand. Students share the page number so rest of class can see the photograph as well.

- *Page 9 (Mojave Desert).*

- *Page 16 (desert in Arizona).*

Remind students that a lake is a large area of water surrounded by land. Instruct students to look through the book to find a photograph of a lake. Students raise a hand when they successfully find a lake. Ask: "What page has a photograph of a lake on it?" Call on a student with a raised hand. Students share the page number so rest of class can see the photograph as well.

- ▪ *Page 10 (Great Lakes).*
- ▪ *Page 15 (Everglades).*

Remind students that a river is a large flow of water that crosses an area of land. Instruct students to look through the book to find a photograph of a river. Students raise a hand when they successfully find a river. Ask: "What page has a photograph of a river on it?" Call on a student with a raised hand. Students share the page number so rest of class can see the photograph as well.

- ▪ *Page 11 (Mississippi River).*
- ▪ *Pages 19, 24 (Hudson River).*

Collect the texts and reorganize students into whole group setting. Explain that students are going to complete a sorting activity.

Land

✔ Distribute Handout 31A. Echo Read the directions at the top. Students draw a line to match illustrations of North American natural features to the correct label. Each label will have two natural feature matches. Use Equity Sticks to call on students to describe how they matched a natural feature to a label. If students disagree on a response, have them explain their thinking.

◾ FOCUSING QUESTION: LESSONS 32–35

What makes the world fascinating?

1 2 3 4 5 6 7 8 9 10 11 12 13 14 15 16 17 18 19 20 21 22 23 24 25 26 27 28 29 30 31 **32 33 34 35** 36

Lesson 32

TEXTS

- All Module Texts
- "The Seven Continents Song," Silly School Songs

Lesson 32: At a Glance

AGENDA

Welcome (3 min.)

Practice Fluency

Launch (5 min.)

Learn (63 min.)

Collect Evidence for the EOM Task (40 min.)

Sort Module Texts (10 min.)

Examine the Importance of Verbal Descriptions (13 min.)

Land (3 min.)

Answer the Content Framing Question

Wrap (1 min.)

Assign Homework

Style and Conventions Deep Dive: Excel at Writing a Sentence (15 min.)

STANDARDS ADDRESSED

The full text of ELA Standards can be found in the Module Overview.

Reading

- RI.K.1, RI.K.7, RI.K.9, RL.K.5

Writing

- W.K.7

Speaking and Listening

- SL.K.1, SL.K.2, SL.K.4

Language

- L.K.5.c
- ↓ L.K.1.f, L.K.2.a, L.K.2.b

MATERIALS

- Assessment 32A: End-of-Module Task
- Handout 32A: Sentence Improvement
- Repeated Language Chart (see lesson for details)
- Handout 8A: Passport Journals
- Evidence Organizers for *Europe*, *Asia*, *Australia*, *Africa*, and *Antarctica*
- Sticky notes
- Speaking and Listening Anchor Chart
- Document camera (if available)

Learning Goals

Recognize common text types and sort module texts into genres. (RL.K.5)

✔ Complete Part 1 of the EOM Task.

Examine the importance of verbal descriptions in providing details. (RI.K.7, SL.K.4)

✔ Verbally describe one animal from *South America*.

↓ Write and expand a complete sentence that begins with a capital letter and ends with the correct punctuation mark. (L.K.1.f, L.K.2.a, L.K.2.b)

✔ Complete Handout 32A.

✔ Checks for Understanding

Prepare

FOCUSING QUESTION: Lessons 32–35

What makes the world fascinating?

CONTENT FRAMING QUESTION: Lesson 32

Know: *How do Module 4 texts build my knowledge of the continents?*

CRAFT QUESTION: Lesson 32

Examine: *Why is it important to describe things in detail when I speak?*

In this lesson, students complete their evidence collection about the different natural features, things to do, and animals. They revisit module texts and demonstrate understanding of these topics as well as their ability to locate evidence in the text. This provides them with a more complete picture of each continent, and prepares them to engage in the written portion of the EOM Task (in the next lesson). Students begin their EOM Task by sorting the module texts into categories, demonstrating an understanding of different text types. Finally, students explore the importance of using descriptive words and details as they discuss the text evidence in preparation for conveying this information to another.

Welcome 3 MIN.

PRACTICE FLUENCY

Display the Repeated Language Chart of the "The Seven Continents Song." Read all four lines of the song and encourage students to Choral Read if they remember the words.

Repeated Language
Song: "The Seven Continents Song," Silly School Songs • North America, South America, • Africa, Europe, and Asia, • Australia, Antarctica, • Seven Continents, back to the startica.

Explain that for the next few lessons students will revisit this song, using it as a way to express knowledge of the different continents.

Play the video of "The Seven Continents Song" (**http://witeng.link/0374**). Prompt students to stand up and dance along with the song. Students say the lyrics with the video.

Launch 5 MIN.

TEACHER NOTE	Prior to the lesson, display the evidence organizers for each continent around the room.

Post and read the Focusing Question aloud, using the agreed-upon hand gestures from earlier in the module. Students Echo Read the Focusing Question using the agreed-upon hand gestures.

Remind students that they have taken a trip around the world with the help of the Module 4 texts. They have learned interesting information about each continent and used photographs from the text to enhance their understanding. Explain that over the next few lessons they will reflect upon what they have learned and share their knowledge with others by completing the EOM Task. If needed, remind students they will be creating a travel brochure about a continent of their choice.

Point to the evidence organizers displayed throughout the room. Ask: "Have we completed our evidence collection?" Volunteers respond.

- *No. There are still blank spots on the evidence organizers.*

Confirm that there is a bit more thinking to do about these continents before they can begin their EOM Task. Explain that in this lesson they will finish their evidence collection and reflect on different ways to express the knowledge they have learned about these continents.

Learn 63 MIN.

COLLECT EVIDENCE FOR THE EOM TASK 40 MIN.

Whole Group

TEACHER NOTE	Consider preparing these sticky notes prior to the lesson using the examples below as a guide. Using preprinted photographs allows students to read back the notes independently, allowing for easier transitions and less wait time between each answer.

Ask: "What topics have we collected evidence on over the course of the module about the continents? How did we find this evidence?" Volunteers respond. As students respond, point to the corresponding column on an evidence organizer.

- *We collected evidence on the natural features.*
- *We found information about things to do and animals, too.*
- *We used the words and the photos in the books.*

Call on volunteers to describe what type of information goes in each of the three categories on the evidence organizers.

Display the front cover of *Europe* and the Evidence Organizer for *Europe* in front of the class. Point to the column labeled "Natural Features." Explain that now they will go back through the text to locate evidence on the natural features in Europe.

If possible, use a document camera to project book pages and prompt students to follow along. Instruct students to make a Nonverbal Signal, such as pointing to their ears, when they hear an example of a "natural feature" in Europe.

Read pages 20–27 of *Europe* aloud. Students make a Nonverbal Signal when they hear evidence in the text. Use Equity Sticks to call on students who signal to share their evidence.

After each response, students consider whether what they just heard is a piece of evidence. They indicate a level of agreement by holding up anywhere from one to five fingers, with one finger showing the lowest level of agreement and five fingers showing the strongest level of agreement.

Use votes to choose one or two refined responses to record in the "Natural Features" column on the Evidence Organizer for *Europe*.

TEACHER NOTE

The exemplars for the Evidence Organizer for *Europe* and the Evidence Organizer for *Asia* are included at the bottom of this section of the lesson. Students collect evidence on the natural features now, and then will return to these texts later to collect evidence on the animals of these two continents.

Display the front cover of *Asia* and the Evidence Organizer for *Asia*. Explain that now they will collect evidence on the natural features in Asia in small groups.

Divide the class into small groups, and distribute copies of the text to each group. Explain that they will go back through a specific section of the text and use the photographs in the text to determine the natural features in Asia.

Prompt groups to turn to pages 22–23 in *Asia*. Point to the photograph on page 22. Ask: "What natural feature do you see in this photograph? How do you know?" Volunteers respond.

- *It is a forest.*
- *I see trees.*
- *It is a forest because I see lots of green.*

Confirm student answers by rereading the text on page 23. Add *forests* to the "Natural Features" column on the Evidence Organizer for *Asia*.

Repeat this same sequence and questioning for the photographs on pages 24 and 26. As students respond, confirm their answers by rereading the corresponding text and add the evidence to the evidence organizer.

Display the Evidence Organizer for *Australia* in front of the class. Reveal and read aloud the title of the second column, "Natural Features." Explain that they will now go back through the text to find evidence on the different natural features in Australia.

If possible, use a document camera to project the pages of the book. Prompt students to follow along with the copy of the text in front of the class. Instruct students to make a Nonverbal Signal, such as pointing to their ears, when they hear an example of a natural feature in Australia.

Read the "Land and Water" section in *Australia* aloud. Students make a Nonverbal Signal when they hear evidence in the text. Use Equity Sticks to call on students who signal to share their evidence.

After each response, students consider whether or not that is a piece of evidence. They indicate a level of agreement by holding up anywhere from one to five fingers, with one finger showing the lowest level of agreement and five fingers showing the strongest level of agreement.

Use votes to choose one or two refined responses to record in the "Natural Features" column on the Evidence Organizer for *Australia*.

Scaffold

If needed, use the questions below to scaffold student learning and understanding as they read these pages.

Page 19: "What other very dry natural feature have we learned about that is like the outback? How do the colors in the picture help you understand how dry the outback is?"

Page 25: "Is this natural feature above or below the water? How do you know?" Explain that a coral reef is hard like a rock, but is home to many plants and fish that make it colorful.

Page 27: "How do you know that a lot of rain falls in this area? What in the picture makes you think so?"

After completing the "Natural Features" section for *Australia*, instruct students to stand up. Explain that now they will act out what it would be like to encounter some of these natural features in Australia.

Point to the evidence labeled "outback." Ask: "How would you feel if you were in the outback? How would you move if you were in the outback?" Students move their bodies as if they were walking through the dry and hot outback. Repeat this same questioning for the other evidence in the natural features columns. After students act out the evidence, ask: "Why did you move your body that way? What about the [natural feature] makes you act that way?" Volunteers respond.

Reveal the title of the first column on the Evidence Organizer for *Australia*, "Things to Do." Read this title aloud. Explain that they will now go back through the text to find evidence on the different things to do in Australia.

Read pages 8–9 and pages 28–29 in *Australia* aloud. Repeat the sequence above to add evidence to the "Things to Do" column.

Evidence Organizer for *Australia*		
Things to Do	**Natural Features**	**Animals**
▪ *ride the monorail* ▪ *visit the opera house*	▪ *outback* ▪ *Uluru Rock* ▪ *forests* ▪ *coral reef* ▪ *waterfalls*	▪ *kangaroo* ▪ *koala* ▪ *platypus*

Explain that finding evidence and recording it is something they will continue to do throughout their time in school—in every grade, whether they are studying storybooks, science, or something else. Reinforce that the world is a big place with a lot of different information, and the more they read and learn, the more likely they are to find the particular things that fascinate them, that they will choose to learn more about.

For now, there is one more category on which they need to collect evidence for their study of the continents Africa, Antarctica, Europe, and Asia. Display the Evidence Organizer for *Africa* and point to the last column. Read the label aloud. Explain that now students will go back through the text in small groups, without teacher help, to locate information on the animals on these last four continents.

Divide the class into four groups. Assign each group one of the four continents listed above. Give each group three to five sticky notes and a few copies of their assigned text. Instruct groups to use sticky notes to annotate evidence on the animals in their assigned continent. Give groups three to five minutes to complete this task.

> ### Scaffold
>
> Circulate as groups discuss the text and annotate the photographs. Encourage students to ask questions if they are not familiar with the name of the animal. For most examples, there is a photograph for each animal. In *Africa*, the photograph on page 22 only shows zebras while the text on page 23 discusses lions and giraffes as well. Read this page aloud to the group assigned *Africa* to help them get a full picture of the animals mentioned in the text.

Call on each group to share the animal evidence they annotated in the text. As groups share their evidence, record their responses on a sticky note and add them to the corresponding evidence organizer.

SAMPLE EVIDENCE ORGANIZER FOR *AFRICA*

Evidence Organizer for *Africa*		
Things to Do	**Natural Features**	**Animals**
▪ *play soccer on the beach* ▪ *hike a tall mountain*	▪ *hot and dry deserts* ▪ *grassy savannas* ▪ *green rainforests* ▪ *long Nile River* ▪ *tall mountains*	▪ *zebras* ▪ *lions* ▪ *giraffes* ▪ *gorillas*

SAMPLE EVIDENCE ORGANIZER FOR *ANTARCTICA*

Evidence Organizer for *Antarctica*		
Things to Do	**Natural Features**	**Animals**
▪ *ski* ▪ *watch animals* ▪ *study the ice and animals*	▪ *icy ocean* ▪ *tall, icy, snowy mountains* ▪ *giant, thick icebergs*	▪ *penguins* ▪ *seals* ▪ *whales*

SAMPLE EVIDENCE ORGANIZER FOR *ASIA*

Evidence Organizer for *Asia*		
Things to Do	**Natural Features**	**Animals**
▪ *visit Burj Khalifa* ▪ *build computer parts* ▪ *grow rice* ▪ *walk the Great Wall of China* ▪ *shop at street market* ▪ *walk in a park*	▪ *forests* ▪ *deserts* ▪ *mountains*	▪ *giant pandas* ▪ *Bengal tigers*

SAMPLE EVIDENCE ORGANIZER FOR *EUROPE*

Evidence Organizer for *Europe*		
Things to Do	**Natural Features**	**Animals**
▪ *ride in boats* ▪ *go to festivals* ▪ *visit museums* ▪ *see pretty buildings* ▪ *visit old castles* ▪ *ski* ▪ *pick grapes*	▪ *forests* ▪ *mountains* ▪ *rivers*	▪ *brown bear*

SORT MODULE TEXTS 10 MIN.

Individuals

Post and read the Essential Question. Reinforce that students have encountered many different texts over the course of this module as they work towards answering this question. Ask: "What are the different text types that you know?" Volunteers respond.

- ▪ *We read informational texts.*
- ▪ *We read storybooks, too.*

Explain that to begin their EOM Task, they will demonstrate this understanding of the different types of text. This will help them understand which module texts they can use to create their travel brochure.

Display page 1 of Assessment 32A. Explain that on this handout there is a list of the text titles from the module. If needed, read the first three texts listed on the assessment. Point to the blank box next to each title. Explain that in this box students will identify what type of text this book is. They will write an I for an informational text or an S for a storybook.

Distribute page 1 of Assessment 32A. Instruct students to turn the assessment over and briefly practice writing the letters I and S. Circulate as students do so to ensure they are writing the correct letters.

Use the teacher-facing version (with key) in Appendix C to administer the assessment. Read each text title aloud one at a time while holding up the text in front of the class. Ask: "Is this an informational text or a storybook?" Students write an I or S next to the corresponding text title to identify which type of text it is.

GK > M4 Assessment 32A WIT & WISDOM™

Name:

Assessment 32A: End-of-Module Task
Part 1
Directions: Identify the type of text for each book below. In the boxes next to each title, write an "I" for an informational text or an "S" for a storybook.

1.	South America	
2.	Australia	
3.	Moon Rope	
4.	Introducing North America	
5.	Africa	
6.	Why Mosquitoes Buzz in People's Ears	
7.	Antarctica	
8.	Europe	
9.	The Story of Ferdinand	
10.	Asia	
11.	World Atlas	

Scaffold

Consider placing copies of the text around the room for students to access during the assessment if needed. Allow them to look at the various text features or pictures to remind them of how they used this text throughout the module. This is not an assessment of student memory.

✔ Students complete Part 1 of the EOM Task. Read each title twice before students fill in answers. Circulate to ensure students follow directions and mark the correct question. Give oral cues as necessary to help students locate the proper row where they should be marking answers.

EXAMINE THE IMPORTANCE OF VERBAL DESCRIPTIONS 13 MIN.

Whole Group

Display the Speaking and Listening Anchor Chart and point to the entry "Give an example." Ask: "Why is it important to give an example? Why is it important to use these examples to show people what we have learned?" Volunteers respond.

- *Then people know what we know.*
- *We can show we understand.*
- *People will know that we understand the question and what we read.*

Post and read the Craft Question. Students Echo Read the question. Explain that today they will look at another way to show they understand a topic: speaking to describe.

Display the Evidence Organizers for *Europe* and *Asia*. Point to the "Natural Features" columns. Instruct students to Think-Pair-Share, and ask: "Is there evidence in these columns that is the same?" Use Equity Sticks to call on students to answer.

- *They both have mountains.*
- *They both have forests, too.*

Confirm that both continents have forests.

Display page 20 from *Europe* and page 22 from *Asia* side by side in front of the class. If possible, use a document camera to display them. Ask: "How are these two forests the same? How are they different?" Volunteers respond.

- *The one from Europe has brown in it.*
- *It only has one tree.*
- *I see a bear, too!*
- *The forest in Asia has lots of trees.*
- *It is really green.*
- *In Asia the trees are tall and skinny. In Europe they have branches and leaves.*

Ask: "If someone has never read these texts or seen these photographs, would they understand these differences if I just said 'They both have forests'?" Volunteers respond.

- *No, because it doesn't tell them what is different.*
- *You need to tell them more about it.*

Instruct students to close their eyes. Explain that now you will describe, or give more detail about, one of these forests. If students know what continent the forest is from they stand up.

Verbally describe the forest from *Europe*, introducing new details one at a time. For example,

This forest has green on the trees. There is grass on the ground. The grass is a little bit brown. The trees have branches. The branches have small pine needles at the end.

Continue describing this scene until every student is standing. Use Equity Sticks to call on students to identify the forest described. Confirm that this forest was from *Europe*.

Ask: "How did I describe the picture? How did describing the details about this forest help you know which forest it was?" Volunteers respond.

- *You used descriptive words.*
- *You told us details about the picture.*
- *You told us what you saw.*
- *It helped because we heard a difference and then we knew.*
- *If you describe it then we can learn more.*

Use responses to reinforce that providing more detail when telling a person information is important because it helps listeners obtain more details about that topic. Describing things and using descriptive words helps provide more information.

Point to the Speaking and Listening Anchor Chart. Add "Speak to describe" to the column "When I speak, I."

When I listen, I	When I speak, I
▪ Listen with my senses.	▪ Use one voice at a time.
▪ Use active listening.	▪ Have conversations.
▪ Listen for order.	▪ Speak with a strong voice.
▪ Listen to remember.	▪ Ask and answer questions.
	▪ Use drawings to add detail.
	▪ Give an example.
	▪ Speak to describe.

Divide the class into pairs and distribute copies of *South America*. Instruct pairs to take turns describing an animal from the text. While one student describes the animal, their partner closes their eyes and tries to guess the animal based on the description. Then, students switch roles.

✔ Pairs describe one animal from the text. Students guess that animal based on their partner's description.

Land 3 MIN.

ANSWER THE CONTENT FRAMING QUESTION

Read aloud the Content Framing Question. Ask: "Why do you think we needed to finish collecting evidence from the rest of the texts? Why couldn't we just collect evidence in one category?" Volunteers respond.

- *We need to think more about the continents.*
- *We need to talk about different topics.*
- *We need to make choices.*

Use responses to reinforce that finishing their evidence collection was very important to being able to engage in their EOM Task. It is important to collect as much information as you can before forming an opinion.

Wrap 1 MIN.

ASSIGN HOMEWORK

Continue the class home-reading routine.

Analyze

Context and Alignment

Students sort module texts into categories to demonstrate understanding of different text types (RL.K.5). Each student:

- Listens to the text title read aloud.

- Writes I or S to label the text type.

Next Steps

If students have difficulty identifying the text type, flip through the pages of the text allowing students to get a better visual of the photographs or illustrations and the text features. Students have worked extensively with these aspects of the text over the course of the year and are familiar with what they signify in a text. If students continue to have difficulty, reread certain pages and ask: "What is happening in this text? Does this text convey information? Does this text have characters and tell a story?" Consider placing copies of the text for students to access while they engage in the assessment.

⬇ **LESSON 32 DEEP DIVE: STYLE AND CONVENTIONS**

Excel at Writing a Sentence

- **Time:** 15 min.

- **Texts:** All Module Texts

- **Style and Conventions Learning Goal:** Write and expand a complete sentence that begins with a capital letter and ends with the correct punctuation mark. (L.K.1.f, L.K.2.a, L.K.2.b)

> **STYLE AND CONVENTIONS CRAFT QUESTION: Lesson 32**
> Excel: *How do I improve at writing a complete sentence?*

Launch

Post and read the Style and Conventions Craft Question.

Reinforce that students have been working hard all module to improve at writing a complete sentence. First they learned how to create and expand a complete sentence.

Ask: "What are the two parts of a complete sentence?" Volunteers respond.

- *Who.*

- *Does what.*

Ask: "How can you expand a complete sentence to tell more information?" Volunteers respond.

- *You can add describing words.*

- *You can tell where or when the action happened.*

Students also learned important rules about how to begin and end their complete sentences.

Ask: "How do you always begin a complete sentence?" Volunteers respond.

- *You start a new sentence with a capital letter.*

Ask: "How do you always end a complete sentence?" Volunteers respond.

- *With a punctuation mark.*

- *With a period, exclamation point, or question mark.*

Explain that students are going to write a complete sentence. They are going to improve the sentence by expanding it and following the rules about beginning and ending a complete sentence correctly.

Learn

Remind students that as they "traveled" to each continent, they learned about interesting things at each place. One thing they explored on each continent was the "Amazing Animals" that live there. They have been practicing their writing skills by sharing complete sentences about some of these amazing animals.

Explain that students are going to improve their writing by expanding a complete sentence about a different animal.

Distribute Handout 32A. Read the directions for the top box of the handout aloud to students. Model how to follow the directions to complete each step. After each step, give students a minute to complete that step on their handout.

Read the directions for the bottom box of the handout aloud. Model how to follow the directions to complete each step. Instruct students to Think-Pair-Share and verbally tell their expanded sentence to their partner.

✔ Allow students several minutes to follow the directions to write an expanded sentence in the bottom box of the handout. Remind students to follow the rules about how to begin and end their sentences correctly. Circulate to provide support as needed and to ensure understanding.

If time allows, use Equity Sticks to call on students to share their improved complete sentences.

Collect completed handouts for assessment.

Land

Redirect student attention back to the Style and Conventions Craft Question.

Ask: "How did you improve your complete sentence?" Volunteers respond.

- *I expanded my complete sentence by describing the animal.*
- *I expanded my complete sentence by telling where or when it happened.*
- *I made sure my sentence began with a capital letter.*
- *I made sure my sentence ended with a period, exclamation point, or question mark.*

What makes the world fascinating?

1 | 2 | 3 | 4 | 5 | 6 | 7 | 8 | 9 | 10 | 11 | 12 | 13 | 14 | 15 | 16 | 17 | 18 | 19 | 20 | 21 | 22 | 23 | 24 | 25 | 26 | 27 | 28 | 29 | 30 | 31 | **32** | **33** | **34** | **35** | 36

Lesson 33

TEXTS

- All Module Texts
- "The Seven Continents Song," Silly School Songs

Lesson 33: At a Glance

AGENDA

Welcome (5 min.)

Practice Fluency

Launch (10 min.)

Learn (56 min.)

Understand the EOM Task (8 min.)

Examine Evidence Organizers (20 min.)

Experiment with Verbal Descriptions (10 min.)

Begin the EOM Task (18 min.)

Land (3 min.)

Answer the Content Framing Question

Wrap (1 min.)

Assign Homework

Vocabulary Deep Dive: Direct Vocabulary Assessment 2 (15 min.)

STANDARDS ADDRESSED

The full text of ELA Standards can be found in the Module Overview.

Reading

- RI.K.1

Writing

- W.K.1, W.K.8

Speaking and Listening

- SL.K.4

Language

- L.K.1.f, L.K.2.a
- ⬇ L.K.6

MATERIALS

- Assessment 32A: End-of-Module Task
- Assessment 33A: Direct Vocabulary Assessment 2
- Repeated Language Chart (see lesson for details)
- Sample travel brochures (paper or digital; see lesson for details)
- All module evidence organizers (excluding *Introducing North America*)
- Speaking and Listening Anchor Chart
- Opinion Sandwich Anchor Chart
- Document camera (if available)

Learning Goals

Express understanding of the unique natural features, animals, and things to do on the different continents. (RI.K.1, W.K.1, W.K.8, L.K.1.f, L.K.2.a)

✔ Begin Part 2 of the EOM Task.

Use descriptive words to verbally describe familiar places. (SL.K.4)

✔ Verbally describe a forest in *Asia* or *Africa*, using a photograph from the text as reference.

⬇ Demonstrate understanding of grade-level vocabulary. (L.K.6)

✔ Complete Direct Vocabulary Assessment 2.

✔ Checks for Understanding

FOCUSING QUESTION: Lessons 32–35

What makes the world fascinating?

CONTENT FRAMING QUESTION: Lesson 33

Know: *How do Module 4 texts build my knowledge of the continents?*

CRAFT QUESTIONS: Lesson 33

Experiment: *How do I describe things when I speak?*
Execute: *How do I use complete sentences in my End-of-Module Task?*

In this lesson students synthesize learning about the continents to begin their EOM Task. They build background knowledge about travel brochures. Students also reflect on their learning through a Gallery Walk of the evidence organizers created during the module. They deepen their understanding of how to use descriptive words when describing something verbally, which prepares them for the upcoming EOM Task presentation. Finally, students complete the first page of their travel brochure by writing and illustrating an opinion statement.

Welcome 5 MIN.

PRACTICE FLUENCY

Display and read aloud the Repeated Language Chart for "The Seven Continents Song." Students Echo Read the chart.

Remind students of the previously agreed-upon dance movements that accompany each line. As a class, determine which movements to keep and which ones to change.

Students Echo Read the chart, line by line, practicing the updated dance moves.

Launch 10 MIN.

Use Google Maps (**http://witeng.link/0445**) to display a satellite image of your school and surrounding neighborhood (Earth view). Zoom in to the image as close as possible to make areas around the school easily visible.

Ask: "What do you see on this map?" Volunteers respond.

- *I see trees.*
- *There's a road.*
- *I see cars.*
- *That looks like a playground.*
- *I think that's our school!*

Explain that students are looking at view of their school from above, as if they were seeing it from the sky. Ask: "Who or what might see the school from this view?" Volunteers respond.

- *Birds.*
- *Someone in an airplane.*
- *Maybe a superhero.*

Then zoom out slowly, pointing out other local landmarks (library, rivers, lakes, parks, etc.). As you zoom out farther, point out nearby cities, states, oceans, and continents. Zoom out all the way, providing a view of Earth from space. Ask: "Who or what might see the school from this view?" Volunteers respond.

- *Astronauts.*
- *The moon.*
- *Aliens.*

Rotate the image of the world around and invite students to identify the continents they see.

Tell students that this map, like the *Earth from Space* image, is created from images taken by satellites that circle around Earth. Explain that satellites are one tool that can help us understand and map our world.

Ask: "What can you see when we zoom way out, and look at the whole world, that you couldn't see when we zoomed in closely on our school?" Volunteers respond.

- *You can see continents.*
- *You can see the oceans.*
- *There are clouds, too.*
- *You can see how it all goes together.*
- *You can see how things are connected.*

Emphasize that, although each continent is different, and some continents seem very far away, they are all part of the same world. We can learn about the world by looking at it close-up, and we can learn about it by zooming out and looking at the bigger picture. Both views are important.

Learn 56 MIN.

UNDERSTAND THE EOM TASK 8 MIN.

Whole Group

Explain that students will continue to reflect on their learning as they begin their EOM Task. Remind students that all the knowledge and skills they have gained over the course of the module have prepared them to answer the module's Essential Question. Post and read the Essential Question aloud, using the agreed-upon hand gestures from earlier in the module. Students Echo Read the Essential Question using these hand gestures.

Tell students that they will respond to the Essential Question by creating a travel brochure. They will think about the ways they have been amazed and fascinated by the continents, and will share their learning and excitement with others through the brochure.

Explain that a brochure is a small collection of pages that give information or advertise something. Build background knowledge by displaying a sample travel brochure and reading key portions of the text aloud (e.g., the headings and introduction).

| **TEACHER NOTE** | Prior to the lesson, gather at least one travel brochure to use as an example. This could be a paper or digital brochure. For example, access the following digital travel brochure: (**http://witeng.link/0446**). |

Ask: "What do you see in this travel brochure? What do you notice?" Volunteers respond.

- *It has beautiful pictures.*
- *It shows different places and things to do.*
- *The words tell about the places and things to do.*
- *I see maps, too.*

Ask: "What can readers learn from a travel brochure?" Volunteers respond.

- *You can learn about a new place.*
- *You can see different places and things to do.*
- *You could decide if you want to visit that place.*

493

Ask: "Why might someone make a travel brochure?" Volunteers respond.

- *They might want to tell someone about a cool place.*
- *Maybe to give information about a place people can visit.*
- *So other people can know if they want to visit that place.*

Use responses to reinforce that travel brochures use words, pictures, and maps to give information about a place and try to convince people to visit that place.

Introduce Part 2 of the EOM Task:

- Students will create a travel brochure about one continent.
- The brochure will have four pages and will follow the Opinion Sandwich writing model.
- Each page will contain a complete sentence and an illustration.

Point out that students can select any continent except North America. Reinforce that they are thinking about which continent they would like to visit. Because they already live in North America, they will need to make another choice. They can use their brochure to explain to family and friends why they should visit another continent.

EXAMINE EVIDENCE ORGANIZERS 20 MIN.

Small Groups

TEACHER NOTE	Prior to the lesson, post the evidence organizers for each continent around the room (excluding *Introducing North America*). Display several copies of the corresponding text next to each organizer. Leave the classroom configured like this until students have completed the EOM Task.

Explain that students will engage in a Gallery Walk of the evidence organizers and texts from this module in order to reflect upon the fascinating things they have learned about each continent and to help them select a continent for their brochures.

Divide students into small groups and assign each group a starting continent. Students rotate through the evidence organizers for each continent, spending about two minutes at each organizer. Instruct students to Mix and Mingle with other students in their group as they rotate through the continents and ask the following questions:

- Which natural feature from this continent interests you most? Why?
- Which animal from this continent most amazes you? Why?
- Which thing to do on this continent would you be most excited to do? Why?

TEACHER NOTE	Consider setting a timer to notify students when to switch to the next continent.

Instruct students to Think-Pair-Share, and ask: "Which continent do you find most fascinating? Which continent would you like to visit? Why?" Use Equity Sticks to call on students to respond.

EXPERIMENT WITH VERBAL DESCRIPTIONS   10 MIN.

Whole Group

Tell students that after they create their brochures they will present them to their classmates. Remind students that when they present their work to others, they should use their best speaking skills.

Display the Speaking and Listening Anchor Chart and highlight "Speak to describe." Explain that today students will explore more about what it means to describe something well in preparation for their presentation.

Display and read aloud the first Craft Question: *How do I describe things when I speak?*

Ask: "Why is it important to describe something well when we speak?" Use Equity Sticks to call on students to respond.

- *It helps people understand what we are talking about.*
- *People can understand what something looks like.*
- *People can understand more details.*

Display the photograph on page 26 of *Africa* and the photograph on page 24 of *Europe* side by side, using a document camera if possible. Instruct students to listen to a description and determine which photograph you are describing. Say:

I see a mountain.

Ask: "Which photograph am I describing, the one from *Africa* or *Europe*?" Volunteers respond.

- *I can't tell!*
- *I don't know, you didn't tell us enough information.*

Acknowledge that simply naming the natural feature is not enough of a description to be able to determine which photograph is being described because both photographs contain a mountain.

Ask: "What kind of words do I need to say to better describe the mountain I am thinking of?" Volunteers respond.

- *You need to say more details.*
- *You should use descriptive words.*
- *You could talk about the snow.*
- *Maybe you could describe the color.*

Instruct students to listen to a new description to determine which photograph you are describing.

I see a tall, snowy mountain. There is so much snow that the mountain looks white! There are also brown and green trees poking up through the snow.

Ask: "Which photograph am I describing, the one from *Africa* or *Europe*?" Students chorally respond.

- *Europe!*

Instruct students to Think-Pair-Share, and ask: "Which descriptive words helped you know the photograph I was thinking of?" Call on several students to respond.

- *Snowy.*
- *White.*
- *Brown and green trees.*

Tell students that it is their turn to practice describing a natural feature. Display the photograph on page 22 of *Asia* and the photograph on page 18 of *Africa* side by side.

✔ Divide students into pairs. One student selects and describes the forest from either *Asia* or *Africa* and the other student guesses which forest is being described. Partners switch roles and repeat.

BEGIN THE EOM TASK 18 MIN.

Individuals

Explain that students will now begin working on their travel brochure for the EOM Task. Direct students to "fly" to the evidence organizer of the continent they want to write about in their brochure.

Students find a partner in their continent group and Think-Pair-Share about the following questions, using the evidence organizer and a copy of the text as a resource. Encourage students to use descriptive words to practice good verbal descriptions.

- Why did you choose this continent?

- What can people do there?

- What can people see there?

Tell students that they will respond to the following prompt to create their brochures.

> Which continent do you think people should visit?

Reference the Opinion Sandwich Anchor Chart and tell students that their brochures will contain an opinion paragraph to explain why people should visit their selected continent.

Display page 2 of Assessment 32A and explain that students will write their opinion statement on the line provided at the bottom of the pages. They will create a drawing in the box to illustrate their brochure.

Ask: "How do we write an opinion statement? How can we make sure our reader knows we are giving our opinion?" Volunteers respond.

- *We tell them what we feel or think.*

- *We can use words from the question so they know that we are answering it.*

- *We tell them when. We tell them why.*

Remind students that their travel brochure should tell other people which continent they should visit. Direct students to imagine creating a brochure to give to someone who is trying to decide which continent to travel to. Instruct students to Think-Pair-Share, and ask: "What will you tell them? What will your opinion statement say?" Use Equity Sticks to call on students to respond.

Name: _____

Assessment 32A: End-of-Module Task

Part 1
Directions: Identify the type of text for each book below. In the boxes next to each title, write an "I" for an informational text or an "S" for a storybook.

1. South America	
2. Australia	
3. Moon Rope	
4. Introducing North America	
5. Africa	
6. Why Mosquitoes Buzz in People's Ears	
7. Antarctica	
8. Europe	
9. The Story of Ferdinand	
10. Asia	
11. World Atlas	

Scaffold

Use a sentence frame to model the structure of the opinion statement. For example: **You should visit _____.**

✔ Students begin the EOM Task, Part 2 by writing and illustrating their opinion statement on page 2 of Assessment 32A. Remind students to write in a complete sentence, making sure to begin the sentence with a capital letter.

Extension

Provide simple stencils of the continents, such as the continent shapes printed out on card stock, for students to trace on the front page of their brochure. Students can also use *World Atlas* as a guide to mark natural features on the drawing of their continent.

Land 3 MIN.

ANSWER THE CONTENT FRAMING QUESTION

Play "Guess the Continent." Provide clues about a continent, pausing between each clue, and invite students to guess the continent you are describing.

If students are ready, invite a volunteer to be the clue-giver.

Wrap <small>1 MIN.</small>

ASSIGN HOMEWORK

Continue the class home-reading routine.

Context and Alignment

Students begin creating a travel brochure to express understanding of the unique natural features, animals, and things to do in the different continents (RI.K.1, W.K.1, W.K.8, L.K.1.f, L.K.2.a). Each student:

- Reflects upon text evidence gathered over the course of the module.

- Forms an opinion about which continent they would most like to visit.

- Writes and illustrates an opinion statement.

- Writes in a complete sentence including capitalizing the first letter of the sentence.

Next Steps

If students have difficulty writing an opinion statement for their brochure, engage in a role-playing activity with small groups to provide additional opportunities for verbal rehearsal. For example, use puppets to role-play a conversation between two friends, trying to decide which continent to visit:

Puppet 1: "I can't decide which continent to visit, they are all so interesting! Which continent should I visit?"

Puppet 2: "You should visit Australia. Then you could see beautiful coral reefs!"

After watching the puppets, have students take turns role-playing the conversation themselves.

⬇ LESSON 33 DEEP DIVE: VOCABULARY

Direct Vocabulary Assessment 2

- **Time:** 15 min.

- **Texts:** All Module Texts

- **Vocabulary Learning Goal:** Demonstrate understanding of grade-level vocabulary. (L.K.6)

Launch

Remind students that they have already completed a Direct Vocabulary Assessment. Explain that they will take the last Vocabulary Assessment for this module to show their understanding of some additional key words.

Learn

Distribute Assessment 33A and pencils (as needed).

Remind students that you will read a question aloud that contains the word listed beside the smiley face. If students think the answer to the question is "yes," they should draw a circle around the smiley face. If they think the answer is "no," they should draw a circle around the frowning face.

Use the teacher-facing version (with key) located in Appendix C to administer the assessment.

Be sure to always read the focus word before reading the question. Read each question twice before students fill out their answers. Circulate as students work, ensuring that they are following directions and on the correct question. Provide oral cues as necessary to help students locate the proper row and where to mark their answers.

✔ Students complete the Direct Vocabulary Assessment 2.

Land

Congratulate students on all their hard work!

■ FOCUSING QUESTION: LESSONS 32–35

What makes the world fascinating?

1 2 3 4 5 6 7 8 9 10 11 12 13 14 15 16 17 18 19 20 21 22 23 24 25 26 27 28 29 30 31 **32 33 34 35** 36

Lesson 34

TEXTS

- All Module Texts
- "The Seven Continents Song," Silly School Songs

Lesson 34: At a Glance

AGENDA

Welcome (5 min.)

Practice Fluency

Launch (5 min.)

Learn (57 min.)

Review the EOM Task (10 min.)

Verbally Rehearse Sentences for the EOM Task (12 min.)

Execute the EOM Task (35 min.)

Land (7 min.)

Answer the Content Framing Question

Wrap (1 min.)

Assign Homework

Style and Conventions Deep Dive: Excel at Opinion Writing (15 min.)

STANDARDS ADDRESSED

The full text of ELA Standards can be found in the Module Overview.

Reading

- RI.K.1

Writing

- W.K.1, W.K.8

Speaking and Listening

- SL.K.1

Language

- L.K.1.f, L.K.2.a
- ⬇ L.K.1.f

MATERIALS

- Assessment 32A: End-of-Module Task
- Handout 34A: End-of-Module Task Checklist
- Repeated Language Chart (see lesson for details)
- Sample travel brochures (paper or digital; see lesson for details)
- All module evidence organizers (excluding *Introducing North America*)
- Opinion Sandwich Anchor Chart
- Wonder Wheel

Learning Goals

Express understanding of the unique natural features, animals, and things to do on the different continents. (RI.K.1, W.K.1, W.K.8, L.K.1.f, L.K.2.a)

✔ Continue the End-of-Module Task.

⬇ With support, evaluate writing and use complete sentences to share reflections. (L.K.1.f)

✔ Reflect on completed EOM Task using complete sentences.

✔ Checks for Understanding

Prepare

FOCUSING QUESTION: Lessons 32–35

What makes the world fascinating?

CONTENT FRAMING QUESTION: Lesson 34

Know: *How do Module 4 texts build my knowledge of the continents?*

CRAFT QUESTION: Lesson 34

Execute: *How do I use complete sentences in my End-of-Module Task?*

In this lesson students continue to synthesize learning from the module as they work on the EOM Task. They use information from the evidence organizers to develop and verbally rehearse two sentences that support their opinion statement. Students then write and illustrate those sentences as part of their travel brochure.

Welcome 5 MIN.

PRACTICE FLUENCY

Display and read aloud the Repeated Language Chart for "The Seven Continents Song." Students Echo Read the chart, line by line, practicing the updated dance moves.

Play the video of "The Seven Continents Song" (**http://witeng.link/0374**). Prompt students to stand up and dance along with the song. Students say the lyrics along with the video.

Launch 5 MIN.

Instruct students to Mix and Mingle, and ask: "We have learned a lot about the world, the continents, and maps over the course of this module. What has helped you learn and explore these ideas?" Invite several students to share responses with the class.

Display and read aloud the Content Framing Question. Ask the following questions. Volunteers respond.

- How do the continent books help build your knowledge about the world?

- How do the storybooks help build your knowledge about the continents? Display copies of *The Story of Ferdinand*, *Why Mosquitoes Buzz in People's Ears*, and *Moon Rope* to reactivate students' memories, as needed.

- Which text fascinates you the most?

Learn 57 MIN.

REVIEW THE EOM TASK 10 MIN.

Whole Group

Explain that students will continue to work on their EOM Task by creating more pages for their travel brochures. Reintroduce the prompt for the EOM Task.

Which continent do you think people should visit?

Display a paper or digital sample of a travel brochure. Ask: "What do you notice about the pictures in this brochure?"

- *They are photographs.*
- *They are colorful and beautiful.*
- *They are big!*

TEACHER NOTE	Consider displaying this digital example of a travel brochure: (http://witeng.link/0446)

Ask: "Why do you think travel brochures use such big, beautiful pictures?" Volunteers respond.

- *To give details about the place.*
- *Maybe the pictures will make people want to go there.*

Encourage students to think about drawing colorful, detailed pictures on their brochures to help convince other people to travel to their selected continent.

Explain that students will share their opinion statement and drawing from the previous lesson with a classmate before they continue working on the brochure. Distribute students' completed page 2 of Assessment 32A. Pairs take turns sharing their opinion statement, giving a compliment and offering a suggestion to improve the drawing. If time permits, students may add to their drawings to improve their writing piece.

Name:

Assessment 32A: End-of-Module Task

Part 1
Directions: Identify the type of text for each book below. In the boxes next to each title, write an "I" for an informational text or an "S" for a storybook.

1.	South America	
2.	Australia	
3.	Moon Rope	
4.	Introducing North America	
5.	Africa	
6.	Why Mosquitoes Buzz in People's Ears	
7.	Antarctica	
8.	Europe	
9.	The Story of Ferdinand	
10.	Asia	
11.	World Atlas	

Scaffold

As needed, use the Sharing Our Writing Anchor Chart to review the procedure for peer-to-peer feedback.

VERBALLY REHEARSE SENTENCES FOR THE EOM TASK 12 MIN.

Pairs

Reference the Opinion Sandwich Anchor Chart, and ask: "We have completed our opinion statements. What do we need to include next in our brochures to support the opinion statement?" Volunteers respond.

- *We need to tell our reasons.*
- *We need to say why we have our opinion.*
- *We need to write details about the continent.*
- *We need to tell our opinion again, too.*

Confirm that students need to write reason sentences to support their opinion paragraph. Explain that today students will write and illustrate two reason sentences for their brochures. They will choose evidence from two of the categories on the evidence organizer (things to do, natural features, or animals).

Remind students that they are creating their brochure to give to someone to convince them to visit their selected continent. When they write their reason sentences, students should write them as if they are addressing another person. For example, a reason sentence for the continent of Africa might say, "You can see grassy savannas."

Direct students to "fly" to the evidence organizer of their selected continent. Provide time for students to examine the evidence organizer and copies of the text and decide which two pieces of evidence they would like to include in their brochures. Emphasize that students should select evidence from two different categories on the organizer.

Explain that before they begin writing, students will verbally rehearse their reason sentences. This will help them think about what they want to say and remember their sentences when they sit down to write them. Divide students into pairs, and ask: "What reasons do you have to support your opinion? What will your reason sentences say?" Pairs take turns sharing their reason sentences.

Remind students to craft sentences as if they are directly addressing another person and to use descriptive words to make their sentences more bright and vivid like the photos in the travel brochure.

Partners give a Nonverbal Signal, such as a thumbs-up or thumbs-down, to confirm if their peer used information from two different categories on the evidence organizer. Repeat the activity as needed for additional verbal rehearsal.

> ### Scaffold
>
> Provide additional support by encouraging students to use a sentence frame, such as **You can _____.**

EXECUTE THE EOM TASK 35 MIN.

Individuals

Display and read aloud the Craft Question: *How do I use complete sentences in my End-of-Module Task?*

Explain that the travel brochures should be written in complete sentences. Ask: "Why is it important to use complete sentences?"

- *Then readers know who did what.*
- *It helps our writing make sense.*
- *Then other people can understand our writing.*

Ask: "What does a complete sentence look like?" Volunteers respond.

- *It has a capital letter at the beginning.*
- *It says "who, does what."*
- *There is a period, exclamation point, or question mark at the end.*

Distribute pages 3–4 of Assessment 32A and explain that students will write one reason sentence per page, on the lines provided at the top of each page. They will create a drawing to support their sentence.

✔ Students work on their EOM Task by completing pages 3–4 of Assessment 32A. Encourage students to insert descriptive words about the things to do, natural features, and animals to add more detail to their sentences.

Extension

Pairs take turns sharing their reason sentences and drawings, giving a compliment and offering a suggestion to improve the drawing. Students add to their drawings to improve their writing piece.

Land 7 MIN.

ANSWER THE CONTENT FRAMING QUESTION

Remind students that their exploration of the world is just beginning. There is much more to explore and learn about the world!

Reference the Wonder Charts created throughout the module and emphasize that as one learns about a subject, some questions are answered and more questions often develop. Divide students into their continent groups and distribute copies of the corresponding text to each group.

Display the Wonder Wheel. Students take turns sharing new questions they have about the continent. Circulate and listen in on student questions. If time permits, use classroom resources or the Internet to research answers to several student questions.

Wrap 1 MIN.

ASSIGN HOMEWORK

Continue the class home-reading routine.

Analyze

Context and Alignment

Students create a travel brochure to express understanding of the unique natural features, animals, and things to do on the different continents (RI.K.1, W.K.1, W.K.8, L.K.1.f, L.K.2.a). Each student:

- Writes and illustrates an opinion statement.

- Writes and illustrates two supporting reason sentences.

- Writes in complete sentences using conventions of initial capitalization.

Next Steps

If students have difficulty supporting their opinion, consider the root of the problem. Are they struggling with the concept of supporting an opinion with reasons? Provide verbal practice with the sentence frame: **I think** _____ **because** _____ and emphasize the relationship between stating what you think and why you think it. Are they struggling to write supporting sentences? Provide additional practice with the evidence organizer. Ask: "Why should someone visit [continent]? What can they see there? What can they do?" Direct students to point to a piece of evidence listed on the evidence organizer. Support students with verbally stating their supporting reason using the sentence frame **You can** _____.

↓ LESSON 34 DEEP DIVE: STYLE AND CONVENTIONS

Excel at Opinion Writing

- **Time:** 15 min.

- **Text:** Student-generated travel brochures

- **Style and Conventions Learning Goal:** With support, evaluate writing and use complete sentences to share reflections. (L.K.1.f)

  STYLE AND CONVENTIONS CRAFT QUESTION: Lesson 34
  Excel: *How do I improve my opinion writing?*

Launch

TEACHER NOTE	Editing completed work is a highly sophisticated skill. Students have practiced using editing checklists at the end of each module but still may need support to do so successfully. Use your knowledge of your students to determine how much support to provide while completing these lessons.

Congratulate students on everything they have learned about writing during this module. Explain that they will look back at their EOM Task and think about how they made their travel brochure.

Post and read the Style and Conventions Craft Question.

Explain that writers use checklists as tools to be sure they have fully responded to a prompt. Distribute Handout 34A.

Learn

Remind students that they used checklists to improve their writing in all the previous modules. Ask: "What is a checklist? What do we use them for?" Volunteers respond.

Reinforce that checklists are tools to help us remember important things. Some people use checklists to make to-do lists; some people use checklists to make a grocery list. Share that authors use checklists to make sure they have included all the important parts in writing.

Name: _____

Handout 34A: End-of-Module Task Checklist

Directions: Circle ☺ Yes or ☹ Not Yet to answer each prompt.

Reading Comprehension	Self	Peer	Teacher
I used words to find evidence about the continents.	☺ Yes ☹ Not Yet	☺ Yes ☹ Not Yet	☺ Yes ☹ Not Yet
I used illustrations to find evidence about the continents.	☺ Yes ☹ Not Yet	☺ Yes ☹ Not Yet	☺ Yes ☹ Not Yet
Structure	**Self**	**Peer**	**Teacher**
I wrote an opinion statement.	☺ Yes ☹ Not Yet	☺ Yes ☹ Not Yet	☺ Yes ☹ Not Yet
I wrote two supporting reason sentences for my opinion.	☺ Yes ☹ Not Yet	☺ Yes ☹ Not Yet	☺ Yes ☹ Not Yet
I wrote an opinion conclusion by stating my opinion again.	☺ Yes ☹ Not Yet	☺ Yes ☹ Not Yet	☺ Yes ☹ Not Yet

Direct students' attention to the self-evaluation column. Explain that this is the column they will be using in this lesson.

> ### *Scaffold*
>
> Lightly shade the self-evaluation column.
>
> Remove the peer evaluation column to avoid confusion.

Ask students to use their travel brochures from the EOM Task. Explain that students will be using the checklist to check the work they have completed thus far.

Direct students' attention to the Reading Comprehension items. Explain that they will be using these criteria to check their work. Use the following steps to support students in evaluating their work:

- Echo Read each criteria.

- Prompt students with concrete questions related to each criteria to help them reflect.

- Circulate as students look for the criteria, offering support as needed.

- Instruct students to circle the "Yes" smiley face if they were able to point to that part of their writing or circle the "Not Yet" neutral face if they are unsure about whether they included that element.

Repeat for the criteria in the Style and Conventions sections.

Remind students that authors write in sentences. Ask: "What are the parts of a sentence?" Volunteers respond.

- *Who, did what.*

Remind students that authors can expand their writing. Ask: "What can we add to give more information?"

- *We can use describing words.*
- *We can tell where or when something happened.*

Instruct students to Think-Pair-Share, and ask: "Think very carefully about your writing. What was something you felt you did well?"

Remind students to start their sentences with I and then describe something they did in their writing. Encourage them to look back at their checklists.

✔ Students use complete sentences to describe what they did well in their EOM Task.

TEACHER NOTE	Students may complete the EOM Task at different rates. If students have not yet completed enough of the EOM Task to use this checklist with their own writing, use this opportunity to allow students to familiarize themselves with the different sections of the checklist and the criteria listed in each section. Circulate and provide support where needed.

Land

Ask: "What tool did we use to check our writing today?" Volunteers respond.

Reinforce that authors use checklists to be sure they have included all the important parts in their writing. Explain that students will continue checking their writing with this checklist in the next Deep Dive.

■ FOCUSING QUESTION: LESSONS 32–35

What makes the world fascinating?

1 | 2 | 3 | 4 | 5 | 6 | 7 | 8 | 9 | 10 | 11 | 12 | 13 | 14 | 15 | 16 | 17 | 18 | 19 | 20 | 21 | 22 | 23 | 24 | 25 | 26 | 27 | 28 | 29 | 30 | 31 | **32** | **33** | **34** | **35** | 36

Lesson 35

TEXTS

- All Module Texts
- "The Seven Continents Song," Silly School Songs

Lesson 35: At a Glance

AGENDA

Welcome (7 min.)

Perform Fluency

Launch (7 min.)

Learn (55 min.)

Complete the EOM Task (20 min.)

Engage in a Socratic Seminar (25 min.)

Add to the Finding Beautiful Graffiti Wall (10 min.)

Land (5 min.)

Reflect on the Module

Wrap (1 min.)

Assign Homework

Style and Conventions Deep Dive: Excel at Opinion Writing (15 min.)

STANDARDS ADDRESSED

The full text of ELA Standards can be found in the Module Overview.

Reading

- RI.K.1

Writing

- W.K.1, W.K.8

Speaking and Listening

- SL.K.1, SL.K.2, SL.K.4, SL.K.6

Language

- L.K.1.f, L.K.2.a
- ⬇ L.K.1.f

MATERIALS

- Assessment 32A: End-of-Module Task
- Handout 34A: End-of-Module Task Checklist
- Repeated Language Chart (see lesson for details)
- Talking chips
- Handout 8A: Passport Journals
- Speaking and Listening Anchor Chart
- All module evidence organizers

Learning Goals

Express understanding of the unique natural features, animals, and things to do on different continents. (RI.K.1, W.K.1, W.K.8, L.K.1.f, L.K.2.a)

✔ Complete EOM Task.

Verbally describe how a detail in one supporting reason from the EOM Task compares to a characteristic of North America. (SL.K.4, SL.K.6)

✔ Verbally describe and compare one detail from a selected continent to a characteristic of North America.

⬇ With support, evaluate writing and use complete sentences to share reflections. (L.K.1.f)

✔ Reflect on a classmate's completed EOM Task with complete sentences.

✔ Checks for Understanding

Prepare

FOCUSING QUESTION: Lessons 32–35

What makes the world fascinating?

CONTENT FRAMING QUESTION: Lesson 35

Know: *How do Module 4 texts build my knowledge of the continents?*

CRAFT QUESTION: Lesson 35

Execute: *How do I describe things in a Socratic Seminar?*

In this lesson, students apply their speaking and listening skills by presenting their EOM Task to the class. They complete their EOM Task by restating their opinion in an opinion conclusion. They then share the travel brochures they have created in small groups by reading their brochures, practicing their language skills by supporting their sentences with references to their illustrations. This reinforces to the class how visual aids add more detail to informative writing. Students demonstrate their ability to verbally describe things as they compare the continent in their brochure to North America. Finally, students reflect upon their knowledge about the continents and add to the Finding Beautiful Graffiti Wall.

Welcome   7 MIN.

PERFORM FLUENCY

Display the Repeated Language Chart of the "The Seven Continents Song."

Explain that now students will demonstrate mastery of this song by performing it for their peers. Divide the class into small groups. Give groups two minutes to practice the song together.

Without playing the video, call each group up to the front of the class. Groups perform the song using the agreed-upon hand gestures.

Launch 7 MIN.

Prompt students to take out their Passport Journals. Ask: "Why did we keep these journals? What information did we include in these journals?" Volunteers respond.

- *We kept track of what we learned.*
- *We wrote down one thing we learned.*
- *It helps us remember all that we learn.*

Remind students that thinking about the knowledge and skills they gain with each text is an important part of learning. Talking about new knowledge helps them remember what they learned and makes it easier to use and build on that knowledge in the future.

Instruct students to take a minute to turn through their Passport Journals and choose a favorite entry. Students share with a partner.

Ask: "Did you and your partner share details about the same continent or a different continent?" Volunteers respond. "What does that tell you about an opinion?" Volunteers respond.

Explain that in this lesson students will complete their work with the EOM Task and share their travel brochure. They will be able to see if other members of their class shared their opinion or had a different opinion!

Learn 55 MIN.

COMPLETE THE EOM TASK 20 MIN.

Individuals

Students take out pages 2–4 of Assessment 32A. Instruct students to share their opinion statement, supporting reason sentences, and drawings with their partner.

Explain that they will now complete their EOM Task by restating their opinion in their opinion conclusion.

Name: _____

Assessment 32A: End-of-Module Task

Part 1
Directions: Identify the type of text for each book below. In the boxes next to each title, write an "I" for an informational text or an "S" for a storybook.

1.	South America	
2.	Australia	
3.	Moon Rope	
4.	Introducing North America	
5.	Africa	
6.	Why Mosquitoes Buzz in People's Ears	
7.	Antarctica	
8.	Europe	
9.	The Story of Ferdinand	
10.	Asia	
11.	World Atlas	

Scaffold

If needed, display the Opinion Sandwich Anchor Chart to remind students of the structure of their paragraph.

Ask: "What does it mean to restate an opinion? How can we do that?" Volunteers respond.

- *It means to say it again.*
- *You can use the same words.*
- *Or, you can use different words.*
- *You can change a descriptive word.*

Ask: "Why do we restate our opinion? Volunteers respond.

- *It is to show our paragraph is over.*
- *We need a conclusion.*
- *It makes an ending.*

Reinforce that an opinion paragraph has an opinion conclusion statement to signal to readers that the paragraph is ending. It also reinforces the opinion statement, which is the main topic of the paragraph.

Ask: "Is an opinion conclusion a complete sentence? How can we make sure it is a complete sentence?" Volunteers respond.

- *We say who does what.*
- *We have a capital letter at the front.*
- *We can put a period or an exclamation point at the end if we want.*

Explain that now they will share their opinion statement again with their partner. Students rehearse their opinion conclusion sentence by verbally restating their opinion. Remind students to use the "who, does what" structure to create a complete sentence.

✔ Distribute the last page of Assessment 32A. Students complete their EOM Task by restating their opinion in an opinion conclusion sentence. Students use complete sentences and capitalize the first letter in the sentence. Students include a drawing to serve as the back cover of their travel brochure.

TEACHER NOTE	As students finish, staple the pages of their brochure together. Students will use these in the next part of the lesson.

ENGAGE IN A SOCRATIC SEMINAR 25 MIN.

Small Groups

Tell students that now they will reflect upon their learning about the continents through a presentation and a Socratic Seminar.

Explain that they will present their brochures aloud to their classmates. This will be a chance for them to show the thinking that went into their work, as well as demonstrate their speaking skills and language abilities.

Instruct students to stand up and, with their travel brochure in hand, "fly" to the evidence organizer for the continent they wrote about in their EOM Task. Divide the class into small groups of four to six, creating groups by pulling one student from each continent.

TEACHER NOTE	Numbers need not be even for each group. The purpose is for students to share with some peers who wrote about a different continent and hear diverse answers.

Explain that now students will take turns sharing their travel brochure with their groups. Model how to share a brochure. For example, using a student's travel brochure as a guide, model reading the sentences, and describing the details in the drawing. Make connections between the supporting reason sentences and the details in the drawing.

Refer back to the Speaking and Listening Anchor Chart and review the important skills that will help students with presenting, such as using a strong voice and listening with their senses.

Students share their travel brochure with their groups. Circulate as needed to help groups navigate how to share in an organized way.

Display and read aloud the Craft Question: *How do I describe things in a Socratic Seminar?*

Ask: "How do we describe things when we speak? How does that help our listeners?" Volunteers respond.

- *We can say what it looks like.*
- *We can use descriptive words.*
- *We can talk about the special details.*
- *It helps our reader learn more and know what we are talking about.*

Use responses to explain that students will verbally describe details about the continents to show their understanding during today's Socratic Seminar.

Display the Speaking and Listening Anchor Chart and highlight the speaking skill students will focus on during the Socratic Seminar: Speak to describe.

As needed, model how to use talking chips to aid discussion:

- Sit in a semicircle with several volunteers, and model how to take turns speaking and listening.

- Each person has one talking chip in front of them.

- When a student is ready to share, they pick up a chip.

- After sharing, the student places the chip in the middle of the circle.

- Only one person can be holding a chip at a time.

- All students use their chips before the process starts again.

Write the first Socratic Seminar question on the board: Think about your home continent, North America. How is North America similar to the continent in your brochure?

Students Echo Read the question.

✔ Groups use talking chips to have conversations about their continent in their brochure and North America. Display the Evidence Organizer for *Introducing North America* in a central location and place a few copies of *Introducing North America* in the center of each circle to support students as they describe.

Scaffold

If needed, review how to identify a similarity and a difference between two topics.

Circulate and record anecdotal notes using the Speaking and Listening Rubric as a guide (see Appendix C).

Midway through the seminar, stop to call attention to the next discussion question: How is North America different from the continent in your brochure?

Small groups use talking chips to discuss the question.

Reread the speaking goal from the Speaking and Listening Anchor Chart. Students use Nonverbal Signals (thumbs-up, thumbs-sideways, thumbs-down) to self-assess the conversations they had. Use anecdotal notes to share notable discussions from the small groups.

ADD TO THE FINDING BEAUTIFUL GRAFFITI WALL 10 MIN.

Individuals

Instruct students to Think-Pair-Share, and ask: "What is something you learned about the continents that you did not know before?" Use Equity Sticks to call on students to answer. Encourage students to think about the texts and the module artifacts.

Instruct students to Mix and Mingle, and ask: "What is something beautiful that you learned in your study of the continents? What is something that is important that you think you should share?" Instead of sharing aloud with the class, students approach the Finding Beautiful Graffiti Wall and draw their answers on the wall.

Land 5 MIN.

REFLECT ON THE MODULE

Post and read the Essential Question. Ask: "What do you think makes the world fascinating?" Volunteers respond.

Ask: "If people are not able to travel the world and visit these places, how can they learn more about the continents and the world?" Volunteers respond.

- *They can read about them.*
- *They can look at maps.*
- *They can look at pictures.*
- *We can tell them about the world.*

Emphasize that the world is a large place—there is so much to learn and you can start anywhere on earth. Encourage students to share their knowledge with others and to continue to collect information about the beauty of the continents, much of which lies in the differences between them.

Wrap 1 MIN.

ASSIGN HOMEWORK

Continue the class home-reading routine.

Analyze

Context and Alignment

Students demonstrate their speaking and listening skills as well as their knowledge of the continents in a Socratic Seminar (RI.K.1, SL.K.4). Each student:

- Shares their EOM Task.
- Verbally describes one similarity between their chosen continent and North America.
- Verbally describes one difference between their chosen continent and North America.

Next Steps

If students have difficulty identifying both a similarity and a difference, allow them to focus on only one comparison. The purpose of this Socratic Seminar is for students to demonstrate their ability to verbally describe familiar people, places, or things. Encourage students to use descriptive words by asking questions such as: "What words can we use to give more detail about this [thing to do/natural feature/animal]?" Support students by helping them locate examples in *Introducing North America* and relating the examples to one of their supporting reason sentences.

⬇ LESSON 35 DEEP DIVE: STYLE AND CONVENTIONS

Excel at Opinion Writing

- **Time:** 15 min.

- **Text:** Student-generated travel brochures

- **Style and Conventions Learning Goal:** With support, evaluate writing and use complete sentences to share reflections. (L.K.1.f)

> **STYLE AND CONVENTIONS CRAFT QUESTION: Lesson 35**
> Excel: *How do I improve my opinion writing?*

Launch

Distribute partially completed Handout 34A. Ask: "What did we use this checklist for?" Volunteers respond. Reinforce that a checklist is a tool that authors use to make sure they have included all the important parts in their writing.

Post and read the Style and Conventions Craft Question.

Explain that students will repeat the same process from the previous Deep Dive to check their writing.

Learn

Distribute completed Assessments 32A. Instruct students to place their fingers on the Self-Evaluation column on Handout 34A.

Direct student attention to the Structure items. Explain that they will be using these criteria to check their work. Use the following steps to support students in evaluating their work:

- Echo Read each criteria.

- Prompt students with concrete questions related to each criteria to help them reflect.

- Circulate as students look for the criteria, offering support as needed.

- Instruct students to circle the "Yes" smiley face if they were able to point to that part of their writing or circle the "Not Yet" neutral face if they are unsure about whether they included that element.

If needed, review the criteria discussed in the Conventions section.

Explain that authors ask other authors to evaluate their work as well. This way they get even more information about how to improve their writing.

Organize students into pairs. Instruct students to exchange their completed EOM Tasks. Students will look at their classmate's travel brochure and give a compliment based on one checklist criterion. Circulate, providing support and prompting as needed.

✔ Use Equity Sticks to call on students to share reflections. Students use complete sentences to describe what a classmate did well on their EOM Task.

Land

Congratulate students on all of the wonderful reading and writing they have done during this module and in all the modules. Express pride in all the hard work they have accomplished.

What is the story of the year?

1 | 2 | 3 | 4 | 5 | 6 | 7 | 8 | 9 | 10 | 11 | 12 | 13 | 14 | 15 | 16 | 17 | 18 | 19 | 20 | 21 | 22 | 23 | 24 | 25 | 26 | 27 | 28 | 29 | 30 | 31 | 32 | 33 | 34 | 35 | **36**

Lesson 36

TEXTS

- All Module 1–4 Core Texts
- *The Cornell Farm*, Edward Hicks (**http://witeng.link/0179**)
- *Washington Crossing the Delaware*, Emanuel Leutze (**http://witeng.link/0205**)
- *Carta Marina*, Olaus Magnus (**http://witeng.link/0409**)

Lesson 36: At a Glance

AGENDA

Welcome (6 min.)

Define Wonder

Launch (8 min.)

Learn (56 min.)

Reflect on the Module Texts (26 min.)

Add to the Finding Beautiful Graffiti Wall (15 min.)

Reflect on the Module Art (15 min.)

Land (4 min.)

Answer the Content Framing Question

Wrap (1 min.)

Assign Homework

STANDARDS ADDRESSED

The full text of ELA Standards can be found in the Module Overview.

Reading

- RL.K.1, RI.K.1

Writing

- W.K.8

Speaking and Listening

- SL.K.1, SL.K.2, SL.K.4

Language

- L.K.2.c, L.K.2.d

MATERIALS

- Speaking and Listening Anchor Chart

- Large sticky notes

Learning Goals

Reflect on learning over the course of the year and verbally describe something from a text that sparked a sense of wonder. (RI.K.1, RL.K.1, SL.K.2, SL.K.4)

✔ Verbally share and describe one detail from a module text that made you want to learn more.

Draw and label one detail from a module text that sparks a sense of wonder. (RI.K.1, RL.K.1, W.K.8, L.K.2.c, L.K.2.d)

✔ Add to the Finding Beautiful Graffiti Wall.

✔ Checks for Understanding

FOCUSING QUESTION: Lesson 36

What is the story of the year?

CONTENT FRAMING QUESTION: Lesson 36

Know: *How do this year's texts build my knowledge?*

In this capstone lesson, students reflect back on their year's learning journey. They begin by exploring the multiple meanings of *wonder*, and consider how the topics of each module have provoked emotions of wonder and curiosity. Next, students hone in on individual module texts as they rotate through stations and think about the texts they found most fascinating. They add a reflective thought about a module text to the Finding Beautiful Graffiti Wall. In closing, students look at selections of the year's artwork and consider how art can also spark a sense of wonder.

Welcome 6 MIN.

DEFINE *WONDER*

TEACHER NOTE	Consider reading *Last Stop on Market Street* prior to the start of the lesson to anchor the concept of *wonder* and refresh the idea of the Finding Beautiful Graffiti Wall. CJ's grandmother's infectious sense of wonder and the quest or desire to learn more about the world has been a unifying thread throughout the modules this year.

Write the word *wonder* where students can see it and read it aloud. Instruct students to Think-Pair-Share, and ask: "What do you think about when you hear the word *wonder*?" Call on several students to respond.

- *I think about our Wonder Charts.*
- *I think about asking questions.*

Confirm that when people <u>wonder</u> about something they are curious and often ask questions to get more information. Students have shared the questions they wonder about many texts and topics over the course of the year.

Explain that *wonder* is also a feeling. When a person feels wonder, they feel surprised and happy because of something that is beautiful, unexpected, or mysterious. Share an example to provide context, such as:

> **Close your eyes. Now imagine that you are at a birthday party. Imagine seeing children wearing birthday hats. Imagine hearing the sound of laughter. Now, imagine that you see a man at the party holding something small and blue. Picture yourself walking up to the man to get a closer look. What is he doing with that blue thing? As you get closer you hear a hissing noise. Then you see the blue getting bigger and bigger! As you step closer you see the man start to bend and twist the thing in his hands faster than your eyes can keep track of. Finally, the man hands you a beautiful puppy, created from a blue balloon! Now, open your eyes.**

Ask: "How did you feel as you imagined that story?" Volunteers respond.

- *I felt excited!*
- *It made me feel curious about what was happening.*
- *I felt happy.*
- *I felt amazed!*

Explain that the feeling of happy surprise and amazement is the feeling of wonder. People might feel wonder because of something they see, or something they learn. Wonder helps students learn and grow because it awakens their curiosity and prompts them to keep asking questions.

Tell students that today they will think about the topics they have explored this year and the books they have read. They will reflect upon how the topics and books filled them with wonder.

Launch 8 MIN.

Remind students of the topics they have explored this year. Post and read aloud the Essential Question from each module, as listed below. After reading each question, pause to ask: "What is something special or important you remember from our lessons on this topic?" Volunteers respond.

- How do our senses help us learn?
- What makes a good story?
- How has life in America changed over time?
- What makes the world fascinating?

Instruct students to Mix and Mingle, and ask: "Which topic most filled you with wonder, and made you curious to learn more?"

Display and read aloud the Content Framing Question. Explain that students will look back over the texts from the module, to reflect on their Kindergarten journey of learning and wonder.

Learn 56 MIN.

REFLECT ON THE MODULE TEXTS 26 MIN.

Small Groups

Prior to beginning the lesson, group all the texts by module, and place each set of module texts in a different location around the room. Tell students that they will do a Gallery Walk to examine and briefly flip through the module texts to remind themselves of all the details in the books.

Explain that as they rotate through each module station, they will reflect upon the texts by answering the following questions:

- What text from this module excites a sense of wonder?

- What in that text fascinates you and makes you excited to learn more?

Display the Speaking and Listening Anchor Chart. Point to various criteria that might help them engage with their group, such as "have conversations," "give an example," and "speak to describe." Remind students that giving an example and verbally describing that example allows their audience to understand what they are trying to say.

Model an example using one of the module texts.

> **(Holding up a copy of a module text, for example *Transportation Then and Now*.) I think this text is so interesting! When I look at this text I want to read it again. This text makes me want to learn more about the different cars over time. I wonder how they went from using horses to using cars because they are so different. I am excited to learn more about transportation and how it changed over time.**

💬 Divide the class into small groups and direct groups to one set of module texts, with one group per module. Give students approximately six to seven minutes at each station. After about three minutes, instruct students to turn to a partner and discuss the previous questions.

✔ Students rotate through the module stations. Students verbally share and describe something from a module text at that station that gives them a sense of wonder or makes them excited to learn more.

After students rotate through each module station, use Equity Sticks to call on one student from each group to share one of their answers.

ADD TO THE FINDING BEAUTIFUL GRAFFITI WALL 15 MIN.

Individuals

Explain that now that they have reflected upon, or thought about, all the module texts, they will catalog this learning by recording one example on the Finding Beautiful Graffiti Wall. Display a copy of *Last Stop on Market Street* and remind students that CJ's grandma taught him how to find beauty in all kinds of experiences and places. Ask: "How might something that is beautiful give us a feeling of wonder? What have you seen or learned this year that has given you a sense of wonder?" Volunteers respond.

Pose the questions again and instruct students to think quietly to themselves for one minute about their answers.

Give each student a large sticky note. Students stand up and walk to the module station that contains the module text they would like to write about.

✔ Students record one detail from a module text that gives them a sense of wonder or makes them excited to learn more about that topic. Students add their answers to the Finding Beautiful Graffiti Wall.

REFLECT ON THE MODULE ART 15 MIN.

Small Groups

Ask: "What have you enjoyed about looking at the various pieces of art throughout the modules?" Volunteers respond.

Ask: "How is a piece of art different than a storybook or informational text?" Volunteers respond.

- *There are no words.*
- *There is only one picture.*
- *Books have lots of pictures and words.*
- *In paintings you have to learn through what you see.*

Use responses to reinforce that a painting often shows one moment in time; it does not have a picture before it that tells what happens before, or one right after—nor does it have words to tell you what is going on.

Display the paintings *Washington Crossing the Delaware*, *The Cornell Farm*, and *Carta Marina* in front of the class. Ask: "How do we know what is happening in these paintings?" Volunteers respond.

- *We can look at the different parts of the painting, like the background.*
- *We can look at what people or animals are doing.*
- *We can use our imagination.*

Reinforce that the artists are not here to answer their questions; they must use their senses to learn what they can from the painting and then use their imagination to think about what is happening.

Instruct students to Think-Pair-Share, and ask: "How do paintings give you a sense of wonder? How do they excite you and make you want to learn more?" Use Equity Sticks to call on three students to answer.

Explain that now they will use this sense of wonder and curiosity to think about "what happens next?" in these paintings. In small groups, they will create a Tableau of their assigned painting. Then, as a group, they will act out what they think happens next!

Divide the class into small groups and assign each group one of the three paintings. Give groups five minutes to practice their Tableaux. After five minutes, pose the question: "What happens next in your painting?" Give groups three more minutes to discuss the question and agree upon a plan for their Moving Tableaux. Circulate as groups discuss and practice to provide support.

Call groups one at a time to come up to the front of the room. Each group performs a Tableau of their assigned painting. Then, prompt groups to stop their Tableau and act out what they think happens next in this scene. After each group finishes, ask: "Why do you think that happens next? What detail in the painting filled you with wonder about what happens next?" Use Equity Sticks to call on one or two group members to answer.

Land 4 MIN.

ANSWER THE CONTENT FRAMING QUESTION

Instruct students to Think-Pair-Share, and ask: "How has wondering or asking questions helped you learn? How can wondering open doors to new ideas and learning?" Volunteers respond.

Instruct students to Think-Pair-Share, and ask: "How will you wonder going forward?" Volunteers respond.

Wrap 1 MIN.

ASSIGN HOMEWORK

Continue the class home-reading routine.

Analyze

Context and Alignment

Students reflect on how all the module texts have built their knowledge. Each student:

- Examines all the module texts as they reflect on what brought them a sense of wonder or prompted them to want to learn more.

- Selects one detail that made them curious or happy to learn more.

- Draws and labels one detail that made them curious or happy to learn more.

Next Steps

If students have difficulty choosing something from the text, allow them to reflect upon what they learned from the module and why they would like to learn more about that topic.

Use this time to reflect upon your own practice. What surprised you about student answers in this lesson? How does that inform your teaching going forward? This can be a group activity as well. Encourage students to think about what they hope to learn more about next year, and consider: do they have any advice for students entering Kindergarten next year?

*Note that there is no Deep Dive in this lesson. Use any additional time to support practice of the vocabulary and/or style and conventions skills introduced in the module.

Appendix A: Text Complexity

Great Minds carefully selects module texts that are both content-rich and complex. Module texts, especially the core texts, must be appropriately challenging so students develop their literacy skills and make progress toward Anchor Standard for Reading 10 by the end of the year. Each module core text is evaluated using quantitative and qualitative criteria as outlined in both the Appendix A **(http://witeng.link/0093)** and the Supplement to Appendix A **(http://witeng.link/0483)** in the CCSS.

Title and Author	*Africa, Antarctica, Asia, Australia, Europe, South America*, Rebecca Hirsch	
Description of Text	These texts introduce readers to the different continents with parallel sections in each text on geographical features, populations, native animals, and modern marvels.	
Complexity Ratings	**Quantitative:**	**Qualitative:**
	410L–500L	Meaning/Purpose: Simple, engaging text and colorful, mesmerizing pictures teach about land features, populations, native animals, technological advances, and more–including how to find each continent on a map.
		Structure: The books employ a predictable structure with photographs on the left and text on the right, making these texts very accessible. Each photo has a caption under it to explain what is happening in the photo. Headings are in blue font.
		Language: Simple sentence structure with two or three sentences on a page allows students to process the information presented to them.
		Knowledge: As students learn the definition of a continent and where it is in relationship to the others, they may require support to help compare and categorize new information.

Title and Author	*Introducing North America*, Chris Oxlade
Description of Text	This book introduces young readers to the continent of North America through age-appropriate maps, engaging photographs, and simple text. Topics covered within the book include the location of the continent; the climate, geography, natural resources, animals and plants of the continent; and the continent's countries, people, languages, cities, and famous places.

Complexity Ratings	**Quantitative:**	**Qualitative:**
	730L	Meaning/Purpose: This nonfiction text, through its differing structure, gives another angle on learning about what is likely to be the most familiar continent of all for young students.
		Structure: Text features such as bolded words, headings, map inserts, and captions are set apart from the text itself. Photographs offer concrete examples of information discussed in the text.
		Language: The text uses many possibly unfamiliar words in context, including *plains*, *swamps*, *prairie*, and *mountain range*. Proper nouns and descriptive words such as *variety*, *tropical*, *vast*, and *famous* may prove difficult.
		Knowledge: Some places are mentioned but not pictured. It will be difficult for students to picture unfamiliar places without an illustration or photo. Students may require support understanding how the text's many sections work together to describe a diverse continent.

Title and Author	*Moon Rope*, Lois Ehlert
Description of Text	Fox wants to go to the moon. Mole is not interested in a trip to the moon until he hears about large worms up there, waiting to be eaten. With help from a rope of grass and some friends, they set off on an adventure to the moon. Bilingual text and bold art add to the meaning of this enchanting tale.

Complexity Ratings	**Quantitative:**	**Qualitative:**
	430L	Meaning/Purpose: This folktale addresses the theme of achieving a goal; it also explains why moles stay underground. Students add this tale to their banks of origin stories and analyze the Peruvian art in the illustrations.
		Structure: This follows a conventional story structure with characters that want something and must solve problems to achieve a goal.
		Language: This is a bilingual English/Spanish book. The English throughout is straightforward and age appropriate.
		Knowledge: The unusual illustrations are inspired by Peruvian textiles, jewelry, ceramics, sculpture, and architecture. Students will use their exposure to South America and Peruvian textiles to better understand the story.

Title and Author	*The Story of Ferdinand*, Munro Leaf; Illustrations, Robert Lawson
Description of Text	This is the story of a bull named Ferdinand who lives in Spain. All the other bulls would run and jump and butt their heads together, but Ferdinand prefers to sit and smell flowers. He is able to do just that until the day a bumblebee and some men from the Madrid bullfights give gentle Ferdinand a chance to go to Madrid and become a star of the *corrida*.

| Complexity Ratings | Quantitative:

710L | **Qualitative:**

Meaning/Purpose: This story is not only enchanting and entertaining but conveys the message that it is acceptable, and perhaps even desirable, to be different. Along with a few other fictional tales from around the world, this storybook adds some cultural enhancement to the informational texts, which form the structure of the module.

Structure: The text has a simple chronological structure, and is well-supported by detailed black and white illustrations that help to tell the story in greater detail.

Language: Conversational language engages the reader, though some vocabulary is specific to Spanish culture: *cork tree, bullfight, Madrid, Banderilleros, Matadors*, and *Picadores*.

Knowledge: Students likely will not have background knowledge about the tradition and violence of bullfighting. Without teacher support, they may not understand why all the other bulls would want to go to a bullfight or be able to understand why Ferdinand is not interested. |

Title and Author	*Why Mosquitoes Buzz in People's Ears*, Verna Aardema; Illustrations, Leo and Diane Dillon
Description of Text	A mosquito brags to an iguana that he spied a farmer digging yams as big as mosquitoes. The iguana, upset by the mosquito's tall tales, refuses to listen to any more nonsense. Grumbling, he puts sticks in his ears and goes about his daily business, setting off a chain reaction among animals in the community.

Complexity Ratings	Quantitative:	Qualitative:
	770L	Meaning/Purpose: This origin story told through an unbelievable chain of events attempts to explain why mosquitoes buzz in people's ears and sheds light on the amazing animals and landscape of Africa.
		Structure: This text presents a common narrative situation where one misunderstanding leads to a series of events. The solution comes about when the problem is better understood. The illustrations add detail to the text and provide reader with an exaggerated perspective of each animal. Brilliant colors with arresting patterns reflect the richness of African animal diversity as well as storytelling.
		Language: This narrative text includes dialogue between the iguana and the other animals in the story. The author also uses unfamiliar words to describe the way that each animal moves: *mek, mek, mek; wasawusu, wasawusu, wasawusu*. Vivid vocabulary adds urgency to the story.
		Knowledge: Students may need support reversing the sequence of events to understand the underlying cause of all the turmoil in the jungle–and also perceiving that this is a fiction text. Students use the illustrations to make sense of the events, but also learn how illustrations can represent a characters perspective and exaggerate the story.

Title and Author	*World Atlas*, Nick Crane; Illustrations, David Dean
Description of Text	Divided by geographic region, this text looks at the way the natural world has shaped communities and cultures, as well as looking at the ideas and initiatives which will shape the future. It shows how all parts of the planet are interconnected and looks at the challenges people face in various regions of the world.

Complexity Ratings	Quantitative:	Qualitative:
	1180L	Meaning/Purpose: The text provides a counterpoint to the smaller individual continent books used in the model, reinforcing some information, providing new information in some instances, and giving a different visual perspective through drawn maps.
		Structure: The text contains complex sentences and punctuation. Labels and map features make the information more accessible to students.
		Language: Complex language (such as with the suffixes *-est*: *largest, remotest*) as well as directional words such as *southeast* and north may challenge students.
		Knowledge: The text references some concepts that may require teacher support, such as continents, population, and land forms such as plateau, fertile belt, plain, desert, and peaks. The scale of maps and landforms might also need to be addressed.

Appendix B: Vocabulary

Wit & Wisdom focuses on teaching and learning words from texts. Students develop an awareness of how words are built, how they function within sentences, and how word choice affects meaning and reveals an author's purpose.

The purpose of vocabulary study in *Wit & Wisdom* is to achieve the following three key student outcomes:

- Improve comprehension of complex texts.
- Increase students' knowledge of words and word parts (including affixes, Latin or Greek roots, etc.).
- Increase students' ability to solve for unknown words on their own.

To achieve these outcomes, vocabulary study in *Wit & Wisdom* emphasizes the following three categories of vocabulary words:

- **Content-Specific Vocabulary:** Necessary for understanding a central idea of the domain-specific text and/or module topic).
- **Academic Vocabulary:** "High-priority" words that can be used across disciplines and are likely to be encountered in other texts. Often abstract and with multiple meanings, these words are unlikely to be known by students with limited vocabularies.
- **Text-Critical Vocabulary:** Words and phrases that are essential to students' understanding of a particular text or excerpt.

Vocabulary study in *Wit & Wisdom* will occur within the following types of instruction:

- **Core 75-min. daily lessons:** Vocabulary study that is essential to understanding the text at-hand. Instructional strategies are explicitly introduced and practiced during vocabulary instruction and put into practice during a reading of a text.
- **Vocabulary Deep Dives:** Vocabulary instruction and practice that advances students' knowledge of high-value words and word-solving strategies, focusing on aspects such as abstract or multiple meanings, connotation, relationships across words, and morphology.

Vocabulary learning is **assessed indirectly** through application, and **directly** through two-question assessments (K–2) and sentence assessments (Grades 3–8).

- **Indirect Assessment:** Students are expected to use and incorporate words from the below list into their academic discourse, through speaking and listening (during Socratic Seminars) and writing (during formal writing tasks, such as the EOM Task).
- **Direct Assessment:** Students' word knowledge will also be evaluated directly through definition assessments. Assessment words are selected because of their importance to the module's content as well as their relevance and transferability to other texts and subject areas. Teachers should make this list of assessed words available to students. (List of assessment words can also be broken down into smaller word banks for ease of use.)

MODULE WORD LIST

The following is a complete list of all words taught and practiced in the module. Those that are assessed, directly or indirectly, are indicated.

World Atlas, Nick Crane; Illustrations, David Dean

Lesson	Word	Content-Specific	Academic	Text Critical	Teaching Strategy	Assessment
1	world	✓	✓	✓	Module Word Wall Nonverbal Signal	
1, 1 DD	continent	✓	✓	✓	Module Word Wall Categorization	Direct Vocabulary Assessment 1 DD 26
1, 8	map	✓	✓	✓	Module Word Wall Student-generated definition	
1 DD	ocean	✓	✓	✓	Module Word Wall Categorization	
8	atlas	✓	✓	✓	Module Word Wall Teacher-provided definition	

Asia, Rebecca Hirsch

Lesson	Word	Content-Specific	Academic	Text Critical	Teaching Strategy	Assessment
2	wild		✓	✓	Teacher-provided definition	
2	monsoon			✓	TDQ Student-generated definition	

Lesson	Word	Content-Specific	Academic	Text Critical	Teaching Strategy	Assessment
2 DD, 6	tallest		✓		Identify opposite Teacher-provided definition	Direct Vocabulary Assessment 1 DD 26
2 DD	busy		✓		Identify opposite	
2 DD	strong		✓		Identify opposite	
2 DD	heavy		✓		Identify opposite	
2 DD	cold		✓		Identify opposite	
2 DD	dry		✓		Identify opposite	
4	modern		✓	✓	TDQ Student-generated definition	
4	marvel		✓	✓	Teacher-provided definition	
4	dunes		✓	✓	Text clues Student-generated definition	
4	mountain		✓	✓	Text clues Student-generated definition	
6	unique		✓	✓	Teacher-provided definition	

The Story of Ferdinand, Munro Leaf; Illustrations, Robert Lawson

Lesson	Word	Content-Specific	Academic	Text Critical	Teaching Strategy	Assessment
3	pasture		✓	✓	Teacher-provided definition	
3 DD	sit		✓	✓	Act out opposite	
3 DD	pick		✓	✓	Act out opposite	
3 DD	shout		✓	✓	Act out opposite	
5 DD, 6 DD	stick		✓	✓	Multiple-meaning word Act out shades of meaning	Direct Vocabulary Assessment 1 DD 26
5 DD	horns		✓	✓	Multiple-meaning word	
6 DD	touch		✓	✓	Act out shades of meaning	
6 DD	poke		✓	✓	Act out shades of meaning	

Europe, Rebecca Hirsch

Lesson	Word	Content-Specific	Academic	Text Critical	Teaching Strategy	Assessment
5	language	✓	✓	✓	TDQ Teacher-provided definition	
5	custom	✓	✓	✓	TDQ Teacher-provided definition	

Lesson	Word	Content-Specific	Academic	Text Critical	Teaching Strategy	Assessment
5	waterway		✓	✓	TDQ Teacher-provided definition	
7	interesting	✓	✓	✓	Student-generated definition	

Africa, Rebecca Hirsch

Lesson	Word	Content-Specific	Academic	Text Critical	Teaching Strategy	Assessment
9 DD	hot		✓	✓	Match opposites	
9 DD	wet		✓	✓	Match opposites	
9 DD	wild		✓	✓	Match opposites	
9 DD, 13	amazing		✓	✓	Match opposites Text evidence	Direct Vocabulary Assessment 1 DD 26
11	dry		✓	✓	Text evidence TDQ	
11	few		✓	✓	Text evidence TDQ	
11	rainforest		✓	✓	Text evidence TDQ	
11 DD	work		✓	✓	Act out opposite	
11 DD	grow		✓	✓	Act out opposite	
11 DD	climb		✓	✓	Act out opposite	

Antarctica, Rebecca Hirsch

Lesson	Word	Content-Specific	Academic	Text Critical	Teaching Strategy	Assessment
10 DD	rocky		✓	✓	Text evidence Opposites	
10 DD	tall		✓	✓	Text evidence Opposites	
10 DD, 12	thick		✓	✓	Text evidence Opposites TDQ	
10 DD, 12	giant		✓	✓	Text evidence Opposites TDQ	Direct Vocabulary Assessment 1 DD 26
12	fierce		✓	✓	Text evidence TDQ	
12 DD	blow		✓	✓	Act out shades of meaning	
12 DD	swirl		✓	✓	Act out shades of meaning	
12 DD	flow		✓	✓	Act out shades of meaning	

Why Mosquitoes Buzz in People's Ears: A West African Tale, Verna Aardema; Illustrations, Leo and Diane Dillon

Lesson	Word	Content-Specific	Academic	Text Critical	Teaching Strategy	Assessment
16, 16 DD, 18 DD	lumbered		✓	✓	Teacher-provided definition Multiple-meaning word Act out opposites	FQT Lesson 21

Lesson	Word	Content-Specific	Academic	Text Critical	Teaching Strategy	Assessment
16	terrified		✓	✓	Text evidence Teacher provided definition	
16	burrow		✓	✓	Text evidence Teacher-provided definition	
16 DD	bear		✓	✓	Multiple-meaning word	
17 DD, 18 DD	returned		✓	✓	Analyzing word parts Text evidence Act out opposite	Direct Vocabulary Assessment 1 DD 26
18	mischief		✓	✓	Text evidence Teacher-provided definition	
18	fetch		✓	✓	Text evidence Student-generated definition	
18	timid		✓	✓	Text evidence Student-generated definition	
18 DD, 19	scurried		✓	✓	Act out opposite Teacher-provided definition TDQ	FQT Lesson 21
19	slithering		✓	✓	Text evidence Teacher-provided definition	

Lesson	Word	Content-Specific	Academic	Text Critical	Teaching Strategy	Assessment
19	bounded		✓	✓	Teacher-provided definition TDQ	
19	leaping		✓	✓	Teacher-provided definition TDQ	
19 DD	uncertainly				Analyzing word parts Text evidence	
20 DD	snap		✓	✓	Multiple-meaning word	
20 DD	mind		✓	✓	Multiple-meaning word	

Australia, Rebecca Hirsch

Lesson	Word	Content-Specific	Academic	Text Critical	Teaching Strategy	Assessment
22 DD, 26	unusual		✓	✓	Analyze word parts Text evidence Examples	Direct Vocabulary Assessment 2 DD 33
24	coral reef			✓	Text evidence Student-generated definition	
26	island	✓	✓		Teacher-provided definition	
26	pouch		✓	✓	Text evidence Student-generated definition	

Moon Rope, Lois Ehlert

Lesson	Word	Content-Specific	Academic	Text Critical	Teaching Strategy	Assessment
23	go		✓		Opposites	New-Read Assessment 2
23	unnoticed		✓	✓	Analyzing word parts	New-Read Assessment 2
23	mad		✓		Opposites	New-Read Assessment 2
23	land		✓	✓	Multiple-meaning word	New-Read Assessment 2
23 DD	hitch		✓	✓	Act out shades of meaning	Direct Vocabulary Assessment 2 DD 33
23 DD	hang		✓	✓	Act out shades of meaning	

South America, Rebecca Hirsch

Lesson	Word	Content-Specific	Academic	Text Critical	Teaching Strategy	Assessment
25	pair		✓		TDQ Student-generated definition	Direct Vocabulary Assessment 2 DD 33
25	textiles		✓		Teacher-provided definition	

Introducing North America, Chris Oxlade

Lesson	Word	Content-Specific	Academic	Text Critical	Teaching Strategy	Assessment
28	introduce		✓	✓	Student-generated definition	
29	culture		✓	✓	Teacher-provided definition	
30	geography	✓	✓	✓	Text evidence Teacher-provided definition	Direct Vocabulary Assessment 2 DD 33
30	flat		✓	✓	Text evidence Student-generated definition	
30, 31 DD	lakes		✓	✓	Text evidence Student-generated definition Categorization	Direct Vocabulary Assessment 2 DD 33
30, 31 DD	rivers		✓	✓	Text evidence Student-generated definition Categorization	
31 DD	mountains		✓	✓	Categorization	
31 DD	deserts		✓	✓	Categorization	Direct Vocabulary Assessment 2 DD 33

Words to Know

Understanding vocabulary and building background knowledge are essential for students' comprehension of complex text. *Wit & Wisdom* students study topics for an extended period of time, building background knowledge. However, students may need additional support with unfamiliar vocabulary as they access complex text.

The words listed here may pose a challenge to student comprehension. Provide definitions or a glossary for these challenging words so students will comprehend complex text. Use a free resource such as Wordsmyth **(http://witeng.link/glossary)** to generate glossaries for students.

Asia, Rebecca Hirsch

- countries (5)
- cities (9)
- factories (11)
- villages (13)

The Story of Ferdinand, Munro Leaf; Illustrations, Robert Lawson

- butt (3, 7, 10, 14, 18, 27)
- lonesome (6, 8)
- roughest (13)
- snorting (14, 18)
- fierce (14, 19, 26, 27, 29)
- pawing (18)
- parade (22)
- Bandarilleros (22, 29)
- Picadores (23, 29)
- spears (23)
- Matador (24, 29)
- proudest (24)
- handsome (24)

Europe, Rebecca Hirsch

- countries (7)
- festival (9)
- royal (11)
- cities (15)
- museums (17)
- castles (19)
- range (25)
- visitors (27)
- travel (27)

Africa, Rebecca Hirsch

- countries (5)
- cities (9)
- crops (11)
- villages (13)
- popular (13)

Antarctica, Rebecca Hirsch

- countries (5)
- scientists (9)
- visitors (11)
- adventurers (13)
- famous (15)
- icebergs (23)
- climate (25)
- protect (27)

Why Mosquitoes Buzz in People's Ears: A West African Tale, Verna Aardema; Illustrations, Leo and Diane Dillon

- grumpily (2)
- reeds (2)
- duty (5)
- alarm (5)
- warn (6)
- hunted (8)
- dawn (8)
- council (9)
- worried (9)
- gathered (9)
- nervously (12)
- fault (12)
- reason (14)
- trembling (17)
- summons (19)
- satisfied (23)
- whining (25)
- honest (25)

South America, Rebecca Hirsch

- countries (5)
- medicine (9)
- snouts (21)
- cities (27)

Australia, Rebecca Hirsch

- country (5, 11)
- cities (9)
- monorail (9)
- ranches (11)
- traditions (13)
- outback (19)

Moon Rope, Lois Ehlert

- digging (1)
- tickled (5)
- loop (5)
- blinked (7)
- crescent (10)
- twirled (10)
- waited (15)
- eager (17)
- followed (17)
- glancing (20)
- creatures (23)
- purpose (23)
- fuss (25)
- avoiding (27)

Introducing North America, **Chris Oxlade**

- stretches (4)

- equator (4)

- connected (5)

- narrow (5)

- landmarks (6)

- popular (6)

- famous (7)

- pyramids (7)

- buildings (7)

- plains (9)

- prairie (9)

- border (10)

- freshwater (10)

- extreme (13)

- hurricanes (13)

- variety (14)

- swamps (15)

- hundreds (15)

- cactus (16)

- vast (17)

- settled (18)

- industry (21, 27)

- business (24)

- thousands (25)

- towns (25)

- cattle (25)

Appendix C: Answer Keys, Rubrics, and Sample Responses

TABLE OF CONTENTS

Key: Representations of Student Writing for Module 3

Bold text represents text provided by teacher

Quotation marks represent text written by students

Italics represent dictation or implied meaning of phonetically written text

Bold italics represent text collaboratively created by the class

( ) represents student drawing

Assessment 7A: Focusing Question Task 1 Sample Response

Texts:

- *Asia*, Rebecca Hirsch

- *Europe*, Rebecca Hirsch

Focusing Question: What interesting things can people do in Europe and Asia?

Prompt: Which continent do you think has the most interesting things to do? (R.I.K.1, W.K.1, W.K.8)

After reading *Asia* and *Europe*, students write an opinion statement about which continent they think has the most interesting things for people to do.

- Students use the evidence organizers to form an opinion and choose between Asia and Europe.

- Students write an opinion statement describing which continent they believe has the most interesting things for people to do.

Sample Response:

"Europe has the most intestrin tins to do." *Europe has the most interesting things to do.*

Assessment 13A: New-Read Assessment 1 Answer Key

Text: "5 Reasons Why Animal Moms Are Awesome," April Capochino Myers (**http://witeng.link/0406**)

Task: After reading "5 Reasons Why Animal Moms Are Awesome," students draw and label two reasons the author gives to support the point: "African Elephant moms are awesome!" (RI.K.8)

Author's Point: African elephant moms are awesome!
Sample supporting reasons (students include two):   ▪ (Drawing of a mother elephant using her trunk to direct her baby; labeled "ster wif tunk" for steer with trunk.)   ▪ (Drawing of a mother elephant using her trunk to lift her baby; labeled "lif bayb wif tunk" for lifts baby with trunk.)   ▪ (Drawing of a mother elephant using her trunk to spray her baby with water; labeled "tunk" for trunk and "giv a baf" for gives a bath.)   ▪ (Drawing of a mother elephant using her trunk to pat her baby on the head; labeled "pats wif tunk" for pats with trunk.)

Assessment 13B: Focusing Question Task 2 Sample Response

Texts:

- *Africa*, Rebecca Hirsch

- *Antarctica*, Rebecca Hirsch

Focusing Question: What interesting natural features can people see in Africa and Antarctica?

Prompt: Which continent do you think has the most interesting natural features? (RI.K.1, W.K.1, W.K.8)

After reading *Africa* and *Antarctica*, students write an opinion paragraph describing which continent they think has the most interesting natural features.

- Students write an opinion statement, making their choice between the continents of Africa and Antarctica.

- Students write and illustrate two sentences to support their opinion with details from the text.

- Students create an opinion conclusion sentence by naming their chosen continent in a sentence frame.

Sample Response:

"Antarctica has the mos interesting natral fetirs." Antarctica has the most interesting natural features.

"Ther ar montans." There are mountains.

"Ther ar isbegs." There are icebergs.

I like the natural features in "Antarctica."

(Drawings of a mountain and iceberg included on the corresponding pages.)

Lesson 15: Socratic Seminar Speaking and Listening Rubric

Kindergarten – Speaking and Listening

	4 (Exceeds expectations)	3 (Meets expectations)	2 (Partially meets expectations)	1 (Does not yet meet expectations)
Structure	• Asks clarifying and probing questions • Answers clarifying and probing questions	• Asks clarifying questions • Answers clarifying questions	• Asks questions sometimes • Answers questions sometimes	• Does not ask questions • Does not answer questions
Development	• Provides examples when speaking	• Provides examples when requested	• Says more when requested	• Does not respond to requests
Style	• Uses drawings to strengthen spoken descriptions	• Uses drawings to add detail to spoken descriptions	• Uses drawings when speaking	• Does not use drawings
Conventions	• Expresses clearly with effective volume	• Speaks audibly and clearly	• Speaks audibly or clearly	• Does not yet speak audibly and clearly
Process	• Alternates speaking and listening in conversations through multiple exchanges • Follows all agreed-upon rules for conversations	• Speaks in conversations through multiple exchanges • Follows most agreed-upon rules for conversations	• Speaks in conversations • Follows some agreed-upon rules for conversations	• Does not speak in conversations • Follows few, if any, agreed-upon rules for conversations
Listening	• Eye contact and body language demonstrate attention • Can repeat back what is heard in sequence from memory	• Tracks speakers with eyes • Can repeat back what is heard	• Sometimes tracks speakers • Can recognize what is heard	• Rarely, if ever, tracks speakers • Doesn't remember what is heard

Assessment 19A: Focusing Question Task 3 Sample Response

Text: *Why Mosquitoes Buzz in People's Ears: A West African Tale*, Verna Aardema; Illustrations, Leo and Diane Dillon

Focusing Question: How can a story transport you to a different place?

Part 1:

Prompt: What is happening in this picture? Does this picture show a real moment from the story or is it imaginary? (RL.K.7, W.K.2)

After reading *Why Mosquitoes Buzz in People's Ears: A West African Tale*, students examine the illustration on pages 17–18 of the text. They write and illustrate a sentence to explain what is happening at this point in the story (e.g., whether the illustration depicts a real event from the story or something imaginary).

- Students write a sentence about what is happening in the illustration.
- Students include a drawing to support their response.

Sample Response:

"Pithon remebrs the igana." Python remembers the iguana.

(Drawing of a snake with a thought bubble. Inside the thought bubble is an iguana with big teeth.)

Part 2:

Prompt: Who is your favorite character in *Why Mosquitoes Buzz in People's Ears*? Why? (RL.K.1, W.K.1, W.K.8)

After reading *Why Mosquitoes Buzz in People's Ears: A West African Tale*, students write an opinion paragraph describing their favorite character from the story.

- Students use a sentence frame to write an opinion statement, making their choice between the characters of the iguana, python, rabbit, crow, or monkey.
- Students write and illustrate two sentences to support their opinion with details from the text.
- Students create an opinion conclusion sentence by naming their chosen character in a sentence frame.

Sample Response:

In **Why Mosquitoes Buzz in People's Ears**, "my favrit karakter is the python." In *Why Mosquitoes Buzz in People's Ears*, my favorite character is the python.

"He has srp tef." He has sharp teeth.

"He is perpl." He is purple.

The "python" **is my favorite character.**

(Drawings of a snake with sharp teeth and a purple snake included on the corresponding pages.)

Part 3:

Task: Students distinguish shades of meaning among verbs by acting out the meaning of the following action verbs: *tiptoe, walk, lumber,* and *scurry.* (L.K.5.d)

Sample scoring tool:

L.K.5.d: Distinguish shades of meaning among verbs describing the same general action (e.g., *walk, march, strut, prance*) by acting out the meanings. Text: *Why Mosquitoes Buzz in People's Ears: A West African Tale*					Date Achieved
Student Name	Tiptoe	Walk	Lumber	Scurry	

Success criteria: To achieve the standard, students must demonstrate their understanding of the shades of meaning among the given action verbs. Students listen to each word read aloud, then use full body movement to act out the given term. For example, students should demonstrate moving slowly to respond to the word *lumber* and moving quickly to respond to the word *scurry.*

Assessment 23A: New-Read Assessment 2 and Answer Key

Task: Students use knowledge of word relationships and the illustrations in *Moon Rope* to define key vocabulary. (RL.K.4, L.K.4.a, L.K.4.b, L.K.5.b)

Directions: Read each question aloud twice. If students think the answer to the question is "yes," they draw a circle around the smiley face. If they think the answer is "no," they draw a circle around the frowning face. Display pages from the book and read the text aloud as directed.

Teacher-Facing Questions and Answer Key	Relevant Standards
Example: Is *Moon Rope* the title of the story? (yes) Read pages 1–4 aloud and ask the following questions: 1. In the story, Fox wanted to go to the moon. Did Fox want to travel to the moon? (yes) 2. In the story, Fox wanted to go to the moon. Did Fox want to stay home? (no) Read pages 21–22 aloud and ask the following questions: 3. In the story, it says, "Mole hung on tightly as he was carried back home. He hoped to land unnoticed." Think about the word *unnoticed*. Did Mole want others to notice him? (no) 4. Think about the word *unkind*. If someone is unkind, are they nice to others? (no) 5. Think about the word *unsafe*. If a place is unsafe, should you play there? (no) Read pages 11–12 aloud and ask the following questions: 6. Fox was mad. Was he upset? (yes) 7. Fox was mad. Was he happy? (no) Read pages 9–10 aloud and ask the following question: 8. What is a crescent moon? (Drawing of a crescent shape) Read pages 21–22 aloud and ask the following question: 9. Which images show the meaning of *land* in the sentence, "He hoped to land unnoticed"?	#1–2: L.K.5.b #3: RL.K.4, L.K.4.b #4–5: L.K.4.b #6–7: L.K.5.b #8: RL.K.4 #9: L.K.4.a

Assessment 26A: Focusing Question Task 4 Sample Response

Text: *South America*, Rebecca Hirsch

Focusing Question: What amazing animals can people see in South America and Australia?

Part 1:

Task: Students use their understanding of the words and pictures in *South America* to respond to questions about the text. (RI.K.7)

Directions: Read each question aloud twice. If students think the answer to the question is "yes," they draw a circle around the smiley face. If they think the answer is "no," they draw a circle around the frowning face. Questions 3 and 5 require students follow a different format as indicated below. Display pages from the book and read the text aloud as directed in Lesson 26.

Example: Is *South America* the title of the text? (yes)

1. Does this photograph show us parrots living in trees? (yes)

2. Does this photograph show us parrots eating fruits and seeds? (no)

3. Did we learn that parrots eat fruits and seeds from the words or the photographs? Circle the image of where you learned this information.

4. Does this photograph show us a monkey in the rainforest? (yes)

5. How do you know this is the rainforest? Draw and label a detail or write a sentence about what in the photograph shows this is the rainforest. (Responses will vary but should include a drawing and label or a sentence identifying green trees.)

Part 2:

Prompt: Which continent do you think has the most amazing animals? (RI.K.1, W.K.1, W.K.5, W.K.8)

After reading *South America* and *Australia*, students write an opinion paragraph describing which continent they believe has the most amazing animals. A sentence frame is provided for the opinion conclusion sentence.

Students write an opinion statement, making their choice between the continents of South America and Australia.

- Students write and illustrate two sentences to support their opinion with details from the text.
- Students create an opinion conclusion sentence by naming their chosen continent in a sentence frame.
- Students share one supporting reason sentence with a peer.
- Students add a descriptive label or details to a drawing based on peer feedback.

Sample Response:

"South America has the mos amzn animls." South America has the most amazing animals.

"Ther ar pik dlfins." There are pink dolphins.

"Ther ar lamas." There are llamas.

Those are the amazing animals in "South America."

(Drawings of a pink dolphin and a llama included on the corresponding pages; labeled "pik dlfin" for *pink dolphin* and "sof lama" for *soft llama*.)

Assessment 26B: Direct Vocabulary Assessment 1 and Answer Key

1. Continent: Is a **continent** a large area of land? (yes)

2. Tallest: Is *happiest* the opposite of **tallest**? (no)

3. Stick: Can you **stick** something with a pillow? (no)

4. Amazing: Can animals be **amazing**? (yes)

5. Giant: Do **giant** chunks of ice make icebergs? (yes)

6. Continent: Is a **continent** a large area of water? (no)

7. Amazing: Does **amazing** mean something is boring? (no)

8. Tallest: Is *shortest* the opposite of **tallest**? (yes)

9. Returned: Does **returned** mean "came back"? (yes)

10. Stick: Can you **stick** something with a pin? (yes)

11. Giant: Do **giant** chunks of ice make ice cubes? (no)

12. Returned: Does **returned** mean "left forever"? (no)

Assessment 30A: Focusing Question Task 5 Sample Response

Text: *Introducing North America*, Chris Oxlade

Focusing Question: Why might people want to visit North America?

Part 1:

Prompt: Why should someone visit North America? What amazing animal, fun thing to do, or interesting natural feature would make North America an interesting place to visit? (RI.K.1, W.K.1, W.K.8, L.K.1.f, L.K.2.a)

After reading *Introducing North America*, students write an opinion paragraph in the form of a letter, to convince someone to visit the continent.

- Students use the Opinion Sandwich writing model to structure their letters.
- Students write an opinion statement.
- Students write and illustrate two sentences to support their opinion with details from the text.
- Students create a conclusion sentence by restating their opinion.
- Students write in complete sentences.
- Students capitalize the first letter in their sentences.

Sample Response:

Dear "Alex,"

"North America is a amsin plas to vizit." North America is an amazing place to visit.

"You can wat basbal." You can watch baseball.

"You can see the gand canun." You can see the Grand Canyon.

"It is fun to vizit North America!" It is fun to visit North America!

From, "Jake."

(Drawings of a people playing baseball and the Grand Canyon included on the corresponding pages.)

Part 2:

Task: Students demonstrate their ability to recognize end punctuation by using different colors to circle a period, exclamation point, and question mark. (L.K.2.b)

Answer Key:

Conifer trees stay green year-round. (Period is circled with blue.)

They grow up to 367 feet high! (Exclamation point is circled with yellow.)

What is the largest mountain range in North America? (Question mark is circled with red.)

Assessment 31A: New-Read Assessment 3 Answer Key

Task: Students use the map on pages 38–39 of *World Atlas* to compare and contrast information that appears on the map of North America with information collected from *Introducing North America*. (RI.K.9)

Directions: In the first box, students draw and label a piece of information that appears in both *Introducing North America* and *World Atlas*. In the second box, they draw and label a piece of information that only appears in *World Atlas*.

Same:
Responses will vary but should include a labeled drawing of an item found in both *World Atlas* and *Introducing North America*. For example: mountains, lakes, football, alligator, bears.
Different:
Responses will vary but should include a labeled drawing of an item found only in *World Atlas*. For example: rocket, eagle, lobster, cherries, flowers.

Assessment 32A: End-of-Module Task Answer Key and Annotated Sample Response

Essential Question: What makes the world fascinating?

Part 1:

Task: Students use knowledge of various text types to sort module texts into one of the following categories: informational text or storybook. (RL.K.5)

Directions: Students identify the type of text for each book listed below. In the boxes next to each title, they write an I for informational text or an S for a storybook.

1.	South America	I
2.	Australia	I
3.	Moon Rope	S
4.	Introducing North America	I
5.	Africa	I
6.	Why Mosquitoes Buzz in People's Ears: A West African Tale	S
7.	Antarctica	I
8.	Europe	I
9.	The Story of Ferdinand	S
10.	Asia	I
11.	World Atlas	I

Part 2:

Prompt: Which continent do you think people should visit?

Students choose from one of the following continents—Asia, Africa, Antarctica, Europe, Australia, and South America—and create a travel brochure to explain why someone should visit that continent. (RI.K.1, W.K.1, W.K.8, L.K.1.f, L.K.2.a)

- Students choose one of the following continents to write about: Asia, Africa, Antarctica, Europe, Australia, or South America.
- Students write and illustrate an opinion statement on the first page of their brochure.
- Students write and illustrate two supporting reason sentences, selecting text evidence from two of the following categories: things to do, natural features, or animals.
- Students create a conclusion sentence by restating their opinion on the last page of their brochure.

- Students write in complete sentences.
- Students capitalize the first letter in each sentence.

Sample Response:

(Page 1)	(Page 2)	(Page 3)	(Page 4)
"You shod vizit Africa."	**"You can see gren ranforsts."**	**"You can see gorilas."**	"You shod cum to Africa!"
You should visit Africa.	**You can see green rainforests.**	**You can see gorillas.**	You should come to Africa!
(Drawing of the shape of Africa and a zebra.)	**(Drawing of green trees.)**	**(Drawing of a gorilla.)**	(Drawing of a happy person with green trees around)

Standard	Annotation
RI.K.1	The supporting reasons sentences in this response demonstrate an understanding of key details from the text (e.g., there are rainforests and gorillas in Africa).
W.K.1	The brochure is written in the format of an opinion piece that identifies a topic (e.g., the continent of Africa) and states an opinion about the topic (e.g., "You should visit Africa.")
W.K.8	Information for the brochure is gathered from text evidence previously recorded on a class chart (e.g., from the Evidence Organizer for *Africa*).
L.K.1.f	The brochure includes student-created complete sentences.
L.K.2.a	Capital letters are used to begin the first word in each sentence.

Assessment 33A: Direct Vocabulary Assessment 2 and Answer Key

1. Unusual: Does *unusual* mean something is very common? (no)

2. Hitch: Can you **hitch** with a rope? (yes)

3. Pair: Does a **pair** mean there are two things? (yes)

4. Geography: Is **geography** the study of flowers? (no)

5. Lakes: Are **lakes** large areas of land? (no)

6. Deserts: Are **deserts** usually covered by sand? (yes)

7. Unusual: Does *unusual* mean something is not common? (yes)

8. Hitch: Can you **hitch** with scissors? (no)

9. Pair: Does a **pair** mean there are 12 things? (no)

10. Geography: Is **geography** the study of places? (yes)

11. Lakes: Are **lakes** large areas of water surrounded by land? (yes)

12. Deserts: Are **deserts** usually covered by grass? (no)

Lesson 35: Kindergarten Opinion Writing Rubric

Kindergarten – Speaking and Listening

	4 (Exceeds expectations)	3 (Meets expectations)	2 (Partially meets expectations)	1 (Does not yet meet expectations)
Structure	Using a combination of drawing, dictating, and writing: ■ Responds thoroughly to all elements of prompt ■ Names topic or book with further information about topic or book ■ States opinion or preference clearly	Using a combination of drawing, dictating, and writing: ■ Responds to all elements of prompt ■ Names topic or book ■ States an opinion or preference	Using a combination of drawing, dictating, and writing: ■ Responds to some elements of prompt ■ Attempts to name topic or book but does so in an unclear or inaccurate way ■ States an unclear opinion or preference	Using a combination of drawing, dictating, and writing: ■ Does not respond to prompt; off-topic ■ Does not name topic or book ■ Does not state an opinion or preference
Development	With guidance and support such as collaborative planning: ■ Supports the opinion with a fact or piece of evidence from text(s)	With guidance and support such as collaborative planning: ■ Supports or explains the opinion with information from text(s)	With guidance and support such as collaborative planning: ■ Attempts to explain or support but support may not relate to the opinion	With guidance and support such as collaborative planning: ■ Does not support or explain opinion
Conventions	The following only applies when using students' own writing: ■ Shows consistent command of end-of-grade-level language standards for conventional written English, including mechanics, usage, and spelling; occasional errors may interfere with meaning but main points are intelligible to reader	The following only applies when using students' own writing: ■ Shows general command of end-of-grade-level language standards for conventional written English, including mechanics, usage, and spelling; some errors interfere with meaning	The following only applies when using students' own writing: ■ Shows partial command of end-of-grade-level language standards for conventional written English, including mechanics, usage, and spelling; errors interfere with meaning and some main points are not intelligible to reader	The following only applies when using students' own writing: ■ Does not show command of end-of-grade-level language standards for conventional written English, including mechanics, usage, and spelling; errors significantly interfere with overall meaning and writing is difficult to follow

Lesson 35: Socratic Seminar Speaking and Listening Rubric

Kindergarten – Speaking and Listening

	4 (Exceeds expectations)	3 (Meets expectations)	2 (Partially meets expectations)	1 (Does not yet meet expectations)
Structure	▪ Asks clarifying and probing questions ▪ Answers clarifying and probing questions	▪ Asks clarifying questions ▪ Answers clarifying questions	▪ Asks questions sometimes ▪ Answers questions sometimes	▪ Does not ask questions ▪ Does not answer questions
Development	▪ Describes familiar people, places, things and events in detail ▪ Provides examples when speaking	▪ Describes familiar people, places, things and events ▪ Provides examples when requested	▪ Names familiar people, places, things, and events ▪ Says more when requested	▪ Does not yet talk about familiar people, places, things and events. ▪ Does not respond to requests
Style	▪ Uses drawings to strengthen spoken descriptions	▪ Uses drawings to add detail to spoken descriptions	▪ Uses drawings when speaking	▪ Does not use drawings
Conventions	▪ Expresses clearly with effective volume	▪ Speaks audibly and clearly	▪ Speaks audibly or clearly	▪ Does not yet speak audibly and clearly
Process	▪ Alternates speaking and listening in conversations through multiple exchanges ▪ Follows all agreed-upon rules for conversations	▪ Speaks in conversations through multiple exchanges ▪ Follows most agreed-upon rules for conversations	▪ Speaks in conversations ▪ Follows some agreed-upon rules for conversations	▪ Does not speak in conversations ▪ Follows few, if any, agreed-upon rules for conversations
Listening	▪ Eye contact and body language demonstrate attention ▪ Can repeat back what is heard in sequence from memory	▪ Tracks speakers with eyes ▪ Can repeat back what is heard	▪ Sometimes tracks speakers ▪ Can recognize what is heard	▪ Rarely, if ever, tracks speakers ▪ Doesn't remember what is heard

¹ The Kindergarten Writing and Language standards do not require strategic application of grammar and vocabulary knowledge in students' writing, so the Kindergarten rubrics do not include the Style feature.

Appendix D: Volume of Reading

Students may select from these recommended titles that support the module content or themes. These texts can be used as part of small-group instruction or as part of an independent and/or choice reading program. Volume of Reading Reflection Questions can be found in the back of the Student Edition document.

Lexile measures are listed below when available. The Lexile code AD (Adult Directed) refers to a book that is usually read aloud to a child and includes difficult language or text elements. A text labeled with NC (Non-Conforming) indicates a developmentally appropriate text that is better suited for high-ability readers.

Picture Books (Informational)

- (660L) *Introducing Antarctica*, Anita Ganeri
- (660L) *Introducing Australia*, Anita Ganeri
- (690L) *Introducing Asia*, Anita Ganeri
- (N/A) *Animal Architects: Amazing Animals Who Build Their Homes*, Daniel Nassar and Julio Antonio Blasco
- (N/A) *Emmanuel's Dream: The True Story of Emmanuel Ofosu Yeboah*, Laurie Ann Thompson

Picture Books (Literary)

- (AD550L) *Koala Lou*, Mem Fox
- (AD580L) *Ganesha's Sweet Tooth*, Emily Haynes and Sanjay Patel
- (870L) *Life Story*, Virginia Lee Burton
- (AD1090L) *Tikki Tikki Tembo*, Arlene Mosel
- (N/A) *The Barefoot Book of Animal Tales*, Naomi Adler
- (N/A) *Wee Gillis*, Munro Leaf
- (N/A) *Follow the Dream*, Peter Sís
- (N/A) *Charles Darwin's Around-the-World Adventure*, Jennifer Thermes

Appendix E: Works Cited

Aardema, Verna. *Why Mosquitoes Buzz in People's Ears: A West African Tale*. Illustrated by Leo and Diane Dillon, Puffin Books, 1975.

"Africa." *Go Wild*, World Wildlife Foundation-UK, Web. Accessed 6 Dec. 2016.

"Americas–Fact Files." *Go Wild*, World Wildlife Foundation-UK, Web. Accessed 6 Dec. 2016.

"Antarctic Sights and Sounds." *YouTube*, uploaded by James Napoli, 13 Jan. 2010, Web. Accessed 6 Dec. 2016.

"Asia and the Subcontinent: 2017." Intrepid Travel, Web. Accessed 6 Dec. 2016.

"Burkina Faso: Music." *Our Africa*, SOS Children, Web. Accessed 6 Dec. 2016.

Crane, Nick. *World Atlas*. Illustrated by David Dean, Barefoot Books, 2011.

Crowfoot. "What is life?" "Crowfoot–Blackfoot Chief," *First People*, Web. Accessed 6 Dec. 2016.

"Duck-Billed Platypus." *National Geographic Kids*, National Geographic Partners, Web. Accessed 6 Dec. 2016.

Ehlert, Lois. *Moon Rope*. 1992. Harcourt, 2003.

"Ethiopian Crazy Head Shake Dance." *YouTube*, uploaded by Steve Young, 2 Mar. 2009, Web. Accessed 6 Dec. 2016.

"Explore Views of the Burj Khalifa with Google Maps." *YouTube*, uploaded by Google Maps, 24 June 2013, Web. Accessed 6 Dec. 2016.

"Grand Canyon Scenic Splendor." *National Park Service*, United States Department of the Interior, United States, Web. Accessed 6 Dec. 2016.

Hicks, Edward. *Cornell Farm*. 1848. Oil on canvas. National Gallery of Art, Washington, D.C. *National Gallery of Art*. Web. 1 July 2016.

Hirsch, Rebecca. *Africa*. Scholastic, 2013.

Hirsch, Rebecca. *Antarctica*. Scholastic, 2013.

Hirsch, Rebecca. *Asia*. Scholastic, 2013.

Hirsch, Rebecca. *Australia*. Scholastic, 2013.

Hirsch, Rebecca. *Europe*. Scholastic, 2013.

Hirsch, Rebecca. *South America*. Scholastic, 2013.

"Jaguar." *National Geographic Kids*, National Geographic Partners, Web. Accessed 6 Dec. 2016.

Leaf, Munro. *The Story of Ferdinand*. Illustrated by Robert Lawson, 1936. Penguin Group, 2011.

Leutze, Emanuel. *Washington Crossing the Delaware*. 1851. Oil on canvas. *The Metropolitan Museum of Art*, New York. The Met. Web. 15 Sept. 2016.

"Lions Roar." "African Songs, Chants, and Games," *CanTeach*, Web. Accessed 6 Dec. 2016.

Magnus, Olaus. *Carta Marina*. 1527–1539. *Wikimedia Commons*, Wikimedia Foundation, uploaded by Fred J, 4 Mar. 2006, Web. Accessed 6. Dec. 2016.

"Moles." *DK Find Out!*, Dorling Kindersley Limited, Web. Accessed 6 Dec. 2016.

Myers, April Capochino. "5 Reasons Why Animal Moms Are Awesome." *National Geographic Kids*, National Geographic Partners, Web. Accessed 6 Dec. 2016.

Oxlade, Chris. *Introducing North America*. Capstone Global Library, 2014.

"Patterns of Chinchero." *Descendants of the Incas*, Center for Traditional Textiles of Cusco, Web. Accessed 6 Dec. 2016.

"Penguin Song." "Music & Songs: Animals > Penguins," *Preschool Education*, Web. Accessed 6 Dec. 2016.

Rylant, Cynthia. *When I Was Young in the Mountains*. Illustrated by Diane Goode, 1982. Dutton Children's Books, 1985.

"The Seven Continents Song | Silly School Songs." *YouTube*, uploaded by Silly School Songs, 23 Jan. 2015, Web. Accessed 6 Dec. 2016.

"Storm-Proofing the World's Biggest Mud Building–Human Planet–BBC." *YouTube*, uploaded by BBC Earth, 2 Oct. 2013, Web. Accessed 6 Dec. 2016.

Stöckli, Reto, et al. *Earth from Space*. Earth Observatory, National Aeronautics and Space Administration, Web. Accessed 6 Dec. 2016.

"Surface of the Earth." *National Geographic*, National Geographic Partners, Web. Accessed 6 Dec. 2016.

"Traditional Chinese Dance–'Flowers Contend in Beauty' by Li Qian, Lin Chen…" *YouTube*, uploaded by tiezi00, 1 Feb. 2014, Web. Accessed 6 Dec. 2016.

"Traditional Weaving, Chincheros Peru." *YouTube*, uploaded by Andean Trails, 19 June 2014, Web. Accessed 6 Dec. 2016.

"*Where in the World Is Carmen Sandiego?* from Smithsonian Folkways." *Smithsonian Folkways*, Smithsonian Institution, Web. Accessed 6 Dec. 2016.

CREDITS

Great Minds® has made every effort to obtain permission for the reprinting of all copyrighted material. If any owner of copyrighted material is not acknowledged herein, please contact Great Minds® for proper acknowledgment in all future editions and reprints of this module.

- All material from the *Common Core State Standards for English Language Arts & Literacy in History/Social Studies, Science, and Technical Subjects* © Copyright 2010 National Governors Association Center for Best Practices and Council of Chief State School Officers. All rights reserved.

- All images are used under license from Shutterstock.com unless otherwise noted.

- For updated credit information, please visit **http://witeng.link/credits**.

ACKNOWLEDGMENTS

Great Minds® Staff

The following writers, editors, reviewers, and support staff contributed to the development of this curriculum.

Ann Brigham, Lauren Chapalee, Sara Clarke, Emily Climer, Lorraine Griffith, Emily Gula, Sarah Henchey, Trish Huerster, Stephanie Kane-Mainier, Lior Klirs, Liz Manolis, Andrea Minich, Lynne Munson, Marya Myers, Rachel Rooney, Aaron Schifrin, Danielle Shylit, Rachel Stack, Sarah Turnage, Michelle Warner, Amy Wierzbicki, Margaret Wilson, and Sarah Woodard.

Colleagues and Contributors

We are grateful for the many educators, writers, and subject-matter experts who made this program possible.

David Abel, Robin Agurkis, Elizabeth Bailey, Julianne Barto, Amy Benjamin, Andrew Biemiller, Charlotte Boucher, Sheila Byrd-Carmichael, Eric Carey, Jessica Carloni, Janine Cody, Rebecca Cohen, Elaine Collins, Tequila Cornelious, Beverly Davis, Matt Davis, Thomas Easterling, Jeanette Edelstein, Kristy Ellis, Moira Clarkin Evans, Charles Fischer, Marty Gephart, Kath Gibbs, Natalie Goldstein, Christina Gonzalez, Mamie Goodson, Nora Graham, Lindsay Griffith, Brenna Haffner, Joanna Hawkins, Elizabeth Haydel, Steve Hettleman, Cara Hoppe, Ashley Hymel, Carol Jago, Jennifer Johnson, Mason Judy, Gail Kearns, Shelly Knupp, Sarah Kushner, Shannon Last, Suzanne Lauchaire, Diana Leddy, David Liben, Farren Liben, Jennifer Marin, Susannah Maynard, Cathy McGath, Emily McKean, Jane Miller, Rebecca Moore, Cathy Newton, Turi Nilsson, Julie Norris, Galemarie Ola, Michelle Palmieri, Meredith Phillips, Shilpa Raman, Tonya Romayne, Emmet Rosenfeld, Jennifer Ruppel, Mike Russoniello, Deborah Samley, Casey Schultz, Renee Simpson, Rebecca Sklepovich, Amelia Swabb, Kim Taylor, Vicki Taylor, Melissa Thomson, Lindsay Tomlinson, Melissa Vail, Keenan Walsh, Julia Wasson, Lynn Welch, Yvonne Guerrero Welch, Emily Whyte, Lynn Woods, and Rachel Zindler.

Early Adopters

The following early adopters provided invaluable insight and guidance for Wit & Wisdom:

- Bourbonnais School District 53 • Bourbonnais, IL

- Coney Island Prep Middle School • Brooklyn, NY

- Gate City Charter School for the Arts • Merrimack, NH

- Hebrew Academy for Special Children • Brooklyn, NY

- Paris Independent Schools • Paris, KY

- Saydel Community School District • Saydel, IA

- Strive Collegiate Academy • Nashville, TN

- Valiente College Preparatory Charter School • South Gate, CA

- Voyageur Academy • Detroit, MI

Design Direction provided by Alton Creative, Inc.

Project management support, production design, and copyediting services provided by **ScribeConcepts.com**

Copyediting services provided by Fine Lines Editing

Product management support provided by Sandhill Consulting